Success in Principles

Success Studybooks

Accounting and Costing

Accounting and Costing: Problems and Projects

Biology

Book-keeping and Accounts

British History 1760–1914

British History since 1914

Business Calculations

Chemistry

Commerce

Commerce: West African Edition

Economic Geography

Economics

Economics: West African Edition

Electronics

Elements of Banking

European History 1815–1941

Financial Accounting

Financial Accounting: Questions and Answers

Geography: Human and Regional

Geography: Physical and Mapwork

Insurance

Investment

Law

Management: Personnel

Mathematics

Nutrition

Office Practice

Organic Chemistry

Physics

Principles of Accounting

Principles of Accounting: Answer Book

Statistics

Twentieth Century World Affairs

Success in
PRINCIPLES
OF ACCOUNTING

Geoffrey Whitehead, B.Sc.(Econ.)

John Murray

to Joan

First published 1974
Reprinted (revised, and with an additional unit) 1977
Reprinted (revised, and with a further additional unit) 1980
Reprinted (revised) 1981
Reprinted (revised) 1982
Reprinted (revised) 1984
Reprinted 1986

Printed and bound in Great Britain
by Richard Clay (The Chaucer Press) Ltd, Bungay, Suffolk

0 7195 2899 2

Foreword

The principles of accounting form the basis of knowledge essential to anyone who has to take part in keeping accurate records of the financial affairs of any business. Today more and more firms use computerized or mechanized systems of accounting, and never has it been so vital for anyone contemplating a business career to understand the methods of book-keeping and accounting that lie behind it. Whether the transactions of a business are recorded and processed by computer, or are hand-written in books of original entry, the basic thinking is the same. No one can hope to understand either the sophisticated programming of a computer, or the simple day-to-day entries in a ledger without a thorough grounding in the accounting system common to both.

This course has been designed to cover syllabus material for most examinations in elementary accounting. It is especially suitable for students working for the following: 16 + and pre-vocational Book-keeping and Accounting courses, BTEC National course Numeracy and Accounting (Accounting aspects), RSA (Stages I and II) and LCCI (Elementary and Intermediate). It is also recommended as an introductory text for students taking Accounting as part of a General Studies course, combining it with other disciplines such as Economics, Science, Engineering, Marketing or Personnel Management.

The book is divided into Units of study, each with its set of Exercises. To get the maximum benefit from the course students should work through the Exercises, then check against the detailed, accurately displayed answers shown in the companion volume, *Success in Principles of Accounting: Answer Book*. This is particularly important for anyone preparing for an examination: it helps to reinforce understanding of the topic concerned; it also illustrates a style of presentation which students should try to achieve if they are to satisfy the high standard of display expected by modern examiners.

The 1981 Companies Act has resolved the longstanding problem of the illogical style in which Balance Sheets have traditionally been presented in the United Kingdom. (The historical background to this situation is described on page 65 of this book.) The 1981 Act states that Balance Sheets must now be presented in one of two formats given in Schedule 1: the logical horizontal style already used in the rest of Europe, with assets on the left and liabilities on the right; or the vertical (or narrative) style. The latter format is favoured by some accountants for technical printing reasons, but is less satisfactory on theoretical accounting grounds. Throughout the book the logical horizontal format is used, but an example of the vertical style is given. The traditional British Balance Sheet is therefore now recognized as incorrect and should no longer be used.

G.W.

Acknowledgments

One of the best ways of preparing for an examination is to study the past papers of examining boards. I am grateful to all the boards which have allowed me to use their questions. I list below the examining bodies I wish to thank, and give their addresses so that students can write to them for specimens of past papers:

Associated Examining Board, Wellington House, Station Road, Aldershot, Hants, GU11 1BQ;
East Anglian Examinations Board, The Lindens, Lexden Road, Colchester, Essex, CO3 3RL;
The Royal Society of Arts, Murray Road, Orpington, Kent, BR5 3RB;
The University of London, Publications Office, 52 Gordon Square, London, WC1H 0PJ.

In preparing this book I have received help from various firms and institutions. I am particularly indebted to:

George Anson & Company Limited, for permission to reproduce a simultaneous records Sales Day Book and a simultaneous records Wages Book (Mr. R. Kemp was very helpful);
Barclays Bank PLC, for permission to reproduce two personalized cheques;
Moore Paragon Limited, for permission to reproduce a pad of invoices;
NCR Limited, for permission to reproduce a mechanized statement and till receipt;
The National Westminster Bank PLC, for permission to reproduce a personalized cheque;
George Vyner Limited, for permission to reproduce a simple Wages Book.

I must express warm appreciation to Irene Slade, who conceived the 'Success' series as a new approach to students of all ages; her guidance and encouragement were invaluable. My sincere thanks also go to Arthur Upson, who read and criticized the text at various stages and re-worked all the questions whose answers appear in the *Answer Book*, and to James Taylor for his constructive criticism and appraisal of the original text.

G.W.

Contents

Unit One

Accounting to the Trial Balance

1.1 A Definition of Accounting

Accounting is the art of controlling a business by keeping accurate book-keeping records, measuring and interpreting the financial results of the business by the preparation of certain statistics called 'accounting ratios' and communicating these results to management and other interested parties.

Every businessman must have an understanding of accounting for it is a major factor in the success of all firms. It is perhaps most important to the very large companies with whom most students and readers will seek employment, for only by the most careful control can these enormous enterprises keep prosperous and successful. Not only their own prosperity, but the prosperity of shareholders, managers, staff, and even the nation itself, depend upon maintaining efficiency and competitiveness in the free-enterprise world.

1.2 Why Start a Business?

The purpose of business is to make a profit, and we may define profit as the *reward for enterprise and risk*. So one of the chief aims of accounting is to reveal whether or not a business is being conducted profitably.

At one time profits were calculated only once in a lifetime—when the owner of the firm died. There was little need to calculate profits more often. If the business was not profitable it soon became obvious for all to see: the premises would not be repaired or redecorated and the owner's family would be seen in shabby clothing. Rumour and gossip would spread news of their difficulties far and wide. By contrast, the prosperous merchant displayed his prosperity. The cities of Europe are filled with the beautiful homes of early merchants.

Today, profit must be calculated at least once a year, for the State requires its share. This contribution to the State is called *taxation*. Individuals pay *income tax* and companies pay *corporation tax*. After taxation has been paid, the shareholders of companies have to be rewarded for investing their money with a *dividend* made up from the remainder of the profits. The *directors* of the company, however, may keep some of the profits back as *reserves* to strengthen the business in the coming year. Even so, an annual calculation of profits is unlikely to keep an efficient check on the business. More frequent calculations of the accounts are necessary, and many companies today actually know how much profit they have made on every day's activities. Such feats of calculation are, of course, only made possible by the use of *computers*.

1.3 Book-keeping—the Basis of Accounting

The true purpose of accounting is to maintain proper control of the finances of a business. Accounting must be based on careful and efficient *double-entry book-keeping*. This is a system of accounting entries devised by the early merchants of Lombardy in Northern Italy. These early accountants, who gave their name to Lombard Street, the banking centre of the City of London, used a book with pages divided down the middle, called the *ledger*. This is still the most important book of account. The name 'ledger' is of Dutch origin, and means 'the book on the ledge'. In early counting houses the book lay open on a ledge under the window, and double entries were made immediately after customers had called at the shop. Fig. 1.1 shows a page from the ledger.

									L 1
Dr. (Debit side)							(Credit side) Cr.		
Date	Details	Folio	£ Amount		Date	Details	Folio	£ Amount	

Fig. 1.1 The ledger

You should note the following points:

(*a*) There is a line at the top of every ledger page for the name, address and telephone number of the person whose transactions with the business are being recorded. Thus the name T. Smith, 29 High Road, Summerville, Hants. (042–29 1347) might appear on this line. Some accounts are not *personal accounts*, but refer to other matters of importance, like assets of the business or losses incurred by the business. Such accounts might be headed 'Typewriters A/c' or 'Light and Heat A/c'.

(*b*) The page is clearly divided down the middle, and the two halves of the page are identical, each having columns for the date, details of transaction, *folio number* (explained below), and the amount of money involved.

(*c*) The two sides of the page are called respectively the *debit side* and the *credit side*. The debit side is always used when the person named at the top receives goods or services or money and thus becomes a *debtor* of the firm. The credit side is used when the person gives goods or services or money to the firm and thus becomes a *creditor*.

(*d*) Every page in the ledger is called an *account*. Since the pages are always used on both sides, an account is really a leaf in the ledger and it is given the name *folio*—from the Latin *folium*, a leaf.

(*e*) Every account is therefore given a *folio number*. In Fig. 1.1 the number is L 1 (Ledger 1) written in the top right-hand corner where it can easily be seen as the pages are turned.

1.4 Double-entry Book-keeping

Whenever a piece of business is arranged, there are always two parties involved: one is the 'giver' and one the 'receiver'. Every piece of business activity is called a *transaction* and millions of them occur every day. If you buy a bar of chocolate from a confectioner, that is a transaction. If the Port of London Authority orders a container crane from a manufacturer that is another transaction. The first involved the payment of twelve pence to the confectioner—it was a *cash transaction*. The other involved a quarter of a million pounds sterling, and was almost certainly not a cash transaction. Such transactions, where there is a time-lag between the contract for the goods and the payment of the money, are called *credit transactions*. This dual nature of transactions—there are two sides to every bargain made —gives rise to the name *double-entry book-keeping*.

Every transaction must be recorded in two accounts, one of which will be debited because it receives value. The other will be credited because it has given value. The rule for double entries is therefore as follows:

Always debit the account that has received goods, or services or money.

Always credit the account that has given goods, or services or money.

Let us now consider the double entries required in a few simple transactions. We will imagine that Arthur Upson has just set up in business in a small way with *capital* of £200·00.

(1) Double Entry No. 1

On January 1st 19. . Arthur Upson contributes the sum of £200·00 as capital for the new business, placing it in a bank account with one of the 'big-four' banks, say Lloyds Bank.

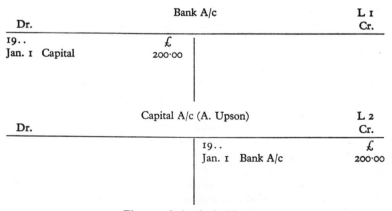

Fig. 1.2 A simple double entry

A very important principle at once arises. In accounting *we always treat the business as quite a different person from the proprietor, or owner, of the business.* The proprietor, when he makes this capital available becomes a creditor of the business *for he has given it £200·00.* The Bank Account is debited with £200·00, *for it has received £200·00.* We therefore have a double entry as shown in Fig. 1.2.

(2) Double Entries Nos. 2 and 3

Upson now pays out £50·00 to a supplier for cloth required in his workshop, and £25·00 each for two second-hand sewing machines.

This requires two further double entries, shown in Fig. 1.3.

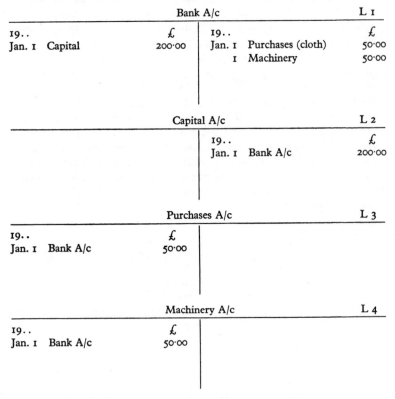

Fig. 1.3 More double entries

Note the following :

(*a*) Whenever we purchase goods for resale, or raw materials to be made up into goods for resale, we call these *purchases* and enter them in the Purchases Account. This is a very important point, because later we shall use the purchases figure as part of the process for finding profit.

(*b*) In contrast to (*a*) above, the purchase of machines is not the purchase of goods to be resold, but is the purchase of an *asset*—something to be kept in the business for regular use by the business.

(*c*) In each of these double entries the Bank Account was credited because it gave money out for the purchase of these items i.e., *credit the account that gives value.*

(*d*) The Purchases Account was debited with £50·00 of cloth, and the Machinery Account was debited with £50·00 of machinery, because they received these items, i.e. *debit the account that receives value.*

You have now seen the basic idea of double entry. There is nothing difficult about it, but of course there are a great many accounts and only with regular practice will you develop a real understanding of all possible entries. Before we go on to consolidate this knowledge, one or two further pieces of vocabulary are necessary. First, the three classes of accounts.

1.5   The Three Classes of Accounts

These are: *personal accounts*, which are the records of our transactions with other firms and individuals, our customers and suppliers; *nominal accounts*, which are records kept of losses and profits of the business (for example Rent and Rates Account or Commission-Received Account); and finally *real accounts*, which are records we keep of the real things the business owns, i.e. the assets of the business. Examples are Land and Buildings Account, Plant and Machinery Account and Cash Account.

Let us consider these in detail.

(1) Personal Accounts

There are many people with whom the business deals. Some are suppliers who make available raw materials and goods for resale, or the assets we need to make the business operate. Others are customers to whom we supply goods or services. All these people are either creditors or debtors. The creditors have given us goods or services, and the debtors have received goods or services from us (Fig. 1.4). Thus we have personal accounts:

Debtors (who have received value)		Creditors (who have given value)	
T. Smith		**R. Jones**	
Sales	£ 50·00		Purchases	£ 75·00

Fig. 1.4 Personal accounts

There is one personal account which is rather special. It is the Capital Account, already mentioned. This is the personal account of the proprietor. In a limited company there are many contributors of capital called *shareholders*. They too have a personal account called, for example, the Ordinary-Share Capital Account (Fig. 1.5). Here all the capital is lumped together in one personal account, but the individual shareholder's share of this is recorded in a special shareholders' register.

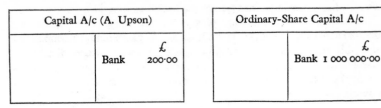

Fig. *1.5 Personal accounts of the proprietor and the shareholders*

(2) Nominal Accounts

The word 'nominal' means 'existing in name only'. This implies that there is nothing really there, so that you might say nominal accounts are the opposite of real accounts. Suppose we decide to mail our customers with a leaflet about a new product. To mail five thousand customers, at the cheapest postage today, will cost £500·00. We send the office boy round to the Post Office to buy stamps for this value. What will the double entry be? It is shown in Fig. 1.6.

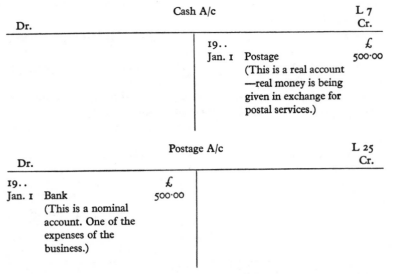

Fig. *1.6 Postage Account—a nominal account*

The Cash Account gave value, so it is credited with £500·00. The money was used to buy postage stamps so it is debited to Postage Account which has received value. In fact where are the stamps? Stuck on the letters now going through the post to our customers. Clearly the £500·00 on the Postage Account does not represent anything real at all; it is only a nominal entry— in name only. It is recorded here for convenience only so that at the end of the year, when we come to work out our profits, we shall remember to deduct from the profits this expenditure of £500·00.

By contrast, suppose we arrange the sale of a piece of property for a customer, and earn commission of £200·00. This will probably be received as a cheque and be paid into the Bank Account. The double entry for it will be in Commission-Received Account as shown in Fig. 1.7.

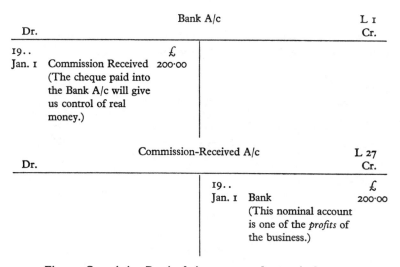

Fig. 1.7 Commission-Received Account—another nominal account

It is clear that this nominal account is quite the opposite of the one in Fig. 1.6, for it is a profit not a loss. The actual money is in the Bank Account, but this nominal record will remind us at the end of the financial year to include this £200·00 as part of the firm's profits.

(3) Real Accounts

When we pay money for postage, the real stamps are stuck on envelopes and are lost to the business as soon as we post the letters in the letter box. If we purchase such things as typewriters, plant and machinery or furniture and fittings they are not lost to the business, but are permanent assets available for use over a period of years. These assets are recorded in the third class of accounts—real accounts. In Fig. 1.8 we have a record of the purchase of a motor vehicle by cheque for £850·00.

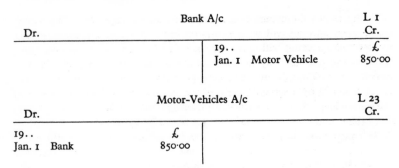

Fig. 1.8 Two real accounts

Notice that both the Bank Account and Motor-Vehicles Account are real accounts. The balance at the bank (not shown in Fig. 1.8) is one of the assets of the business, just like the motor vehicle we have purchased.

1.6   Rules for Entering Items in the Three Classes of Accounts

Table 1.1 The commonest accounts

Personal Accounts		Nominal Accounts		Real Accounts	
Dr.	Cr.	Dr.	Cr.	Dr.	Cr.
T. Smith A/c	J. Brown A/c	Rent-Paid	Rent-	Cash A/c	There are
R. Jones A/c	P. Green A/c	A/c	Received	Bank A/c	no real
and all	and all	Wages A/c	A/c	Motor-	accounts
other	other	Salaries A/c	Commission-	Vehicle	with
trade	'trade'	Light and	Received	A/c	credit
debtors;	creditors	Heat A/c	A/c and	Furniture	balances
also the	and	Telephone-	all other	and	
Drawings	'expense'	Expenses	profits	Fittings	
A/c of the	creditors;	A/c	of the	A/c	
prop-	also the	Motor-	business.	Land and	
rietor(s)	Capital	Vehicle	Also the	Buildings	
	A/c of the	Expenses	Sales A/c	A/c and all	
	prop-	A/c and	and the	other asset	
	rietor(s).	all other	Purchases-	accounts	
	Loan A/cs,	losses of	Returns		
	Mortgage	the	A/c		
	A/cs and	business;			
	any other	also the			
	admissions	Purchases			
	of debts	A/c, the			
	like	Sales-			
	Reserves	Returns			
	or unap-	A/c and			
	propriated	the Stock			
	profits	(at start)			

Table 1.1 shows the commonest accounts in each of the three classes. Of course every account will have entries on both the debit and credit sides, because every account will eventually be cleared off the books in some way or other, and the only way to 'clear' an account is to have an entry on the other side of it. Thus the motor vehicles purchased in Fig. 1.8 will be cleared from the books by a series of depreciation entries over a number of years, and eventually it will be traded in as a second-hand car to some garage in part-exchange for a new one. In Table 1.1 the listing is only intended to show the side of the account, debit or credit, which will usually have a balance.

Clearly we must have rules for making the entries in this very large collection of accounts. The learner in accounting, rather like the learner-driver, faces a very involved pattern of new ideas. He cannot expect to learn everything at once. The very best thing to grasp firmly at first is the idea of debit and credit, the two sides of the ledger page. Let us look at this in pictorial form again (Fig. 1.9).

							L 1
Dr.							Cr.
Date	Details	Folio	Amount	Date	Details	Folio	Amount
	The Debit Side An entry here means that the person or thing named at the top of the account has *received* goods, or services, or money *from* the business.				*The Credit Side* An entry here means that the person or thing named at the top of the account has *given* goods, or services, or money *to* the business.		

Fig. 1.9 The meaning of debit and credit entries

A simple rule for debit and credit entries is as follows:

Debit the receiver—credit the giver.

This is short for:

Debit the account of the person or thing that receives goods, or services or money from the business.

Credit the account of the person or thing that gives goods, or services or money to the business.

More detailed rules for each of the classes of accounts are as follows:

(1) Personal Accounts

Debit the person who receives value (goods, services or money). He will thus become a *debtor* of the business.

Credit the person who gives value (goods, services or money). He will thus become a *creditor* of the business.

(2) Nominal Accounts

Debit the loss accounts, which have received 'in name only' the benefits from money expended. Examples are Postage Account and Motor-Vehicle Expenses Account.

Credit the profit accounts, which have given 'in name only' benefits to the business. Examples are Commission-Received Account and Fees-Received Account.

(3) Real Accounts

Debit the asset account when the stock of the assets is increased. The asset concerned has received an increased share of the resources of the business because money has been expended on a further supply.

Credit the asset account when the stock of the asset is reduced either by fair wear and tear or because we dispose of a worn-out or obsolete asset. The asset has given up some of its value in the service of the business.

1.7 An Exercise in Double-entry Book-keeping

We are now ready to make a set of entries following double-entry rules. Try the following exercise as an example.

Make appropriate entries in a set of accounts. Remember that every transaction will appear in two accounts so that the six transactions require twelve entries.

(a) On January 1st 19.. T. Smith starts business with capital of £500·00 which he puts in the bank.

(b) The same day he buys goods for resale £200·00, by cheque.

(c) He also pays by cheque for the hire of a market stall and lighting, etc., for one month, £25·00.

(d) He buys an account book for £0·90, by cheque.

(e) On January 2nd he buys a second-hand motor van for £65·00, by cheque.

(f) Sales for the week by January 6th total £385·00, which he banks.

Notes on the six transactions:

(a) This is the contribution of capital by the proprietor. Bank Account has received £500·00; Capital Account (T. Smith) has given value. Debit Bank Account, credit Capital Account.

(b) All goods purchased for resale are called purchases, and are recorded in Purchases Account. Bank Account has given £200·00. Debit Purchases Account, credit Bank Account.

(c) This payment of £25·00 is one of the expenses, or losses, of the business. Bank Account has given £25·00. The debit entry will be made in an expense account. You can give such accounts any name you like, but as rent of a business place is a regular item which will recur every month, we will call the expense account Rent of Stall Account. Debit Rent of Stall Account, credit Bank Account.

(d) An account book is a necessary office expense. It will not occur too frequently but we will enter it in Stationery Account. Bank Account has given £0·90. Debit Stationery Account, credit Bank Account.

(e) This is the purchase of an asset of the business. Debit Motor-Vehicles Account (always debit the asset account when you purchase an asset), credit Bank Account.

(f) Cashing up his takings at the end of the week T. Smith sees that what he has sold has realized £385·00. No doubt he still has some goods in stock, so that it has been a profitable week. When the Bank Account is debited because it has received £385·00, we shall credit the Sales Account. Sales Account is always credited with the sales figure; it is the opposite of Purchases Account mentioned in (b).

Looked at in ledger form (Fig. 1.10) we have:

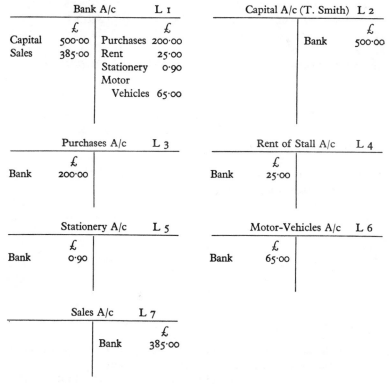

Fig. 1.10 Double-entry book-keeping for T. Smith

1.8   The Trial Balance—a Check on the Accuracy of the Double Entries

This first Unit is called 'Accounting to the Trial Balance'. It is a most important section of accounting, and many people spend their entire business lives carrying out book-keeping transactions which only go as far as the Trial-Balance level. If you examine the 'situations-vacant' columns of any newspaper, you will find many requests for book-keepers who can keep records 'to the Trial Balance'. You may then ask 'Do you really mean I have now learned enough book-keeping to go out and get a job?'. Well, not quite, but by the end of this chapter you will have learnt the *principles* underlying work to the Trial-Balance level. You will only then need a little more knowledge, chiefly connected with books of original entry, and you will certainly be ready for useful, if perhaps routine, employment.

What is a Trial Balance? It is an attempt to check the accuracy of the book-keeping by striking a balance of the books. Since a debit entry is never made without a corresponding credit entry, a list of all the items entered on the debit side should balance, or agree, with a list of items on the credit side. This is called 'striking a balance', and any mistake of double entry should be revealed by it. It would, however, be rather boring to extract all the entries we have just made and draw up two lists of debit and credit entries. Instead we take the opportunity of clearing up one or two little difficulties that exist on the accounts, and we draw up a Trial Balance *which consists only of the balances on the accounts.*

(1) Balancing-off an Account

Look at Fig. 1.10 and consider which accounts are difficult to understand. Six of them are perfectly clear, because they have only one item on the account. But the first account, the Bank Account, is very muddled at present, for it has six entries on it. We cannot tell at a glance how much money is in the account; we need pencil and paper to work out the balance. Let us look at this account again, and balance it off so that it is clear.

	Bank A/c		L 1
	£		£
Capital	500·00	Purchases	200·00
Sales	385·00	Rent	25·00
		Stationery	0·90
		Motor Vehicles	65·00

Fig. 1.11 An account that is unclear

If we add up the two sides (Fig. 1.11) we find:

Debit side (money received by the Bank A/c)   = £885·00
Credit side (money given out by the Bank A/c)   = £290·90
Difference   = £594·10

We now add the difference to the credit side—the smaller side—and that balances off the account level at £885·00. We then bring the balancing figure down to the debit side to show the true balance on the account. The account now looks like Fig. 1.12.

Bank A/c			L 1
	£		£
Capital	500·00	Purchases	200·00
Sales	385·00	Rent	25·00
		Stationery	0·90
		Motor Vehicles	65·00
		Balance	594·10
	£885·00		£885·00
Balance	594·10		

Fig. 1.12 An account that is easy to understand

Note the following:
(a) The balancing figure is called 'the balance on the account'.
(b) This balance is first entered on the side which is smallest in value, but is brought down on to the proper side of the account to show the true position, which in this case is that we have £594 10 in the bank.
(c) These two balancing entries are a 'double entry'.
(d) To make the account look neat we use a currency sign—a £, $ or whatever your currency sign is—and underline it, above and below.
(e) Since we balance the sides at the same level, we must leave some empty lines on the shorter side. There is a rule in accounting which says: *never leave empty lines*. Fill them in with ruled lines in red so that no one can enter sums of money by mistake on the lines. Alternatively some people fill in the lines where wording is written, that is, under the word 'sales'.

(2) A further note on Balancing Accounts
Some students think that it is necessary to balance off every account. This is not so. It is only necessary to balance off an account if there are items on both sides of the account, so that the balancing off makes the account simpler to understand. Consider Fig. 1.13. Here the balancing off has not simplified the picture at all. The picture was perfectly clear anyway. Motor vehicles worth £450·00 are recorded on the books as an asset of the business.

Motor-Vehicles A/c			L 5
	£		
Bank	450·00		

(contd. on page 14)

Motor-Vehicles A/c			L 5
	£		£
Bank	450·00	Balance	450·00
	£450·00		£450·00
Balance	450·00		

Fig. 1.13 An account that need not be balanced off

Even in the following example (Fig. 1.14) it is not necessary to balance off the account. A much simpler process is to add it up and pencil in the total figure to one side.

R. Brown A/c		L 21
19..	£	
Jan. 4 Sales	242·75	
11 Sales	36·50	
19 Sales	16·18	
(Pencil note:		
Total=£295·43)		

Fig. 1.14 An account that can be clarified without balancing off

Only accounts that have items on both sides of the page, as in Fig. 1.11, need to be balanced off before preparing a Trial Balance.

We are now ready to prepare the Trial Balance: it is shown in Fig. 1.15.

Trial Balance of T. Smith's ledger
(as at January 6th 19..)

		Dr.	Cr.
		£	£
Bank A/c	L 1	594·10	
Capital A/c	L 2		500·00
Purchases A/c	L 3	200·00	
Rent of Stall A/c	L 4	25·00	
Stationery A/c	L 5	0·90	
Motor-Vehicles A/c	L 6	65·00	
Sales A/c	L 7		385·00
		£885·00	£885·00

Fig. 1.15 A simple Trial Blance

Note the following :
(a) The book-keeping would appear to have been well done because the debits and credits agree, so it seems that a proper double entry has been done in each case.

(b) A currency sign is used to make the total stand out.

(c) All the accounts with a debit balance are listed in the debit column.

(d) All the accounts with a credit balance are listed in the credit column.

(e) The heading should always show the date the Trial Balance was extracted.

You should now attempt several exercises in double-entry book-keeping to the Trial Balance.

1.9   Exercises Set 1: Accounting to the Trial Balance

1. M. Thomas begins to trade in motor vehicles on March 1st 19.. with a capital of £10 000·00 which he banks. Record this opening capital and then the following transactions. Balance off the accounts where necessary and extract a Trial Balance as at March 7th 19..

March 2nd   Buys second-hand vehicle for £50·00 which he intends to resell. Buys spare parts for repair work £10·00. Pays for both by cheque.

March 3rd   Buys second-hand vehicle, £1 450·00, for resale; pays by cheque. Draws £50·00 cash from bank (enter in Cash A/c).

March 4th   Resells first vehicle for £120·00 to A. Debtor who will pay on March 31st.

March 5th   Sells second vehicle £1 595·00 for cash.

March 6th   Banks £1 550·00 from cash received on previous day.

2. On May 1st 19.. R. Brown goes into business as a scrap metal dealer with capital of £1 000 which he banks. He rents a yard that day for £20·00 per month, paying by cheque for the first month.

May 2nd   Purchases scrap boiler and spare piping, £55·00 by cheque.

May 3rd   Withdraws cash from bank £100·00 (record the cash in Cash A/c). Purchases two cars for scrap, paying cash £10·00 for one and £5·00 for the other.

May 4th   Purchases scrap aluminium £75·00 by cheque from US Army depot.

May 5th   Sells scrap copper £180·00. Sells scrap aluminium £110·00. Payment received for both by cheque.

Record these items in R. Brown's ledger; balance off those accounts that need to be balanced and extract a Trial Balance as at May 5th 19..

3. M. Whiteside begins business as a market trader on March 20th 19.. as a dealer in transistor radio sets, etc., with a capital of £200·00 in cash. Record this capital and enter the following items in his ledger accounts,

March 20th   Buys transistor radios for £85·00. These are for resale.

March 21st   Cash sales for the day £46·00. Buys hi-fi equipment for resale, £22·50, pays in cash.

March 22nd   Pays for hire of stall (Rent A/c) £10·00. Pays deposit on electricity bill (Light and Heat A/c) £5·00. Purchases batteries, £10·00, for resale.

March 23rd   Sales for the day £86·00 cash.

March 24th   Banks £100·00 for safe keeping. Purchases for £16·00 cash hi-fi equipment for resale.

March 25th   Sales for the day £58·00 cash.

March 26th   Balance off the accounts where necessary and prepare a Trial Balance.

4. On April 1st 19.. M. Logan begins business as a decorator with a capital of £100·00 in cash. He purchases second-hand ladders, trestles and other equipment for £35·00, also materials for use in the business (Purchases A/c) for £23·00. Enter these items in his ledger and then the following.

April 2nd   Receives payment for redecorations in cash £6·00 (Fees Received A/c), sells materials, £4·50 cash.

April 3rd   Purchases wallpaper, £6·40 cash.

April 4th   Receives payment for redecorations, £9·50 by cheque (Bank Account opened). Sells materials, £11·20 (receives cheque).

April 5th   Receives for shop alterations £3·50 cash.

April 6th   Pays for hire of power spray (Equipment-Hired A/c) £3·00 cash. Sale of materials £4·40 cash.

April 7th   Receives for redecoration work £8·00 cheque. Buys ledger and other stationery, £1·25 cash.

Balance off the accounts where necessary and extract a Trial Balance as at April 7th.

5. D. Lobley sets up in business as a master locksmith with a capital of £1 000 which he banks on January 1st 19.. He then pays by cheque for two copy-cut machines for £185·00, tools for £35·00 and a supply of blank keys and other goods for resale, £120·00. Enter these items and then record the following transactions in his ledger.

January 2nd   Draws cash from bank, £50·00. Pays signwriter for supplying sign and painting name on door (General Expenses A/c), £5·50 cash.

January 3rd   Cash sales of cut keys £4·25.

January 4th   Receives for repairs of antique casket (Fees-Received A/c) £6·50 by cheque.

January 5th   Cash sales of cut keys £3·30. Sale of metal cash boxes £4·50 cash.

January 6th   Pays rent by cheque £10·00. Sales of storage chests and other items £22·55 cash.

Balance off those accounts which require it and extract a Trial Balance.

6. R. Sparrow is a market gardener who sets up in business on April 1st 19.. He has capital in cash of £50·00 and also brings in as part of his capital the following items: land and buildings £1 500·00; tools and equipment £240·00; a delivery van £85·00. Enter these items and then the following transactions.

April   5th Purchases artificial fertilizer in cash £8·50, also seeds £1·50.

April 13th Purchases garden fork £2·40 cash.
April 21st Sells seedling lettuces £4·25 cash.
April 28th Sells seedling cabbages, etc., £8·30.
April 30th Pays wages for casual worker £3·45.
Extract a Trial Balance as at April 30th 19. .

7. Complete these sentences:
   (a) Accounting is . . . . (see Section 1.1).
   (b) The purpose of business in a free-enterprise society is . . . .
   (see Section 1.2).

8. Complete the sentences below by inserting the correct word from the list
   in italics.
   (a) The government's share in the rewards of enterprise is called . . . .
   (b) A person running a business of his own pays a tax called . . . .
   tax.
   (c) A limited company pays a tax called . . . .
   (d) The basis of accounting is a very careful record of transactions called
   . . . . book-keeping.
   (e) The chief book of account is called the . . . .
   (f) A . . . . is a person who owes our firm money.
   (g) A person or firm to whom we owe money is said to be our . . . .
   (h) A number written in the top corner of a page is called a . . . .
   number.
   (i) The three classes of ledger accounts are called . . . . accounts,
   . . . . accounts and . . . . accounts.
   (j) Every business deal of any sort in which goods or services are supplied,
   or money is paid, is called a . . . .
   Word list: *transaction, taxation, double entry, corporation tax, income,
   personal, creditor, nominal, debtor, real, ledger, folio.*

Unit Two

A More Detailed Look at the Ledger

2.1 Book-keeping to the Trial Balance

We have already learned seven important points:

(a) Accounting records are kept by a system of *double-entry book-keeping*.
(b) The chief book of account is the *ledger*.
(c) Every leaf in the ledger is called *an account*.
(d) The left-hand side of an account is called the *debit side* and is used whenever the person or thing named at the top of the account *receives* goods, or services or money from the firm whose records are being kept in the ledger.
(e) The right-hand side of an account is called the *credit side* and is used whenever the person or thing named at the top of the account *gives* goods, or services or money to the firm whose records are being kept in the ledger.
(f) There are three classes of account: *personal accounts, nominal accounts* and *real accounts*.

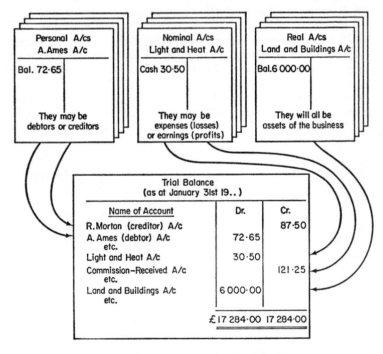

Fig. 2.1 Book-keeping to the Trial Balance

(g) At the end of any accounting period a *Trial Balance* may be struck. The various balances are listed in two columns, debit and credit, and the accuracy of the double entry checked by seeing that the two columns agree.

Diagrammatically the whole of *book-keeping to the Trial Balance* may be illustrated as in Fig. 2.1.

We must now go on to look more closely at these accounts and have some practice in making entries in typical accounts.

2.2 Traditional Accounts and Mechanized Accounts

The accounts already shown in Unit One, and illustrated again in Fig. 2.3 may be described as *traditional accounts,* that is, they have debit and credit sides to the account, and are balanced off at the end of the month, ready for the Trial Balance. This type of account has been improved upon in the last twenty-five years since the adoption of book-keeping machines which add up and subtract automatically. While it would be a terrible labour for a human book-keeper to balance off an account every time he made an entry in it, a machine can do it with no trouble at all. A machine can perform the calculations either mechanically or electronically, which means that accounts might as well be balanced off to a new balancing figure every time we make an entry in an account. This has, in recent years, brought about a change in the style of accounting. Where a business has a mechanized system, accounts are laid out as shown in Fig. 2.2. Accounts in this form are called *'continuous-balance accounts'*. Read the notes about this illustration carefully so that you can be sure you follow the revised layout of the debit and credit sides. However, the student, who cannot leave it to the machine to do the adding and subtracting and to work out all the arithmetic involved, would waste a good deal of time, so we must return to traditional accounts for our study of the ledger. (*See overleaf for notes to Fig. 2.2.*)

Ledger Name: Smith, L. R. Address: 37 High Road, Leigh-on-Thames, Essex.					
Date	*Details*	*Debit*	*Credit*	*Balance*	*Verification*
		£	£	£	£
Mar. 2 19..	Balance		12·30	12·30	24·60
Mar. 3 19..	Invoice No. 1712		184·40	196·70	393·40
Mar. 15 19..	Returns 165	7·70		189·00	378·00
Mar. 19 19..	Cheque 4146	12·30		176·70	353·40
Mar. 27 19..	Invoice No. 1758		15·40	192·10	384·20

Fig. 2.2 A continuous-balance mechanized account

Note the following:
(*a*) The page is no longer divided down the middle but instead the debit and credit columns are side by side.
(*b*) When the account receives value, as on March 15th and 19th, the account is debited.
(*c*) Since this is the account of a creditor, in other words a supplier, these debit entries are deducted from the running balance which is what we owe him at any given time.
(*d*) When the supplier gives goods to our firm the account is credited, as on March 3rd and 27th. These supplies increase the amount owed on the running balance.
(*e*) The 'verification' column is simply a safety device; it is, in fact, twice the running balance. It simply checks that the operator picks up the balances properly when she changes from one ledger card to another as she goes through her day's work.

2.3   Cash Transactions and Credit Transactions

(1) Cash Transactions
These take place whenever the goods supplied are paid for immediately, as in a shop. Clearly a person who pays in this way cannot become a debtor of the business, and the proprietor of the business cannot suffer any bad debts. There is no need to record the transaction at all, so that book-keeping time is saved. As the money is struck up on the cash register, it will usually be printed on the till roll, which gives, at the end of the day, a total 'daily cash takings' or 'daily cash-sales' figure. This figure will be recorded in the Sales Account to enable profits to be calculated later on. Many small businessmen prefer to keep all transactions in cash and many large firms, like supermarkets, deal similarly in cash only. We even have, these days, 'cash and-carry' warehouses, where retailers may purchase goods in bulk for *spot cash*, carrying them away in their own vans. Naturally they are able to purchase very cheaply, getting good *cash discounts* on purchases, because they are not asking the wholesaler for the usual services he supplies, i.e. transport and *credit*.

(2) Credit Transactions
The word 'credit' sometimes confuses students, for it has several common uses, some of which appear to conflict with others. The following explanations of the word 'credit' are worth a moment's consideration.
(*a*) *Credit*—the name given to the right-hand side of the ledger page, on which entries are made when a person, or thing, has given goods, services or money to the business.
(*b*) *Credit*—the name given to the transaction for which immediate payment is not made, but is postponed to some future time. The usual period of credit in business is one month. The person receiving goods or services pays for them at the end of the month, when a *statement of account* is sent

out requesting payment for all those transactions that have occurred in the last thirty days. This kind of trading is said to be on *monthly credit terms.*

(*c*) *Long-term credit*—often called 'hire-purchase credit' or 'extended credit' —requires payment to be made over a longer period of time, often up to three years. Hire-purchase credit terms are sometimes controlled by Government orders since they can be used to control the economy.

What is confusing about the use of the term 'credit' is that the person concerned becomes a '*debtor*'. Some students find this muddling, but it is not really difficult. The point is that the one who holds out the credit as an inducement to others to do business with him, becomes one of their 'creditors'. When inviting firms to do business with you on 'monthly credit terms' you are offering to become a creditor until the end of the month. They will therefore become your debtors, and you will incur some risk of bad debts. The small businessman, fearful of bad debts, often exhibits a notice reading 'Please do not ask for credit as a refusal may offend'. He prefers to deal in cash only.

2.4 Debtors' Personal Accounts

The people to whom we sell goods, or to whom we give services of some sort, become debtors of the business and must eventually pay for the goods or services received. They also occasionally return goods which are unsatisfactory for some reason, or they may be made an allowance for some overcharge or as compensation for some dissatisfaction they feel about the service provided. It follows that any debtor's account may have the following entries:

(1) Debit Entries in a Debtor's Account
(*a*) *The opening balance.* This will almost always be a debit balance at the start of the month, since the debtor is in debt (debit).
(*b*) *Invoice entries.* Invoices are made out whenever goods or services are supplied (see Section 10.2) showing how much the debtor must pay for the goods or services he has received.
(*c*) *Debit-note entries.* Very much like invoices; generally used to correct some under-charge on an invoice, or to charge the debtor with carriage, packing expenses, etc.

(2) Credit Entries in a Debtor's Account
(*a*) *Credit-note entries.* Credit notes are made out when goods are returned, or when allowances are made after some complaint.
(*b*) *Cash or cheques.* When these are received by the firm, the debtor is given credit as he has paid some of his debt.
(*c*) *Discount entries.* These may be cash or settlement discounts given for prompt payment (see Section 14.2). They reduce the debtor's debt.

(d) *The closing-balance*. This will be carried down to the debit side as the outstanding debt at the end of the month.

Fig. 2.3 shows such a debtor's account.

M. Rostov, 15 High Road, Saltsea, Sussex. Dr.							DL 18 Cr.
19..			£	19..			£
Apr. 1	Balance	B/d	145·50	Apr. 7	Bank		138·22
2	Sales		36·80	7	Discount		
3	,,		12·50		Allowed		7·28
3	Carriage			12	Sales Returns		8·40
	Outwards		1·50	30	Balance	c/d	383·80
8	Sales		45·50				
11	,,		149·00				
17	,,		65·00				
29	,,		80·50				
29	Insurance		1·40				
		£	537·70			£	537·70
May 1	Balance	B/d	383·80				

Fig. 2.3 A debtor's account

Note :

(a) The year is written at the top of the date column. To save constant alteration only the figures 19.. have been shown here. You should read this as if it were the current year.

(b) The words used in the details column are sometimes a source of some difficulty. The correct word to use in every case *is the name of the account where the double entry will be found*. Thus on April 2nd the double entry would be on the Sales Account, since Rostov has been sold goods to the value of £36·80. On April 7th the payment was by cheque, which will have been entered in the Bank Account, and the discount allowed to Rostov for prompt payment will have been entered in the Discount-Allowed Account.

(c) Only three *folio numbers* have been entered here. They are B/d, c/d, and B/d. These refer to 'Brought down' and 'carried down', and are used whenever an account is balanced off. (Traditionally a capital letter was always used for 'Brought down', but not for 'carried down'.) An explanation of folio numbers is given later (see Section 3.5) where the division of the ledger into several parts is discussed. But you should note that this account, which is a debtor's account, is in the *Debtor's Ledger*, and has a folio number DL 18.

(d) The balancing off of the account is carried out on the same line so that the two sides are level, and a currency symbol has been inserted to emphasize that a 'balance' has been struck at this point. This must leave the shorter side with some unused lines. These are struck through, in red ink, to prevent later entries being made in the spare lines.

(e) An account with a balance on it must have the balance brought down before it can be called complete. *It would be quite wrong to leave the account levelled off*—in this case at a total of £537·70. This would give the impression that the account was clear, when in fact Rostov still owes us the sum of £383·80.

(*f*) As the balance is brought down the date is changed to May 1st, i.e. the first day of the next month to show clearly what the debtor owes at this date.

Do the following exercises without worrying about the double entry for each transaction you are entering. Of course in real business you would never make an entry in one account without making an equal and opposite entry in some other account, but here we are just concerned about practising the keeping of a single account.

Remember the rules for entries in a debtor's account:

Debit the debtor's account when he receives goods, or services or money from your business.

Credit the debtor's account when he gives back goods, or deserves an allowance off his debt because of some dis-service you have done to him, or when he gives money in payment.

2.5   Exercises Set 2: Debtors' Personal Accounts

1. C. Hadland is a debtor of ours, whose account has the folio number DL 17. On January 1st 19. . he has a debit balance of £402·97. Then these transactions take place:

January 2nd Hadland pays us the amount owed on January 1st, by cheque, less discount of £20·15.

January 3rd Hadland orders goods which he collects by private messenger, value £47·50.

January 14th He orders more goods, value £72·50. We charge him carriage £4·25.

January 16th Hadland orders goods, value £285·00, and agrees to pay £100·00 on account. His cheque for this amount is brought by his van driver when he collects the goods.

January 27th Hadland returns packing cases, value £4·50.

Balance off the account on January 31st and bring down the balance.

2. G. Wakeman is a debtor of ours for the sum of £5·25 on May 1st 19. . His account number is DL 32. During May the following transactions take place.

May 2nd   Wakeman pays the balance owing by cheque, less discount of £0·13.

May 5th   Wakeman orders goods valued at £27·55.

May 7th   He orders further goods for £62·50 and is charged for insurance £1·50.

May 18th   Wakeman returns goods sold to him on May 5th. Their value is £8·50.

May 29th   Wakeman orders goods for £12·25.

May 31st   We balance off the account and bring down the balance.

3. (a) M. Watts is a debtor of ours for the sum of £720·50 on July 1st 19. .
His account number is DL 194. During July the following transactions
take place. Enter them into Watts's account after you have opened it
with the balance shown above. Close the account on July 31st and bring
down the balance.

July   3rd   Watts pays the balance owing on July 1st by cheque, less a
              discount of 2½ per cent = £18·01.

July   4th   Watts is sold goods valued at £41·25.

July   5th   Watts returns goods, damaged in transit, worth £7·77.

July 15th   Watts purchases more goods value £142·50. He is charged
              carriage £1·25 and insurance £0·75.

July 29th   Watts agrees to sell us a surplus machine, valued at £650, the
              sum to be set against his account.

July 30th   Watts is sold goods valued at £380·50.

(b) Explain what is unusual about this balance in the debtor's account on
July 31st.

4. (a) Here is a ledger account in the books of Peter Lee. Copy it out on a
piece of ledger paper, balance it off on March 31st and bring down the
balance. Then answer the questions below.

R. T. Crafty, 14 High Street, Rowford, Essex.							DL 31
19. .			£				£
Mar. 1	Balance	B/d	405·75	Mar. 3	Bank		395·61
11	Sales		274·50	3	Discount		10·14
19	Sales		100·00	27	Returns		12·50
20	Carriage		5·50	28	Motor Vans		150·00

(b) On March 1st was Crafty a debtor or a creditor?

(c What happened on March 27th according to this account?

(d) What happened on March 28th according to this account?

(e) On March 31st was Crafty a debtor or a creditor?

5. (a) Here is M. Fisher's account in W. Sandon's books. Copy it out and
complete it for the month of May 19... Then answer the questions
below.

M. Fisher, 87 Peartree Way, Newtown, Herts.							DL 72
19. .			£	19. .			£
May 1	Balance	B/d	15·25	May 2	Bank		14·49
14	Sales		10·50	2	Discount		0·76
29	,,		12·25	30	Sewing		
29	Carriage		0·55		Machines		68·50

(b) On May 1st was Fisher a debtor or a creditor?
(c) What happened on May 2nd?
(d) What happened on May 30th?
(e) What is unusual about the balance on May 31st?

2.6   Creditors' Personal Accounts

When we buy from a supplier he becomes a creditor of the business. The personal account of a creditor is exactly the same as the personal account of a debtor but the items appear on the opposite side. Instead of receiving goods from our business (a debit entry) the creditor is giving goods to our business, so we must *credit the giver*. Fig. 2.4 shows such a creditor's account.

19..			£	19..			£
Jan. 2	Purchases			Jan. 1	Balance	B/d	490·55
	Returns		9·55	17	Purchases		235·60
30	Bank		481·00	17	,,		71·90
31	Purchases			19	Interest due		4·81
	Returns		5·50	28	Purchases		64·50
31	Balance	c/d	500·36	28	Purchases		125·30
				29	Carriage		3·75
			£ 996·41				£ 996·41
				19..			£
				Feb. 1	Balance	B/d	500·36

R. Michaelson, 17 Low Road, Upper Hilton, Staffs.   CL 27 Dr.   Cr.

Fig. 2.4 A creditor's account

Notice the item 'interest due' on January 19th. Michaelson has charged us one per cent interest on the balance still owing from January 1st. It appears we should have paid more promptly.

You should now practise the keeping of creditor's accounts by making the entries for the exercises below.

Remember the rules for entries in a creditor's account.

Credit the creditor whenever he gives goods, or services or money to your business.

Debit the creditor when he receives payment from your firm or receives back goods you have returned to him, or makes you an allowance because you are dissatisfied.

2.7   Exercises Set 3: Creditors' Personal Accounts

1. R. Bolton is a supplier of ours, to whom we owe a balance of £40·75 on August 1st 19.. Open his ledger account CL 21 and then enter the following transactions for the month.

   August   2nd We pay the outstanding balance by cheque, less £2·04 discount.

   August 13th Bolton supplies goods valued at £85·00.

   August 17th He supplies more goods valued at £16·50.

   August 18th We return goods to Bolton £5·75.

   August 19th He makes us an allowance on goods that need repolishing because of damage in transit £8·40.

   August 27th He supplies goods value £132·50 and also charges insurance on transit £1·50.

   August 31st Account balanced off and brought down.

2. R. Lucas is in business as a manufacturer and the following are his transactions with T. Robertson for the month of January 19..

   January   1st Balance due to Robertson £500·00.

   January 10th Buys from Robertson 30 tonnes scrap at £95 per tonne = £2 850·00.

   January 12th Pays Robertson, by cheque, the balance due to him, on January 1st, less five per cent settlement discount.

   January 14th Buys from Robertson 4 tonnes scrap zinc at £97 per tonne = £388·00.

   January 16th Returns to Robertson 5 tonnes scrap purchased on January 10th.

   January 16th Pays carriage on above return, £12·50 chargeable to Robertson.

   January 27th Sells to Robertson a bulldozer at agreed valuation £880·00.

   January 29th Buys from Robertson aluminium scrap sheeting valued at £42·00.

   You are required to open Robertson's account in Lucas's books CL 47; balance off the account and bring down the balance.

3. A. Miller is in business in the household durable-goods trade and is supplied by Universal Warehouses Ltd. On January 1st 19.. the supplier is owed £729·54 by Miller. Open the supplier's account in Miller's book CL 94 and make the following additional entries.

   January   2nd Miller pays the full amount owing by cheque.

   January   4th Goods supplied to Miller £248·50.

   January 11th Goods supplied to Miller £320·75. Miller returns empties, etc., £4·55.

   January 18th Goods supplied to Miller £452·65. Miller returns discoloured goods £16·75 and empties £4·05.

January 19th   Miller buys for use in the shops a cash register (Furniture
and Fittings A/c) valued at £215·50.

January 25th   Goods supplied £184·55. Returned empties £15·25.

January 31st   Account balanced off and brought down.

4. Here is the Ledger Account of R. Jones as it appears in the books of Lee
Bros. Copy out the account and balance it off at the end of the month.

R. Jones.							CL 55
19..			£	19..		B/d	£
Jan. 2	Purchases			Jan. 1	Balance		234·70
	Returns		7·70	14	Purchases		48·60
3	Bank		221·32	15	Carriage		4·40
3	Discount		5·68	17	Purchases		133·10
23	Purchases			18	Insurance and		
	Returns		4·12		Carriage		7·12
30	Motor Lorry						
	(Exchange)		150·00				

Now answer these questions:

(a) What does each line mean? Deal with them in date order.

(b) Who owes the balance to whom?

5. Here is a ledger account in the books of M. Bright. Copy out the account
on a piece of ledger paper; balance it off on February 28th 19.. and
bring down the balance. Then answer the questions below.

P. B. Rowe, 27 Hill Road, Canewdon, Essex.							CL 39
19..			£	19..		B/d	£
Feb. 2	Bank		702·39	Feb. 1	Balance		720·40
2	Discount		18·01	11	Purchases		425·50
14	Returns		25·50	19	Purchases		285·50
18	Motor Vehicles		1 650·00	20	Carriage		12·50

(a) On February 1st, was Rowe a debtor or a creditor?

(b) What happened on February 14th according to this account?

(c) What happened on February 18th according to this account?

(d) On February 28th, was Rowe a debtor or a creditor?

More Advanced Accounting to the Trial Balance

3.1 Business Documents

If a transaction is a cash transaction, for instance when a child buys an ice-cream from a hawker's van, no accounting records are kept, and no documents pass between the two parties. Where a transaction is a credit transaction an accounting record will have to be kept at least until payment is received, and generally much longer. The law says that a legal action on a simple bargain may be brought at any time within six years of the bargain being struck (Limitations Act, 1939). Therefore if the transaction is a credit transaction, requiring records to be kept of the bargain, these records should be preserved for at least six years. The usual documentary record of a bargain is an *invoice*, but of course there are more formal agreements which are drawn up by lawyers—deeds and leases are examples. Other documents are: *credit notes*, for returns, cheques and credit-transfer slips for payments; *receipts* for acknowledging payments, and so on. Not all documents lead to book-keeping records—for instance an *order* is an offer to buy, but it does not become a bargain between the parties until it is accepted by the supplier, who prepares an *invoice*. The documents that lead to book-keeping records are called *original* documents and lead to entries in books of original entry. These books are discussed later (see Units Nine to Sixteen).

3.2 The Documents that Lead to Book-keeping Entries

The documents that lead to book-keeping entries are shown in full in Sections 10.2 and 11.2. Briefly they are:

(1) Invoices
These are made out by the supplier (seller) of goods and given to the receiver (buyer) as evidence of the bargain struck.

They are prepared with the names and addresses of both parties to the transaction and include a description of the goods and their value. Then the ledger entries are as shown in Figs. 3.1 and 3.2. Here we are keeping the books of A. Retailer.

(2) Credit Notes
These are always printed in red and are made out (again) by the seller of goods when customers send back goods which are unsatisfactory. They may also be used to give an allowance where goods are not actually returned but are

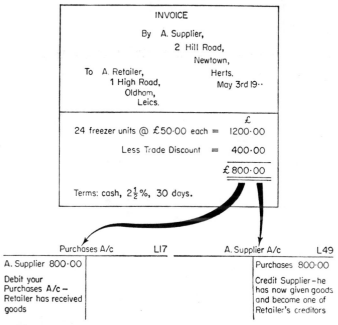

Fig. 3.1 Double entries for purchases invoices for goods received

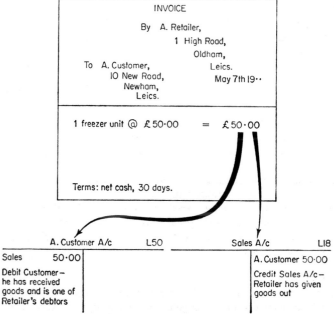

Fig. 3.2 Double entries for sales invoices for goods dispatched

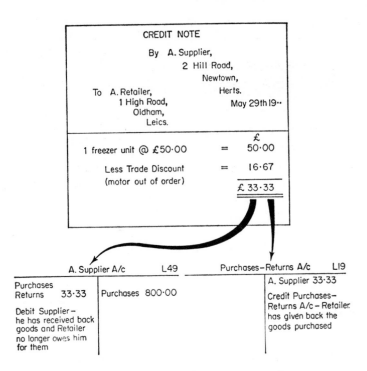

Fig. 3.3 Double entries for returns outwards

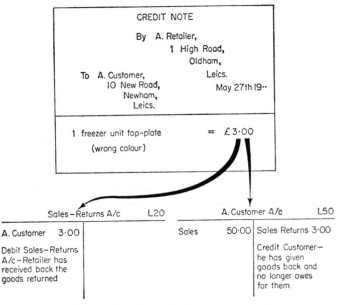

Fig. 3.4 Double entries for returns inwards

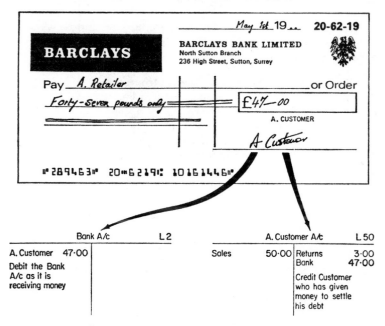

Fig. 3.5 Double entries for a cheque received

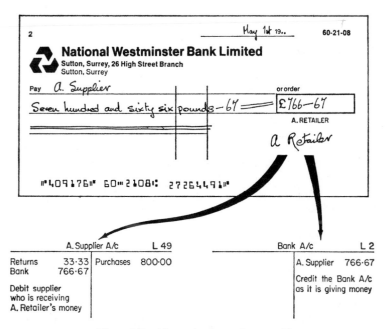

Fig. 3.6 Double entries for a cheque paid

for some reason not worth the full invoice price—for example where they were slightly damaged in transit. The ledger entries are as shown in Figs. 3.3 and 3.4.

(3) Cheques, Credit Transfers, Postal Orders, etc.
These are used to settle indebtedness between businessmen. They lead to entries in the Bank Account as shown in Figs. 3.5 and 3.6.

Having looked at some of the most important accounting documents, a further word on the use of accounting paper is helpful here. There are many rulings of paper used, but the three chief ones are: *ledger paper, journal paper* and *three-column cash paper*. The first two are all that need concern us for the moment; three-column cash paper is discussed in Section 14.2.

3.3   The Use of Ledger Paper when Studying Accounting

As we said earlier, in a ledger in a business office every leaf of the book—that is both sides of a sheet of paper—are reserved for the transactions with the one person, or thing, named at the top. We must never put Tom Smith's transactions on Peter Brown's page. But this is not possible when students are doing exercises involving, perhaps, twenty accounts which will have only one or two entries on them. It would waste too much ledger paper. The usual solution is to put about six accounts on a page, but pretend that they are separate accounts and give them separate folio numbers. An alternative way is demonstrated in the model exercise in Section 17.2.

3.4   Journal Paper in Accounting

'Journal' comes from the French word 'le jour', which means 'day', and journal paper is often called 'day-book' paper. The Journal, or Day Book, is a very important book which we must learn about later (see Section 9.2), but the ruling is shown here because it is very useful for Trial Balances. The two columns on the right-hand side are used for the Dr. and Cr. balances. The columns can be ruled across at the end of the Trial Balance and neat totals can be prepared, as shown in the model exercise on page 37.

Month	Day	Details	Folio	Dr.	Cr.

Fig. 3.7 Journal (Day-Book) paper

3.5   Folio Numbers

All book-keeping papers have special columns for folio numbers. These are used as cross references for page numbers. In the ledger of the model exercise that follows, the folio numbers have been inserted as cross references. On every line of this example there appears the folio number of the ledger account where the other half of the double entry will be found. In your own exercises from now on you should put in the folio numbers. You should also use these numbers throughout the model exercise and check the accuracy of the cross references given.

The exercises in this Unit are a little longer than those in Unit One. They use the new knowledge you will have acquired in this Unit by referring to documents such as invoices, credit notes and cheques, and they introduce a wider variety of expenses of the business. In every case, however, simple double-entry book-keeping is all that is required. *If you need to revise, you should do so at this point* so that you gain more confidence. The model exercise shown below will help you in your revision of double entry.

3.6   Model Exercise to the Trial Balance

R. Peabody sets up in business on January 1st 19.. as a retail grocer, with the following assets: land and buildings £3 850·00; equipment £720·00; stock £350·00; cash at bank £650·00 and cash in hand £35·00. Open up the necessary accounts, including the Capital Account, and then enter the following items.

January   4th   Cash Sales £32·50. Sales on credit to R. Johnston £42·50. Pays rate demand by cheque, £12·50.

January 11th   Buys shop shelving and equipment from Dexter Ltd. by cheque £27·00. Pays signwriter (General-Expenses Account) £4·35 by cheque. Buys goods for resale from Ivor Brown Ltd. on credit £234·50.

January 15th   Cash sales £78·50. Pays travelling expenses in cash £3·25. Pays for repairs to premises in cash, £4·20. Returns goods to Ivor Brown Ltd., £15·50.

January 24th   Cash sales £42·60. Purchases goods for resale from Mohican Bros. Ltd., £105·25, on credit.

January 31st   Pays Ivor Brown's outstanding account by cheque. Cash sales £93·75. Banks £200·00 from cash till.

Notes:

The double entries would be as shown below, and may be followed in the accounts of Fig. 3·8.

January   1st   For the opening situation, all the assets brought in are real items, and must be debited in their real accounts; the Capital A/c will be credited with the total value contributed to the business. We therefore have:

Debit	Land and Buildings	£3 850·00
	Equipment	£ 720·00
	Stock	£350·00
	Cash at Bank	£650·00
	Cash in Hand	£35·00
Credit	Capital A/c	£5 605·00

January 4th Debit Cash A/c £32·50; credit Sales A/c £32·50.
Debit R. Johnston A/c £42·50; credit Sales A/c £42·50.
Debit Rates A/c £12·50; credit Bank A/c £12·50.

January 11th Debit Equipment A/c £27·00; credit Bank A/c £27·00.
Debit General-Expenses A/c £4·35; credit Bank A/c £4·35.
Debit Purchases A/c £234·50; credit Ivor Brown Ltd. A/c £234·50.

January 15th Debit Cash A/c £78·50; credit Sales A/c £78·50.
Debit Travelling-Expenses A/c £3·25; credit Cash A/c £3·25.
Debit Repairs A/c £4·20; credit Cash A/c £4·20.
Debit Ivor Brown Ltd., £15·50; credit Purchases-Returns A/c £15·50.

January 24th Debit Cash A/c £42·60; credit Sales A/c £42·60.
Debit Purchases A/c £105·25; credit Mohican Bros. Ltd. £105·25.

January 31st Debit Ivor Brown Ltd. £219·00; credit Bank A/c £219·00.
Debit Cash A/c £93·75; credit Sales A/c £93·75.
Debit Bank A/c £200·00; credit Cash A/c £200·00.

			Land and Buildings A/c				L 1
19..		F	£				
Jan.	1 Capital	L 6	3 850·00				

			Equipment A/c				L 2
19..		F	£				
Jan.	1 Capital	L 6	720·00				
	11 Bank	L 4	27·00				

			Stock A/c				L 3
19..		F	£				
Jan.	1 Capital	L 6	350·00				

			Bank A/c				L 4
19..		F	£	19..		F	£
Jan.	1 Capital	L 6	650·00	Jan. 4 Rates	L 9	12·50	
	31 Cash	L 5	200·00	11 Equipment	L 2	27·00	
				11 General Expenses	L 10	4·35	
				31 Ivor Brown	L 11	219·00	
				31 Balance	c/d	587·15	
			£850·00			£850·00	
19..							
Feb. 1		B/d	587·15				

Fig. 3.8 A model exercise to the Trial Balance

Cash A/c   L 5

19..		F	£	19..		F	£
Jan.	1 Capital	L 6	35·00	Jan. 15 Travelling			
	4 Sales	L 7	32·50		Expenses	L 13	3·25
	5 Sales	L 7	78.50		15 Repairs	L 14	4.20
	24 Sales	L 7	42·60		31 Bank	L 4	200·00
	31 Sales	L 7	93·75		31 Balance	c/d	74·90
			£282·35				£282·35
Feb.	1 Balance	B/d	74·90				

Capital A/c   L 6

				19..		F	£
				Jan.	1 Sundry assets	L 1–5 5	605·00

Sales A/c   L 7

				19..		F	£
				Jan.	4 Cash	L 5	32·50
					4 R. Johnston	L 8	42·50
					15 Cash	L 5	78·50
					24 Cash	L 5	42·60
					31 Cash	L 5	93·75

R. Johnston A/c   L 8

19..		F	£
Jan.	4 Sales	L 7	42·50

Rates A/c   L 9

19..		F	£
Jan.	4 Bank	L 4	12·50

General-Expenses A/c   L 10

19..		F	£
Jan.	11 Bank	L 4	4·35

Fig. 3.8 A model exercise to the Trial Balance (continued)

Ivor Brown Ltd. A/c   L 11

19..		F	£	19..		F	£
Jan.	15 Purchases			Jan.	11 Purchases	L 12	234·50
	Returns	L 15	15·50				
	31 Bank	L 4	219·00				
			£234·50				£234·50

Purchases A/c   L 12

19..		F	£
Jan.	11 Ivor Brown		
	Ltd.	L 11	234·50
	24 Mohican Bros.	L 16	105·25

Travelling-Expenses A/c   L 13

19..		F	£
Jan.	15 Cash	L 5	3·25

Repairs A/c   L 14

19..		F	£
Jan.	15 Cash	L 5	4·20

Purchases-Returns A/c   L 15

				19..		F	£
				Jan.	15 Ivor Brown Ltd.	L 11	15·50

Mohican Bros. Ltd. A/c   L 16

				19..		F	£
				Jan.	24 Purchases	L 12	105·25

Fig. 3.8. A model exercise to the Trial Balance (continued)

Trial Balance
(as at January 31st 19. .)

	F	Dr.	Cr.
		£	£
Land and Buildings	L 1	3 850·00	
Equipment A/c	L 2	747·00	
Stock A/c	L 3	350·00	
Bank A/c	L 4	587·15	
Cash A/c	L 5	74·90	
Capital A/c	L 6		5 605·00
Sales A/c	L 7		289·85
R. Johnston A/c	L 8	42·50	
Rates A/c	L 9	12·50	
General-Expenses A/c	L 10	4·35	
Purchases A/c	L 12	339·75	
Travelling-Expenses A/c	L 13	3·25	
Repairs A/c	L 14	4·20	
Purchases-Returns A/c	L 15		15·50
Mohican Bros. Ltd.	L 16		105·25
		£6 015·60	6 015·60

3.7   Exercises Set 4: More Practice in Double-Entry Book-keeping to the Trial-Balance Level

1. On June 1st 19. . E. Saxby, who has experience in the clothing industry sets up in business with a capital of £3 500·00, made up of land and buildings £2 000·00, furniture and fittings £300·00 and the rest in cash, which he banks except for £50·00. Open up the necessary accounts to record these matters and then enter the following further transactions:

June 1st   Buys goods for resale on credit from R. Marsh, value £280·00.
June 2nd   Pays rates £15·50, electric-light deposit £5·00, and telephone connexion fee £3·50, all by cheque.
June 3rd   Buys materials for use in making up goods for resale, £35·00 cash.
June 4th   Cash sales £65·00. Credit sales to R. Lebon £68·50.
June 5th   Pays for postage £2·25, cottons and threads (Purchases A/c) £7·50, and buys goods for resale, £15·00, all in cash.
June 6th   Sends invoice to R. Johnson for goods sold to him on credit, £27·50. Receives invoice from M. Walker for goods supplied by him on credit, for resale, £42·00.

Balance off the accounts and extract a Trial Balance as at June 6th.

2. On July 1st 19. . G. Parker sets up in business as a stationer with capital of £4 800·00, consisting of furniture and fittings £1 000·00, stock £2 000·00, cash at bank £1 000·00 and the rest in cash. Open the necessary accounts and then enter the following transactions:

July 1st   Pays rent £30·00 in cash, purchases goods for resale on credit from H. Roach £285·50, and pays for hire of till and scales in cash, £27·50.

July 2nd   Cash sales £18·55, credit sales to Rose and Frank Ltd., £37·50.

July 3rd   Postage £4·50 cash, travelling expenses £3·65 cash, and cash sales £42·65. Agrees to employ assistant for £45·00 per week; gives him a £25·00 advance on salary.

July 5th   Receives invoice from T. Law for goods supplied by him on credit, £120·00.

July 6th   Cash sales £84·75. Cash purchases of goods for resale £3·75. Purchases on credit from T. Yates goods valued at £75·50.

Balance off the accounts and extract a Trial Balance.

3. On April 1st 19.. T. Lawrence sets up in business with a capital of £1 500·00, made up of land and buildings £1 000·00, furniture and fittings £200·00, and the rest in cash which he banks, except for £25·00. Open the necessary accounts to record these matters and then enter the following further transactions:

April 1st   Buys goods for resale on credit from R. Sims, value £56·50.

April 2nd   Pays rates £15·00, electric-light deposit £5·50, and telephone connexion fee £3·50, all by cheque.

April 3rd   Buys materials for use in making up goods for resale, by cheque £125·00.

April 4th   Cash sales £48·00. Credit sales to R. Morton £15·00.

April 5th   Pays for postage £5·50 cash, travelling expenses £4·20 cash, and buys goods for resale, £275·00, on credit from R. Large.

April 6th   Sends invoice to R. J. Moss for goods sold to him on credit £50·00. Receives invoice from M. Rowe for goods supplied by him for resale £45·00.

Balance off the accounts and extract a Trial Balance as at April 6th.

4. On July 1st 19.. M. Rowcliffe sets up in business as a stationer with capital of £850·00, consisting of furniture and fittings £200·00, equipment £135·00 and the rest in cash. Open the necessary accounts and then enter the following transactions.

July 1st   Banks £500·00 for safe keeping. Pays rent £25·00 by cheque, purchases goods for resale on credit from H. Rogerson £142·00, and pays for hire of till and scales, £12·00, cheque.

July 2nd   Cash sales £18·55, credit sales to Roach and Lane Ltd., £48·50.

July 3rd   Postage £5·50 cash, travelling expenses £3·25 cash and cash sales £14·75. Agrees to employ assistant for £55·00 per week; gives him £27·50 cash advance on salary.

July 5th   Receives invoice from R. Lyons for goods supplied on credit, £50·00.

July 6th   Cash sales £27·25. Cash purchases of goods for resale £5·30. Purchases on credit from M. Loman goods valued at £47·50.

Balance off the accounts and extract a Trial Balance.

5. On November 1st 19. . R. Turf sets up in business as a landscape gardener with a capital made up of tools and equipment, £320·00, stock of materials £172·00 and cash £550·00 of which £500·00 is banked. Open up the accounts necessary to record these matters and then record also the following transactions.

November   6th Purchases materials for use in draining land, £42·00 cheque. R. Coombes agrees to settle his account on November 30th for work done, £50·00. Recorded him as a debtor, and credited Fees Received Account.

November 13th Purchases materials £30·00 by cheque. Sale of rock for decorative work, £25·50 cash. Pays wages to casual worker £6·00 cash.

November 20th Purchases materials, £84·00 by cheque. Receives cash for work done (Fees-Received A/c) £80·00. Banks £50·00.

November 27th Wages to casual worker, £10·00 cash. Pays for materials, £35·00 cheque, and for transport £4·50 cash.

November 30th Balances off accounts and prepares a Trial Balance.

6. R. Tilehurst is a smith and wrought-iron specialist who sets up in business on June 1st 19. . making decorative ironwork. He has a capital consisting of premises £1 550·00, stock £820·00, and equipment £200·00. He also has a bank balance of £270·00 and £30·00 in cash. Record these items, then enter the following transactions:

June   2nd   Pays telephone connexion fee, £3·50 cash.

June   3rd   Pays for small fittings in cash, £12·25. Receives invoice from Imperial Iron Co. for metal, £250·00, on credit until June 30th. Sells iron gates £22·35 for cash.

June   4th   Pays wages of part-time assistant, £10·00 cash. Pays for charcoal and solder £3·00 cash. Sends invoice to Ocean Hotel Ltd., £37·50, for goods supplied.

June 10th   Cash sales £18·50. Purchases raw materials at auction, £27·50, for use in making up goods for resale, cheque. Pays carrier £5·50 and casual helper £2·00, both in cash.

June 17th   Cash sales £27·35. Invoices Alhambro Garden Works for goods supplied, £86·50. Pays carriage £4·50 in cash.

June 23rd   Receives invoice from Imperial Iron Co. Ltd. for goods supplied by them on credit, £186·50.

June 30th   Pays wages to part-time assistant £24·50 by cheque. Pays for fuel oil £7·20 cash, small items for use in making up goods for resale £11·50 cash. Balances off accounts and draws up a Trial Balance.

Accounting to Final-Accounts Level
Part One: The Trial Balance

4.1 Accounting to Final-Accounts Level

In Unit One we saw that the first level of maturity in accounting is to reach the Trial-Balance level of work, where the student can enter transactions in the ledger, balance off the accounts at the end of a month and prepare a Trial Balance of the ledger, getting the two sides to agree.

The second level of work in accounting is called 'Final-Accounts' level, because the student moves on past the Trial Balance to prepare two Final Accounts: the *Trading Account* and the *Profit and Loss Account*. The first of these is used to discover what is known as the *gross profit* or overall profit. The second is used to prepare the *net profit* or clean profit of the business. This net profit of course belongs to the owner, or owners, of the business, and will be handed over to the *sole proprietor*, or shared among the *partners* or *shareholders*, as a reward for the enterprise they have shown.

Final-Accounts work is therefore concerned with *discovering the profits of an enterprise, and paying them over to the person or persons entitled to enjoy them.*

The starting point for the preparation of these Final Accounts is the Trial Balance. We must now analyse a typical Trial Balance very carefully to make quite sure we understand exactly what it consists of.

4.2 Analysing the Trial Balance

Figure 4.1 shows a typical Trial Balance, prepared on December 31st 19.., after D. Webster has been in business for one month. Also provided is a set of notes, arranged in two columns. Study these notes carefully.

The reader will notice that a summary of the notes reveals that the debit and credit columns contain the following types of item.

Dr.	Cr.
3 Trading A/c items	2 Trading A/c items
Loss items	Profit items
Assets	Liabilities
A special asset	A special liability
(drawings of the proprietor)	(capital of the proprietor)

To make the picture complete, we should point out that outside the Trial Balance, not yet recorded on the books of the business, is the closing stock which, like the opening stock shown, is a Trading-Account item.

Trial Balance of D. Webster's books (as at December 31st 19..)

Accounts	Dr. £	Cr. £	Notes (Dr.)	Notes (Cr.)
Purchases	1 400·00		Trading A/c	
Sales		1 865·50		Trading A/c
Purchases-Returns		100·00		Trading A/c
Sales-Returns	65·50		Trading A/c	
Stock (as at Dec. 1st 19..)	200·00		Trading A/c	
Warehouse Wages	100·00		Loss	
Warehouse-Expenses	56·00		Loss	
Light and Heat	28·50		Loss	
Repairs	5·50		Loss	
Rent (Branch shop)	50·00		Loss	
Discount-Allowed	42·50		Loss	
Discount-Received		32·50		Profit
Commission-Received		12·00		Profit
Land and Buildings	8 750·00		Asset	
Furniture and Fittings	1 250·00		Asset	
Motor-Vehicles	1 500·00		Asset	
Sundry-Debtors	650·50		Asset	
Sundry-Creditors		430·50		Liabilities
Plant and Machinery	880·00		Asset	
Cash	164·75		Asset	
Bank	2 047·25		Asset	
Drawings (D. Webster)	220·00		Special Asset	
Mortgage on Premises		2 000·00		Liability
Loan (Finance Co.)		1 000·00		Liability
Capital (D. Webster)		12 000·00		Special Liability
Carriage In	30·00		Loss	
	£17 440·50	17 440·50		

The closing stock was found to be worth £300·00.

Fig. 4.1 A Trial Balance (with notes)

It is very important to realize where all these balances belong. The outstanding balance of an asset account, for example, will always be a debit balance and will appear in the debit column of the Trial Balance. If a Trial Balance had an asset account with a credit balance it would clearly be wrong, for assets never appear in the credit column. The liabilities, which are the opposite of assets, appear in that column. Similarly the losses are all debit items, and the profits of the business all credit items.

4.3   The Drawings Account—a Special Type of Asset

As we saw in Section 1.5, the Capital Account is a liability, because the business owes back to the proprietor the amount contributed by him. Normally he will not be repaid unless the business closes down, or, for example, if he retires. However, the proprietor needs to live, to pay his personal bills, and to keep up his domestic establishment. He cannot draw wages, for the proprietor is not an employee, even if he works in the business full-time. He is entitled to the profits of the enterprise when they are discovered at the end of the financial year. In the meantime how shall he support his family? The answer is by 'drawings', that is the withdrawal of such sums of money as he needs in expectation of profits. He may draw in cash from the cash box (credit Cash Account and debit Drawings Account) or he may draw by cheque from the bank (credit Bank Account and debit Drawings Account). He may even draw 'goods', taking home goods from work, which have been bought for re-sale but which instead he decides to take for his own use. Because of a decision in the House of Lords (Sharkey *v.* Wernher (1953))— a decision which is contrary to common sense and sound accounting principles—we have to treat the matter as a 'sale' to himself at Selling Price. This means we must credit Sales Account and debit Drawings Account. Whatever the type of drawings, the proprietor becomes a debtor of the business for that amount until the end of the trading year. At the end of the year, if the business has been profitable, he will be entitled to the profits made, less the sums already drawn. If the business has made a loss, the proprietor will be in debt to the business for the amount drawn, which will have to be set against the capital originally contributed. He has been 'living off his capital', which consequently *reduces by the amount of both his Drawings Account, and of his losses.*

4.4   The Trading-Account Items

There are five items in the Trial Balance (and a sixth item outside it, the closing stock) which are described as Trading-Account items. These are the raw data from which profits are calculated, and which form the basis of the *Trading Account*, discussed fully in Section 5.2. For the present it is sufficient if you remember the following points:

(*a*) Purchases and sales are opposites: one brings goods into the business to fill the shelves, the other removes them into the consumers' baskets.

(*b*) Sales returns and purchases returns are also opposites. The former brings back into the business goods formerly sold because for some reason the customer is dissatisfied with them. The latter removes goods from the business because of defects, and returns them to his supplier.

(*c*) Opening stock is an asset—at least it is on the first day of the year. It may be sold by the end of that day, or the next day. It is a rather special item. Closing stock is similarly rather special, and does not appear on the books at all: it is found by stock-taking.

Now practise drawing up Trial Balances by doing Exercises Set 5.

4.5   Exercises Set 5: Drawing up Trial Balances

1. Prepare a Trial Balance from the following accounts which appear in R. Fowler's books on March 31st 19. .
   Discount allowed £26·45; capital £1 500·00; rent and rates £250·00; office expenses £142·50; loan from M. Castle £1 000·00; stock in hand at April 1st 19. . £600·00; sundry creditors £845·00; cash at bank £1 970·55; plant and machinery £1 750·00; returns inwards £45·50; trade expenses £248·50; Sales A/c £6 560·00; purchases £1 580·50; cash in hand £65·50; freehold property £2 000·00; sundry debtors £1 225·50.

2. The following accounts in A. Dealer's books have balances on them at April 30th 19. . You are asked to arrange them in Trial-Balance form.

Sundry-Debtors' A/cs	£2 516·50	Office-Salaries A/c	£265·50
Sundry-Creditors' A/cs	£4 826·50	Light and Heat A/c	£104·40
Land and Buildings A/c		Telephone A/c	£76·70
	£13 000·00	Warehouse-Wages A/c	£1 595·50
Plant and Machinery A/c		General-Expenses A/c	£295·50
	£11 550·00		

Furniture and Fittings A/c £825·00			
Opening Stock at		Rates A/c	£462·90
April 1st 19. .	£3 266·00	Insurance A/c	£380·50
Cash A/c	£175·00	Drawings A/c	£228·00
Bank A/c	£2 475·00	Loan A/c (R. Thomas)	£1 000·00
Purchases A/c	£16 875·00	Capital A/c	£10 000·00
Sales A/c	£38 265·00		

3. The following accounts have balances on them in J. Brown's ledger at December 31st 19. . Draw up the Trial Balance as at that date.
   Returns Inwards £175·50; Returns Outwards £195·90; Cash in Hand £40·00; Machinery £1 640·00; Salaries £1 522·00; Audit Fee £27·50; Sales £7 261·40; Stock £800·00; Telephone Expenses £45·20; Bank Overdraft £506·00; Factory Wages £4 676·00; Discount Received £27·50; Creditors £4 726·50; Debtors £3 871·60; Carriage Outwards £42·40; Bad Debts £165·60; Capital £5 000·00; Rent and Rates £240·00; Purchases £2 535·50; Commission Received £1 864·00; Furniture £300·00; Premises £3 500·00.

4. The following accounts have balances on them in J. Fisher's books on December 31st 19. . Draw up a Trial Balance from them.
   Warehouse Wages £850·00; Office Salaries £1 750·00; Debtors £2 462·50; Creditors £4 861·50; Furniture and Fittings £250·00; Commission Received £1 755·00; Capital £4 000·00; Drawings £1 500·00; Returns Outwards £75·00; Returns Inwards £250·00; Rent and Rates £450·00; Light and Heat £600·00; Carriage In £48·50; Carriage Out £72·60; Opening Stock at January 1st £1 575·00; Cash in Hand £42·50; Cash at

Bank £1 664·60; Sales £17 404·70; Purchases £11 160·50; Motor Vehicles £1 420·00; Land and Buildings £5 000·00; Loan from Bank £1 000·00.

5. From the following figures draw up the Trial Balance of I. Cooper as at December 31st 19.. Purchases £37 000·00; Sales A/c £56 000·00; Purchases-Returns A/c £194·50; Sales-Returns A/c £2 004·00; Stock A/c at January 1st 19.. £8 850·50; Warehouse Wages £250·90; Warehouse Expenses £56·00; Discount-Allowed A/c £36·50; Discount-Received A/c £79·80; Light and Heat A/c £198·40; Travelling Expenses £34·50; Repairs A/c £18·50; Rent-Paid A/c £450·00; Rent-Received A/c £150·00; Commission-Received A/c £185·55; Furniture and Fittings A/c £2 650·00; Plant and Machinery A/c £13 840·70; Motor-Vehicles A/c £6 825·50; Debtors' A/cs £675·50; Creditors' A/cs £12 133·00; Cash A/c £1 383·50; Bank A/c £4 718·35; Mortgage A/c £3 000·00; Loan from Bank Finance Ltd. £1 000·00; Drawings A/c £1 750·00; Capital A/c £8 000·00.

6. Prepare a Trial Balance as at December 31st 19.. from the following ledger accounts of David Cann, exporter of manufactured goods.

	£
Goodwill (asset)	5 000·00
Bad Debts	426·00
Commission Received	1 285·00
Motor Vehicles	750·00
Furniture	450·00
Premises	3 800·00
Warehouse Wages	1 150·00
Discount Received	24·50
Creditors	1 284·00
Debtors	2 562·00
Carriage In	82·00
Returns In	141·00
Returns Out	60·50
Cash in Hand	248·00
Machinery	1 250·00
Office Salaries	2 376·00
Sales	17 987·00
Stock at January 1st	1 450·00
Postage	56·50
Office Expenses	275·50
Bank Loan	2 000·00
Capital	6 916·50
Rates and Insurance	450·50
Light and Heat	276·80
Purchases	8 572·60
General Expenses	240·60

Unit Five

Accounting to Final-Accounts Level
Part Two: The Gross Profit on Trading

5.1 What is Profit?

Once the Trial Balance is properly understood the Final Accounts of a business may easily be prepared and the profits for the year discovered. We must now consider carefully the question, 'What is profit?'.

Profit has already been defined as the reward for entering into business activity. The sole trader or partners who set up a small business, and the shareholders who contribute the capital for companies, are running certain risks. They may eventually lose the capital they have contributed if the enterprise is a failure. They immediately lose the enjoyment and use of their funds, which are now tied up in the business. Profit is their reward for surrendering the use of their money, and for running the risks of business life.

To determine the profit it is necessary to find the difference between the costs of the enterprise and its earnings. This is an involved process with many hidden difficulties, since different ideas exist as to what are the true costs and what are the true earnings. We shall be discussing these difficulties more fully later. Here we are interested in more simple ideas. The first of these tells us how to find the rough profit of the business, which in accounting is called the *gross profit*. Gross means 'fat', but in the accounting sense it means 'overall' profit, without deductions of any sort. The best definition of gross profit is:

$$\text{Gross profit} = \text{sales} - \text{cost of sales}$$

We shall now follow a simple example through in four stages to find a perfect gross-profit figure. (The example relating to Fig. 5.1 is on the next page.)

5.2 Finding the Gross Profit: Stage 1

	Trading A/c		L 205
	£	Sales	£ 32·00
Purchases			
(Cost of Sales)	25·50		
Gross Profit	6·50		
	£32·00		£32·00
		Gross Profit	6·50

Fig. 5.1 Calculating the-gross profit—1

Sales less Purchases

A shopkeeper sells a bicycle to Mrs Jones for her son's birthday present. She pays £32·00 for it. The bicycle cost the shopkeeper £25·50. The gross profit, which is found in the *Trading Account,* would be discovered as shown in Fig. 5.1.

5.3 Finding the Gross Profit: Stage 2

Net Sales less Net Purchases

Unfortunately the example shown in Fig. 5.1 is too simple, for it overlooks several difficulties that are met with in all businesses. First, we often find that some of the goods we sell are returned to us, so that the sales figure on our Sales Account must usually have some *sales returns* deducted from it to arrive at the true sales figure. Similarly we often return goods we have purchased which for some reason are unsatisfactory: these are known as *purchases returns*. It follows that a normal Trading Account will have both sales returns and purchases returns deducted from the appropriate sides, to give us the *net-sales* and *net-purchases* figures. (The word 'net' comes from the French, and means 'clean' or 'clear'. Net sales are therefore 'clear sales' and net purchases are 'clear purchases'—free of any returns.)

If we take slightly more sensible figures than the single items shown in Fig. 5.1, for example the figures given in the Trial Balance in Section 4.2, we have a Trading Account on December 31st 19.. like that in Fig. 5.2.

Trading A/c (for month ending December 31st 19..)				L 205
19..	£	£	19..	£
Dec. 31 Purchases	1 400·00		Dec. 31 Sales	1 865·50
Less Purchases			*Less* Sales	
Returns	100·00		Returns	65·50
Net Purchases			Net Sales	
(Cost of Sales)		1 300·00	(Turnover)	1 800·00
Gross Profit		500·00		
		£1 800·00		£1 800·00
			Gross Profit	500·00

Fig. 5.2 Calculating the gross profit—2

Notes:

(*a*) The word 'turnover', or 'net turnover', is often used for the net-sales figure. The *turnover of a business* is a very important figure in accounting, since every purchaser of a business, and every bidder in the take-over of a company, considers the turnover of the business very seriously before deciding what price he will pay.

(*b*) The gross profit is once again the difference between the sales and the cost of sales, but we now have more accurate figures for both these items, since returns have been taken into account on both.

(c) Notice that the purchases-less-returns figures have been indented a little towards the left of the page. This style is adopted to enable stock to be taken into account. This brings us to Stage 3, but before we deal with stock we must notice the double entries of the transactions in Fig. 5.2.

Double Entries and the Trading Account

Two points arise which are of importance in following the double entries in a Trading Account. They are: 'good style' and the Trading Account, and the 'closing-off' of revenue accounts.

(a) Good style and the Trading Account

The Trading Account, like every other account, must observe the rules of double entry. We cannot debit the Trading Account unless we credit some other account at the same time, and we cannot credit the Trading Account unless we debit some other account. However, the Trading Account is not just *any* ledger account, it is one of the two *Final Accounts*, which are only made out once a year to determine the profits of the business. It follows that *good style* on the Trading Account becomes more important than anything else. By 'good style' we mean a clear presentation of how the profits were achieved. We do therefore, while sticking to the rules of double entry, still adopt a few variations in a stylish Trading Account. These variations will be explained as they are introduced.

(b) The 'closing-off' of expense accounts and receipts accounts

Consider the Trading Account of Fig. 5.2. It has had the entry 'Purchases £1 400·00' entered on the debit side, and the entry 'Sales of £1 865·50' entered on the credit side. Clearly neither of these entries can be made unless equal and opposite entries are made in the accounts named. The effect of these entries is to 'close-off' the Purchases Account and the Sales Account and leave them with no balances at all; the accounts are cleared into the Trading Account. Fig. 5.3 illustrates what has happened to these accounts.

(a)	Purchases A/c		L 27
19..	£		
Sundry Purchases	1 400·00		

	Sales A/c		L 28
		19.	£
		Sundry Sales	1 865·00

(b)	Purchases A/c		L 27
19..	£	19..	£
		Dec. 31 Transfer to Trading	
Sundry Purchases	1 400·00	A/c	1 400·00

(contd. on page 48)

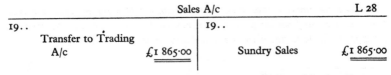

Fig. 5.3 *Purchase and Sales Accounts (a) before closure, (b) after closure*

The chief point to note here is that when the Final Accounts are prepared, a 'closing Journal entry' is made in the Journal. The effect is to close off any accounts that are transferred to them. These accounts, which are either expenses (losses of the business) or receipts (profits of the business) cease to have any balances on them *and consequently disappear from the Trial Balance as soon as they are absorbed into the 'final' account concerned.*

(c) *Good style and the 'returns' entries on the Trading Account*

Let us repeat both the points explained above by considering the purchases-returns and sales-returns entries. On the Trial Balance (Section 4.2) we see that these accounts have balances as shown in Fig. 5.4.

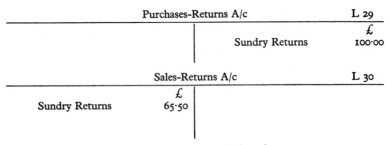

Fig. 5.4 *Returns accounts before closure*

The entry necessary to clear the Purchases-Returns Account is clearly a debit entry, as shown in Fig. 5.5.

Purchases-Returns A/c			L 29
19..			
Dec. 31 Transfer to			
Trading A/c	£100·00	Sundry returns	£100·00

Fig. 5.5 *Closing off of the Purchases-Returns Account*

We would therefore expect the double entry in the Trading Account to appear on the credit side as in Fig. 5.6.

Trading A/c			L 205
	£		£
Purchases	1 400·00	Purchases-Returns A/c	100·00

Fig. 5.6 *'Strict double-entry' in the Trading Account*

Instead *we improve the style in the Trading Account by deducting the purchases returns from the purchases figures on the debit side. To deduct something from the debit side is the same as adding it to the credit side.*

Trading A/c			L 205
	£		
Purchases	1 400·00		
Less Purchases			
Returns	100·00		
Net Purchases	£1 300·00		

Fig. 5.7 'Better style' on the Trading Account—1

The advantage is that we are now able to see clearly what we actually did purchase, that is the net-purchases figure. Similarly, on the credit side, we are able to bring out clearly that very important figure, net turnover, as in Fig. 5.8.

Trading A/c			L205
	£		£
Purchases	1 400·00	Sales	1 865·50
Less Purchases Returns	100·00	*Less* Sales Returns	65·50
Net Purchases	1 300·00	Net Turnover	1 800·00

Fig. 5.8 'Better style' on the Trading Account—2

We are now ready to proceed to Stage 3 in the discovery of the gross-profit figure—the question of stock.

5.4   Finding the Gross Profit: Stage 3

The Question of Stock

We have still not arrived at a perfect figure for the cost of sales, since in real life we rarely sell everything that we purchase in the trading period. Instead we still have in stock at the end of the year (or whatever period for which we are trying to discover the profits) some of the goods purchased. Clearly we must take away from the net-purchases figure any *closing stock* which we have not yet sold, and this stock will become the *opening stock* for the new period just about to begin. It must therefore be added to the purchases of the new period when the time comes to decide the profits of that period.

Before looking at the Trading Account with opening stock and closing stock we must make one point about stock valuation.

The *valuation of stock* is a subject of some controversy in the world of accounting, since different accountants might place different values upon the stock in hand. In one celebrated take-over bid the accountants of the two firms differed about the valuation to be placed upon the stock by as much as four million pounds sterling. These matters are discussed later (see Section 25.1), but for the present we will just say that before the Trading Account can be worked out we must first count the stock to find the number of units in hand, then value each line of goods and finally multiply this figure by the number of units to find the total value of that line of goods in stock. (The number of people who actually do the stock-taking varies from a small business where one person can do it, to a big firm like a supermarket where a large staff is needed to count stocks of possibly 10000 different lines on the shelves.)

The Trial Balance we are using shows an opening-stock figure of £200·00, and a closing-stock figure of £300·00. Using these figures we now find that the Trading Account looks like Fig. 5.9.

Trading A/c
(for month ending December 31st 19..)   L 205

19..		£	19..		£
Dec. 31	Opening Stock	200·00	Dec. 31	Sales	1 865·50
	Purchases 1 400·00			Less Returns	65·50
	Less Returns 100·00			Net Sales (Turnover)	1 800·00
	Net Purchases	1 300·00			
	Total Stock				
	Available	1 500·00			
	Less Closing Stock	300·00			
	Cost of Stock Sold	1 200·00			
	Gross Profit	600·00			
		£1 800·00			£1 800·00
			19..		
			Jan. 1	Gross Profit	600·00

Fig. 5.9 Calculating the gross profit—3

Notes:
(a) The indentation of the purchases-less-returns figure makes a very clear presentation of the account. As in real life the goods actually purchased are added to the stock in hand, giving 'total stock available' during the year of £1 500·00. When the unsold stock is deducted from this we arrive at the cost of the stock sold. What was purchased for £1 200·00 and sold for £1 800·00, earned a profit of £600·00.
(b) The phrase 'cost of stock sold' has been used here instead of 'cost of sales'. The reason is made clear in Stage 4.

Double Entries for Stock Account
The stylish Trading Account shown in Fig. 5.9 has required some adaptation of double entry, similar to the adaptations made in bringing out the net-

purchases and net-sales figures. Let us consider the Stock Account carefully. On the Trial Balance the Stock Account has a date written by it, Stock Account (at December 1st 19. .). Here it is.

		Stock A/c		L 49
19. .		£		
Dec. 1 Opening Balance		200·00		

Fig. 5.10 The Stock Account as it appears throughout the Trading period

Notes:

(*a*) The opening balance was found at the stock-taking at the end of the previous trading period and it does not vary during the trading period.

(*b*) Any stock that is purchased is not entered in Stock Account, but in Purchases Account. (If firms do keep 'running' Stock Accounts they are only memorandum accounts kept for their own convenience in doing quick stock-taking checks.)

To clear the Stock Account to the Trading Account is a simple double entry shown in Fig. 5.11.

	Stock A/c		L 49
19. . £	19. .		£
Dec. 1 Opening Balance 200·00	Dec. 31 Trans. to Trading A/c		200·00

	Trading A/c		L 205
19. . £			
Dec. 31 Opening Stock 200·00			

Fig. 5.11 Closing the Stock Account

The Stock Account is now clear, and disappears, for a few minutes, from the Trial Balance. However, it immediately reappears as a different figure, because we need now to bring the stock-taking figure—just discovered by our stock-takers—on to the books. The 'closing-stock' figure in this case is £300·00. Clearly this is an asset, and must come on the debit side of the Stock Account. The double entry must be a credit entry in the Trading Account. Here it is, in Fig. 5.12, by strict double entry.

	Stock A/c		L 49
19. . £	19. .		£
Dec. 1 Opening Balance 200·00	Dec. 31 Trans. to Trading A/c		200·00
Jan. 1 Opening Balance 300·00			

(contd. on page 52)

Trading A/c

(for month ending December 31st 19..)   L 205

19..		£	19..		£
Dec. 31	Opening Stock	200·00	Dec. 31	Sales	1 865·50
	Purchases 1 400·00			*Less* Returns	65·50
	Less Returns 100·00			Net Sales (Turnover)	1 800·00
				Closing Stock	300·00
	Net Purchases	1 300·00			
	Total Stock	1 500·00			
	available				

Fig. 5.12 'Strict double entry' for stock in the Trading Account

Note:
The entry in the Stock Account is dated for the first day of the new trading period, and the Stock Account will now reappear on the Trial Balance—*but at a new figure.*

It would be much better style (because it would bring out clearly the cost-of-stock sold figure) to transfer the closing stock over to the debit side *and deduct it.* Once again the deduction of an item from the debit side is the same as adding it to the credit side. We have adapted the double-entry system, but it is a good double entry just the same. This gives us a Trading Account as shown in Fig. 5.9.

5.5   Finding the Gross Profit: Stage 4

Trading Expenses

A great many expenses are incurred in the course of business, such as rent, light and heat, advertising, postage and telephone expenses. We shall see shortly that most of these expenses are deducted from the gross profit in an account called the Profit and Loss Account. However some of these expenses are looked upon as being so directly connected with the actual trading activities that they are deducted from the profits in the Trading Account. Later on we shall also see that manufacturing expenses are similarly deducted in a Manufacturing Account. The items treated as Trading Account items may be divided into two groups:

(*a*) Those expenses that are best looked upon as an additional cost of our purchases, the commonest of these are 'carriage in' and 'customs duty on imported purchases'.

(*b*) Those expenses that are truly an expense involved in the trading activities, such as warehouse wages and warehouse expenses.

The former (*a*) should really be added to purchases before the returns are deducted—for example:

	£	£
Purchases	1 400·00	
+Carriage In	30·00	
	1 430·00	
Less Returns	100·00	
		1 330·00

The point here is that if we pay either 'carriage in' or 'customs duty on purchases', the goods really cost us both the purchase price on the invoice and the expenses incurred in bringing the goods to us. The true cost of the purchases above is £1 330·00, not £1 300·00.

The latter (*b*) are added to the 'cost of stock sold' to give the final figure for the cost of sales.

When all these matters have been attended to we may confidently say we have reached as accurate a gross-profit figure as is possible. Fig. 5.13 shows such a Trading Account.

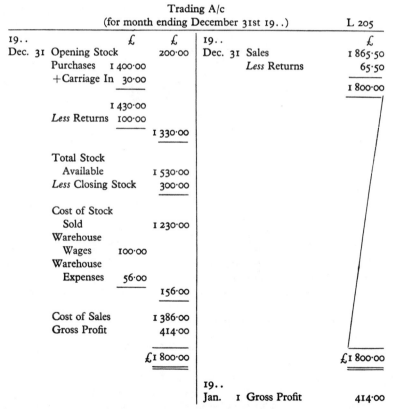

Trading A/c
(for month ending December 31st 19..)   L 205

19..		£	£	19..		£
Dec. 31	Opening Stock		200·00	Dec. 31	Sales	1 865·50
	Purchases 1 400·00				*Less* Returns	65·50
	+Carriage In 30·00					1 800·00
		1 430·00				
	Less Returns 100·00					
			1 330·00			
	Total Stock					
	Available	1 530·00				
	Less Closing Stock	300·00				
	Cost of Stock					
	Sold	1 230·00				
	Warehouse					
	Wages 100·00					
	Warehouse					
	Expenses 56·00					
		156·00				
	Cost of Sales	1 386·00				
	Gross Profit	414·00				
		£1 800·00				£1 800·00
				19..		
				Jan. 1	Gross Profit	414·00

Fig. 5.13 An accurate gross profit—4

Double Entry and the Expense Accounts

In each case as we transfer these items to the Trading Account the double entry will close-off the expense account concerned, leaving the account clear, as shown in Fig. 5.14.

	Carriage-Inwards A/c		L 36
19..	£	19..	£
Sundry Cash		Dec. 31 Transfer to	
Items	30·00	Trading A/c	30·00

	Warehouse-Wages A/c		L 37
19..	£	19..	£
Sundry Cash		Dec. 31 Transfer to	
Items	100·00	Trading A/c	100·00

	Warehouse-Expenses A/c		L 38
19..	£	19..	£
Sundry Cash		Dec. 31 Transfer to	
Items	56·00	Trading A/c	56·00

Fig. 5.14 Closing off the expense accounts

Notes:

(*a*) The use of the word 'sundry' indicates that in fact there may have been several entries making up the figure shown (which is the total expense for the trading period under consideration).

(*b*) The closing-off of these accounts removes them automatically from the Trial Balance—since there is no longer a balance on the account.

You should now prepare several Trading Accounts in the style shown in Fig. 5.13 from the information given in Exercises Set 6.

5.6 Exercises Set 6: The Trading Account

1. At the end of his trading year, on December 31st 19.., R. Hudson has the following balances on his accounts: opening stock £325·00; purchases £785·00; sales £2 725·00; purchases returns £15·00; sales returns £125·00. A check on his stock in hand gives a total for closing stock of £295·00. Prepare his Trading Account and discover the gross profit for the year.

2. At the end of his trading year, on June 30th 19.. I. Brunel has the following balances on his accounts: sales £17 250·00; purchases £12 520·00; sales returns £120·00; purchases returns £1 520·00. Opening stock had been £1 500·00 on July 1st the previous year. Stock-taking revealed a closing-stock figure of £2 370·00. Prepare his Trading Account and hence calculate his gross profit for the year.

3. When T. Turner closes his books for the year on March 31st 19.. he has the following balances on his accounts: purchases £66 275·00; sales £184 000·00; purchases returns £1 275·00; sales returns £2 500·00; opening stock £17 280·00; warehouse wages £3 400·00. Stock-taking revealed a closing stock of £14 180·00. Prepare his Trading Account and thus find his gross profit.

4. On March 31st 19.. J. Metcalfe has the following balances on his books: opening stock £12 500·00; purchases £105 000·00; carriage inwards £500·00; sales £175 200·00; sales returns £3 700·00; purchases returns £1 800·00; closing stock £14 700·00; warehouse wages £3 500·00; warehouse expenses £1 500·00. Prepare his Trading Account and find the gross profit of his business.

5. R. Miller's accounts show the following balances, among others, at March 31st 19.. when he prepares his Trial Balance. Prepare his Trading Account and discover the gross profit of his business. Sales £65 700·00; purchases £38 440·00; sales returns £255·50; purchases returns £262·75; carriage in £130·00; opening stock £2 350·50; closing stock £2 535·40; warehouse wages £2 565·00; trade expenses £370·35.

6. When the Trial Balance of G. Poole's books is prepared on June 30th 19.. the following balances are found to exist. Use them to prepare his Trading Account and hence discover the gross profit of his business. Opening stock £15 750·00; closing stock £16 726·60; purchases £105 002·00; sales £196 000·00; purchases returns £1 280·50; sales returns £2 500·00; customs duty on imported purchases £620·00; carriage in £150·00; warehouse wages £1 650·70; warehouse expenses £752·30; warehouse redecoration £249·60.

Accounting to Final-Accounts Level Part Three: The Net Profit of the Enterprise

6.1 Taking Account of Expenses and Receipts

(1) Expenses

In Unit Five certain expenses of the business—carriage in, warehouse wages and warehouse expenses—were deducted from the profits of the business. The majority of the expenses of the business, particularly the items usually known as 'overheads', such as rent, rates, insurance and telephone expenses are deducted from the profits in the Profit and Loss Account. It is usual to arrange them in some logical order, which may be appropriate to the type of business concerned. A common choice is to group them under three headings: administrative expenses, financial expenses and selling and distribution expenses.

(2) Receipts

Similarly, where a business earns fees, commissions or rents of any kind these receipts are brought into the profit calculations as part of the Profit and Loss Account.

6.2 Up-dating the Trial Balance

Before seeing how this is done we must up-date the Trial Balance which is being used as the basis of our calculations. The Trading Account prepared in Unit Five has resulted in the closing of many accounts, which consequently have disappeared from the Trial Balance. We are therefore left with a smaller list of balances. The Trial Balance shown in Fig. 4.1 (see Section 4.2) has now become:

Trial Balance of D. Webster's books
(as at December 31st 19..)

Accounts	Dr. £	Cr. £	Notes
Light and Heat	28·50		Loss
Repairs	5·50		Loss
Rent	50·00		Loss
Discount-Allowed	42·50		Loss
Discount-Received		32·50	Profit
Commission-Received		12·00	Profit
Land and Buildings	8 750·00		Asset
Furniture and Fittings	1 250·00		Asset
Motor-Vehicles	1 500·00		Asset
Sundry-Debtors	650·50		Asset
Sundry-Creditors		430·50	Liability
Plant and Machinery	880·00		Asset
Cash	164·75		Asset
Bank	2 047·25		Asset
Drawings (D. Webster)	220·00		Special Asset
Mortgage on Premises		2 000·00	Liability
Loan (Finance Co.)		1 000·00	Liability
Capital (D. Webster)		12 000·00	Special Liability
Stock (at Dec. 31st 19..)	300·00		Asset
Trading (Gross Profit)		414·00	Special Liability
	£15 889·00	15 889·00	

Fig. 6.1 The revised Trial Balance

Notes:
(a) The stock has changed to the new stock figure. It can also be correctly described as an asset, because this time it really does describe the actual goods on the shelves; it is a real account, not a nominal account.
(b) The Trading-Account balance is a special type of liability, because it is owed to the owner of the business, just like the capital he originally contributed.

6.3 The Profit and Loss Account

The Profit and Loss Account is very simply prepared, for there are less special points of style than in the Trading Account. The first item to be transferred is the gross profit, which is transferred from the Trading Account. Then the various expenses are transferred to the debit of the Profit and Loss Account, and the various receipts are transferred to the credit side. When totalled the difference between the two sides is the profit (or loss) of the business. Using the modified Trial Balance of Fig. 6.1 as the source of our figures we may prepare the Profit and Loss Account as in Fig. 6.2.

Profit and Loss A/c
(for month ending December 31st 19..)   L 206

19..		£	19..		£
Light and Heat A/c		28·50	Gross Profit		414·00
Repairs A/c		5·50	Discount-Received A/c		32·50
Rent A/c		50·00	Commission-Received A/c		12·00
Discount-Allowed A/c		42·50			
Total Expenses		126·50	Total Profits		458·50
Net Profit	c/d	332·00			
		£458·50			£458·50
			19..		
			Dec. 31 Net Profit	B/d	332·00

Fig. 6.2 The Profit and Loss Account of a business

6.4   Double Entries in the Expense and Receipts Accounts

As these items are transferred into the Profit and Loss Account the double entries in every case will be in the various accounts named, and will result in the closure of these accounts. They will be left without any balance, and consequently will disappear from the Trial Balance. The closure of these accounts is illustrated in Fig. 6.3.

Light and Heat A/c   L 8

19..		£	19..		£
	Sundry items	28·50	Dec. 31 Transfer to P & L A/c		28·50

Repairs A/c   L 9

19..		£	19..		£
	Sundry items	5·50	Dec. 31 Transfer to P & L A/c		5·50

Rent A/c   L 10

19..		£	19..		£
	Sundry items	50·00	Dec. 31 Transfer to P & L A/c		50·00

(contd. on page 59)

	Discount-Allowed A/c		L 11
19..	£	19..	£
Sundry items	42·50	Dec. 31 Transfer to P & L A/c	42·50

	Discount-Received A/c		L 12
19..	£	19..	£
Dec. 31 Transfer to P & L A/c	32·50	Sundry items	32·50

	Commission-Received A/c		L 13
19..	£	19..	£
Dec. 31 Transfer to P & L A/c	12·00	Sundry items	12·00

Fig. 6.3 Closing the expense accounts, etc.

You should now prepare several Profit and Loss Accounts in the style shown in Fig. 6.2.

6.5 Exercises Set 7: Profit and Loss Accounts

1. Prepare the Profit and Loss Account from M. Lawrence's books, for the year ending December 31st 19.. Figures are as follows: Trading A/c Balance (gross profit) £2 755·00; Rent and Rates A/c £850·00 Light and Heat A/c £230·50; Office Salaries A/c £945·00.

2. Prepare the Profit and Loss Account of W. Sandon, for the year ending March 31st 19.. His Trial Balance shows: Gross Profit £18 655·00; Rent and Rates A/c £2 560·00; Light and Heat A/c £426·00; Commission-Received A/c £2 065·00; Office Salaries A/c £7 956·00; Rent-Received A/c £240·00; Telephone-Expenses A/c £236·50; Sundry-Expenses A/c £32·50; Postage A/c £125·50.

3. Prepare from the following list of balances the Profit and Loss Account of M. Chesterfield for the year ending June 30th 19..

	£
Gross Profit	78 561·75
Rent Paid	2 865·50
Rent Received	525·25
Office Salaries	9 589·50
Office Expenses	2 361·00
Office Light and Heat	854·60
Advertising Expenses	7 965·50
Interest on Loans	450·00
Interest on Bank Overdraft	65·50
Entertainment of Visitors	2 725·50

4. From the following figures prepare R. Burton's Profit and Loss Account for the year ending December 31st 19. .

	£
Gross Profit	12 840·00
Rent and Rates	800·00
Office Expenses	1 440·00
Lighting and Heating	240·00
Discount Received	60·00
Commission Received	180·00
Loan Interest	400·00
Mortgage Interest	664·00
Discount Allowed	400·00
Advertising Expenses	886·00
Transport Costs	1 106·00
Rent Received	360·00

5. From the following particulars prepare the Trading Account and the Profit and Loss Account of L. Lucerne, for the year ending March 31st 19. .

	£
Opening Stock at April 1st 19. .	3 521·10
Purchases	9 101·00
Sales	17 033·20
Sales Returns	33·67
Purchases Returns	24·25
Closing Stock	3 171·30
Discount Received	4·00
Discount Allowed	34·50
Insurance	8·30
Office Expenses	853·50
Printing and Stationery	51·76
Rent and Rates	885·00
General Expenses	649·80
Telephone Expenses	51·00
Interest Paid	61·10
Light and Heat	49·20

6. From the following particulars taken from B. Grant's records prepare the Trading Account and Profit and Loss Account for the year ending December 31st 19. ., using such figures as you consider appropriate.

	£
Capital	42 000·00
Rent and Rates	1 000·00
Purchases	46 550·00

Sales	82 500·00
Stock at January 1st 19..	12 000·00

Bad Debts	1 150·00
Carriage Outwards	1 300·00
Debtors	8 000·00
Creditors	4 550·00
Office Salaries	9 450·00

Telephone Expenses	750·00
Bank Overdraft	1 650·00
Returns Inwards	350·00
Returns Outwards	1 500·00
Cash in Hand	100·00

Machinery	15 050·00
Stock at End of Year	11 500·00
Land and Buildings	6 500·00

Accounting to Final-Accounts Level Part Four: The Balance Sheet of the Business

7.1 Introduction: the Balance Sheet Idea

A Balance Sheet is a list of balances outstanding on the accounts after the Trading Account and Profit and Loss Account have been completed. We have already seen that as these two accounts are prepared, a number of other accounts are removed, and the Trial Balance is left, therefore, with only a few accounts. Most of these are either assets or liabilities, but we do have one special asset, Drawing Accounts (the proprietor's temporary debts to the business), and a special liability, the Capital Account (the amount of money contributed by the proprietor to the business). There is also now another special liability: the Profit and Loss Account. This shows the profits earned during the year and these, of course, belong to the proprietor. Soon we shall see how these special items are dealt with, and how a Balance Sheet, or list of assets and liabilities, can be drawn up.

This list of assets and liabilities is very important, because *it forms the basis on which businesses are bought and sold*. A new owner, anxious to purchase an existing business, needs to know what assets are being purchased, and what liabilities are being incurred. The Balance Sheet helps him to judge what price he should pay for the business he is acquiring. The purchase price will be the value of the assets acquired less the total of the liabilities incurred, but in practice an additional payment for the *'goodwill'* of the business will also be paid. (Goodwill is dealt with later in Section 26.11.) Here it is sufficient to note that the Balance Sheet, provided it is prepared from honest figures, is a *statement of the affairs of the business*, which enables a purchaser to judge a proper purchase price.

Before preparing a Balance Sheet let us clarify what happens to the special items mentioned above.

7.2 The Appropriation of Profits

The owner of the business *appropriates the net profit*. The word 'appropriate' means to take possession of. Since the whole purpose of the business is to make profit, the owner takes possession of the profits which are added to his account, the Capital Account. This does not mean that he actually takes all the profits out as money. If he takes out some of his profit in money this is called drawings and the amounts are recorded in the Drawings Account. The balance of undrawn profit remains in the business and enables the business to 'grow'. The transfer of net profit to the Capital Account would be effected by the double entries shown below, closing off the Profit and Loss Account.

	Profit and Loss A/c			L 206
19..		£	19..	£
Dec. 31 Trans. to Capital A/c		332·00	Dec. 31 Balance B/d	332·00

	Capital A/c (D. Webster)		L 1
		19..	£
		Dec. 1 Balance	12 000·00
		31 Profit and Loss A/c	332·00

Fig. 7.1 Appropriation of profit by the owner of the business

In more advanced forms of business, partnerships and limited companies, the profits in the Profit and Loss Account would be appropriated by the partners, or the shareholders, in the manner proposed either in the partnership agreement or by resolution of the company as proposed by the directors at the annual general meeting. This requires a slightly more sophisticated treatment than in Fig. 7.1. However, in Fig. 7.1 we see that at the end of the trading period the owner's capital increases by the amount of net profit made during that period.

7.3   Closing the Drawings Account

The sums withdrawn by the owner of the business, usually in cash, but sometimes in the form of goods, are debited to Drawings Account throughout the trading period. They are often looked upon as capital withdrawn from the business, but it is better to regard them as withdrawals in expectation of profits. A prudent owner would limit his drawings to the amount of profit he could reasonably expect to make in the trading period. To exceed this figure would be to consume capital—an undesirable state of affairs. Whether the owner is prudent or imprudent his drawings, collected in the Drawings Account, will be transferred to the Capital Account as a debit item, to reduce the balance on that account. The double entry is shown in Fig. 7.2.

	Drawings A/c (D. Webster)			L 9
19..		£	19..	£
Dec. 7 Bank		55·00	Dec. 31 Capital Account	220·00
14 Bank		55·00		
21 Bank		55·00		
28 Bank		55·00		
		£220·00		£220·00

(contd. on page 64)

		Capital A/c (D. Webster)		L 1

19..		£	19..		£
Dec. 31 Drawings A/c		220·00	Dec. 1 Balance		12 000·00
31 Balance	c/d 12 112·00		31 Profit and Loss A/c		332·00
	£12 332·00			£12 332·00	
			19..		
			Jan. 1 Balance B/d		12 112·00

Fig. 7.2 Closing the Drawings Account

The final situation is that the owner's Capital Account has increased by the difference between the net profit made in the period and the drawings made from the business in the period.

7.4   The Residual Trial Balance

The Trial Balance of D. Webster's books, originally including all the ledger accounts (see Section 4.2) and subsequently reduced by the closure of the accounts absorbed into the Trading Account and the Profit and Loss Account, has now been further reduced by the closure of the Profit and Loss Account and the Drawings Account. We are left with a residue of accounts which cannot be closed, *but must be carried on into the next trading period.* All these accounts are either assets or liabilities and form the raw data from which a *Balance Sheet* may be prepared. Fig. 7.3 shows this residual Trial Balance of D. Webster's books.

Trial Balance of D. Webster's books
(as at December 31st 19..)

Accounts	Dr. £	Cr. £	Notes
Land and Buildings	8 750·00		Asset
Furniture and Fittings	1 250·00		Asset
Motor-Vehicles	1 500·00		Asset
Sundry-Debtors	650·50		Asset
Sundry-Creditors		430·50	Liability
Plant and Machinery	880·00		Asset
Cash	164·75		Asset
Bank	2 047·25		Asset
Mortgage on Premises		2 000·00	Liability
Loan (Finance Co.)		1 000·00	Liability
Capital (D. Webster)		12 112·00	Liability
Stock (at close)	300·00		Asset
	£15 542·50	15 542·50	

Fig. 7.3 A residual Trial Balance after the preparation of the Final Accounts

Before displaying this information in Balance-Sheet form it is necessary to explain the historical development of the Balance Sheet, from its origin in the sixteenth century.

7.5 The History of the Balance Sheet

Simon Stevin of Bruges first devised what he called a statement of affairs of a business early in the sixteenth century, using the data provided by the residue of the Trial Balance such as is given in Fig. 7.3. The name 'statement of affairs' is still used in book-keeping today (see Section 30.3) but the more modern term is Balance Sheet, since it is a list of the outstanding balances on the ledger accounts. As may be seen in the Trial Balance of Fig. 7.3 the asset accounts all have debit balances, and the liabilities all have credit balances. It would therefore have been logical to display the balances as shown in Fig. 7.4.

Balance Sheet
(as at December 31st 19..)

	£		£
Assets	15 542·50	Liabilities	15 542·50

Fig. 7.4 Assets and liabilities logically displayed

Unfortunately Stevin reversed the sides, as in Fig. 7.5. There was no sensible reason for doing this, indeed it was positively misleading, but as a statement of affairs is not part of double-entry book-keeping, no one could say that it was 'wrong'—it was just illogical.

Balance Sheet
(as at December 31st 19..)

	£		£
Liabilities	15 542·50	Assets	15 542·50

Fig. 7.5 Stevin's illogical display

When the British Parliament introduced the Companies Act of 1856, it was stated that a Balance Sheet should be prepared for all companies at the end of their financial year in the style shown in the Schedule to the Act. This Schedule showed a Balance Sheet in exactly the style laid down by Simon Stevin three centuries before. In obeying the Act accountants established the British practice, later copied by Commonwealth and Colonial countries, of displaying the Balance Sheet in Stevin's way. Belgium, Stevin's own country, and other continental countries, as well as the United States of America, have long abandoned Stevin's illogical display and always present their Balance Sheets logically, as in Fig. 7.4.

Fortunately, harmonization of accounting practices in the European Economic Community has led Parliament to enact formats for the Balance Sheet which conform with the European style, with assets stated first (on the left-hand side) and liabilities stated on the credit side, as in the actual accounts. For printing reasons some accountants prefer to produce a Balance Sheet in vertical style, and this format also appears in Schedule 1 of the Companies Act 1981. In this textbook assets are shown on the left-hand side, and liabilities on the right-hand side, in the correct manner.

7.6   Stylish Balance Sheets 1: Marshalling the Assets

It is a principle of modern accounting that the accountant should arrange the accounts in such a way that anyone reading them—providing he has some understanding of accounts—can immediately appreciate the important aspects of the business, and be able to assess the firm's true position. In former times a chief preoccupation of some accountants was to hide the true state of affairs from interested parties. This was particularly undesirable with limited companies, since innocent shareholders were often unable to discover weaknesses in the business until too late, and were left with worthless shares on their hands. Today the Companies Acts of 1948–1981 require auditors to certify that in their opinion the accounts do give 'a true and fair view' of the business.

One of the ways in which a clear picture can be presented is by dividing the assets into separate classes. There are about four types of assets, but here we shall only consider the two chief types: *current assets* and *fixed assets*.

(1) Current Assets
These are sometimes called *circulating assets* as they are assets which are continually being turned over. The word current comes from the French word 'courrant' meaning running. Fig. 7.6 illustrates the way in which stock

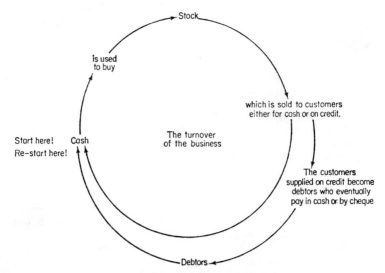

Fig. 7.6 Circulating or current assets

which has been manufactured or purchased for resale is marketed and sold, either for cash or on credit terms. The cash received or eventually received is then used to purchase further stock for resale.

The current assets from the Trial Balance of Fig. 7.3 may therefore be listed as follows:

Current Assets	£
Stock	300·00
Sundry Debtors	650·50
Cash at Bank	2 047·25
Cash in Hand	164·75
	3 162·50

Equally well they could have been presented as follows:

Current Assets	£
Cash in Hand	164·75
Cash at Bank	2 047·25
Sundry Debtors	650·50
Stock	300·00
	3 162·50

The two alternative presentations are discussed later (see Section 7.8).

(2) Fixed Assets

These are assets which are not 'turned over' and sold at a profit, but are 'fixed' in the business and retained over a very long period. They are often called *capital assets*, since they form part of the permanent capital equipment in use. The longest-lasting item is land, which may be said to be eternal. Plant and machinery lasts many years, while assets like motor vehicles last only a few years.

The fixed assets listed in Fig. 7.3 may be shown like this:

Fixed Assets	£
Land and Buildings	8 750·00
Plant and Machinery	880·00
Furniture and Fittings	1 250·00
Motor Vehicles	1 500·00
	12 380·00

Alternatively they may be grouped in the opposite order, as follows:

Fixed Assets	£
Motor Vehicles	1 500·00
Furniture and Fittings	1 250·00
Plant and Machinery	880·00
Land and Buildings	8 750·00
	12 380·00

These alternative presentations are discussed later (see Section 7.8).

7.7   Stylish Balance Sheets 2: Marshalling the Liabilities

Just as the arrangement of the assets in clear groups, current assets and fixed assets, is helpful in presenting a simple picture to the public, a clear division of the liabilities is also helpful. There are three groups to whom any business owes funds. They are:

(*a*) The owner himself, who expects eventually to be repaid the capital he originally contributed, plus any profits retained in the business over the course of the years. The amounts owing to the owner are contained in his Capital Account, but by convention it is usual to display the capital at the start of the trading period, adding the net profit and deducting the drawings as already shown in Figs. 7.1 and 7.2. This enables anyone studying the Balance Sheet to see the profits earned in the trading period.

(*b*) Long-term creditors who will usually have made a special contract with the owner of the business, and whose repayment terms are specified in the contract. Examples are those who lend for mortgages and personal loans. We call such liabilities *long-term liabilities*.

(*c*) Short-term creditors who may expect to be paid almost at once. These liabilities are called *current liabilities*. The commonest Balance-Sheet items of this sort are creditors and bank overdrafts.

Listing these liabilities from Fig. 7.3 they may be presented as follows:

	£	£
Capital (at start)		12 000·00
Add Net Profit	332·00	
Less Drawings	220·00	
	———	
		112·00
		———
		12 112·00
Long-term Liabilities		
Mortage on Premises	2 000·00	
Loan A/c (Finance Co.)	1 000·00	
	———	
		3 000·00
Current Liabilities		
Creditors		430·50
		———
		£15 542·50

These items could also have been presented in the reverse order. As shown above they are presented in the *order of permanence*. The reverse order would be the *order of liquidity*.

7.8   Stylish Balance Sheets 3: The Order of Permanence and the Order of Liquidity

When a Balance Sheet is arranged in the order of permanence, the most enduring item is entered first. Then successive items are positioned in the list in decreasing order of permanence, finishing up with cash in hand, which is a perfectly liquid item. 'Liquid' in business means 'available in cash form', so that land, which is difficult to turn into cash—because it must be 'conveyed' by deed to a new owner—is illiquid, while stock is more liquid, since it can be sold without any formal transfer.

Some businesses, to whom liquidity is very important, arrange their Balance Sheets in the order of liquidity. The best examples are the banks. Ask a major bank for its published accounts, available free to anyone interested, and note the order of liquidity used. Most manufacturing businesses, with many capital assets of a very permanent nature, use the order of permanence, while small traders are free to choose whichever presentation they prefer.

Fig. 7.7 presents the Balance Sheet of D. Webster in both forms, to display the two alternative presentations. Compare the two. Note that a Balance Sheet always has the date clearly indicated, in the same way as the Trial Balance.

(a)   *Order of Permanence*
                        Balance Sheet of D. Webster's books
                            (as at December 31st 19..)

	£	£		£	£
Fixed Assets			Capital		
Land and Buildings		8 750·00	At Start		12 000·00
Plant and Machinery		880·00	*Add* Net Profit	332·00	
Furniture and			*Less* Drawings	220·00	
Fittings		1 250·00			112·00
Motor Vehicles		1 500·00			12 112·00
		12 380·00	*Long-term Liabilities*		
Current Assets			Mortgage on		
Stock	300·00		Premises	2 000·00	
Sundry Debtors	650·50		Loan A/c (Finance		
Cash at Bank	2 047·25		Co.)	1 000·00	
Cash in Hand	164·75				3 000·00
		3 162·50	*Current Liabilities*		
			Creditors		430·50
		£15 542·50			£15 542·50

(contd. on page 70)

(b)   *Order of Liquidity*
                      Balance Sheet of D. Webster's books
                         (as at December 31st 19. .)

	£	£		£	£	£
Current Assets			*Current Liabilities*			
Cash in Hand		164·75	Creditors			430·50
Cash at Bank		2 047·25	*Long-term Liabilities*			
Sundry Debtors		650·50	Loan A/c (Finance			
Stock		300·00	Co.)		1 000·00	
		———	Mortgage on			
		3 162·50	Premises		2 000·00	
					———	3 000·00
Fixed Assets			*Capital*			
Motor Vehicles	1 500·00		At Start		12 000·00	
Furniture and			*Add* Net			
Fittings	1 250·00		Profit	332·00		
Plant and Machinery	880·00		*Less*			
Land and Buildings	8 750·00		Drawings	220·00		
	———	12 380·00		———	112·00	
					———	12 112·00
		£15 542·50				£15 542·50

Fig. 7.7 Balance Sheet showing (a) order of permanence and (b) order of liquidity

You should now draw up several balance sheets from the exercises given below, presenting them in good style, and in the order indicated in the question.

7.9   Exercises Set 8: the Balance Sheet of a Business

1. Prepare a Balance Sheet from the following information drawn from R. Long's books. He presents his Balance Sheet in the order of permanence.

Trial Balance (R. Long)
(as at December 31st 19. .)

	Dr.	Cr.
	£	£
Cash in Hand	1 000·00	
Cash at Bank	9 000·00	
Stock at Close	10 000·00	
Land and Buildings	10 500·00	
Office Equipment	4 500·00	
Creditors		1 500·00
Debtors	2 000·00	
Motor Vehicles	2 000·00	
Capital (at start)		30 000·00
Drawings	2 500·00	
Net Profit		5 000·00
Bank Loan		5 000·00
	£41 500·00	41 500·00

2. Prepare J. Triton's Balance Sheet in the order of permanence from the Trial Balance given below.

Trial Balance (J. Triton)
(as at December 31st 19..)

	Dr. £	Cr. £
Cash in Hand	150·00	
Cash at Bank	6 850·00	
Stock at Close	4 500·00	
Debtors	1 600·00	
Motor Vehicles	5 000·00	
Land and Buildings	10 000·00	
Office Equipment	2 000·00	
Plant and Machinery	3 000·00	
Capital (at start)		25 000·00
Net Profit		3 000·00
Mortgage on Premises		5 000·00
Creditors		1 850·00
Drawings	1 750·00	
	£34 850·00	34 850·00

3. Prepare T. North's Balance Sheet from the Trial Balance given below, arranging the items in the order of liquidity.

Trial Balance (T. North)
(as at December 31st 19..)

	Dr. £	Cr. £
Cash in Hand	36·50	
Cash at Bank	548·50	
Trade Debtors	1 036·50	
Stock at Close	1 245·00	
Short-term Investments	400·00	
Motor Vehicles	1 500·75	
Furniture and Fittings	515·55	
Plant and Machinery	1 400·00	
Land and Buildings	3 000·00	
Creditors		997·20
Mortgage on Premises		1 000·00
Capital		4 185·00
Bank Loan		3 000·00
Drawings	1 750·00	
Net Profit for year		2 250·60
	£11 432·80	11 432·80

4. Prepare M. Twain's Balance Sheet in the order of liquidity from the figures given below in his Trial Balance.

Trial Balance (M. Twain)
(as at March 31st 19..)

	Dr. £	Cr. £
Cash in Hand	38·50	
Cash at Bank	720·50	
Debtors and Creditors	1 434·25	919·25
Closing Stock	1 500·00	
Motor Vehicles	1 675·50	
Furniture and Fittings	2 565·50	
Land and Buildings	9 000·00	
Mortgage on Premises		4 000·00
Capital		11 765·00
Drawings	1 500·00	
Profit and Loss A/c balance		1 750·00
	£18 434·25	18 434·25

Accounting to Final-Accounts Level Part Five: Exercises to Final-Accounts Level

8.1 Introduction

You are now ready to carry out some consolidating work to ensure that you have fully assimilated the arguments and ideas developed in the first seven Units. You should now be able to carry out the following accounting activities:

(*a*) Make double entries in the ledger accounts for every type of transaction.

(*b*) Extract a Trial Balance of the ledger and, if the sides do not agree, check the double entries until agreement is achieved.

(*c*) Prepare from the Trial Balance a set of Final Accounts, i.e. a Trading Account and a Profit and Loss Account, closing off in the process all the nominal accounts in the ledger.

(*d*) Prepare a Balance Sheet, in good style, from the remaining accounts, the *real accounts* and the *personal accounts*, i.e. the residue of the Trial Balance.

You should now prepare several sets of records from the opening of the accounts right through to the Balance Sheet. To assist you, and to recapitulate all we have said, look at the specimen exercise in accounting to Final-Accounts level in Section 8.2.

8.2 A Specimen Exercise in Accounting to Final-Accounts Level

R. Brown starts in business on January 1st 19.. contributing these assets: motor vehicles £530·00; furniture and equipment £650·00; cash in hand £30·00; cash at bank £980·00. Open the ledger accounts to record these items. The following transactions then take place. Record them by double entries.

January   1st   Purchased postage stamps £1·20 in cash and goods for resale, £78·00, on credit from T. Jones.

January   2nd Purchased scales for use in shop, £15·00 cash. Purchased goods for resale £36·50 cheque.

January   5th   Cash sales £99·50. Pays cleaning expenses, £5·00 cash.

January   8th   Postage £0·75 cash. Purchases on credit from R. Freedom goods for resale, £125·95.

January 10th Sells on credit to I. Slade goods valued at £95·50.

January 12th Cash sales £150·60. Pays into bank £200·00.

January 15th Purchases on credit from T. Jones goods for resale £285·50.

January 16th Postage £1·25 cash. Pays A. Builder cash for shelving £36·00

January 19th Cash sales £88·75. Pays insurance by cheque £24·50.

January 22nd Pays T. Jones by cheque £78·00.
January 24th Pays rates for half-year to Urban District Council £78·50, cheque.
January 26th Cash sales £195·25.
January 29th Postage £2·25 cash.
January 31st Cash sales £64·75. Pays into bank from cash till £150·00.

Extract a Trial Balance as at January 31st 19.. Then prepare Trading and Profit and Loss Accounts for the month, and a Balance Sheet as at January 31st 19.. The closing-stock figure was valued at £144·00.

Model Answer: Part 1
Entering the opening items in the ledger accounts we have these entries:

Motor-Vehicles A/c			L 1
19..		£	
Jan. 1 Capital	L 5	530·00	

Furniture and Equipment A/c			L 2
19..		£	
Jan. 1 Capital	L 5	650·00	

Cash A/c			L 3
19..		£	
Jan. 1 Capital	L 5	30·00	

Bank A/c			L 4
19..		£	
Jan. 1 Capital	L 5	980·00	

Capital A/c			L 5
	19..		£
	Jan. 1 Sundry Asset		
	A/cs	L 1–4	2 190·00

Fig. 8.1. Opening entries

Notes:
(a) Each asset has been debited in an account.
(b) The entry in the Capital Account—to save making several entries—is simply the total value of the assets contributed by the proprietor, R. Brown.
(c) The folio numbers indicate where the other half of a particular double entry is to be found.

Model Answer: Part 2

Continuing with the transactions which took place in January, we have the following set of accounts. You should work through the set to make sure you follow each double entry.

	Motor–Vehicles A/c			L 1
19..			£	
Jan. 1 Capital	L	5	530·00	

	Furniture and Equipment A/c			L 2
19..			£	
Jan. 1 Capital	L	5	650·00	
2 Cash	L	3	15·00	
16 Cash	L	3	36·00	

	Cash A/c							L 3	
19..			£	19..				£
Jan. 1 Capital	L	5	30·00	Jan. 1 Postage	L	6	1·20
5 Sales	L	9	99·50	2 Furniture and			
12 Sales	L	9	150·60	Equipment	L	2	15·00
19 Sales	L	9	88·75	5 Cleaning			
26 Sales	L	9	195·25	Expenses	L	10	5·00
31 Sales	L	9	64·75	8 Postage	L	6	0·75
				12 Bank	L	4	200·00
				16 Postage	L	6	1·25
				16 Furniture and			
				Equipment	L	2	36·00
				29 Postage	L	6	2·25
				31 Bank	L	4	150·00
				31 Balance	c/d		217·40
			£628·85				£628·85
Jan. 31 Balance	B/d		217·40				

	Bank A/c							L 4	
19..			£	19..				£
Jan. 1 Capital	L	5	980·00	Jan. 2 Purchases	L	7	36·50
12 Cash	L	3	200·00	19 Insurance	L	13	24·50
31 Cash	L	3	150·00	22 T. Jones	L	8	78·00
				24 Rates	L	14	78·50
				31 Balance	c/d		1 112·50
			£1 330·00				£1 330·00
31 Balance	B/d		1 112·50				

(contd. on page 76)

Capital A/c   **L 5**

		19..		
		Jan. 1 Sundry-Asset		£
		A/cs	L 1–4	2 190·00

Postage A/c   **L 6**

19..				£
Jan.	1	Cash	L 3	1·20
	8	Cash	L 3	0·75
	16	Cash	L 3	1·25
	29	Cash	L 3	2·25

Purchases A/c   **L 7**

19..				£
Jan.	1	T. Jones	L 8	78·00
	2	Bank	L 4	36·50
	8	R. Freedom	L 11	125·95
	15	T. Jones	L 8	285·50

T. Jones A/c   **L 8**

19..			£	19..			£
Jan. 22	Bank	L 4	78·00	Jan. 1	Purchases	L 7	78·00
31	Balance	c/d	285·50	15	Purchases	L 7	285·50
			£363·50				£363·50
				Feb. 1	Balance	B/d	285·50

Sales A/c   **L 9**

				19..			£
				Jan.	5 Cash	L 3	99·50
					10 I. Slade	L 12	95·50
					12 Cash	L 3	150·60
					19 Cash	L 3	88·75
					26 Cash	L 3	195·25
					31 Cash	L 3	64·75

Cleaning-Expenses A/c   **L 10**

19..			£
Jan. 5	Cash	L 3	5·00

(contd. on page 77)

	R. Freedom A/c		L 11
	19.. Jan. 8 Purchases	L 7	£ 125·95

I. Slade A/c			L 12
19.. Jan. 10 Sales	L 9	£ 95·50	

Insurance A/c			L 13
19.. Jan. 19 Bank	L 4	£ 24·50	

Rates A/c			L 14
19.. Jan. 24 Bank	L 4	£ 78·50	

Fig. 8.2 The accounts

Model Answer: Part 3

If we tidy up the accounts where necessary by balancing off those that have items on both sides, and total (in pencil) those that have two or three entries on one side only, the Trial Balance may be extracted like this:

Trial Balance (R. Brown's Accounts)
(as at January 31st 19..)

	Dr. £	Cr. £
Motor-Vehicles A/c	530·00	
Furniture and Equipment A/c	701·00	
Cash A/c	217·40	
Bank A/c	1 112·50	
Capital A/c		2 190·00
Postage A/c	5·45	
Purchases A/c	525·95	
T. Jones A/c		285·50
Sales A/c		694·35
Cleaning-Expenses A/c	5·00	
R. Freedom A/c		125·95
I. Slade A/c	95·50	
Insurance A/c	24·50	
Rates A/c	78·50	
	£3 295·80	3 295·80

Fig. 8.3. The Trial Balance

Model Answer: Part 4

Using the closing-stock figure given, £144·00, the Trading Account, Profit and Loss Account and Balance Sheet can be prepared.

Trading A/c
(for month ending January 31st 19...)

	£		£
Purchases	525·95	Sales	694·35
Less Closing Stock	144·00		
Cost of Stock Sold	381·95		
Gross Profit	312·40		
	£694·35		£694·35

Profit and Loss A/c
(for month ending January 31st 19...)

	£		£
Postage	5·45	Gross Profit	312·40
Cleaning Expenses	5·00		
Insurance	24·50		
Rates	78·50		
Total Expenses	113·45		
Net Profit	198·95		
	£312·40		£312·40

Balance Sheet
(as at January 31st 19...)

	£	£		£	£
Fixed Assets			*Capital*		
Furniture and Equipment		701·00	At Start	2 190·00	
Motor Vehicles		530·00	*Add* Profit	198·95	
		1 231·00			2 388·95
Current Assets			*Current Liabilities*		
Closing Stock	144·00		R. Freedom	125·95	
I. Slade	95·50		T. Jones	285·50	
Cash in Bank	1 112·50				411·45
Cash in Hand	217·40				
		1 569·40			
		£2 800·40			£2 800·40

Fig. 8.4 The Final Accounts

The exercises which follow are in two sets. Set 9 provides a number of examples of transactions by sole traders, from which you may gain a complete mastery of accounting to Final-Accounts level. Set 10 provides a number of Trial Balances, from which you may achieve real facility in the preparation of Final Accounts.

8.3 Exercises Set 9: Accounting to Final-Accounts Level—Part One

1. On July 1st R. Todd starts in business with capital of £500·00 which he banks. He then buys by cheque a market stall (Stall and Equipment A/c), £25·00; goods for resale, £34·00; and equipment £12·50. His transactions are as follows:

   July 2nd Cash sales £36·00. Purchase of goods for resale, £8·00 cash. Wages of assistant in cash £2·00.

   July 3rd Cash sales £42·00. Purchase of goods for resale £26·50 cash. Electric-light connexion fee £2·00 cash. Tip to dustman £0·25 cash.

   July 4th Cash sales £13·00. Purchase in cash of goods for resale £21·50. Wages of assistant £2·00 cash.

   July 5th Cash sales £84·00. Purchase by cheque of goods for resale £16·50. Wages of assistants £3·50 cash. Banked £50·00.

   July 6th Cash sales £62·50. Wages of assistants £3·50 cash. Todd takes £50·00 from cash box as personal drawings.

   Record the above items, extract a Trial Balance as at July 6th and from it prepare a Trading Account and Profit and Loss Account for the week, and a Balance Sheet as at that date. Stock at the close was valued at £17·50. Wages are to be charged in the Profit and Loss Account.

2. On July 1st E. Carr starts in business with capital of £1 500·00 which he banks. He then buys by cheque a market stall (Stall and Equipment A/c), £75·00; goods for resale £120·00; and equipment £67·50. His transactions are as follows:

   July 2nd Cash sales £84·00. Purchase in cash of goods for resale £18·00. Wages of assistant £3·00 cash.

   July 3rd Cash sales £142·00. Purchase in cash of goods for resale £36·50, Electric-light fee £3·00 (cash). Tip to dustman £0·25 (cash).

   July 4th Cash sales £113·00. Purchase by cheque of goods for resale £85·00. Wages of assistant £2·00 cash. Paid to bank £100·00.

   July 5th Cash sales £94·00. Purchase in cash of goods for resale £62·50. Wages of assistants £8·50 cash.

   July 6th Cash sales £164·00. Wages of assistants £17·20 cash. Carr takes £40·00 as personal drawings from cash.

   Record the above items, extract a Trial Balance as at July 6th and from it prepare a Trading Account and Profit and Loss Account for the week, also a Balance Sheet as at that date. Stock at the close was valued at £34·00. Wages are to be charged to Profit and Loss Account.

3. On January 1st 19.. M. Tapley starts in business with assets as follows: Cash in hand £50·00; cash at bank £730·00; premises £6 250·00; motor vehicle £720·00; and furniture and fittings £380·00. Enter these opening items, then record the following transactions for the first two weeks of

January. After that, balance such accounts as require it, prepare a Trial Balance and a full set of Final Accounts. Then advise Tapley whether he should continue in business. (The closing stock was valued at £48·00. Wages are to be charged to Profit and Loss Account.)

January 1st   Purchases goods for resale by cheque £72·00. Purchases goods for resale on credit from Wholesale Suppliers Ltd. £325·00.

January 2nd   Postage £0·50 cash. Entertainment of commercial traveller £1·75 cash. Purchases fittings £24·50 by cheque.

January 3rd   Sells goods on credit to M. Jones £42·50. Pays telephone connexion charge £2·50 cash.

January 4th   Purchases typewriter in cash £24·00. Purchases goods for resale by cheque £34·80.

January 5th   Cash sales for week £263·00. Pays to bank £200·00. Pays wages of assistants £17·50 in cash. Drawings for self, cheque £40·00.

January 8th   Jones pays £10·00 on account in cash. Purchases goods for resale on credit from W. Grossmith £240·00.

January 9th   Sells goods on credit to M. Jones £62·30.

January 11th   Pays motor-vehicle expenses £25·00 cash.

January 12th   Cash sales for week £130·00. Pays to bank £80·00. Pays wages of assistants £17·50 in cash. Drawings for self, cheque £40·00.

4. On January 1st 19. . R. Quilp starts in business with assets as follows: cash in hand £50·00; cash at bank £350·00; premises £3 500·00; motor vehicle £650·00; and furniture and fittings £240·00. Enter these opening items, then record the following transactions for the first two weeks of January. Now, (a) balance such accounts as require it, and (b) prepare a Trial Balance and a full set of Final Accounts. Then advise Quilp whether he should continue in business. (The closing stock was valued at £472·00.)

January 1st   Purchases goods for resale by cheque £42·00. Purchases goods for resale on credit from Wholesale Suppliers Ltd., £465·50.

January 2nd   Travelling £1·25 cash. Entertainment of Finance-House representative £2·40 cash. Purchases goods from Universal Shop Suppliers on credit £380·00.

January 3rd   Sells goods on credit to M. Freeman £68·50. Pays for improvements to premises (Premises Account) cheque £100·00.

January 4th   Purchases goods for resale in cash £24·50. Sells goods on credit to M. Wilde £25·40.

January 5th   Cash sales for week £385·00. Pays to bank £200·00. Pays wages £13·50 cash. Drawings for self, cheque £50·00.

January 8th   Purchases goods for resale, cash £38·50. Purchases goods on credit from Wholesale Suppliers Ltd., £525·50.

January 9th Sells goods on credit to M. Freeman £95·65.

January 11th Pays Wholesale Suppliers Ltd. on account £300·00 by cheque.

January 12th Cash sales for week £620·00. Banks £400·00. Pays wages of assistants £13·50 cash. Drawings for self, cheque £50·00.

5. R. Bingham starts in business on April 1st 19.. with the following assets: motor vehicles £530·00; furniture and fittings £275·00; premises £3 800·00; cash in hand £24·50; and cash at bank £725·50. Open the ledger accounts to record these items, also the following transactions:

April 1st Purchases stock for resale by cheque, £150·00. Buys cash register £25·50, cheque.

April 2nd Purchases goods for resale, on credit from T. Lines, £75·00. Purchases shelving and equipment £70·00 by cheque.

April 6th Cash sale £165·50. Pays travelling expenses £1·25 cash.

April 8th Sells goods on credit to R. French £25·50. Purchases goods (for resale) at auction of a bankrupt's property, £65·50 by cheque.

April 10th Purchases typewriter £32·50 cash. Purchases stationery £6·55 cash.

April 12th Sells goods on credit to T. Tozer £42·50. Purchases goods for resale £240·00 by cheque.

April 13th Cash sales £238·25. Banks £200·00 from cash till.

April 16th Pays wages £42·00 in cash.

April 20th Cash sales £167·75. Purchases goods for resale on credit from T. Lines £185·50.

April 23rd Pays fares £2·25 in cash.

April 27th Cash sales £245·50. Pays £200·00 into bank.

April 29th Recorded letter £0·25 cash. Pays for repairs £1·65 cash.

April 30th Draws cash for personal use by cheque £120·00. Pays wages £42·00 cash. Pays T. Lines £75·00 by cheque.

Extract a Trial Balance as at April 30th and from the Trial Balance prepare a Trading Account and Profit and Loss Account for the month ending April 30th, and a Balance Sheet as at that date. (Closing stock was valued at £116·00.) Wages are to be dealt with in the Profit and Loss A/c.

6. M. Day starts in business on January 1st 19.. with the following assets: motor vehicles £650·00; furniture and fittings £230·00; premises £4 200·00; cash in hand £35·00; and cash at bank £475·00. Open the ledger accounts to record these items, also the following transactions.

January 1st Purchases stock for resale by cheque £250·00. Purchases scales and weights £3·55 cash.

January 2nd Purchases goods for resale, on credit from R. Lyons £75·50. Purchases typewriter from Remington's Ltd., on credit £48·50.

January 6th Cash sales £84·75. Postage £0·25 cash. Pays telephone connexion fee, £2·50 cheque.

January 8th   Cleaning materials £2·55 cash. Sales on credit to Mowler
                Tooth and Co. £42·50.
January 10th   Repairs to window fitting £2·25 cash.
January 12th   Pays for electric fittings and installation £12·25 by cash.
January 13th   Cash sales £172·50. Pays into bank £150·00.
January 16th   Purchases goods for resale on credit from R. Lyons
                £160·00.
January 20th   Cash sales £163·80. Pays into bank £100·00.
January 22nd   Pays wages to casual worker £3·25 in cash.
January 23rd   Pays cash for fittings bought at bankruptcy sale, £27·50.
January 27th   Cash sales £236·50. Pays £200·00 into bank.
January 29th   Recorded letter £0·35 cash. Sells on credit to R. White
                goods £55·00.
January 30th   Pays cash wages £7·50. Draws cash for personal use by
                cheque £100·00. Pays for advertisement by cheque £12·10.
                Pays by cheque to Remington Ltd., £48·50.

Extract a Trial Balance as at January 31st and from the Trial Balance
prepare a Trading Account and Profit and Loss Account for the month
ending January 31st 19.. and a Balance Sheet as at that date. (Closing
stock was valued at £55·50.) Wages are to be dealt with in the Profit and
Loss Account.

8.4   Exercises Set 10: Accounting to Final-Accounts Level—Part Two

1. M. Davies's Trial Balance at December 31st 19.. shows the following balances. Prepare from them Trading and Profit and Loss Accounts for 19.., and a Balance Sheet as at that date.

	Dr.	Cr.
	£	£
Purchases A/c	5 840	
Sales A/c		9 726
Purchases-Returns A/c		140
Sales-Returns A/c	126	
Opening Stock (January 1st 19..)	2 000	
Sundry-Expenses A/c	426	
Rent and Rates A/c	550	
Light and Heat A/c	230	
Discount-Allowed A/c	85	
Discount-Received A/c		65
Land and Buildings A/c	4 500	
Furniture and Fittings A/c	380	
Motor-Vehicles A/c	750	
Debtors	495	
Creditors		1 295
Drawings	1 500	
Capital		6 656
Cash in Hand	200	
Cash at Bank	800	
	£17 882	17 882

Closing stock was valued at £1 780·00 on December 31st 19..

2. P. Robinson's Trial Balance at March 31st 19.. shows the following balances. From this Trial Balance prepare a Trading Account and Profit and Loss Account for the year and a Balance Sheet as at that date.

	Dr. £	Cr. £
Purchases and Sales	10 250	21 155
Sales Returns and Purchases Returns	355	650
Opening Stock (April 1st 19..)	2 175	
Warehouse Wages	2 135	
Warehouse Expenses	108	
Sundry Expenses	2 640	
Selling Expenses	1 255	
Interest Paid	65	
Discount Allowed and Received	172	88
Commission Received		255
Cash in Hand	50	
Cash at Bank	950	
Premises	5 240	
Motor Vehicles	1 850	
Fixtures and Fittings	430	
Debtors and Creditors	1 555	1 795
Drawings	950	
Capital		4 937
Loan from A. Colleague		1 300
	£30 180	30 180

Closing stock was valued at £2 250·00 on March 31st 19..

3. T. Ford's Trial Balance is given below as it was drawn up on December 31st. From it you are asked to prepare a Trading Account and a Profit and Loss Account for the year ending December 31st 19. . and a Balance Sheet as at that date.

	Dr. £	Cr. £
Purchases and Sales	11 800	17 550
Sales Returns and Purchase Returns	150	100
Opening Stock (as at January 1st 19. .)	1 850	
Carriage In	40	
Warehouse Expenses	895	
Rent, Rates and Insurance	725	
Light, Heat and Fuel	480	
Petrol and Oil	254	
Motor-Vehicle Repairs	126	
Cleaning Expenses	72	
Repairs and Redecorations	234	
Commission Received		285
Fees Received		1 245
Land and Buildings	5 000	
Furniture and Fittings	840	
Fork-Lift Trucks	1 220	
Debtors and Creditors	425	1 385
Mortgage on Premises		3 000
Interest Paid	420	
Drawings	1 850	
Capital		3 816
Cash in Hand	150	
Cash at Bank	850	
	£27 381	27 381

Closing stock was valued at £2 000·00 on December 31st 19. .

4. R. Maycock's Trial Balance is given below as it was drawn up on December 31st 19.. From it you are asked to prepare a Trading Account and a Profit and Loss Account for the year ending December 31st 19.. and a Balance Sheet as at that date.

	Dr.	Cr.
	£	£
Purchases and Sales	5 725·50	11 246·50
Sales Returns and Purchases Returns	146·50	125·50
Opening Stock (as at January 1st 19..)	850·75	
Carriage In	35·75	
Warehouse Expenses	425·25	
Rent, Rates and Insurance	136·50	
Light, Heat and Fuel	149·75	
Petrol and Oil	235·25	
Motor-Vehicle Repairs	62·50	
Cleaning Expenses	148·50	
Repairs and Redecorations	230·65	
Commission Received		175·50
Fees Received		1 250·00
Land and Buildings	6 250·00	
Furniture and Fittings	1 385·80	
Fork-Lift Trucks	1 485·50	
Debtors and Creditors	247·35	656·50
Mortgage on Premises		4 000·00
Interest Paid	336·50	
Drawings	1 450·00	
Capital		2 848·05
Cash in Hand	25·00	
Cash at Bank	975·00	
	£20 302·05	20 302·05

Closing stock was valued at £1 000·00 on December 31st 19..

5. From the following Trial Balance of A. Brewis's books prepare a Trading Account and Profit and Loss Account for the year ending March 31st 19..; also a Balance Sheet as at that date.

	Dr. £	Cr. £
Purchases and Sales	27 246	44 725
Sales Returns and Purchases Returns	725	1 266
Carriage In	180	
Carriage Out	325	
Opening Stock at April 1st 19..	4 650	
Rent and Rates	1 420	
Insurance	148	
Light and Heat	1 630	
Discount Allowed and Discount Received	125	86
Commission Paid and Commission Received	1 095	2 469
Salaries	5 854	
Debtors and Creditors	2 760	1 000
Land and Buildings	10 750	
Furniture and Fittings	1 250	
Motor Vehicles	1 480	
Drawings	1 625	
Cash in Hand	138	
Cash at Bank	2 745	
Loan from R. Petworth		5 000
Capital		9 600
	£64 146	64 146

Closing stock was valued at £5 450·00 on March 31st 19..

6. From the following Trial Balance of E. London's books prepare a Trading Account and Profit and Loss Account for the year ending December 31st 19.., and a Balance Sheet as at that date.

	Dr. £	Cr. £
Purchases and Sales	12 580·50	25 624·30
Sales Returns and Purchases Returns	624·30	580·50
Opening Stock at January 1st 19..	2 000·00	
Carriage In	120·50	
Warehouse Wages (Trading Account)	1 480·50	
Warehouse Expenses (Trading Account)	338·75	
Light and Heat	240·50	
Rent and Rates	1 248·00	
Telephone Expenses	86·55	
Insurance	48·50	
Selling Expenses	726·30	
Motor-Vehicle Expenses	241·55	
Travellers' Salaries	3 865·25	
Office Salaries	1 585·50	
Rent Received from Sub-tenant		240·00
Land and Buildings	11 250·00	
Furniture and Fittings	870·50	
Plant and Machinery	3 150·00	
Drawings	1 650·00	
Debtors and Creditors	842·00	1 736·00
Cash in Hand	142·70	
Cash at Bank	1 150·00	
Mortgage		7 250·00
Bank Loan		1 000·00
Capital (E. London)		7 811·10
	£44 241·90	44 241·90

. Closing stock was valued at £2 500·00 on December 31st 19..

Books of Original Entry
Part One: The Journal

9.1 The Antiquity of Accounting

Accounting is essential to all advanced civilizations which have moved beyond barter as a means of exchange, and have devised some sort of monetary system of payments. It follows that accounting records are some of the oldest records available to us, inscribed on cuneiform tablets from Mesopotamia, or papyri and ostraca from Ancient Egypt. Even the puzzling Minoan scripts from Knossos in Crete were eventually found to consist largely of kitchen bills for supplies to the royal commissariat.

Double-entry book-keeping was devised towards the end of the first millennium A.D. by merchants in Northern Italy. It was included in a textbook by the mathematician Pacioli in 1494. The double-entry system which he described used two books, a *Journal*, which was the *book of original entry*, and the ledger, the main book of account.

At the very moment that this first formal statement of the double-entry system of accounting was being published, commerce was spreading from the Mediterranean basin, via the Iberian Peninsula to Northern Europe. Columbus was just returning from the New World, and Vasco da Gama, embarking for India. The ancient camel routes across Asia and the Near East were about to be replaced by sea-borne trade, and the *Italian method* of keeping accounts was copied by the merchants of Spain, the Low Countries and England. It was Simon Stevin of Bruges who developed the idea of the Balance Sheet in the 1530s, and British and American accountants who devised the later improvements. These included the development of other books of original entry, to reduce the number of Journal entries, such as the *Purchases Day Book*, the *Sales Day Book*, the *Purchases-Returns Book* and *Sales-Returns Book*, *Bill Books*, etc. Later still, *simultaneous records*—particularly for wages, sales, purchases and tax—were developed. Finally, the computer has made these labour-saving books of original entry unnecessary. Routine double-entry work can now be done on the computer, and entries are made direct into the electronic records, shuffled, sorted, analysed and aggregated effortlessly.

The next few chapters describe the books of original entry, which are still in use by many firms which do not employ computerized or mechanized systems. If you work in a large company using computerized systems, you will find it useful to see how these books were used to reduce work and perfect the accounting records.

9.2 The Journal

The Journal is a 'day book', in which transactions are recorded in chrono-
logical order, day by day, as they occur. It is the most important of the
subsidiary books. Subsidiary means 'giving additional help to'. The Journal
gives additional help to the *ledger*, which is *the main book of account*.
Journal paper is ruled as shown in Fig. 9.1.

Month	Day	Details	Folio	Debit Column (in which the accounts to be debited are listed)	Credit Column (in which the accounts to be credited are listed)

Fig. 9.1 Journal paper

Originally there was only one Journal, where all original entries were
made. These entries were then transferred into the ledger accounts, a
process known as *posting* the Day Book to the ledger. A typical Journal entry
is shown in Fig. 9.2.

19.. Jan.	1	Motor-Vehicles A/c Dr. Danehole's Garage Being new motor vehicle XOO 127N purchased at this date	L 5 L 7	£ 1 270·50	£ J 1 1 270·50

Fig. 9.2 A typical Journal entry

Posted to the ledger accounts these entries would appear as shown in Fig.
9.3.

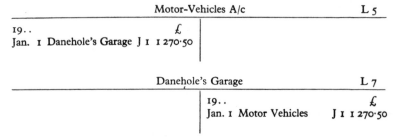

Motor-Vehicles A/c   L 5

19..   £
Jan. 1 Danehole's Garage J 1 1 270·50

Danehole's Garage   L 7

                              19..   £
                              Jan. 1 Motor Vehicles J 1 1 270·50

Fig. 9.3 Posting the Journal to the ledger

Notes :

(*a*) The Journal entry simply records the transaction as a double entry. The abbreviation Dr. appears at the end of the line to show the account to be debited. The name of the account to be credited is indented a little way along the line.

(*b*) A short explanation, called the *narration*, is written below each entry to remind the accountant of the circumstances. It usually starts with the word 'Being'.

(*c*) The journal entry is then posted to the ledger, that is to say the original entry is transferred to the respective ledger accounts, the account to be debited having its entry made on the debit side and the account to be credited having its entry on the credit side.

(*d*) The folio numbers J 1 indicate the page of the Journal from which the transfers were made.

As the years went by it became clear that this Journal system was rather tiresome, in that a great many of the Journal entries were exactly alike, recurring repeatedly throughout the month or the year. In general the entries were found to consist of the following types:

(i) Many *purchases* of goods from suppliers, in which Purchases Account was debited and the supplier was credited.

(ii) Many *sales* of goods to customers, in which the customer was debited and Sales Account was credited.

(iii) Many purchases returns, in which the supplier was debited as he received back the goods purchased which for some reason were unsatisfactory, and the Purchases-Returns Account was credited.

(iv) Many sales returns, in which the customer was credited with the goods given back, and Sales-Returns Account was debited.

(v) Many cash payments and payments by cheque.

(vi) A variety of other items, much more rarely occurring, but including the following: opening entries at the start of the business; the purchase of assets, the depreciation of assets and the sale of worn-out assets; the correction of errors; the writing-off of bad debts; the arrangement of loans and mortgages, the payment of interest due and the receipt of interest receivable; the treatment of dishonoured cheques; and the closing entries made when the final accounts are being prepared.

New ideas were therefore introduced to reduce the number of entries in the Journal, which now became known as the *Journal Proper*, and only contained the relatively rare items like those listed in (vi) above. Instead of putting the other repetitive items in the Journal Proper, a whole battery of Journals, or Day Books, was opened. These were the *Purchases Day Book*, the *Sales Day Book*, the *Purchases-Returns Book* and the *Sales-Returns Book*. These books are illustrated and described in Sections 10.3, 10.5 and 11.3, 11.5. Here we are concerned to learn the layout and use of one of the Journal entries for the rarer types of entries which are still entered in the Journal Proper, because they do not occur frequently and therefore do not merit having a book opened especially for them.

The first such entry, made when a business first starts to use double-entry book-keeping, is the *opening Journal entry*.

9.3 Journal Proper Entries 1: Opening Entries

Whenever a business is established, the first entry made is the contribution of the proprietor, in the form of capital. This contribution may be in money form, but more often it consists of a variety of assets, some cash, a balance at the bank, premises, motor vehicles, etc. The new business may also already have a few debtors or creditors, for varying amounts. Such an opening entry involves a Journal entry of the type shown in Fig. 9.4.

Example

R. Grimshaw sets up in business on July 1st 19. ., with the following assets. Cash in hand, £25·00, cash at bank £156·00, premises £2 500·00, furniture and fittings £850·00 and a motor vehicle £400·00. He has a creditor, Long Loans Ltd, for £1 500·00. Draw up the Journal entry and open the ledger accounts.

In preparing this Journal entry the assets are listed, and totalled as shown below. The liabilities are then set beside them.

Assets	£	Liabilities	£
Cash	25·00	Long Loans Ltd.	1 500·00
Bank	156·00		
Premises	2 500·00		
Furniture	850·00		
Motor Vehicles	400·00		
	£3 931·00		£1 500·00

The assets and liabilities of any business must always balance, yet clearly this is not so in the example shown above. What is missing? The answer is, the Capital Account. We must always calculate the Capital Account and include it in the Journal entry. The calculation is:

		£
Total assets	=	3 931·00
Less amounts financed by external creditors	=	1 500·00
Capital	=	£2 431·00

Although opening entries are usually done on the first day a business starts they are also necessary at other times. For example, a business which has not kept proper records of its affairs, (see *Incomplete Records*, Section 30.2) may change to using the double-entry system. The first stage of such a change is to open the necessary accounts from an opening Journal entry.

You should now attempt several opening Journal entries from Exercises Set 9.4. Further work on Journal entries will be found in Units Twelve, Thirteen and Sixteen.

19.. July 1	Cash Dr.	L 1	£ 25·00	£	J 1
	Bank Dr.	L 2	156·00		
	Premises Dr.	L 3	2 500·00		
	Furniture and Fittings Dr.	L 4	850·00		
	Motor Vehicles Dr.	L 5	400·00		
	Long Loans Ltd.	L 6		1 500·00	
	Capital A/c	L 7		2 431·00	
	Being assets and liabilities at this date		£3 931·00	£3 931·00	

Cash A/c   L 1

19.. July 1	Capital	J 1	£ 25·00	

Bank A/c   L 2

19.. July 1	Capital	J 1	£ 156·00	

Premises A/c   L 3

19.. July 1	Capital	J 1	£ 2 500·00	

Furniture and Fittings A/c   L 4

19.. July 1	Capital	J 1	£ 850·00	

Motor-Vehicles A/c   L5

19.. July 1	Capital	J 1	£ 400·0	

Long Loans Ltd. A/c   L 6

		19.. July 1	Capital	J 1	£ 1 500·00

Capital A/c   L 7

		19.. July 1	Capital	J 1	£ 2 431·00

Fig. 9.4 An opening Journal entry posted to the ledger accounts

9.4   Exercises Set 11: Opening Journal Entries

1. R. Marshall sets up in business on January 1st 19.., with a capital of £1 000·00, in cash, which he puts into the bank. Record this opening Journal entry and post it to ledger accounts opened for the purpose.

2. M. Léghorn sets up in business on June 1st 19.. with a capital of £2 500·00, in cash, which he puts into the bank. Record this opening Journal entry and post it to ledger accounts opened for the purpose.

3. M. Tyler sets up in business on January 1st 19.. with the following assets: cash in hand £24·00; cash at bank £125·00; premises £2 500·00; motor vehicles £472·00 and office equipment £350·00. Calculate his capital, and draw up the opening Journal entry. Give a suitable narration.

4. R. Lucas sets up in business on January 1st 19.. with the following assets: cash in hand £48·00; cash at bank £225·00; premises £3 800·00; motor vehicles £740·00 and office equipment £520·00. Calculate his capital and draw up the opening Journal entry. Give a suitable narration.

5. G. Porter sets up in business on January 1st 19.. with the following assets: cash in hand £32·00; cash at bank £250·00; premises £3 300·00; motor vehicles £655·00 and office equipment £256·00. Calculate his capital, and draw up the opening Journal entry. Give a suitable narration.

6. M. Larkin sets up in business on April 1st 19.. with the following assets and liabilities: cash in hand £256·00; cash at bank £325·00; premises £7 000·00; plant and machinery £485·00; stock £480·00. He has two debtors, P. Rose £52·00 and M. Groves £37·00, and one creditor R. Beeden £285·50. Draw up an opening Journal entry showing the total capital contributed. Post it to the ledger accounts, opening them up for this purpose.

7. M. Lawson sets up in business on April 1st 19.. with the following assets and liabilities: cash in hand £8·00; cash at bank £192·00; premises £1 600·00; plant and machinery £85·00; stock £240·00. He has two debtors P. Rogers £47·00 and M. Graves £29·00, and one creditor R. Bell £162·50. Draw up an opening Journal entry showing the total capital contributed. Post it to the ledger accounts.

8. S. Thompson sets up in business on April 1st 19.. with the following assets and liabilities: cash in hand £82·00; cash at bank £1 156·00; premises £2 958·00; plant and machinery £440·00; stock £650·00. He has two debtors R. Lyons £276·50 and A. Moore £550·50. His only creditor Lyle Finance Co. is owed £268·50. Draw up an opening Journal entry showing the total capital contributed. Post the opening entry to the ledger accounts.

9. Peter Martin has been in business for some time, but has not been keep-

ing proper books of account. As a result he feels that the tax payment required last year by the Inspector of Taxes was excessive, but he is unable to prove his point. He decides to keep a proper set of books in future and asks you to draw up an opening Journal entry to record his position, which is as follows on January 1st 19..: cash in hand £24·00; cash at bank £1 756·00; premises £8 500·00; stock £1 750·00; motor vehicles £840·00. Debtors: R. Long £27·50, B. Short £42·75, T. Wide £36·85. Creditors: Imperial Loan Co. £1 500·00, Longlife Finance Co. £800·00. It is not necessary to post the opening entry to the ledger accounts.

10. Steptoe's son, having completed his education at a local technical college, is about to join his father in the family business. He persuades the old man, who has never kept proper books of account, to agree to this practice in future. Draw up the opening Journal entry for Steptoe and Son on July 1st 19.., the senior partner to have £5 000·00 of the capital allocated to him. The following assets and liabilities exist: cash in hand £85·00; cash at bank £1 876·00; premises and yard £2 800·00; stock of scrap materials £185·00; motor vehicles £1 050·00; scales and other equipment £42·50. Debtors: A. Scrapiron £285·00, B. Ragdealer £155·50. A bill for motor-vehicle repairs is owing to A. Welder £25·00.

Books of Original Entry
Part Two: The Purchases and Sales Day Books

10.1 Trading Businesses—Goods for Resale

One of the commonest business activities is the purchase of goods for resale at a profit. This is the activity known as *trade*, and comprises *wholesale trade* and *retail trade*. The former of these may also involve importing and exporting. Another business activity, *manufacturing*, also means purchasing raw materials and components, which are eventually resold as part of the finished product which is being manufactured.

It follows that purchases of goods and sales of goods are repeatedly taking place in such firms and that the number of entries required in the accounting records is very great. As they occur daily they will be recorded in a Journal, but since they are so numerous it is usual to have a special Day Book for purchases—the Purchases Day Book—and a special Day Book for sales—the Sales Day Book. We will look at these books shortly, but first it is necessary to explain the special meaning given in business to the words 'goods', 'purchases' and 'sales'.

Goods refers to items forming part of the stock in trade of a firm, which are purchased to be resold at a profit. A firm may purchase other items for use in the business, but they are not purchases of 'goods'. They may be purchases of *assets*, which will last a long time, or purchases of *consumables*, which only last a short time, being used up in the business. A few examples will illustrate the point. A draper purchases sheets, pillow cases, towels, etc., as goods for resale, but a cash register for use in the business would be an asset, and paper bags and wrapping paper would be consumables. Filing cabinets, typewriters and adding machines would be goods to a supplier of office equipment, but capital assets to everyone else. To a garage, cars are goods since they form part of the stock in trade. To everyone else they are assets, recorded in the Motor-Vehicles Account.

Purchases refers to the purchase of goods for resale, and not to the purchase of assets or consumables. The Purchases Account therefore only contains purchases of goods for resale. It is an *error of principle* to record purchases of assets and consumables in the Purchases Account.

Sales refers to sales of goods which have formed part of the stock-in-trade of the business. Sales of other items, such as worn-out or obsolete assets, or assets surplus to requirements are not 'sales' in the accounting meaning of that word. It would again be an error of principle to record sales of assets in the Sales Account.

10.2 The Invoice—The Document for Sales and Purchases

An invoice is a document which is made out whenever one person sells goods to the other. It is made out by the seller, and at least one copy is sent to the buyer. More often two copies reach the buyer: the top copy, which is sent by post, and a further copy called the *advice note*, which accompanies the goods so that the buyer's stock department can check the contents of the packages.

A typical invoice is illustrated in Fig. 10.1.

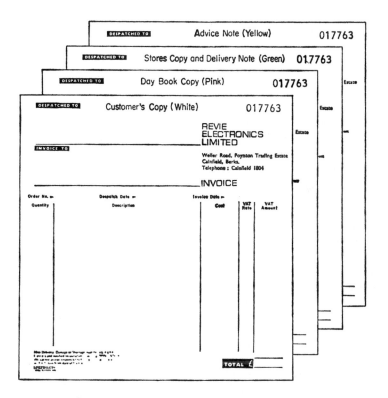

Fig. 10.1 An invoice with a four-copy distribution

(1) Characteristics of an Invoice
An invoice is a document for the sale of goods, made out by the seller and used to inform the buyer of the type, number, price and value of the goods

supplied. There may be as many as twenty copies of it, but more usually three, four or five copies are sufficient. While it may not actually form the contract between the two parties to the transaction, it is very good evidence of the contract and is often produced in court in cases where disputes over contracts for the sale of goods are being decided. It should have the following details:

(a) The names and addresses of both parties to the contract.

(b) An exact description of the goods, including the number, unit price and total value of the consignment.

(c) The terms and conditions of sale, or a reference to the place where the terms and conditions of sale may be discovered.

(d) It often has the letters E and OE (errors and omissions excepted). This is an old-fashioned practice, which recognizes the legal maxim that written evidence cannot be varied by oral evidence. It was formerly thought that a mere slip of the pen, or a typists' error, would have to be honoured if the invoice was the contract. Thus an invoice in which a machine valued at £1 000·00 was incorrectly made out for £100·00 might have bound the seller at the cheaper figure. However the case of Webster *v.* Cecil (1861) decided that a mere slip of the pen may be corrected, so that the letters E and OE are not strictly necessary now.

(2) Distribution of Invoices

The *top copy* always goes to the purchaser, and becomes his accounting record, entered—with any other purchases invoices—in his *Purchases Day Book*.

The *second copy* stays with the seller, and becomes his accounting record, entered—with any other sales invoices in his *Sales Day Book*.

The *third and fourth copies*, often called the 'delivery note' and the 'advice note', are sent down to the seller's dispatch department. Goods are obtained for dispatch from the stock department, and the advice note is packed with these goods for the customer's information. The delivery note is then used by the carman to obtain a signature from the customer acknowledging delivery of the goods in sound condition.

The fifth copy, if there is one, is often used as a 'file copy' or 'representative's copy'. It informs the representative, about to call on a customer, that his previous order for that customer has been fulfilled by Head Office.

(3) Trade Discount

Frequently a type of discount called *trade discount* is given to traders. A discount is a reduction in price. The granting of trade discount has developed because it often happens that it is more convenient for all those concerned with a product to think of it in terms of the final price to the consumer. Thus a vacuum cleaner manufacturer may turn out two models— a standard model at £20·00 and a *de luxe* model at £30·00. Although he does not sell these to retailers at these prices—because these are the final prices to the consumer—it is convenient for him to invoice them to the retailer at this value.

Such an invoice might read:

8 *de luxe* vacuum cleaners at £30·00 each = £240·00
Less Trade Discount 40 % = 96·00

£144·00

Note the high rate of trade discount granted to the retailer in this case. Trade discount tends to be high when goods are expensive and slow-moving, and low when the turnover is more rapid. As you will see this discount represents the profit to which the retailer is entitled and may be defined as follows.

Trade Discount is a reduction made in the catalogue price of an article to enable the retailer to make a profit.

It does not enter the ledger accounts, but may be recorded in the Purchases and Sales Day Books as shown in Fig. 10.2.

(4) Debit Notes

It sometimes happens that an invoice is made out incorrectly, the value of the transaction being *understated*. When this occurs it is usual to correct the error by sending a *debit note* to the customer. This document is treated exactly like an invoice, and is entered in the Day Books in exactly the same way.

10.3 Recording Purchases Invoices—The Purchases Day Book

During the nineteenth century the volume of goods produced in fields and factories rose and it became clear that the Journal was inadequate as the sole book of original entry. Too many clerks wanted to make entries in the same book at the same time. It became easier to have a separate book for the commoner activities, like purchases, sales, purchases returns and sales returns. Not only that, but the use of these special Journals, or Day Books, was simplified. Instead of making a double entry for every invoice, the clerk would make only a single entry at that time, leaving the double entry until the end of the month. For example in the Purchases Day Book, every invoice entered was for purchases. It required a credit entry in the supplier's account (the supplier had given goods) and a debit entry in Purchases Account (Purchases Account had received goods). There was little point in making the second of these entries in the Purchases Account separately for each entry. A simpler way was to add up the whole book at the end of the month, and make one entry of the total figure in the Purchases Account. The two columns of the Journal (see Section 9.2) were no longer needed, and the inner column became merely an addition column for invoices with several items on them. The last column became the important column, showing how much should be credited to each supplier's personal account, and the total of the book on the last day of the month showed the total to be debited to Purchases Account. This is illustrated clearly in Fig. 10.2.

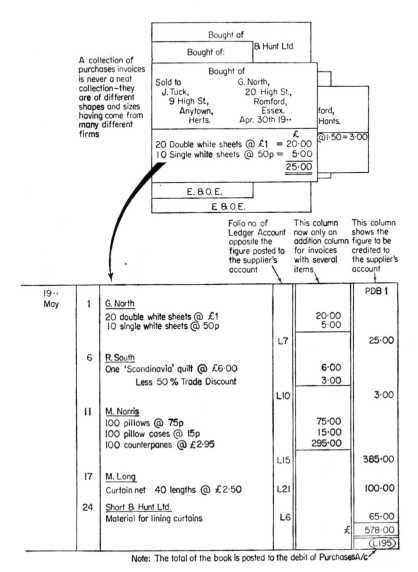

Fig. 10.2 The Purchases Day Book

Posting the Purchases Day Book to the Ledger

When posted to the ledger, the entries would be as shown in Fig. 10.3. In each case the supplier is credited (credit the giver) and the firm whose books are being kept is debited with the *total* purchases in the Purchases Account. This debit entry is the double entry for *all* the entries in the suppliers' accounts.

	G. North A/c		L 7
	19		£
	May 1 Purchases	PDB 1	25·00

	R. South A/c		L 10
	19..		£
	May 6 Purchases	PDB 1	3·00

	M. Norris A/c		L 15
	19..		£
	May 11 Purchases	PDB 1	385·00

	M. Long A/c		L 21
	19..		£
	May 17 Purchases	PDB 1	100·00

	Short and Hunt Ltd. A/c		L 6
	19..		£
	May 24 Purchases	PDB 1	65·00

Purchases A/c			L 195
19..	£		
May 31 Sundry			
Creditors PDB 1	578·00		

Fig. 10.3 Posting the Purchases Day Book

The reader should now practise one or two entries in the Purchases Day Book, using the examples given in Exercises Set 12.

10.4 Exercises Set 12: The Purchases Day Book

1. Enter the following items in the Purchases Day Book of M. Sibthorpe, and post the book to the ledger accounts. Total the book on May 31st 19..

   May 1st   F. Ball sells Sibthorpe 3 sets of golf clubs @ £42·50 per set (£127·50).

May 2nd   B. Bannerman sells Sibthorpe 20 badminton sets @ £1·55 each (£31·00) and 20 comeback tennis trainers @ £2·25 each (£45·00).

May 11th   R. Downs supplies Sibthorpe with 100 golf balls @ 25p each (£25·00).

May 17th   P. Roberts supplies Sibthorpe with 40 leather footballs @ £1·80 each (£72·00) and 200 plastic footballs @ 85p each (£170·00).

May 24th   G. Wright supplies Sibthorpe with 200 'Homesocca' games @ £2·35 each (£470·00).

2. Enter the following items in the Purchases Day Book of R. Beech, and post the book to the ledger accounts. Total the book on May 31st 19. .

May 1st   M. Benton sells Beech 5 sets of 'Home Painter' equipment @ £5·50 per set (£27·50).

May 3rd   D. Cade sells Beech 20 drums of paint @ £1·85 each (37·00) and 20 litres thinners @ 65p per litre (£13·00).

May 14th   S. Carter supplies Beech with 100 rolls wallpaper @ 55p each (£55·00).

May 27th   D. Cade supplies Beech with 40 tins white gloss paint @ £1·60 each (£64·00) and 200 plastic paint trays @ 45p each (£90·00).

May 29th   G. Wright supplies Beech with 100 rolls wallpaper @ 85p each (£85·00).

3. M. Lawson is invoiced for the following goods by the suppliers shown. Record them in his Purchases Day Book and post to the ledger accounts. Total the book on January 31st 19. .

January 4th   R. Davy supplies 12 Barracuda fish tanks @ £3·20 each (£38·40).

January 10th   K. Adcock supplies 12 mini-tank aeration pumps @ £1·55 each (£18·60).

January 13th   M. Bridger supplies assorted tropical fish, valued at £18·50, and submarine landscape features (24 sets) @ £0·85 per set (£20·40).

January 21st   D. De'ath supplies garden fish tanks valued at £184·50.

January 23rd   R. Lawrence supplies freshwater fish valued at £12·50 and weed (assorted) valued £6·00.

4. R. J. Upfold is in business as a grocer and is supplied with the following supplies in May 19. . Record them in his Purchases Day Book and post the entries to the ledger accounts. Total the book on May 31st 19. .

May 1st   R. Biggs supplies fresh tomatoes valued at £17·50 and 2 000 hens' eggs at 1·5p (£30·00).

May 7th   Golden Freezers Ltd. supplies butter £42·50, margarine £36·50 and various bacon packs valued at £45·00.

May 8th   California Fruit Co. Ltd. supplies tinned peaches £40·00, tinned pears £36·00 and blueberries £5·50.

May 11th Danish Produce Ltd. supplies bacon £50·00, cheeses £32·00 and butter £43·50.

May 17th Shropshire Cooperative Producers Ltd. supplies eggs £48·50, milk products £32·50 and cheese £16·50.

May 29th London Import Co. supplies assorted Canadian produce valued at £248·00.

5. R. Davison is in the ironmongery business and is supplied with the following items in June 19.. Record them in his Purchases Day Book and post the entries to the ledger accounts. Total the book at June 30th 19..

June 1st P. Ketley supplies assorted prepacked brassware £15·60 and ironware £27·30.

June 7th Safety Fires Ltd. supplies the following: 12 oil stoves @ £3·75 each (£45·00), 10 cooking stoves @ £7·95 each (£79·50) and spare wicks and mantels £8·55.

June 11th Sheffield Cutlers Ltd. supplies stainless-steel cutlery totalling £185·00 in value.

June 13th Plastico Ltd. supplies the following: tea sets £42·00, bowls £36·00 and buckets £32·00.

June 23rd A. E. Plant supplies goods (tools and equipment) valued at £234·50.

June 29th K. J. Adlam invoiced for copper fittings £48·50, chromium fittings £77·50 and mirror wares £12·85.

10.5 Recording Sales Invoices—The Sales Day Book

Just as the purchase of goods for resale is a frequent occurrence, the sale of goods is an everyday transaction. A single invoice typist may type as many as one hundred invoices every day. She will, in addition, separate the top copy from each set and send it to the customer, who will enter it in his Purchases Day Book. The third and fourth copies will be sent down to the dispatch department for processing. The second copy becomes the accounts-department copy, for entry into the Sales Day Book. The illustration Fig. 10.4 shows the entries in this book, which are identical to those made in the Purchases Day Book. Only the pile of invoices is neater, since this time they have not come from many different firms but are all from our own firm, and therefore identical in shape, size and colour.

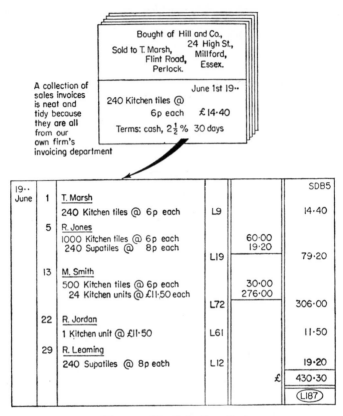

Fig. 10.4 The Sales Day Book

Posting the Sales Day Book to the Ledger

When posted to the ledger, the entries would be as shown in Fig. 10.5. Each customer is debited with the goods he has received (debit the receiver) and the firm whose books are being kept is credited with the sales figure.

			T. Marsh A/c			L 5
19..			£			
June	1 Sales	SDB 5	14·40			

			R. Jones A/c			L 19
19..			£			
June	5 Sales	SDB 5	79·20			

(contd. on page 105)

M. Smith A/c				L 72
19..			£	
June 13 Sales	SDB 5	306·00		

R. Jordan A/c				L 61
19..			£	
June 22 Sales	SDB 5	11·50		

R. Leaming A/c				L 12
19..			£	
June 29 Sales	SDB 5	19·20		

Sales A/c				L 187
	19..			£
	June 30 Sundry			
	Debtors	SDB 5	430·30	

Fig. 10.5 Posting the Sales Day Book

Notice that every customer has been debited with the goods invoiced to him, becoming a debtor for that amount. The total of the Sales Day Book, posted to the Sales Account on the credit side is the double entry for *all* the entries made in the debtors' personal accounts. The folio number of this entry in the Sales Day Book is usually written below the total figure, to mark its posting to the Sales Account at the end of the month.

You should now do some Sales Day Book entries as shown in Figs. 10.4 and 10.5. Exercises Set 13 gives five for you to to try.

10.6 Exercises Set 13: The Sales Day Book

1. R. Hall, who is in the timber trade supplies the following customers in May 19..
   May 1st R. Whitechurch is supplied with 2 chicken sheds at £45·50 each (£91·00).
   May 13th M. Lamb is supplied with 'Peep-proof' garden fencing— 20 × 2-metre panels at £2·50 per panel (£50·00) and 3 × 1-metre panels at £1·50 per panel (£4·50).
   May 17th R. Marshall is supplied with a lean-to greenhouse frame £13·50.
   May 19th R. Shaw buys 12 kits for garden sheds at £13·80 per kit (£165·60).
   May 27th M. Lever buys 4 chicken sheds at £45·50 (£182·00).
   Enter these items as invoices in Hall's Sales Day Book and post them to the ledger accounts so that a proper double entry is achieved.

2. M. Thomas is in the catering trade. During June 19. . he caters for the following functions, supplying goods as shown. Enter the invoices in Thomas's Sales Day Book and post it to the ledger to achieve a proper double entry.

June 4th M. Allen (wedding)

        200 assorted sandwiches @ 5p each = £10·00

        400 pastries @ 5p each   = £20·00

        1 three-tier cake   = £18·50

June 11th R. Cross (Golden Wedding)

        400 bridge rolls @ 1p each   = £4·00

        300 assorted sandwiches @ 5p each = £15·00

        300 pastries @ 5p each   = £15·00

        1 single-tier cake   = £12·00

June 24th R. Diamond Ltd. (Annual conference of sales representatives).

        200 filled rolls @ 4p each   = £8·00

        200 sandwiches @ 5p each   = £10·00

        500 pastries @ 5p each   = £25·00

        Decorated *petit fours*   = £10·00

3. R. Larch is a nurseryman wholesaling plants to shops in his locality. He invoices the following sales in April 19. . Enter these invoices in Larch's Sales Day Book and post them to the ledger to achieve a proper double entry.

April 2nd Garden Traders Ltd. 25 boxes antirrhinums @ 20p per box (£5·00); 25 boxes salvias @ 25p per box (£6·25).

April 9th Fine Gardens Co. 200 boxes dahlias @ 20p = £40·00.

April 21st Green, Finger & Co. 100 boxes each of dahlias @ 20p (£20·00), salvias @ 25p (£25·00), lobelia @ 20p (£20·00), mesembryanthemums @ 20p (£20·00), and alyssum @ 20p (£20·00).

April 28th Garden Traders Ltd. 50 boxes alyssum @ 20p (£10·00), and 50 boxes lobelia @ 20p (£10·00).

4. M. Paterson supplies specialized decorative office fittings. During May he invoices the following:

May 4th Plant stands of assorted types to the Colossal Insurance Company—total value £85·00.

May 11th Showcases for their foyer to Pharmaceutical Specialities Ltd. as follows:

        1 display cabinet @ £90·50.

        2 display cabinets @ £35·00 each (£70·00).

May 19th Reproofed Concrete Ltd. purchases one fish-tank display @ £250·50.

May 27th International Exporters Ltd. purchases a world-map wall display £234·00 and a motorway display model £165·00 for their office foyer.

Enter these items in the Sales Day Book and post them to the ledger to achieve a proper double entry.

5. R. Lawes is a supplier of pet foods. His invoices for the month of January 19.. are given below. Record them in his Sales Day Book.

January 3rd R. Smith

      200 tins of Kumficat @ 5p each = £10·00.

      60 packets of dog biscuits @ 25p per packet = £15·00.

January 7th M. Lyons

      144 packets fish food @ 5p per packet = £7·20.

      1 litre live daphnia @ £3·15.

January 8th R. Jayson

      200 tins of Kumficat @ 5p each = £10·00.

      120 tins of Bestfriend dog meat @ 25p per tin = £30·00.

January 19th M. Lord

      60 packets of dog biscuits @ 25p per packet = £15·00.

      120 tins of Bestfriend @ 25p per tin = £30·00.

January 29th R. Countryman

      Assorted pet foods—total value £15·00.

      120 packets of dog biscuits @ 25p per packet = £30·00.

Books of Original Entry
Part Three: The Purchases and Sales Returns Books

11.1 Returns

Any trading business that supplies goods to customers must inevitably at times receive back goods which for some reason are unsatisfactory to the customer. Contracts for the sale of goods cannot be cancelled at the customer's whim; this would constitute *breach of contract*. Goods may however be returned if there is some genuine complaint as to their quality, colour, size, etc. A businessman may also allow a customer to return goods which he has decided he does not require, if he feels that the customer's goodwill in the future is worth more than the loss of profit on this particular transaction. A further reason for *returns* is the movement of empty containers, crates, etc., which are charged out to the customer when goods are dispatched, on the understanding that they are returnable when empty.

Whenever goods or containers are returned, for whatever reason, the appropriate document is the *credit note*.

11.2 Credit Notes

A credit note is a business document which is made out whenever one person returns goods to another. The credit note is made out by the original supplier of the goods, after the returned goods have reached his warehouse. Credit notes are always *printed in red*, to distinguish them from invoices. Like the invoice, they constitute written evidence on the returns transaction, and may be produced in the courts in the event of a dispute over the contract.

Credit notes are also used in the following circumstances:

(*a*) Where an error has been made on an invoice, resulting in an *overcharge*. Clearly the excessive charge made must be cancelled in some way. The simplest method is to issue a credit note, even though no returns have actually occurred.

(*b*) Where goods are damaged in some minor way it is a common practice to make the customer an allowance on the goods. Thus a piece of furniture which has lost its polish might not merit return to the factory. The protesting customer is greeted with a suggestion that it be repolished, and an allowance against the invoice price is suggested. The customer may be only too happy to carry out the work because he is paying less money. The allowance is made by sending the customer a credit note for the agreed sum. A second copy of this credit note is kept for the use of the accounts department. There are fewer copies of credit notes than of invoices.

11.3 Entering Credit Notes Inwards—The Purchases-Returns Book

Credit notes sent to us by suppliers, to whom we have returned goods or containers, are entered into the Purchases-Returns Book. This is a Day Book ruled exactly like the Purchases Day Book, as is illustrated in Fig. 11.1. Note that there is rarely more than one item on a credit note, so that the inner column falls to some extent into disuse.

(1) Returns at Catalogue Price

As already pointed out (see Section 10.2) goods are often invoiced at catalogue price, trade discount being deducted to give the retailer his margin of profit. This may result in difficulties when goods are returned, since they may be returned at their nominal catalogue price. A supplier who has only charged a customer at the 'trade-discount' price, but gives credit on the full retail price will be giving his customer a profit on the returned item. Care should be taken to deduct trade discount.

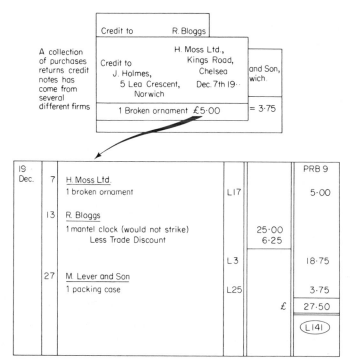

Fig. 11.1 Entering credit notes in the Purchases-Returns Book

(2) Posting the Purchases-Returns Book to the Ledger

When posted to the ledger, the entries are as shown in Fig. 11.2. The suppliers, who have received back the unsatisfactory items are debited (debit the receiver) and the Purchases-Returns Account is credited. The firm whose ledger is being kept, our firm, has given these items back and must be credited with the total returns at the end of the month.

		H. Moss Ltd. A/c					L 17
19..			£	19..			£
Dec. 7 Purchases Returns	PRB 9	5·00		Dec. 4 Purchases	PDB 4	155·00

		R. Bloggs A/c					L 3
19..			£	19..			£
Dec. 13 Purchases Returns	PRB 9	18·75		Dec. 3 Purchases	PDB 4	37·50

		M. Lever and Son A/c					L 25
19..			£	19..			£
Dec. 27 Purchases Returns	PRB 9	3·75		Dec. 17 Purchases	PDB 4	48·50

	Purchases-Returns A/c					L 141
			19..			£
			Dec. 31 Sundry Creditors	PRB 9	27·50

Fig. 11.2 Posting the Purchases-Returns Book to the ledger

The reader should now practise entering groups of credit notes in the Purchases-Returns Book, and posting the entries to the ledger.

11.4   Exercises Set 14: The Purchases-Returns Book

1. R. Lutterworth is in business as a retail draper. He receives the following credit notes from suppliers in May 19..

May   4th Lustre Colour Ltd.—one set of ready-manufactured curtains (colour faded) £27·50.

May 11th C. E. Montrose—returned sheets 3 sets @ £2·25 per set (faulty design pattern) £6·75.

May 29th E. A. Phillips—returned curtain lining material—damaged by water in transit £5·50.

Enter the credit notes in R. Lutterworth's Purchases-Returns Book and post to the appropriate ledger accounts.

2. E. S. Oliver is a garage proprietor. During July 19.. he receives the following credit notes from suppliers:

July 7th — Miniparts Ltd. one set of chrome-plated mudguards—chrome imperfect—£8·75.

July 22nd — Accessories Ltd.—one chronometer £8·95 (defective mechanism) and one oil pressure gauge—engine mounting badly machined £4·25.

July 30th — Battery Wholesale Supply Co. Ltd.—one 12-volt battery (leaking) £4·35.

Enter the credit notes in Oliver's Purchases-Returns Book and post the entries to the appropriate ledger accounts.

3. C. Hosking is in the confectionery trade and during June 19.. receives the following credit notes. Enter them in his Purchases-Returns Book and post the entries to the appropriate ledger accounts.

June 1st — Seager's Sweet Co. One jar bullseyes @ £2·50 (suspected contamination with noxious fluid).

June 13th — The Liquorice Allsorts Co. Empty jars and tins £3·45.

June 14th — Read's Liqueur Chocolates Ltd.—one box liqueur chocolates damaged in transit £0·55.

June 27th — Seager's Sweet Co. Empty jars and tins £3·20.

4. R. Robertson is a footwear retailer. During August 19.. he receives the following credit notes:

August 4th — Norwich Traders Ltd.—one pair brown size 12 children's shoes, stitching faulty, £2·25.

August 5th — Northampton Leather Dealers—one pair 'Country cumfi' walking boots (discoloured) £4·35. One pair dress boots (inner lining defective) £7·25.

August 25th — Shoe Importers Ltd. One case plastic beach sandals—no buckles fitted £25·00.

Enter the credit notes in Robertson's Purchases-Returns Book and post to the ledger.

5. T. New and Son are outfitters. During November 19.. they receive the following credit notes:

November 13th Hall Brothers send a credit note for one blazer—machined imperfectly £4·75.

November 22nd Lamark Trading Company. One car coat (badly torn) £6·50 and one pair of car blankets (wrong colour) £8·95.

November 25th Lutz and Co. Three sets of men's underwear (not as ordered) £2·75.

November 29th Hall Brothers. One blazer (pocket torn) £3·35.

Enter these credit notes in Robertson's Purchases-Returns Book and post to the ledger.

11.5   Entering Credit Notes Outwards—The Sales-Returns Book

When a firm receives goods returned from a dissatisfied customer, it draws up a credit note and sends off the top copy to the customer. The second copies of all the credit notes are used to complete the accounting records in the books of the seller, who has now received back the goods returned. As shown in Fig. 11.3 the credit notes form a neat pack, because they are all prepared by the same firm, the seller. Entries are exactly similar to those for the Purchases-Returns Book, but the postings are different, as shown in Fig. 11.4. The customers' accounts are credited, and the Sales-Returns Account is debited with the total returns for the month.

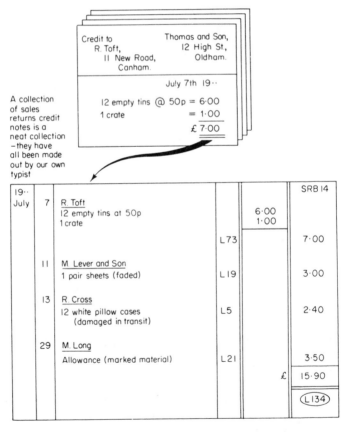

Fig. 11.3 Entering credit notes in the Sales-Returns Book

Posted to the ledger the entries appear as shown in Fig. 11.5.

			R. Toft A/c				L 73
19..			£	19..			£
July	1 Sales	SDB 6	25·00	July	7 Sales		
					Returns	SRB 14	7·00

			M. Lever and Son A/c				L 19
19..			£	19..			£
July	3 Sales	SDB 6	106·00	July	11 Sales		
					Returns	SRB 14	3·00

			R. Cross A/c				L 5
19..			£	19..			£
July	12 Sales	SDB 8	70·50	July	13 Sales		
					Returns	SRB 14	2·40

			M. Long A/c				L 21
19..			£	19..			£
July	20 Sales	SDB 15	65·50	July	29 Sales		
					Returns	SRB 14	3·50

			Sales-Returns A/c			L 134
19..			£			
July	31 Sundry					
	Debtors	SRB 14	15·90			

Fig. 11.4 Posting the Sales-Returns Book to the ledger

You should now attempt Exercises Set 15: entering credit notes in the Sales-Returns Book.

11.6   Exercises Set 15: The Sales-Returns Book

1. T. Cratchett is a wholesaler supplying goods to customers in the domestic-appliances field. In June 19.. he issues the following credit notes. Enter them in his Sales-Returns Book and post the entries to the appropriate ledger accounts.

    June 4th Pram Centre Co. One 'Slumbercot' damaged in transit £14·50.

    June 6th E. Proctor and Co. Ltd. One coach-built pram, wheels strained £13·45 and one pram basket, damaged by paint in transit £3·00.

    June 16th R. Rudd. One electric toaster, faulty switch £3·25.

June 27th   T. W. Russell. One 'Vacumetric' vacuum cleaner, motor
                 burnt out £34·65.

2. Paul Luscombe supplies toys to retailers. During January 19. . the
   following were credited by him for goods, etc., returned. Record these
   credit notes in his Sales-Returns Book and post the entries to the appropriate ledger accounts.

January 4th   Macaulay and Co. One train set, motor mechanism
                 faulty £8·25.
January 11th   Petersen and Co. One 'Hobbyhorse' scooter and trailer,
                 painting defective £7·25.
January 19th   T. Barr. A set of twelve boxes of bricks, contents in-
                 correctly packed £8·58.
January 29th   T. R. Portray Ltd. One train set, motor mechanism
                 faulty £8·25.

3. A. Robens is a supplier of office equipment. Record the following credit
   notes in his Sales-Returns Book and post to the ledger to achieve a correct
   double entry for the month.

February   1st   T. MacAndrew and Co. Ltd. returned goods as follows.
                 One typist's chair £5·50 (metalwork rough), one filing
                 cabinet (lock faulty) £19·75.
February   4th   R. Robertson returned a cabinet (wrong colour) £33·95.
February 14th   M. Loach returned crates charged to him at £5·50.
February 25th   R. Ingrams returned a filing cabinet (lock faulty) £19·75
                 and metal trays (swivel mechanism faulty) £5·50.

4. A. W. Manser is a wholesale supplier of pot plants to florists and nursery-
   men. In July he has the following returns for which credit notes are drawn
   up. Enter them in his Sales-Returns Book. Post it to the ledger accounts.

July 4th   John Mansfield. Assorted packets of seeds sold on a sale-
                 or-return basis—value £5·48.
July 11th   Garden Beauty Co. Two fruit trees @ £0·40; six dead
                 standard roses @ £0·60.
July 19th   Kilmuir Landscape Co. Ltd. Twenty-four bedding plants
                 @ £0·20 each—wrong variety.
July 29th   Kent Window Box Co. were given an allowance of
                 £5·00 against agreed poor quality of plants supplied
                 earlier this month.

5. M. Lancaster supplies meat to the retail butchery trade. He never accepts
   returns, but occasionally issues credit notes to customers who complain
   that meat delivered to them is below the quality ordered. In June 19. . he
   issues credit notes as follows. Enter them in his Sales-Returns Book and
   post the entries to the appropriate ledger accounts to achieve a correct
   double entry.

June 7th   M. Rooselar. Argentine beef agreed to be only third
                 quality, made an allowance of £65·00.

June 19th M. Candler. English prime beef agreed to be second quality only; allowance given £8·00.

June 21st R. T. Jones. Frozen produce agreed to be possibly defrosted; dealer to destroy; credit note £44·00.

June 29th M. Johnson. Australian ewe mutton agreed to be poor quality; allowance of £10·50 given.

Books of Original Entry
Part Four: More Journal Proper Entries—
Assets and Depreciation

12.1 Assets

Many of the things we purchase in business are not *goods for resale*, to be entered in the Purchases Day Book. They may be, instead, either *assets* of the business or *consumables*. The difference between assets and consumables is that assets last a long time, while consumables are soon used up in the course of the activities. The dividing line between the two is drawn at one year. If items last longer than a year they are regarded as assets of the business, conferring some permanent benefit upon the business. Items lasting less than one year are regarded as consumables, conferring only temporary benefits upon the business. Common assets are land and buildings, furniture and fittings, plant and machinery, motor vehicles and typewriters. Common consumables are postage stamps, stationery and motor-vehicle expenses.

Assets may therefore be defined as items purchased which bring some long-term benefit to the business and permanently increase its profit-making capacity.

12.2 Recording the Purchase of Assets

When assets are purchased, it is usual to enter the asset in a Journal entry, which is then posted to the ledger. The rules are:

(a) Always debit the asset account (for it has received value).

(b) Always credit (i) Cash Account—if cash was paid for the asset,

or (ii) Bank Account—if the asset was paid for by cheque,

or (iii) the supplier if the asset was supplied on credit, the account being payable at a later date.

It is usual to record in the narration any details which will help prove ownership at some future date. Typewriters, for example, are often stolen, as indeed are motor cars and other items. Here is an example of such an entry:

19..					£	£ J1
Jan.	15	Furniture and Fittings A/c Dr.	L 77		32·50	
		Sheer Beauty Ltd.	L 85			32·50
		Being the purchase on credit				
		of a showcase for the foyer				
		(Ref. No. stl/50,874)				

Fig. 12.1 The purchase of an asset

Posted to the ledger, the accounts would read as shown in Fig. 12.2.

			Furniture and Fittings A/c			L 77
19..			£			
Jan.	1	Balance	B/d	875·00		
	15	Sheer Beauty Ltd.	J 1	32·50		

		Sheer Beauty Ltd. A/c			L 85
		19..			£
		Jan. 15 Furniture and Fittings		J 1	32·50

Fig. 12.2 Ledger entries for the purchase of an asset

You should now try some 'purchase-of-asset' entries from the exercises given below.

12.3   Exercises Set 16: The Purchase of Assets

1. R. Lever is in business as a stationer. He purchases twelve Bettaview display cabinets at a total invoice price of £156·00, paying by cheque. The serial numbers of the cabinets are A1856 to A1867. Record the purchase in Lever's Journal Proper, and post the entry to the ledger accounts.

2. M. Robertson is in business as an accountant. On July 16th 19.. he purchases from British Olivetti Ltd., an electric typewriter valued at £186·00, on the usual monthly credit terms. Record this entry in Robertson's Journal Proper. The reference number of the machine is El/20785. Post the entry to the ledger accounts.

3. A. Printz is an exporter to the European market. On August 1st 19.. he purchases a motor vehicle for roll-on, roll-off services to Holland and Germany. The price is £9 500·00, payable on monthly credit terms to Heavy Autos Ltd. The vehicle number is AJN 187L, the engine number 32Z/7146 and the chassis number E8/47.625. Record the purchase in Printz's Journal Proper, and post to the ledger.

4. S. Debbotista is in the fur trade. On May 31st 19.. he purchases a security vehicle, RJO 125M, for transporting furs to clients' premises. It costs £1 656·00. Half is paid at once by cheque and the balance at the end of the month. It is supplied by Special Motors Ltd. Record the entries in the Journal Proper.

5. J. Scaggs runs a boutique. She purchases a till for £220·00, paying half in cash. The balance on credit is payable to Shop Fittings Ltd. The till has

a serial number: Automatic 38.754. Record the entry in the Journal Proper.

6. M. Lucien purchases the following items on credit on December 1st 19. . from the General Supplies Co.: two filing cabinets @ £35·00 each; six electric typewriters @ £90·00 each; desks, chairs and other furniture £425·00. Serial numbers are as follows: filing cabinets E12 745 and E12 746, typewriters A1075-80. Record these entries in the Journal Proper and post to the ledger accounts.

12.4   Depreciation of Assets

Although assets last a long time, and confer some lasting benefit upon the business, they do not last for ever. They gradually wear out, and decline both in value and usefulness to the enterprise. It is necessary to recognize this *depreciation* in value, and the usual practice is to reduce the asset value each year by an amount that corresponds with the 'fair wear and tear' it 'has suffered. Since all assets suffer this depreciation, it is usual to collect together all the losses by depreciation, in a *Depreciation Account*. There are many different ways to calculate a 'correct' figure for depreciation. These are dealt with in Unit Twenty-two. For the moment all that is necessary is to illustrate the principle of depreciation by a simple example.

The rule for simple depreciation entries is:
   Debit the Depreciation Account with the decline in value suffered.
   Credit the Asset Account to reduce the asset's book value.

Example of Depreciation Entry

J. Smith purchased a crane on July 1st 19. ., at a cost of £5 800·00. Depreciation is calculated on a basis of 20 per cent *per annum* on the original cost. Do the depreciation entry in the Journal on December 31st of that year, and show the Crane Account as it would appear on January 1st, next day.

In this example it is clear that only half a year's depreciation is necessary at December 31st 19. ., for the crane was only purchased on July 1st of that year. It follows that £580·00 has to be written off the value of the crane. The Journal entry appears as shown in Fig. 12.3, and the accounts as shown in Fig. 12.4.

19.. Dec.	31	Depreciation A/c Dr. Crane A/c Being depreciation at 20% *per annum* on crane purchased July 1st 19..	L 61 L 60	£ 580·00	£ J 27 580·00

Fig. 12.3 A depreciation entry in the Journal

		Crane A/c				L 60

19..			£	19..			£
July 1	Heavy Machines Ltd.	J 1	5 800·00	Dec. 31	Depreciation	J 27	580·00
				31	Balance	c/d	5 220·00
			£5 800·00				£5 800·00
19..							
Jan. 1	Balance	B/d	5 220·00				

		Depreciation A/c		L 61

19..			£
Dec. 31	Crane A/c	J 27	580·00

Fig. 12.4 Depreciation on an asset account

12.5 Exercises Set 17: Simple Depreciation Exercises

Note: A full treatment of depreciation is given in Unit Twenty-two.

1. A. Reeve's assets include an executive-type motor car which cost £5 500·00 on January 1st 19.. At the end of the first year it was decided to depreciate the vehicle by one-third of its original cost (calculated to the nearest £10·00). Do the necessary Journal entry and post it to the Executive Motor-Car A/c and Depreciation A/c.

2. P. Senior has office equipment on his books valued at January 1st at £1 350·00. His policy is to depreciate office equipment on December 31st each year by 20 per cent of its value at the beginning of the year. Draw up the Journal entry for this depreciation and post it to the ledger accounts.

3. C. Blythe is a hairdresser. She has on her books at January 1st 19.. a Fittings and Equipment Account which values the fittings and equipment in her premises at £1 800·00. She writes off one-third of this original cost each year, since it is her policy to up-date layout and equipment every third year. Show the depreciation entry in the Journal, at the end of the first year.

4. M. Larkins is a fruit and vegetable wholesaler. His vehicles were valued at £6 300·00 on January 1st 19.. and it is his policy to have them re-valued by a local garage owner on the last day of every year. On December 31st this valuer gives it as his opinion that the vehicles are worth £4 700·00. Larkins asks you to make the depreciation entry in his Journal, to take account of the fall in value over the year. Show this entry, and also the Motor-Vehicles A/c for the year.

5. Howden Ironware Co. have premises valued at £12 000·00 on January 1st 19. . On July 1st they purchased the property next door valued at £6 000·00, by cheque. On December 31st they decided to depreciate premises at 10 per cent *per annum*. Draw up the necessary Journal entry and show the Premises Account for the year.

6. M. Burns is a quarry owner, whose quarry is valued at £23 000·00 on January 1st 19. . This represents £1 for every tonne of stone estimated to be available on that date. During the year he quarries 5 800 tonnes of rock, but a geologists' report confirms that his earlier figure of reserves (23 000 tonnes) was an under-estimate, and should have been 25 000 tonnes. He decides to depreciate the quarry on December 31st, and to take account of the true remaining tonnage at £1 a tonne. Show the necessary Journal entry.

12.6   The Sale of Worn-out Assets

When an asset comes to the end of its useful life, it is disposed of at the best price it will fetch. The useful life of an asset may come to an end for several reasons. It may break down, and be sold for scrap. It may be constantly needing attention, so that production is interrupted. In such cases the time comes when it is cheaper to buy a new machine. It may have been rendered obsolete by more modern devices, so that although it is still in good working condition a newer model will raise productivity.

Practically always there will be some final adjustment to the Profit and Loss Account as the asset is disposed of. The following situations may exist at the time of sale.

(*a*) The *book value* of the asset at the time of sale may be greater than the price we can obtain for it. For example a motor vehicle may be valued at £300·00 on the Motor-Vehicles Account but the most the garage will give us as trade-in value is £230·00. Clearly we have under-estimated the depreciation over the years and the extra £70·00 will have to be written off as a loss. It is usual to debit it to the Sale of Vehicles Account.

(*b*) The book value of the asset may be exactly the same as the final sum offered by the purchaser of the asset. This is rather unlikely; it means our estimates of profit over the years have been exactly right. No final adjustment is necessary.

(*c*) The book value of the asset may be less than the actual value on the day of disposal. This frequently happens, because some firms follow a policy of reducing assets to a very nominal value of £1. When finally disposed of, even for scrap, most machinery and equipment will fetch more than £1. Some readjustment of profit is made on disposal to take account of the over-depreciation in earlier years. Examples of these three situations are given below, with the appropriate Journal entries.

The rules for these entries are:

(i) Always remove the asset completely from the Asset Account. This means credit the asset account with the book value.

(ii) Debit the Cash Account, or the Bank Account, with any cash, or cheque received. If the person purchasing the old asset is not paying at once, but only in the usual course of business (i.e. at the end of the month), debit him as a debtor for the amount due.

(iii) Adjust the Profit and Loss Account by taking the profit on sale, or the loss on sale, to a suitable account, such as the Sale of Machinery Account. This will be cleared to Profit and Loss Account in due course.

Example 1: Asset Overvalued on the Books

T. Hodges has a motor vehicle valued at January 1st 19.. at £250·00. He disposes of it to a friend at the best price he can get, £180·00 in cash, on that day. Show the Journal entry.

19..					£	£ J 1
Jan.	1	Cash A/c Dr.	CB 1	180·00	
		Sale of Vehicles A/c Dr.	L 72	70·00	
		Motor-Vehicle A/c	L 8		250·00
		Being sale of motor vehicle SJN 375 at this date for the best price obtainable			

Fig. 12.5 Disposal of an over-valued asset

Example 2: Asset Valued Correctly on the Books

R. Bines has a sewing machine valued at £5·00 on the Small-Machines Account. He disposes of it for cash to an employee at that figure. Show the Journal entry on July 1st 19..

19..					£	£ J 1
July	1	Cash A/c Dr.	CB 1	5·00	
		Small-Machines A/c	L 15		5·00
		Being sale of sewing machine S 12,745 at book valuation to Miss R. Jones (employee)			

Fig. 12.6 Disposal of a correctly-valued asset

Example 3: Asset Undervalued on the Books

M. Blanchflower has a Mobilmix cement mixer valued on his books on June 30th at £180·00. He disposes of it on that date in exchange for a stock of motor-vehicle tyres valued at £300·00. Show the Journal entry on June 30th 19..

19..					£		£	J 1
June	30	Motor-Vehicle Spares A/c Dr.	L 27		300·00			
		Plant and Machinery A/c	L 5				180·00	
		Sale of Machinery A/c	L 72				120·00	
		Being exchange of Mobilmix						
		cement mixer for spare tyres						
		at this date						

Fig. 12.7 Disposal of an asset that has been over-depreciated in earlier years

You should now attempt the simple exercises given below on the disposal of worn-out assets.

12.7   Exercises Set 18: The Disposal of Assets

1. John Kelleher is in possession of a motor vehicle, XYT997H, valued at £50·00 on December 31st 19.. He is approached by a fellow trader who wishes to purchase it at that figure. The offer is accepted. Do the Journal entry for the transaction, which is settled by cheque.

2. A. Hancock is a retail tobacconist who has a mechanized till surplus to requirements. On July 31st it is valued on his books at £45·00. He disposes of it, for cash, to A. Streetseller at the book valuation. Do the Journal entry for the transaction.

3. D. Heywood runs a boutique and is about to undertake a major redesign of her premises. On January 1st 19.. she disposes of fixtures and fittings, valued at £300·00 on her books, to A. Junkbuyer for £85·00 cash. Show the Journal entry required.

4. J. Scaggs is a furrier, who disposes of premises which are now inconveniently situated, due to the introduction of a one-way system, for £2 800·00. They were valued at £3 250·00 on her books. Payment was by cheque. Do the Journal entry necessary to record this transaction on August 1st 19..

5. Allen Motors Ltd. have premises at a particularly valuable corner site. These premises are valued on their books at August 31st 19.. at their original cost price of £10 000·00. On this date they sell the premises for £38 000·00, recording the increased value, caused by a rise in land values, in a special account called Site-Appreciation Account. Do the Journal entry, and show the ledger accounts. The sale price of £38 000·00 was settled by cheque.

6. A motor vehicle, valued on John Briggs' books at £180·00, was sold on January 1st 19.. for £230·00, cash. Show the Journal entry required to record this transaction.

7. Paul Watts disposes of a steam engine, valued on his books at £30·00, to the National Industrial Museum of America for £380·00. This profit will be credited to Sale of Machinery Account. Show the Journal entry to record this transaction on December 31st 19.. The museum authorities have asked him to allow them credit until next April 1st, when their funds will benefit from a legacy due to be settled on that date.

8. F. Azouqua is a ship owner who owns a vessel valued at £2 800·00 on his books. He disposes of it to Greek Liners Ltd. for £5 900·00, the sum to be settled three months after delivery of the vessel. Azouqua regards the difference between book value and true value as a profit caused by a demand for ships of this type. Make the Journal entry dated September 15th 19..

Books of Original Entry
Part Five: More Journal Proper Entries—
Bad Debts

13.1 'Bad' Debtors

Whenever a businessman supplies customers on credit, the person supplied becomes a *debtor* of the business. Clearly no one gives credit to customers that are considered unreliable, and when asked to supply goods in this way a trader would usually take up *references* from other suppliers, or from the customer's bankers. If these references prove satisfactory the trader will then allow goods to be supplied on credit—usually on monthly terms. This means that goods will be supplied as ordered for one month, a *statement of account* being rendered at the end of the month. The customer must then pay within the specified period, say seven days, fifteen days or perhaps a further month.

It may happen, though, that debtors who have been good customers in the past may find themselves in unforeseen difficulties. Sickness of the proprietor may affect the business, or a change in the general prosperity of the area may affect the purchasing power of the business's customers. A debtor who for some reason cannot meet his obligations is called a 'bad' debtor and the debt is spoken of as a 'bad' debt.

The action taken when a debt becomes bad depends upon the circumstances. If the debtor is a rogue, or even just inept at running his business, legal proceedings are often instituted for recovery of the money, if only to prevent the debtor doing the same thing to other businessmen at a later date. The result of such proceedings is *bankruptcy*, a process whereby the debtor's assets are taken and sold for the benefit of the creditors. In return he is set free from all debts, and can start again to earn his living. He will not however be able to set up in business again without the approval of the court, and if he gets this approval he must, over a period, repay all his former debts with five per cent interest per annum.

In other circumstances bankruptcy proceedings might be inappropriate. For example, where a debtor has had a bad accident, it might not be appropriate to sue for the debt for fear of losing public goodwill. It is also unlikely you would sue the widow of a debtor who died attempting to stop a criminal attack. You would probably write off the debt as a gesture of sympathy and support for his bereaved family.

Whatever the decision made, the clearing of the debtor's account will require a Journal entry of some sort. There are three possibilities:

(a) A debt which is entirely bad.

(b) A debt which is partially bad—some settlement being arrived at in which part payment only is received.

(c) A debt written off at an earlier date may be recovered.

These three aspects of bad debts are dealt with below.

13.2   A Debt which is Entirely Bad

On August 1st R. Jones is a debtor for the sum of £50.00. He is found to have left the country, and it is decided to write the debt off as bad.

The solution is to clear the debtor's account by writing it off to Bad-Debts Account. A simple Journal entry would be made as in Fig. 13.1.

19..					£	£	J 5
Aug.	1	Bad-Debts A/c Dr.	L 21		50·00		
		R. Jones A/c	L 57			50·00	
		Being bad debt written off					
		after discovering that Jones					
		had left the country.					

Fig. 13.1 Writing off a bad debt

The ledger accounts would appear as shown below. Note that the debtor's account is marked clearly (in red ink) BAD DEBTOR to prevent any further credit being made available.

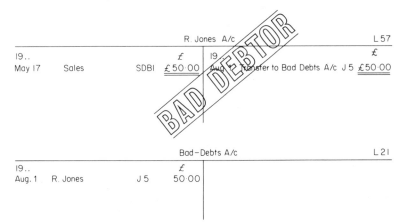

Fig. 13.2 Posting the bad-debt entry to the ledger

13.3   A Debt which is Partially Bad

Sometimes a debtor may make an arrangement with his creditors whereby he makes a certain sum available in full settlement of his debts. This is called a '*composition*' with the creditors, i.e. a voluntary agreement to settle the debt by payment of a smaller sum. In other cases the debtor will be bank-rupted, his assets will be seized and sold for the benefit of the creditors, and the proceeds will be shared up among them. In both cases outlined above the sums received will be debited in the Bank Account or Cash Account, the unpaid portion being written off to Bad-Debts Account. The result is a three-lined Journal entry as shown in Fig. 13.3. Here, P. Rossiter is adjudged bankrupt on July 5th 19.., and a payment of 10 pence in the £1·00 is author-ized from the funds available after the sale of his assets. R. Long Ltd. are his creditors for £40·00. Show the journal entry for this matter, and post it to the ledger and cash book.

19..					£	£ J 5
July	5	Bank A/c	Dr.	CB 7	4·00	
		Bad-Debts A/c	Dr.	L 21	36·00	
		P. Rossiter		L 69		40·00
		Being bad debt written off at				
		this date on payment by				
		Official Receiver of £4·00 in				
		full settlement.				

Fig. 13.3 A Journal entry for a partially bad debt

Posted to the ledger the accounts would be as shown in Fig. 13.4.

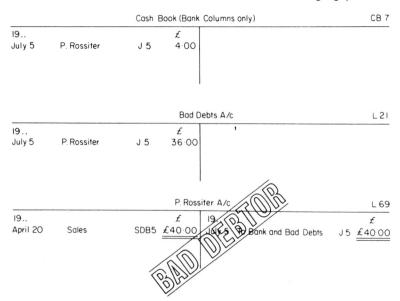

Fig. 13.4 Posting the Journal entry for a partially bad debt

13.4   A Bad Debt Recovered

When a debtor's account has been cleared off and the debtor has ceased to trade, the debtor's account will be removed from the ledger and will be stored in a file of 'dead' accounts. Suppose such a debtor wishes to clear his name by paying up his debts with interest. The payment will be most acceptable, but there is little point in reviving the 'dead' account. Instead the unexpected profit may be recorded on a special Bad-Debts Recovered Account, or on the credit side of the Bad-Debts Account where it will offset any bad debts that occur this year. Note that no entry at all is made in the debtor's 'dead' account. An example is given in Fig. 13.5.

M. Lucas, whose debt of £54·00 was written off last year, pays £55·35 in cash in full settlement on August 4th 19. ., being the sum of £54·00 due, plus interest at 2½ per cent for one year. Show the Journal entry for this transaction.

19. . Aug.	4	Cash A/c Dr.	CB 197	£	£	J 1
				55·35		
		Bad-Debts Recovered A/c	L 72		54·00	
		Interest-Received A/c	L 73		1·35	
		Being debt due plus interest at 2½ per cent *per annum*				

Fig. 13.5 A bad debt recovered

Posted to the ledger accounts these entries would now appear as shown in Fig. 13.6.

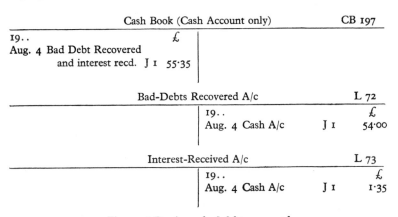

Cash Book (Cash Account only)		CB 197
19. .	£	
Aug. 4 Bad Debt Recovered and interest recd. J 1 55·35		

Bad-Debts Recovered A/c		L 72
	19. .	£
	Aug. 4 Cash A/c J 1	54·00

Interest-Received A/c		L 73
	19. .	£
	Aug. 4 Cash A/c J 1	1·35

Fig. 13.6 Posting a bad debt recovered

You should now try the following exercises.

13.5 Exercises Set 19: Bad Debts

1. R. Porter, who owes your firm £50·40, dies tragically in a fire at a local cinema. It is decided to write the debt off as a gesture of sympathy to his family. Do the Journal entry dated July 19th 19.. and post it to the ledger.

2. It is your policy to pursue bad debtors in every case where it will be economic to do so. A. Student owes £3·50 and has left his lodgings without trace. You decide to write this debt off as an uneconomic case, since the costs of collection are likely to exceed the sum recovered. Do the Journal entry dated June 29th 19.. and post it to the ledger.

3. Anne Oldlady owes you £35·00. She is unable to pay, and an Aged-Persons Charitable Association asks you to agree to a payment of half the sum in full settlement of her debt. You agree to the composition, and they pay by cheque. Do the Journal entry dated October 19.. and post it to the ledger.

4. Solar Ventures (Moortown) Ltd. are debtors for £2 300 for equipment supplied. They go into voluntary liquidation and you eventually receive £0·25 in the £1·00 by cheque. Do the Journal entry dated July 4th 19.. and the ledger postings.

5. R. Pettifogger sends only £98·50 on August 29th 19.. in settlement of his debt of £100·00, claiming that the balance is due to him because of an inconvenient late delivery. It is decided to write off the remainder of the debt, since the sum concerned is small compared with the profit on the transaction. Do the Journal entry dated August 31st 19.. and post to the ledger accounts.

6. Carnival Productions (Westlake) Ltd. are debtors for goods supplied for £34·50. They are insolvent, and the liquidator pays £0·80 in the £1·00 by cheque. Show the Journal entry dated July 11th 19.. and post to the ledger accounts.

7. A. Slowsettler sends a postal order on February 14th 19.. for £3·50 to clear his debt, which has been written off some time ago. Show the Journal entry for the recovery of this bad debt, and post it to the ledger accounts.

8. M. Lipsey, a former director of a liquidated private company, wishes to settle the debts of the company although he has no personal liability at law. He sends a cheque for £42·00 on April 5th 19.., being payment of one-tenth of the debt, with interest £2·00. The account was written off completely a year ago. Record this receipt in the Journal and post the entry to the ledger accounts.

9. A. Partner, whose debt of £30·00 was written off five years ago, sends a payment of £38·25 cash on December 8th 19. . representing payment in full with 5 per cent compound interest. Record the payment in the Journal Proper and post the entry to the ledger accounts.

10. A. Sloman sends a money order on June 1st 19. . for £113·00, being a debt of £100·00, interest £5·00 and legal expenses £8·00. The debt, which was written off one year ago is thus fully recovered, as are the legal charges incurred. Draw up a suitable Journal entry and post it to the Cash Book and the ledger.

Books of Original Entry
Part Six: The Three-Column Cash Book

14.1 Two Busy, Vulnerable Accounts—Cash Account and Bank Account

The simple accounts which we have considered in earlier chapters are perfectly satisfactory for keeping a record of transactions with debtors and creditors, or a record of assets purchased or expenses paid. Any clerk usually has access to the ledger and performs a variety of entries in it as and when required. There are two accounts—the Cash Account and the Bank Account —where it is much less desirable to permit everybody in the office to make entries. These accounts are very vulnerable, and a skilled clerk might make entries which would enable him to extract either cash, or cheques, for his own use. Such losses are called *defalcations*. To prevent such losses it is usual to remove the Cash Account and the Bank Account from the ledger and put them instead into a special book called a Cash Book. The person appointed to keep this book is called the cashier and generally speaking will be a mature and trusted member of staff. This book is the *book of original entry* for all payments and receipts, whether in cash or by cheque.

As a further safeguard against defalcations, it is a common practice to insure the firm against theft by the cashier. This type of insurance is called a Fidelity Bond (fidelity means faithfulness) and is usually taken out for a sum such as £10 000. Losses suffered by the firm will be repaid provided the firm presses criminal charges against the offending cashier and makes every attempt to recover sums stolen.

14.2 The Three-column Cash Book

If the Cash Account and Bank Account are to be in use frequently throughout the day as cash and cheques are entered, there is little point in having them on separate pages with a consequent need to turn over from one account to another continually. It is much better to have them set out side by side and have both accounts visible at once. This will enable the cashier to make his entries as they occur in the appropriate account without the need to turn over when the items dealt with change from cash to cheques, or vice versa. At the same time a third column can be added in which the discount allowed or discount received can be recorded. Fig. 14.1 shows such a ruling, which is called a 'three-column cash book'. The reader must obtain a supply of this type of paper from a stationer. It is best to obtain a small booklet, rather than a loose-leaf pad, since loose-leaf paper of this sort is very inconvenient unless a proper binder is available. When opening the booklet the first page is only half a page of a three-column cash book, and must be left blank. Let us consider the various entries shown in Fig. 14.1.

(1) Debit Side

(Money or cheques being received by the business of B. Jones.)

January 1st Opening balances. Note that there are two opening balances because there are two accounts, side by side on the page. Both may be written on the same line, and the folio number J1 indicates that the entry has come from the Journal Proper.

January 1st, etc. Cash sales. Every day the till has been cashed-up, and the cash-sales figure entered into the cash column. These are the daily takings of the business.

January 1st R. Miles. Clearly R. Miles must have been a debtor, who has paid Jones £4·75. The entry of £0·25 in the discount column indicates that the total amount of his debt was really £5·00, but Jones allowed him discount of 5 per cent. This is known as a *settlement discount*. Similar entries also occur on January 2nd. 3rd, 4th and 5th from other debtors.

January 2nd and 5th. Two *contra entries*. First consider very carefully the entry of £80·00, *which appears on both sides of the book*. On the debit side, £80·00 is received by the Bank Account from the Cash Account. On the credit side £80·00 is given by the Cash Account to the Bank Account. Clearly these two entries are connected; money is taken out of the till and banked for safe keeping. This is one of the commonest activities in business, since supermarkets and other shops take large amounts of cash every hour. You may have seen supervisors collecting the notes from the tills in numbered linen bags; this is for the cashier to count and pay into the bank. In this way there is never more than an hour's takings in the tills, and the chances of serious losses from a robbery are reduced. Such entries appear on both sides of the cash book, because both the Cash Account and Bank Account are affected in opposite ways. The name *contra entries* is given to these entries (*contra* is Latin for 'opposite') since the two entries appear opposite one another. This is the only place in the accounts where both halves of a double entry are visible on the same page, for it is the only place where two ledger accounts appear side by side.

On occasions, of course, the contra entry could be of the opposite type. Instead of paying surplus money into the bank we could at times need to withdraw funds from the bank to ease a shortage of cash. This would be particularly likely to happen on days when employees were paid wages, or when the proprietor needed sums of cash to attend sales or auctions. On these occasions a cheque would be presented at the bank and

The Three-column Cash Book (B. Jones)

CB 1

Dr.

Date	Details	Folio	Discount Allowed £	Cash A/c £	Bank A/c £
19.. Jan. 1	Opening Balances	J 1		37·50	4 050·00
1	Sales	L 5		42·80	
1	R. Miles	L 29	0·25		4·75
2	Sales	L 5		62·60	
2	P. Marchant	L 30			47·95
2	Cash	C			80·00
3	R. Marshall	L 31	1·00		39·00
3	M. Runes	L 32	0·30		11·70
3	Sales	L 5		25·80	
4	Lomax Ltd.	L 33		7·70	
5	Sales	L 5		135·50	
5	Coral and Co.	L 34	1·25		48·75
5	Sales	L 5		240·80	
5	Cash	C			250·00
			£ 2·80	552·70	4 532·15
			L 48		
Jan. 8	Balance	B/d		146·20	4 274·90

Cr.

Date	Details	Folio	Discount Received £	Cash A/c £	Bank A/c £
19.. Jan. 1	Signwriters Ltd.	L 15			16·30
1	Cash Purchases	L 19		24·50	
1	M. Lodge	L 37			3·85
1	Soloman and Co.	L 26			1·50
2	Hedell and Co.	L 38	1·80		34·20
2	Bank	C		80·00	
2	Postage	L 16		2·50	
3	Cash Purchases	L 19		12·25	
3	M. Liversy	L 39	3·25		126·75
4	R. Sterling	L 40			1·40
4	Repairs	L 20		3·50	
4	Travelling Expenses	L 21		16·25	
4	M. Rostov	L 41	1·75		33·25
5	Bank	C		250·00	
5	Drawings	L 131			40·00
5	Wages	L 22		17·50	
5	Balance	c/d		146·20	4 274·90
			£ 6·80	552·70	4 532·15
			L 49		

Fig. 14.1 A three-column cash book

the sums of cash required would be withdrawn. The effect on the Cash Book would be the opposite of the entry shown on January 2nd, the Bank Account being credited and the Cash Account debited.

The entry of £250·00 on January 5th is exactly similar to the entry of £80·00 on January 2nd.

(2) Credit Side
(Money or cheques being paid out by B. Jones.)

January 1st Signwriters Ltd. were paid by cheque an amount of £16·30.

January 1st and 3rd. On each of these occasions goods were purchased for cash.

January 1st, 2nd, 3rd and 4th. Various creditors were paid by cheque. Some of them gave discount since Jones had paid promptly.

January 2nd, 4th and 5th. Payments for postage, repairs, travelling expenses and wages were made in cash.

January 5th Jones, the proprietor, drew a cheque (Drawings) for his own use.

January 5th The cash book was totalled, the balances discovered, and carried down ready to start the next week's records. The till would also be checked to ensure that the cash balance was in fact correct in the till.

(3) The Cash Book Totals
Note that when the cash book is totalled, one side will normally have more entries than the other. The shorter side is filled in with a 'Z' in the details column, to prevent an entry being made inadvertently in these blank lines after the book has been balanced off and brought down. The discount columns are simply totalled, but no balance is struck on these columns, which are not accounts but only *memorandum columns*.

14.3   Double Entry and the Three-column Cash Book

Throughout this book, we always try to think in double-entry terms, since this is the basic principle behind accounting. However, the practical needs of the office require that cashiers, book-keepers, etc., specialize in particular aspects of the work, and do not stop what they are doing to go and do the other half of a double entry. For example the cashier may have over a hundred cheques in the post each morning. He records them one after the other in the cash book, two or three pages of entries perhaps. He then sends George—the messenger—down to the bank with the paying-in book and the cheques. He also calls Fred—a trainee accountant—and asks him to 'post the cash book' for him. So Fred is the one who actually carries the cash book upstairs to the office where the debtors' ledger is, and posts the ledger. In some offices this task will be performed by staff working a mechanized system, or will be fed into a computer in some way. In these cases Fred will

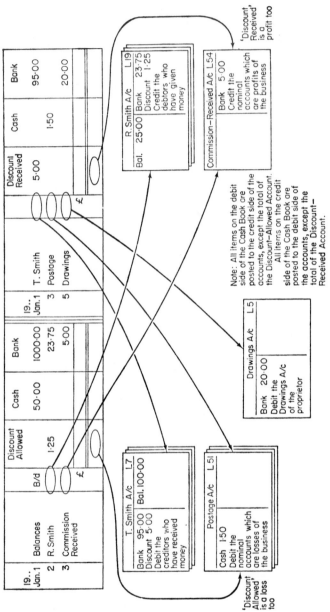

Fig. 14.2 Posting the three-column cash book

probably just prepare a list of amounts to be entered in the various accounts, which will then be posted mechanically or electronically.

So, although you should always think in double entries, you should not make the mistake of imagining that every debit entry is immediately followed by a credit entry. The accountant will have devised a system which ensures that these double entries are always done, but in a way which is economical of effort in the office.

The posting of the three-column cash book is illustrated in Fig. 14.2. Note especially that the totals of the Discount-Allowed Account and Discount-Received Account are the only items that do not cross over to the opposite sides of the ledger accounts. An explanation of this is given below, but first you should look at the ledger accounts of Figs. 14.3 and 14.4. These are the ledger postings from the three-column cash book shown in Fig. 14.1.

				Sales A/c				L 5
				19..				£
				Jan.	1	Cash	CB 1	42·80
					2	Cash	CB 1	62·60
					3	Cash	CB 1	25·80
					4	Cash	CB 1	135·50
					5	Cash	CB 1	240·80

				R. Miles A/c				L 29
19..			£	19..				£
Dec. 31 Balance		B/d	5·00	Jan.	1	Bank	CB 1	4·75
					1	Discount Allowed	CB 1	0·25

The accounts of P. Marchant, R. Marshall, M. Runes, Lomax Ltd. and Coral and Co. will be similar.

			Discount-Allowed A/c		L 48
19..			£		
Jan.	5 Sundry Debtors	CB 1	2·80		

Fig. 14.3 Posting the debit side of the cash book to the accounts

				Sign Writers Ltd. A/c			L 15
19..			£	19..			£
Jan.	1 Bank	CB 1	16·30	Dec. 31 Balance	J 1		16·30

The accounts of M. Lodge, Soloman and Co., Hedell and Co., M. Liversy, R. Sterling and M. Rostov will be similar.

(contd. on page 136)

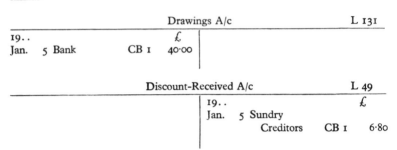

Purchases A/c   L 19

19..			£
Jan.	1 Cash	CB 1	24·50
	3 Cash	CB 1	12·25

The Postage A/c. Repairs A/c, Travelling-Expenses A/c and Wages A/c will be similar.

Drawings A/c   L 131

19..			£
Jan.	5 Bank	CB 1	40·00

Discount-Received A/c   L 49

			19..		£
			Jan.	5 Sundry	
				Creditors CB 1	6·80

Fig. 14.4 Posting the credit side of the cash book to the accounts

14.4 Why the Totals of the Discount Accounts do not Change Sides

One of the commonest causes of an incorrect Trial Balance is the mis-posting of the totals of the Discount-Allowed and Discount-Received Accounts. These are the only two accounts which are *not* posted from the Cash Book to the opposite side of the nominal accounts. The explanation is as follows.

Consider the entries relating to R. Miles's payment of £4·75, in full settlement of his account of £5·00, on January 1st 19.. The double entries are as follows:

Debit entry in cash book	Credit entries in Debtors Ledger
£4·75 (Bank A/c)	(R. Miles A/c): £4·75 Cash
	£0·25 Discount

Clearly this is not a proper double entry, because the entry in the cash book of £0·25 in the Discount-Allowed column is only an entry in a Memorandum column. It is not an entry in an account. Therefore, to correct this lack of a proper double entry we need an entry on the debit side of some account. As we can see in Fig. 14.3, the double entry is achieved when we *debit* the Discount-Allowed Account with £2·80, which is the total discounts allowed during the week, and includes the £0·25 allowed to R. Miles. This debit is a loss of the business.

The complete double entry therefore is as follows:

Debit entry:	Credit entry
£4·75 in the Bank A/c	(R. Miles A/c): £4·75 cash
£0·25 in the Discount-Allowed	£0·25 discount
A/c (part of the £2·80)	

Similarly the Discount-Received Account must be *credited* with the profit made when discounts are received for prompt payments.

14.5   Documents and the Three-column Cash Book

The documents chiefly connected with the cash book are the cheque, the statement and the receipt.

(1) Cheques

A cheque is defined as an unconditional order in writing addressed to a banker, signed by the person giving it, requiring the banker to pay on demand a *sum certain* in money either to the bearer of the cheque, or to a particular named person, or to that person's order.

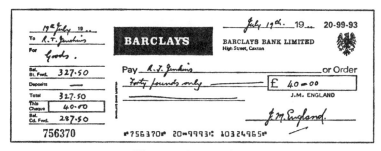

Fig. 14.5 An open cheque

In the cheque illustrated in Fig. 14.5 J. M. England is instructing the banker to pay R. T. Jenkins the sum of £40, or order. This is an 'order' cheque, which means that if R. T. Jenkins cares to do so, he can pass the cheque on to a third person, after ordering the bank to pay that third person by writing 'Pay A. N. Other, signed R. T. Jenkins' on the back of the cheque.

The number of cheques in use is so enormous (to a value of over £1 000 millions cleared every day) that the Cheques Act 1957 gives certain protections to the paying banker and the collecting banker. Generally speaking, the legal aspects of cheques need not concern us here, but it is important to consider the distinction between 'open' cheques, 'crossed' cheques and 'special crossings'.

(*a*) *Open cheques.* The cheque in Fig. 14.5 is an open cheque, that is to say it has no crossing. A crossing is effected by drawing two parallel lines across the face of the cheque. Traditionally the words 'and Co.' were inserted between the lines but this is no longer necessary. An open cheque may be cashed over the counter of a bank, and so it is difficult to stop a thief from enjoying the proceeds of a stolen cheque.

(*b*) *Crossed cheques.* These may only be cleared into a bank account, but there is no restriction on a simple crossed cheque as to the account into which they may be paid. Thus a cheque sent to Mrs Brown, who does not have a bank account, may be paid into T. Smith's account if she endorses the cheque over to him (i.e. writes on the back of it 'Please pay T. Smith' and signs her name). Crossed cheques are cheques which have two parallel lines across them, with or without the words 'and Co.'. The cheque is said to be 'crossed generally' and the effect of the crossing is to make the cheque payable only through a banker for entry into a bank account. Another type of general crossing is one where the words 'A/c Payee' are written between the lines. This puts the banker on his guard if the cheque is to be paid into any account other than that of the payee. He must check that the person named to receive the payment has really authorized another person to receive the money.

(c) *Special crossings.* A cheque may be crossed in such a way as to restrict its free transfer. This is called a 'special crossing'. Here the bank is named between the crossing lines.

These crossings are illustrated in Fig. 14.6.

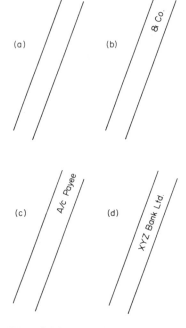

Fig. 14.6 (a), (b) and (c), general crossings; (d) special crossing

(2) Statements
A statement is usually sent out on the last day of each month, to all customers who are debtors on that date. It is a request for payment. These days it is

usually in a mechanized form, showing all the transactions that have occurred in the month, in running-balance style. The statement shown in Fig. 14.7 illustrates the way in which the figures are presented. Before paying the account the customer will deduct discount if he is entitled to any, and will pay the balance due. This cheque, when received by the cashier in the mail inwards, will be entered into the three-column cash book and presented to the bank for payment through the bankers' clearing system.

STATEMENT

NCR

ELECTRONIC ACCOUNTING SYSTEMS
ELECTRONIC DATA PROCESSING SYSTEMS
CASH AND CREDIT CONTROL SYSTEMS

F.G. CAVENDISH & CO.
WEYMOUTH ROAD.
LONDON. EC.

206 Marylebone Road London NW1 6LY Telephone 01-723 7070
Telegrams Nacareco London Telex 261250

Sales and Service Centres throughout the UK
Factories at Kingsway West Dundee

DATE	DETAILS		GOODS	TAX	CASH, ETC.	BALANCE
01MAR 19	B/FWD	0	0.00		Balance from last Statement	147.50
02MAR 19	GDS	1034	130.37			277.87
4MAR 19	GDS	2114	60.00			337.87
5MAR 19	CSH	53			147.50	190.37
5MAR 19	CSH	79			15.50	174.87

NCR N C R
Systemedia 2 9 9
299

ELECTRONIC
ACCOUNTING
SYSTEM

RM No. 25873

NCR Systemedia 49280 ER 9693

The last amount in
this column is now due

PLEASE NOTE: CHEQUES SHOULD BE MADE PAYABLE TO **NCR** ELECTRONIC ACCOUNTING SYSTEMS

Fig. 14.7 A monthly statement in mechanized form

(3) Receipts

At one time a receipt was made out for every sum of money paid, as proof of payment. Every debtor is entitled to demand a receipt but under the Cheques Act 1957 the cheque itself, if stamped 'paid' by the banker, is itself a receipt for the money. This has rendered many receipts unnecessary, although the debtor is still legally entitled to demand one. Most firms who receive payments by cheque do not send a receipt unless specifically requested to do so.

14.6 Exercises Set 20: The Three-column Cash Book

1. Enter the following in D. Swann's cash book; ledger postings are not required.

19..

March 1st — Swann has balances as follows: cash £72·50, bank £1 550·75. Pays A. Driver his account, £100·00 less 5 per cent cash discount, by cheque.

March 2nd — Pays R. Jones £38·00 by cheque, receiving £2·00 discount off the account.

March 3rd — Pays travelling expenses £3·25 (cash) and rates to Urban District Council £14·75, by cheque.

March 4th — Pays carriage inwards £1·55 cash. R. Hope pays by cheque £4·75. Gives him discount £0·25.

March 5th — Cash sales £103·55. Banks from till £100·00 (contra entry). Pays wages to part-time helper, cash £8.50.

Balance off the book on March 5th and bring the balances down ready for business on March 8th 19...

2. Enter the following in D. Hunter's three-column cash book. Invent suitable folio numbers but do not post the entries to the ledger accounts.

19..

May 1st — Balances: cash £28·55, bank £275·65. Pays R. Benjamin £6·50 in cash. Pays postage £1·25 in cash.

May 2nd — R. Long pays his account of £80·00, which was overdue, in full by cheque.

May 3rd — Pays rent £25·00 by cheque. Pays M. Morgan's account £72·00 less 5 per cent cash discount by cheque.

May 4th — Draws cash from bank for office use, £50·00. Cash purchases £45·00.

May 5th — D. Lester sends a cheque for £85·50, being settlement in full of his debt of £90·00. Cash sales for the week £275·50. Banks £180·00 for safe keeping. Pays wages in cash £27·50 and postage £1·15. Balances off the books and brings the balances down ready for the next week's work on May 8th.

3. B. Gale's cash book is a three-column cash book. Make the following entries in it for the week shown below. Then balance the book and bring down the balances. Invent suitable folio numbers, but do not draw up the ledger accounts.

19..

November 11th Balances in hand: cash £72·65, bank £1 250·50. Buys goods for resale, cash £36·50.

November 12th R. Levis pays cash £9·75 in full settlement of his account of £10·00. Pays L. Robbins cheque, £42·50. Receives discount from Robbins, £2·25.

November 13th Pays for meter hire and connexion charges in cash, £7·50 (Light and Heat A/c). Sundry expenses £0·42, postage £0·85, both in cash.

November 14th Draws cash from bank for office use £80·00. Receives from D. Delderfield cheque for £92·63 in full settlement of his account of £95·00.

November 15th Pays wages in cash £35·00. Pays for fuel oil in cash £17·50. Pays postage £2·50 cash.

4. E. Stapleton has a three-column cash book. On December 1st 19. . he has £25·00 in his cash till, but is overdrawn at the bank by £326·55. Open his cash book with these balances (one will be a credit balance) and enter the following items:

19. .

December 1st He receives a loan from the bank of £500·00.

December 2nd R. Hopkinson is paid £42·56 by cheque, in full settlement of his account of £44·80. M. Giles pays £39·00 to Stapleton, by cheque in full settlement of a debt of £40. Stapleton withdraws £30·00 from the bank for the cash till. He also pays for repairs to a window, £5·35, in cash.

December 3rd R. Lawton pays £117·00 cheque to Stapleton. The balance of his account, £3, is treated as cash discount. M. Glyndeborne, a creditor, is paid £7·25 in cash. Stapleton pays by cheque £5·60 for stationery, and train fares in cash £3·35.

December 4th Stapleton purchases goods for resale, £29·50, by cheque. He also pays by cheque £95·00 P. Roche's account of £100·00—the rest is discount.

December 5th He draws a cheque for drawings £30·00, pays wages in cash £24·60. Cash sales for the week total £275·00. He banks £250·00 from the cash till, for safe keeping.

Balance off the cash book and bring down the balances. Invent suitable folio numbers, but do not post the entries to ledger accounts.

5. W. Allen's three-column cash book has balances on July 15th of £5·00 cash and £1 047·15 at the bank. Enter these balances, and the items shown below. Balance off the cash book and bring down the balance. Then post the cash book to the ledger accounts.

July 15th Pays postage £1·35 cash. M. Long pays by cheque £23·75 in full settlement of his account for £25·00. Draws £20·00 from Bank A/c for office use.

July 16th Purchases in cash of goods for resale £12·50, travelling expenses £3·50 in cash.

July 17th Allen pays M. Treegrove by cheque £128·70. Also postage

£1·85 in cash and repairs £4·25 in cash. R. Lightfoot clears his account of £200·00 by cheque for £195·00.

July 18th   M. Hudson is paid by cheque £28·50, discount received £1·50. R. Thomas pays his account £5·65 by cheque.

July 19th   Cash sales £112·75. R. Johnson is paid £42·75 by cheque after deducting £2·25 discount from his account. Allen draws £30·00 for personal use from the Bank A/c. Wages paid, £16·50 in cash.

6. From the relevant entries given in the ledger account of Joseph Cotton and from the additional information given, you are required to construct his cash book for the month of March 19.., carrying down the balances at the end of the month. Insert folio numbers in your answer.

K. Jones — L 1

19..		£	19..		£
March 8	Bank	67·00	March 1	Purchases	70·00
March 8	Discount	3·00			

S. Rolf — L 2

19..		£	19..		£
March 12	Sales	74·00	March 14	Bank	72·00
March 25	Sales	13·00	March 14	Discount	2·00
			March 29	Bank	13·00

Wages — L 3

19..		£
March 8	Cash	10·00
March 22	Cash	20·00

Office Expenses — L 4

19..		£
March 28	Cash	8·00

Rent Received — L 5

			19..		£
			March 29	Cash	15·00

Discount Received — L 6

			19..		£
			March 29	Sundry Discounts	3·00

Discount Allowed		L 7
19..	£	
March 29 Sundry Discounts	2·00	

Additional information:

(a) On March 1st the cash in hand was £10·00 and the balance at the bank £540·00.

(b) On March 4th £40·00 was drawn from the bank for office cash and on March 29th £25·00 of the cash in hand was paid into the bank.

(c) On March 29th a statement of account was obtained from the bank and it was found that £7·00 had been debited in respect of bank charges.

Note:

You are *not* required to reproduce the above ledger accounts in your answer.

(RSA 1 adapted)

Books of Original Entry
Part Seven: The Petty-Cash Book

15.1 The Imprest System

There are many minor items of expenditure in any office which are too trivial for an entry in the main cash book. It would interrupt the cashier's work to be asked for money for bus fares, postage and other small items. At the same time all such expenditures must be honestly and accurately accounted for. The solution is to appoint a *petty cashier*, who will be responsible for paying for all such minor items. Usually it is convenient to appoint the person in charge of the post as petty cashier.

The petty-cash book is kept on the *imprest system*, which is a system whereby a certain sum of money is advanced for a particular purpose. The sum advanced will be deemed adequate for the purpose, say £10·00 for a week, or £20·00 for a week. The cashier credits the cash book with this amount and it is debited in the petty-cash book. The petty cashier then pays the money out as need arises for postage, telegrams, travelling expenses, etc. and at the end of the week balances the book and takes it to the cashier for checking. The cashier then 'restores the imprest', making it up again to the original sum.

Advantages of the Imprest System

The advantages of the imprest system are as follows:

(*a*) It saves the time of the chief cashier, who is a busy person with heavy responsibilities.

(*b*) It trains young staff to be responsible about money and accurate in accounting for it.

(*c*) The sum impressed is small, and unlikely to prove a temptation either to the person in charge of it or to others in the office.

(*d*) It enables a great saving to be effected in the posting of small items to the ledger accounts, since it uses an analysis system which collects these small items together into weekly or monthly totals. These are then posted to the ledger accounts. Where items are individual in nature, for example small payments to creditors, these are entered in a column called Ledger Accounts.

15.2 The Petty-cash Book

This may be described as an extension of the three-column cash book. It is definitely part of the double-entry system, for the sums debited into it from the cash book are then credited out for the various purposes required. The items spent thus become losses of the business, or if spent on durable items they become assets of the business. As such, in both cases, they become debits in the respective accounts. An example of the petty-cash book is given in Fig. 15.1.

The following points are worth noting.

(a) The pages are not divided down the centre since there are very few entries where money is received. Hence the debit side is reduced, in most rulings, to a single money column, or perhaps a date column, details column and money column. In the ruling shown, the details are written in the right-hand column for both sides of the book, but cash received is placed over on the debit side.

(b) The chief item received is the original imprest, £20·00. Other items include the money paid for private staff telephone calls, and the sale of brochures and similar small items, which may be recorded in this way in some firms.

(c) Moneys disbursed are recorded on the credit side and then analysed out into a number of analysis columns which serve as collection columns for a large number of small items. Thus all the postage is collected together in the 'postage' column.

(d) Certain payments cannot be added together in this way, for example the payments to Smith and Lorrimer must be posted to the personal accounts of these creditors. Similarly the purchase of any small asset for office use would be posted to Office-Equipment Account. A special column at the end headed Ledger Accounts, which has a folio column alongside, enables these items to be posted separately to their respective accounts.

(1) Balancing off the Petty-cash Book

When balancing off the petty-cash book, a line is drawn right across the figures on the credit side, and all the columns are added up. Then the analysis columns *only* are closed with a double line, the total column being left open. The analysis columns are cross-totted, to check that they total the same as the total column. If they do not, the error must be discovered.

The balance of cash in hand can now be calculated by taking the total spent from the total received. The answer to this calculation should be the sum of money left in the petty-cash till. This is inserted in the credit column, the book is balanced off and the balance brought down.

(2) Restoring the Imprest

On presenting the book and the till to the cashier, the petty cashier's work will be checked, and the imprest will be restored by the cashier refunding the money paid out, less any sums recovered for private phone calls, etc. The restored imprest gives the petty cashier, for the new week, the sum the management has authorized to be advanced each week. It is bad accounting practice to give a further £20·00 since this would raise the sum in the care of the petty cashier to £22·87 in this case, which is more than the management deems necessary for this particular function.

Dr. £	Date	Details	PCV	Total	Postage	Travelling Expenses	Stationery	Sundry Expenses	Folio	PCB 27 Cr Ledger Accounts
20·00	19.. Dec. 1	Imprest	CB 5							
	1	Stamps	PCV 1	2·50	·2·50					
	1	Bus fares	PCV 2	0·23		0·23				
	2	Postage	PCV 3	0·55	0·55					
	2	Envelopes	PCV 4	1·25			1·25			
	2	Refreshments	PCV 5	0·65				0·65		
	3	R. Smith	PCV 6	3·25					L27	3·25
0·48	3	Private telephone call	L5							
	4	Postage	PCV 7	1·05	1·05					
	5	Postage	PCV 8	0·65	0·65					
	5	E. Lorrimer	PCV 9	5·28					L32	5·28
	5	Train fares	PCV 10	2·20		2·20				
				17·61	4·75	2·43	1·25	0·65		8·53
	5	Balance	c/d	2·87						
£ 20·48				£20·48						
2·87	Dec. 5	Balance	B/d		L7	L8	L9	L10		
17·13	8	Restored Imprest	CB7							

The cash impressed for petty cash purposes and debited in the Petty-Cash Book is credited to the Three-column Cash Book

This debit entry is posted to the credit side of Telephone-Expenses A/c – reducing the loss incurred

These totals are posted to the debit side of the 'loss' accounts, Postage A/c, etc.

These credit items are posted to the debit side of the creditors' accounts

Fig. 15.1 The petty-cash book

(3) Posting the Petty-cash Book

As shown in Fig. 15.1, every item on the debit side of the petty-cash book must appear in the credit side of an account elsewhere, while every credit entry must be debited to some loss, or asset account. Considering these postings, the debit side has only three items, two of them receipts of imprest money from the chief cashier. Each must have its credit entry elsewhere. This credit entry will be in the Bank Account as far as the original imprest is concerned, while the money for the telephone call, and any other sums received at any time by the petty cashier, will be entered as credit entries in the account affected. As shown in Fig. 15.2 the sums received for staff private telephone calls are credited to Telephone-Expenses Account, reducing the losses suffered on this account.

				£						L 5
	Telephone-Expenses A/c									
19..			£		19..					£
Mar. 31	Post Office		172·50		Apr.	4	Petty-Cash			
June 30	Post Office		166·45				Receipt	PCB	5	1·24
Sept. 30	Post Office		171·90		July	10	Petty-Cash			
							Receipt	PCB	9	1·31
					Dec.	3	Petty-Cash			
							Receipt	PCB	27	0·48

Fig. 15.2 Petty-cash receipts reducing the losses to be charged to Profit and Loss Account

The credit entries on the petty-cash book are debited into the accounts concerned. Now it can be seen how useful the analysis system is for collecting together the tiny disbursements for postage, travelling expenses, etc. These items are posted to the debit side of the 'loss' accounts concerned, while the items in the special column headed 'Ledger Accounts' which cannot be posted as one figure, are posted separately to their ledger accounts, the folio number being inserted in the folio column alongside each amount posted.

15.3 Original Documents for Petty Cash—the Petty-cash Voucher

Every transaction has its original document, which is entered in the book of original entry and leads to postings to the ledger accounts. This is still true of the petty-cash book, but the documents may be very small—for example bus tickets, receipts for registered letters, etc. All such items are carefully preserved, pasted or clipped to larger pieces of paper or perhaps to books which can be preserved for inspection by the auditors or senior members of staff.

Wherever possible, a petty-cash voucher should come from outside the business, since it is more likely to be genuine. Where this is impossible, for

```
                    11 JUN ..

    Envelopes.       00 0.12  I

    Paper clips      00 0.07  I

    Rubber           00 0.05  I
    bands
    Pencils          00 0.09  I

    Wrapping         00 0.14  I
    paper
    Gummed           00 0.07  I
    labels.
    String           00 0.16  I

                     00 0.70  TL


                     00 1.00  AT
                        0.30  CH


        AT – Amount Tendered
        TL – Total
        CH – Change
```

Fig. 15.3 An external petty-cash voucher

petty cash voucher

date.......27ᵗʰ March, 19..

required for travelling expenses	£	p.
Fares to London airport	0	35
" " Ware	1	24
total	1	59

signature..........G. M. Hopkinson

folio.........PCV 9..........   passed by.........ERP

Fig. 15.4 An internal petty-cash voucher

example where train fares are concerned—the tickets being collected on arrival at the destination—the completion of an *internal petty-cash voucher*, duly signed by some authorized person, provides the necessary documentation. Many external vouchers today are till receipts from a mechanized till, such as the one shown in Fig. 15.3. An internal voucher is shown in Fig. 15.4. Note that in both cases the petty cashier or the member of staff concerned has written in enough details for the voucher to be understood by the senior member of staff authorizing or checking the payments.

Petty-cash vouchers are numbered, and filed in numerical order so that the vouchers for any given month can be inspected as required.

You should now attempt a number of the exercises given below. It is necessary to rule up petty-cash paper, unless you buy paper that is already ruled.

15.4   Exercises Set 21: The Petty-cash Book

1. State briefly what you would do if you were asked to check the accuracy of the entries in a firm's analytical petty-cash book kept on the imprest system.

2. What are the advantages of a petty-cash book kept on the imprest system? Explain how the various entries are posted to the ledger accounts, using as illustrations the following items:
   (a) The total of the analysis column headed 'Postage'.
   (b) An entry in the ledger-accounts column reading L. Shire £4·25.
   (c) The entry on the debit side which reads 'restored imprest'.
   (d) An entry on the debit side reading 'staff purchases £4·25'.

3. Using petty-cash paper open D. Benson's petty-cash book on April 7th, 19. ., with an initial balance of £4·35. Then enter the cash given to the petty cashier by the proprietor to restore the imprest to £10·00, and the following transactions:
   19. .
   April   7th Pays postage £0·22 and bus fares £0·08; pays R. Collins's Account £1·32.
   April   8th Receives from a member of staff £0·57 for a private telephone call; pays postage £0·36, stationery £0·10.
   April   9th Pays postage £0·24, train fares £0·65; gives dustman £0·10.
   April 10th Purchases for office use, letter scales for post department £1·27; pays office cleaner £1·25, also cleaning materials £0·26.
   April 11th Pays postage £0·49; buys cakes for typist's birthday £0·28.
   The petty-cash book has analysis columns for postage, travelling expenses, office-cleaning expenses, stationery, sundry expenses and a ledger-accounts column where payments to creditors, or for the purchase of assets, are recorded. Balance the book at the end of the week, ready to

present to the proprietor for checking. Invent suitable folio and petty-cash voucher numbers.

4. Enter the following items in R. Norris's petty-cash book which has five columns, for postage, fares, office sundries, repairs, and ledger accounts. Invent sensible folio numbers and petty-cash voucher numbers.

19..

July 15th	Draws petty cash imprest £25·00; pays postage £3·50.
July 16th	Pays fare £0·28; buys ball of string £0·25; pays plumber to clear drain £2·75, and a creditor, T. Bright, £4·75.
July 17th	Pays postage £1·55; buys stationery £0·50; buys cleaning materials £0·25.
July 18th	Pays R. Jones £1·45; member of staff pays £0·35 for private telephone call; pays fares £0·16.
July 19th	Pays fares £2·35; pays for repairs to door £0·85; pays M. Knight £3·25; pays postage £0·50.

Balance the book and restore the imprest to £25·00.

5. (a) M. Jobling runs his office petty cash on the imprest system, giving the petty cashier a basic imprest of £25·00. The book has five columns for postage, travelling expenses, cleaning, sundry expenses and ledger accounts. Enter the following items, balance off the book at the end of the week and restore the imprest.

(b) Explain the postings to be made for the entries on March 20th.

19..

March 19th	Balance on book £20·00; imprest restored by proprietor; postage £0·45; bus fares £0·65.
March 20th	Pays postage £0·36; a debtor, Tom Jones, calls in and pays a small account £1·35, which the petty cashier accepts and for which she gives a receipt; fares £0·15.
March 21st	Postage £1·05. Envelopes and wrapping paper £0·23. Soap and detergents £1·65.
March 22nd	Pays M. Brogan £3·75. Purchases spirit lamp for postal clerk £0·65 (Office-Equipment Account).
March 23rd	Postage stamps £1·25. Telegram £0·65.

6. M. Clarke employs a cashier who keeps a petty-cash book on the imprest system. It has five analysis columns for postage, travelling, stationery, general expenses and ledger accounts. Rule special petty-cash paper and record the following week's transactions, inserting appropriate folio numbers and petty-cash voucher numbers:

19..

January 11th	Draws imprest of £20·00 from cashier; pays postage £1·45; pays M. Hemstock's Account £2·48.
January 12th	Pays fares £0·26; pays for notepaper £0·55; collects from staff for private telephone calls £2·32.
January 13th	Pays for cleaning materials £0·28; pays for tea and cakes for typist's birthday £0·36.

January 14th Pays L. Smith's Account £2·25; pays for cleaning materials £1·30.

January 15th Pays cleaner's wages £5·00; pays fares £0·12; pays window cleaner £0·25.

Rule off the book, bring down the balance in hand, and restore the imprest to £20·00.

7. A petty cashier was given an imprest of £25·00 and his book and the balance in hand were checked on the first working day of each month. On February 1st 19. . the petty cashier's balance in hand was £2·91. At the end of February the analytical columns showed the following totals: Postage—£3·27; Cleaners—£8·00; General Expenses—£7·12 and the Ledger column—£4·13. The last-named item was the cost of a special container bought on behalf of E. Robbins, a debtor. You are asked to answer the following questions:

   (a) How much should the chief cashier hand his junior on February 1st and on March 1st?

   (b) State in which accounts and on which side of them entries should be made to ensure double entry in respect of the totals £7·12 and £4·13.

8. A petty-cash book is kept on the imprest system, the amount of the imprest being £15·00. It has five analysis columns: postage and stationery, travelling expenses, carriage, office expenses and ledger accounts. Give the ruling for the book and enter the following transactions:

   19. .

   January 14th Petty cash in hand £2·25; receives cash to make up the imprest; buys stamps £2·00.

   January 15th Pays railway fares £0·25; bus fares £0·85; telegrams £1·25.

   January 16th Pays carriage on small parcels £0·45; pays railway fares £0·86; buys stationery £0·68.

   January 17th Pays for repairs to window £1·65; pays T. Smith's account for December £2·55.

   January 18th Pays office tea lady £1·16.

   Balance the petty cash book as on January 18th and bring down the balance. Invent suitable folio numbers and petty-cash voucher numbers.

9. R. Duncan keeps a petty-cash book with three analysis columns: postages, cleaning and sundries. On June 29th 19. ., the petty cashier reaches the bottom of a page, and carries forward the following totals:

	£
Imprest	10·00
Total Expenditure	6·30
Postage	4·14
Cleaning	1·22
Sundries	0·94

The following payments were made on the last two days of the month:

$£$

		$£$
June 29th	Postages	0·13
30th	Window cleaner	0·22
	Bus fare	0·07
	Postages	0·15

Write up the petty-cash book as it would appear for the last two days of the month, balance the book and restore the imprest. Post to the ledger accounts, and invent sensible petty-cash voucher numbers.

10. (a) Enter the following items in R. Lyons's petty-cash book which is kept on the imprest system. At the end, balance off the book and restore the original imprest. Use analysis columns for fares, postage, sundry expenses, cleaning and ledger accounts. Post the book to the ledger accounts and invent suitable petty-cash voucher numbers.

19. .

January 21st   Receives imprest from cashier £25·00; pays for postage stamps £2·50.

January 22nd   Repairs to lock £2·45; pays window cleaner £0·30; pays for postage £0·25.

January 23rd   Pays sundry expenses £0·50; cleaner's wages £1·50; pays R. Thompson £2·35.

January 24th   Pays postage £0·36; travelling expenses £0·25.

January 25th   Sundry expenses £0·55; stamps £1·25; postage £1·43; travelling expenses £2·25.

(b) Explain where the double entries are for the following items:

(i) Imprest received on January 21st.

(ii) Pays R. Thompson £2·35 on January 23rd.

(iii) Travelling expenses £2·25 on January 25th.

More Journal Proper Entries— Unusual Bank Transactions

16.1 Introduction

Most of the transactions which take place with our bank are current-account items, handled in the way shown in Unit Fourteen through the three-column cash book. There are many other special items which are of such importance that they deserve to be recorded through the Journal Proper, which you will remember is a book where the original record is made of all the more unusual transactions that take place.

Among these items may be listed the following types:

(a) Loans made by the bank, to be repaid over a given period—often two or three years.

(b) Interest payable on such loans.

(c) Dishonoured cheques.

Some firms would also do Journal entries for:

(d) Bank charges.

(e) Bank interest payable on overdrafts.

(f) Bank interest receivable on deposit accounts.

We will now look at the entries necessary for each of these types of entry.

16.2 Bank Loans and Interest Payable

When a bank lends money to a customer it may do so in two ways. First it may *permit an overdraft* which simply means that it will allow the customer to draw cheques to a greater value than the amounts paid in to his current account. Overdrafts are only intended to be short-term affairs, helping the customer to overcome a temporary shortage of cash. They may be recalled at any time, which means that the customer can be required to pay in the amount of his overdraft. It is most unlikely that he can do so, otherwise he would not be overdrawn, so that where a bank calls in overdrafts, they may in fact have to formalize the overdraft by making a proper loan to the customer.

When a *bank loan* is arranged, the customer enters into a formal arrangement (i.e. he signs an agreement) to borrow a sum of money and repay it over several years. The sum of money is then entered into his current account (extinguishing an overdraft if one already existed), but a second Loan Account is opened. Interest arrangements vary these days. In the case shown in Fig. 16.2 the interest has been added for the full period. The Loan Account is debited with the loan and interest, repayable by monthly instalments. The customer will take similar action in his own accounts. The Journal entry would be as follows.

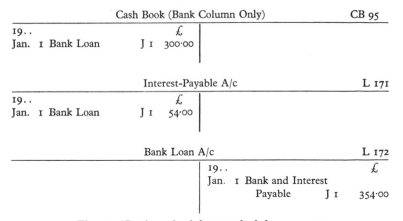

19..					£	£ J 1
Jan.	1	Bank A/c	Dr.	CB 95	300·00	
		Interest Payable A/c	Dr.	L 171	54·00	
		Bank Loan A/c		L 172		354·00
		Being loan negotiated with				
		Barclays Bank at this date,				
		at 9 per cent over two years.				

Fig. 16.1 A bank loan

Posted to the ledger and the cash book the entries would be:

Cash Book (Bank Column Only)   CB 95

19..		£	
Jan. 1 Bank Loan	J 1	300·00	

Interest-Payable A/c   L 171

19..		£	
Jan. 1 Bank Loan	J 1	54·00	

Bank Loan A/c   L 172

	19..		£
	Jan. 1 Bank and Interest		
	Payable	J 1	354·00

Fig. 16.2 Posting a bank loan to the ledger accounts

The *repayments on the loan* would be deducted by the bank at the agreed dates, the customer crediting his cash book and debiting Bank-Loan Account so that the loan is gradually extinguished. Such a bank loan is, of course, a long-term liability on the balance sheet.

16.3 Dishonoured Cheques

When a customer pays by cheque, the cheque is debited in the cash book and credited to the customer's account. Very often the cheque is not for the full amount of the debt, since the customer deducts discount for paying promptly. Sometimes the cheque is returned by the bank, marked with the phrase 'refer to drawer'—in other words 'Ask the debtor why he has given you a cheque when he has no funds to cover it in his account'. Usually the debtor will then see his bank and arrange to have the cheque honoured at a subsequent presentation.

In the meantime the creditor should take action to *restore the debt, in full, to the debtor*. Clearly he has not paid, and the debt should be restored to his account. This requires not only the restoration of the value of the cheque, but discount as well, i.e. the value of the original debt, since he is not entitled to any discount now that the cheque has been dishonoured. The effect of this is to restore the full debt to the debtor's account, and at the same time recover the discount on the Discount Allowed Account. We shall not lose this discount now, as the debtor will have to pay in full. Remember, discount is only given to debtors who pay promptly. A typical Journal entry would be as follows:

19..					£	£ J 7
Jan.	19	A. Debtor	Dr.	L 57	150·00	
		Bank A/c		CB 9		142·50
		Discount-Allowed A/c		L 168		7·50
		Being dishonoured cheque				
		returned marked refer to				
		drawer at this date				

Fig. 16.3 Journalizing a dishonoured cheque

These entries would then be posted to the account as follows. In each case the folio number J 7 indicates the journal entry—the other figures have been put in to make the account sensible and as it would appear in practice.

			A. Debtor A/c			L 57
19..				£		
Jan.	1	Balance	B/d	150·00		
	19	Bank and				
		Discount	J 7	150·00		

19..				£
Jan.	15	Bank	CB 5	142·50
	15	Discount		
		Allowed	CB 5	7·50

Cash Book (Bank Column Only) CB 9

				£
19..				
Jan.	19	Dishonoured		
		Cheque		
		A. Debtor	J 7	142·50

Discount-Allowed A/c L 68

19..				£
Jan.	8	Sundry Discounts	CB 3	142·50
	15	Sundry Discounts	CB 5	138·65

19..				£
Jan.	19	A. Debtor	J 7	7·50

Fig. 16·4 Dishonoured-cheque entries in the accounts

16.4   Bank Charges and Bank Interest on Overdrafts

Strictly speaking, Journal entries are not necessary for items which appear as original entries in the cash book, for this book is unique in having a dual function—it is both a book of original entry and a part of the ledger. However, as we have already seen, bank loans and dishonoured cheques are matters of such importance that some formal record of them is desirable, and the Journal entry—with its narration explaining the circumstances—constitutes a formal record by the accountant of the transaction.

Some accountants would also regard a simple Journal entry for bank charges and bank interest on overdrafts as desirable. Many examining bodies regard the ability to think in Journal-entry form essential to accounting, and they ask the student in the rubric—the instructions to a question—to 'journalize all transactions'. This is not an unreasonable request, as the Journal entry is indeed essential to a clear understanding of double entry.

Double entries for bank charges and bank interest payable on overdrafts would arise usually as a result of receiving a bank statement. Unit Twenty deals fully with bank statements, and their *reconciliation* with the cash book. Part of this reconciliation usually involves the discovery on the statement that the bank has deducted bank charges from the balance on the account. If the account is overdrawn, the bank will increase the overdraft by the amount of the charges and these will also include a considerable charge for interest—payable at from 2–5 per cent above base-rate. These charges must now be entered in the cash book, crediting the cash book and debiting Bank-Charges Account or Interest-Payable Account. If it is decided to journalize these entries, typical Journal entries would be as follows:

19..					£	£ J 1
June	30	Bank-Charges A/c Dr.	L 72		4·50	
		Bank A/c	CB 4			4·50
		Being charges as per bank statement at this date				
June	30	Interest-Payable A/c Dr.	L 71		7·21	
		Bank A/c	CB 4			7·21
		Being interest on overdraft payable as per bank statement				

Fig. 16.5 Journalizing bank charges

16.5   Interest Receivable on Deposit Accounts

A *deposit account* is one where surplus funds are deposited with the bank. These accounts earn interest, usually at 2 per cent below minimum lending rate, and in theory are not supposed to be drawn upon without giving the bank seven days' notice. In fact the bank will usually make funds available if requested, but charges seven days' interest on the money withdrawn. Normally the deposit account is left untouched by the depositor and interest is added at intervals. This interest is added at the bank's convenience, and it is unlikely that they will notify the depositor, but should he ask, and a statement is sent to him, he will add the interest received to his Deposit Account, and credit it as a profit to Interest-Received Account. The Journal entry will be:

19.. June	30	Bank-Deposit A/c Dr. Interest-Received A/c Being interest received on Deposit A/c at 10 per cent for quarter ended June 30th	L 37 L 52	£ 25·00	£ J 1 25·00

Fig. 16.6 Interest received on a bank deposit

16.6 Exercises Set 22: Bank Loans, Interest and Charges

1. On December 15th 19.. R. Piggott arranges a loan with Lloyds Bank Plc for £500·00, at 7 per cent, to be repaid over two years. Interest is added to the loan on that date for the whole period. Show the Journal entry in R. Piggott's books, and the ledger accounts affected.

2. On August 4th 19.. M. Smith is overdrawn at the bank £132·50. The bank asks him to regularize this by agreeing to a loan of £150·00 at 8 per cent interest repayable over a period of one year. M. Smith signs the necessary agreement and makes appropriate entries in his Journal, ledger and cash book. Interest is added for the full period of the loan. Show the entries made in M. Smith's books.

3. On April 8th 19.. the Loamshire Quarry Co. were overdrawn at the bank £231 729·00. The bank insisted on clearing this overdraft at once, but agreed to make a loan of £300 000·00 available at 8 per cent interest repayable over three years. This was agreed, and the accountant of the Quarry Co. made an appropriate Journal entry, interest being added for the full period. Show this Journal entry and post it to the ledger accounts affected.

4. On May 4th 19.. M. Dawson received a cheque from a debtor, P. Hawkins, for £120·25 in settlement of his debt of that sum. On May 7th the cheque was returned 'refer to drawer'. Show the Journal entry necessary to restore the debt to the debtor.

5. On July 17th M. Rookes pays B. Barnard a cheque for £38·50, in full settlement of his debt of £40·00. The cheque is passed through Barnard's cash book and is then paid into the bank. The cheque is returned marked 'refer to drawer' on July 21st 19. . Show the Journal entry necessary to restore the debt to the debtor, and post it to the ledger accounts.

6. M. Kelley receives a cheque on May 12th 19. . from R. Boniface for £72·20, in full settlement of his account of £76·00. Kelley enters the cheque in his Bank Account but it is returned dishonoured on May 17th 19. . Show the Journal entry restoring the debt to the debtor, and post it to the relevant accounts.

7. On July 15th 19. . R. Hope discovers from his bank statement that charges of £8·75 were deducted from his account. He decides to record this as a Journal entry. Show this Journal entry.

8. M. Hall discovers the following matters from his bank statements on March 31st 19. .
   (a) The bank have deducted £4·25 for bank charges;
   (b) They have added £6·25 to his deposit account as interest on the deposit.
   Show Journal entries for these matters.

9. R. Homberger discovers that his bank have credited his Deposit Account with £6·50 interest on deposit. He decides to journalize this entry. Show the Journal entry. (Be careful—when a bank credits your account they are viewing the matter from their point of view.)

10. Home Loans (London) Ltd. have given B. Charles interest of £42·80 on his deposit account with them. He decides to make a Journal entry for this item. Show the Journal entry, dated March 31st 19. . and post it to the ledger.

A Full Set of Accounts

17.1 From Original Entries to Final Accounts

We have now followed the accounting processes through the full range of accounting activities from the original entries for individual transactions to the final calculation of net profit and the preparation of a Balance Sheet at the end of the financial year. There are many further aspects of accounting to consider. but these only develop the basic principles as they are applied to different institutions—to partnerships, clubs, limited companies and public corporations.

Fig. 17.1 presents diagrammatically the complete development of double-entry accounting. There are six stages:

(a) Every transaction has its original document.

(b) These documents are posted into the books of original entry, which are:

  (i) the Sales Day Book,
  (ii) the Sales-Returns Book,
  (iii) the Purchases Day Book,
  (iv) the Purchases-Returns Book,
  (v) the Journal Proper,
  (vi) the cash book (which is also part of the ledger),
  (vii) the petty-cash book (which is an extension of the cash book and therefore also part of the Cash Account).

(c) These original entries are then posted to the ledger;

(d) A Trial Balance is extracted from the ledger;

(e) The Trial Balance is used to prepare a set of final accounts, i.e.

  (i) a Trading Account,   ⎱ Sometimes these are joined into a
  (ii) a Profit and Loss Account, ⎰ single Trading and Profit and Loss
  (iii) a Balance Sheet.   Account.

(f) Finally these ideas are modified to meet the needs of particular business units such as partnerships, clubs, limited companies and other incorporated bodies like nationalized industries and the local and central government agencies.

You should now follow the diagram through and make sure that you understand every part of it. Then you should try at least one, and preferably several, of the exercises given at the end of this Unit. These will help you make sure that you know all that is required to keep the books of any sole trader enterprise. You will start with original information about transactions, and pass through all the stages to a Balance Sheet at the end of a financial period, which for our purpose here is taken to be one month.

(a) Every transaction has its original document   (b) Every document is entered in its book of original entry

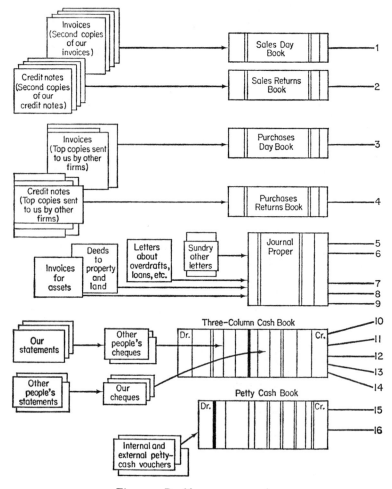

Fig. 17.1 Double-entry accounting

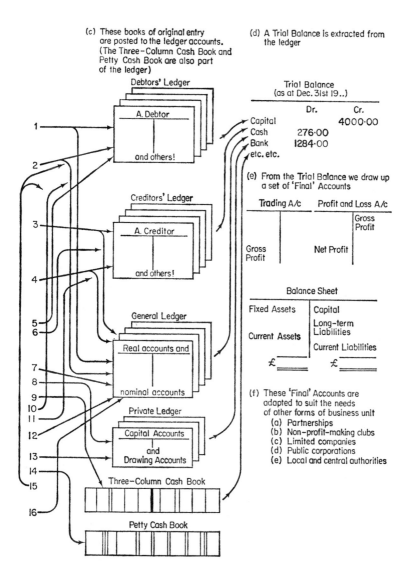

(c) These books of original entry are posted to the ledger accounts. (The Three-Column Cash Book and Petty Cash Book are also part of the ledger)

Debtors' Ledger

A. Debtor

and others!

Creditors' Ledger

A. Creditor

and others!

General Ledger

Real accounts and

nominal accounts

Private Ledger

Capital Accounts

and

Drawing Accounts

Three-Column Cash Book

Petty Cash Book

(d) A Trial Balance is extracted from the ledger

Trial Balance
(as at Dec. 31st 19..)

	Dr.	Cr.
Capital		4000·00
Cash	276·00	
Bank	1284·00	
etc. etc.		

(e) From the Trial Balance we draw up a set of 'Final' Accounts

Trading A/c | Profit and Loss A/c

Gross Profit

Gross Profit

Net Profit

Balance Sheet

Fixed Assets | Capital

Current Assets | Long-term Liabilities

Current Liabilities

£ ___   £ ___

(f) These 'Final' Accounts are adapted to suit the needs of other forms of business unit
  (a) Partnerships
  (b) Non-profit-making clubs
  (c) Limited companies
  (d) Public corporations
  (e) Local and central authorities

17.2   A Model Exercise—Double-Entry Accounting with a Full Set of Books

To help you keep a full set of books the following model exercise will show the stages of the work. To accommodate all the entries on pages of the size used in this book we have used a sequence of work based on the following plan:

(a) The starting point is the model exercise.

(b) First an opening Journal entry must be done (see Fig. 17.2 (a)).

(c) This is then posted to the three-column cash book (see Fig. 17.2 (b)).

(d) It is also posted to the ledger accounts (see Fig. 17.2 (c)).

(e) Then the transactions are taken one at a time. You must decide what book of original entry to enter them in. To help, an explanation is given under the heading, 'Notes on Model Exercise' and the Day Books are shown as Fig. 17.2 (d) and (e).

(f) When all transactions have been entered, the books of original entry are posted to the ledger. Be careful to total the Day Books and post them to Sales Account, Purchases Account, etc.

(g) Extract a Trial Balance from the ledger after all the postings have been completed (see Fig. 17.2 (f)).

(h) Prepare from the Trial Balance a Trading Account, Profit and Loss Account and Balance Sheet (see Fig. 17.2 (g)).

Model Exercise

On April 1st 19.. R. Marshall's books disclosed the following balances: cash in hand £25·50; cash at bank £450·00; furniture £1 250·00; stock £600·00; premises £6 500·00. Debtors M. Lupin £150·00, J. Jordan £130·00. Creditors R. Grimes £75·00.

Transactions for the month are as follows:

April   1st   Sells to M. Tapley on credit goods £135·00.

April   3rd   Purchases on credit from R. Grimes, goods £90·00 less 15 per cent trade discount.

April   6th   Cash sales £75·15.

April   7th   Pays R. Grimes the sum due on April 1st by cheque, less cash discount 5 per cent.

April   8th   Pays office expenses in cash £14·50.

April   9th   Purchases goods on credit from R. Grimes £28·60, less 15 per cent trade discount.

April 10th   Receives a credit note from Grimes for goods returned, *catalogue value £22·60.*

April 14th   Purchases by cheque a typewriter for office use £35·00.

April 16th   Pays salaries by cheque £100·00.

April 17th   Sends a credit note to M. Tapley for goods returned £15·00.

April 19th   Cash sales £230·15.

April 22nd   Marshall draws cash from till for his personal use £20·00.

April 25th   Sells M. Lupin goods on credit £100·00.

April 27th   Pays warehouse wages £42·50 in cash.

April 29th   Sells goods to P. Brown on credit £24·50.

April 30th J. Jordan is bankrupt. Writes his account off as a bad debt.
April 30th Banks £100·00 from cash.
Note: Closing stock on April 30th is valued at £520·00.

Notes on Model Exercise

April 1st This is a Sales Day-Book entry.
April 3rd This is a Purchases Day-Book entry.
April 6th Debit the cash sales in the Cash Account.
April 7th Credit Bank Account and enter the discount in the discount column.
April 8th Credit the Cash Account with £14·50.
April 9th This is a Purchases Day-Book entry.
April 10th This is a Purchases-Returns Book entry.
April 14th A Journal-Proper entry—purchase of an asset.
April 16th Credit Bank Account in the cash book.
April 17th This is a Sales-Returns Book entry.
April 19th Debit the cash sales in the Cash Account.
April 22nd Credit the Cash Account with these drawings.
April 25th This is a Sales Day-Book entry.
April 27th Credit the Cash Account.
April 29th This is a Sales Day-Book entry.
April 30th This is a Journal-Proper entry.
April 30th This is a contra entry in the cash book.

The opening Journal entry will appear as shown in Fig. 17.2(a).

19..						£	£
April	1	Cash in Hand	Dr.	CB	5	25·50	
		Cash at Bank	,,	CB	5	450·00	
		Furniture	,,	L	1	1 250·00	
		Stock	,,	L	2	600·00	
		Premises	,,	L	3	6 500·00	
		M. Lupin	,,	L	4	150·00	
		J. Jordan	,,	L	5	130·00	
		R. Grimes		L	6		75·00
		Capital		L	7		9 030·50
		Being assets and liabilities at this date.				£9 105·50	9 105·50
	14	Typewriters A/c	Dr.	L	8	35·00	
		Bank A/c		CB	5		35·00
		Being purchase of typewriter D/27 106 at this date.					
	30	Bad-Debts A/c	Dr.	L	9	130·00	
		J. Jordan		L	5		130·00
		Being bad debt written off at this date.					

Fig. 17.2 (a) The Journal Proper

19.. Apr.			£	£	£
1	Balances	J 1	—	25·50	450·00
6	Cash Sales	L 12		75·15	
19	Cash Sales	L 12		230·15	100·00
30	Cash	C			
				330·80	550·00
				153·80	343·75
19.. May 1	Balance	B/d			

19.. Apr.			£ 3·75	£	CB 5 £
7	R. Grimes	L 6		14·50	71·25
8	Office Expenses	L 16			
9	Typewriters	J 1			35·00
16	Salaries	L 17		20·00	100·00
22	Drawings	L 18		42·50	
27	Wages	L 19		100·00	
30	Bank	C		153·80	
30	Balance	c/d			343·75
			£ 3·75	330·80	550·00
			L 20		

Fig. 17.2 (b) The Three-column Cash Book

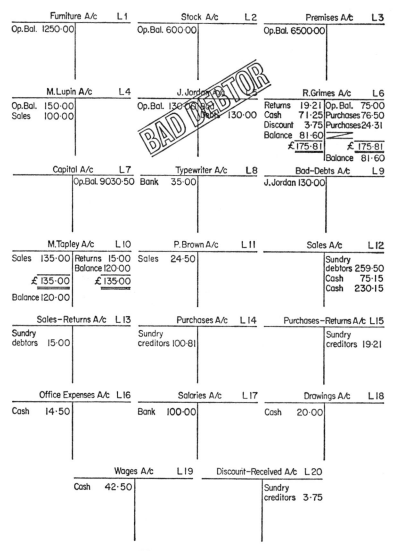

Fig. 17.2 (c) The Ledger

19.. April	1	M. Tapley			SDB 10
		Goods	L 10		£
					135·00
	25	M. Lupin			
		Goods	L 4		100·00
	29	P. Brown			
		Goods	L 11		24·50
					£259·50
					L 12

19.. April	17	M. Tapley			SRB 4
		Goods	L 10		£
					15·00
					£15·00
					L 13

Fig. 17.2 (d) The Sales Day Book and Sales-Returns Book

19.. April	3	R. Grimes				PDB 11
					£	£
		Goods			90·00	
		Less Trade Discount			13·50	
			L 6			76·50
	9	R. Grimes				
		Goods			28·60	
		Less Trade Discount			4·29	
			L 6			24·31
						£100·81
						L 14

19.. April	10	R. Grimes				PRB 7
					£	£
		Goods Returned			22·60	
		Less Trade Discount			3·39	
			L 6			19·21
						£19·21
						L 15

Fig. 17.2 (e) The Purchases Day Book and Purchases-Returns Book

Trial Balance (as at April 30th 19..)

	Dr. £	Cr. £
Cash	153·80	
Bank	343·75	
Furniture	1 250·00	
Stock	600·00	
Premises	6 500·00	
M. Lupin	250·00	
R. Grimes		81·60
Capital		9 030·50
Typewriter	35·00	
Bad Debts	130·00	
M. Tapley	120·00	
P. Brown	24·50	
Sales Returns and Sales	15·00	564·80
Purchases and Purchase Returns	100·81	19·21
Office Expenses	14·50	
Salaries	100·00	
Drawings	20·00	
Wages	42·50	
Discount Received		3·75
	£9 699·86	9 699·86

Fig. 17.2 (f) The Trial Balance

As the transactions are entered in the cash book and the Day Books these books will become as in Figs. 17.2 (b), (d) and (e). The extra Journal entries dealing with the more unusual items will be made as in Fig. 17.2 (a). Then the posting of these books into the ledger will give us the ledger accounts as in Fig. 17.2 (c).

From these ledger accounts, and from the cash book balances, the Trial Balance of Fig. 17.2 (f) will be prepared. From this Trial Balance, and using the closing stock figure given at the end of the model exercise, the Final Accounts shown in Fig. 17.2 (g) will be prepared. Ledger entries to clear the ledger accounts have not been shown.

Readers trying this type of difficult exercise will find that the crucial test of the correctness of their work is whether the Trial Balance, Fig. 17.2(f), balances. If it does not there is an error somewhere. For a procedure to follow, when checking a Trial Balance that does not agree, see page 176, Section 18.2.

Trading A/c
(for month ending April 30th 19..)

	£	£		£	£
Opening Stock		600·00	Sales		564·80
Purchases	100·81		Less Returns		15·00
Less Returns	19·21		Net Turnover		549·80
Net Purchases		81·60			
Total Stock available		681·60			
Less Closing Stock		520·00			
Cost of stock sold		161·60			
Warehouse Wages		42·50			
Cost of sales		204·10			
Gross Profit		345·70			
		£549·80			£549·80

Profit and Loss A/c
(for month ending April 30th 19..)

	£		£
Bad Debts	130·00	Gross Profit	345·70
Office expenses	14·50	Discount Received	3·75
Salaries	100·00		349·45
	244·50		
Net Profit	104·95		
	£349·45		£349·45

Balance Sheet
(as at April 30th 19..)

	£	£		£	£
Fixed Assets			*Capital*		
Premises		6 500·00	At Start		9 030·50
Furniture		1 250·00	Net Profit	104·95	
Typewriter		35·00	Less Drawings	20·00	
		7 785·00			84·95
					9 115·45
			Long-term Liabilities		—
Current Assets			*Current Liabilities*		
Stock	520·00		Creditors		81·60
Debtors	394·50				
Bank	343·75				
Cash	153·80				
		1 412·05			
		£9 197·05			£9 197·05

Fig. 17.2 (g) The Final Accounts

17.3   Exercises Set 23: Accounting with a Full Set of Books to Final-Accounts Level

1. Paul Brickhill had the following balances on his books on May 1st 19. .
Cash in hand £12·00; cash at bank £132·00; premises £4 800·00; furniture £450·00; stock £1 450·00. Debtors R. Lyons £56·50; B. Forte £116·25. Creditors M. Hague £420·00, R. Wright £270·00.

Make the opening Journal entry, post it to the cash book and the ledger and record the following transactions for the month in the books of original entry. Post these books to the ledger accounts and extract a Trial Balance. Use this Trial Balance to prepare a Trading Account and Profit and Loss Account for the month just ended and a Balance Sheet as at May 31st 19. .

May   1st   Cash Sales £42·50.
May   2nd   Sells goods on credit to R. Lyons £36·50.
May   4th   Loan from bank arranged £500·00. (*Disregard interest.*)
May   5th   Pays wages in cash £9·30.
May   8th   Cash sales £262·50; banks £200·00 from till.
May   10th   Purchases goods on credit from M. Hague £325·00.
May   11th   Purchases typewriter for office use (Ref. No. D/71258) by cheque £55·00.
May   12th   Pays wages in cash £9·30; pays M. Hague's account as at May 1st, by cheque, less 5 per cent cash discount.
May   15th   Buys goods on credit from R. Wright £125·00.
May   16th   R. Lyons pays his account as at May 1st, net, by cheque.
May   18th   Sells goods on credit to B. Forte £25·50.
May   19th   Cash sales £245·00; pays wages in cash £9·30; banks £200·00 from till.
May   22nd   Pays R. Wright by cheque the amount owing on May 1st, less 5 per cent cash discount.
May   23rd   Pays office expenses £5·25 cash.
May   25th   Sends credit note to B. Forte £25·50—goods returned.
May   26th   Cash sales £148·50; pays wages in cash £10·00.
May   29th   Pays cash for goods to be resold £37·50.
May   30th   Pays office cleaning expenses £7·25 cash; banks £200·00 from till.
May   31st   Cash sales £49·50; draws for personal use from bank £50·00.
Note: Closing stock on May 31st valued at £1 300·00.
Wages are to go in the Trading Account.

2. Martin Lawrence had the following balances on his books on October 1st 19. . Cash in hand £27·00; cash at bank £525·00; premises £9 500·00; furniture £850·00; stock £1 500·00. Debtors M. Lowe £27·50, R. Lark £38·60. Creditors M. Thomas £272·60, R. Peacock £162·50.
Make the opening Journal entry, post it to the cash book and the ledger

and record the following transactions for the month in the books of original entry. Post these books tó the ledger accounts and extract a Trial Balance. Use this Trial Balance to prepare a Trading Account, and Profit and Loss Account for the month just ended and a Balance Sheet as at October 31st 19. .

October 1st Cash sales £127·50.
October 2nd Sells goods on credit to M. Lowe £85·50.
October 4th Purchases showcases on credit from Office Display Co. Ltd., £86·50.
October 5th Pays wages in cash £44·50.
October 8th Cash sales £136·50; banks £200·00 from till.
October 10th Purchases goods on credit from M. Thomas £28·75.
October 11th Purchases calculator for office use (Ref. No. M/727a) by cheque £34·00.
October 12th Pays wages in cash £44·50.
October 15th Sells goods on credit to R. Lark £16·50.
October 16th Pays M. Thomas his account dated October 1st, less 5 per cent discount, by cheque.
October 18th R. Lark pays his account as at October 1st by a cheque for £36·67 (full settlement).
October 19th Cash sales £172·75; pays wages in cash £44·50.
October 22nd Purchases goods on credit from R. Peacock £140·00.
October 23rd Pays Peacock's account as at October 1st, net, by cheque.
October 25th Sends a credit note to M. Lowe £45·00, goods returned.
October 26th Cash sales £175·50; banks £200·00 from till.
October 29th Pays for minor repairs £4·25 cash.
October 30th Pays office-cleaning expenses £7·50 cash.
October 31st Cash sales £38·50; draws for personal use from bank £120·00.

Notes: Closing stock on October 31st valued at £1 400·00.
Wages are to go in the Trading Account.

3. Martin Candler was in business as a fishmonger and his financial position on July 1st was as follows: cash in hand £138·50; cash at bank £3 250·00; stock £320·00; furniture and fittings £650·00. Debtors M. Truelove £15·75, R. Carter £21·60. Creditors M. Perkins £184·60. Make the opening Journal entry, enter the following transactions and, after tidying up such accounts as require it, prepare a Trial Balance as at July 31st 19. . Then draw up a set of Final Accounts for the month and a Balance Sheet as at that date—bearing in mind that closing stock was valued at £165·00. Wages are to be entered in the Trading Account.

July 1st Cash purchases £26·50; M. Truelove pays his account by cheque in full.
July 2nd Purchases goods on credit from M. Perkins £68·50.

July 4th Pays M. Perkins's account at July 1st less 5 per cent discount, by cheque.

July 5th Cash sales for week £142·46; banks £120·00 for safe keeping.

July 8th Cash purchases £45·50.

July 9th R. Carter pays his account by cheque less 5 per cent cash discount.

July 11th Purchases new scales for shop £28·40 on credit from True-charge Ltd.

July 12th Cash sales for week £165·60; banks £100·00.

July 15th Cash purchases £36·85; pays for repairs to refrigerators £8·25 cash.

July 19th Cash sales for week £132·80.

July 22nd Cash purchases £72·50; banks £50·00 from till.

July 23rd Sells goods on credit to R. Carter £27·80.

July 24th Pays casual worker £5·00 cash.

July 25th Pays accountant's charges £8·40 by cheque.

July 26th Cash sales for week £224·26; banks £250·00 from till.

July 29th Cash purchases £40·45.

July 30th Paid casual workers £6·50 in cash.

July 31st Cash sales £65·20; drawings £120·00 by cheque.

4. John Walker was in business as a furniture retailer and his financial position on July 1st was as follows: cash in hand £138·50; cash at bank £2 752·50; stock £7 250·00; furniture and fittings £260·00. Debtors M. Tankerton £275·00, R. Cartier £16·50. Creditor: Union Supply Co. £1 048·80. Make the opening Journal entry, enter the following transactions and after tidying up such accounts as require it, prepare a Trial Balance as at July 31st 19.. Then draw up a set of Final Accounts and a Balance Sheet as at that date, bearing in mind that closing stock was valued at £6 450·00. Wages to go in Trading Account.

July 1st Purchases on credit from Union Supply Co. goods valued at £650·00.

July 2nd M. Tankerton pays £75·00 on account by cheque.

July 4th Cash purchases £42·50.

July 5th Pays Union Supply Co. their account as at July 1st, less 5 per cent discount, by cheque.

July 6th Cash sales for week £825·50; banks £600·00 from till.

July 8th R. Cartier pays his account in full by cheque.

July 9th Purchases goods on credit from Carson's Furniture Co. £828·50.

July 10th Buys motor vehicle for deliveries £650·00 by cheque.

July 11th Purchases goods from Union Supply Co. £248·50 on credit.

July 12th Pays wages £32·50 in cash.

July 13th Cash sales for week £630·55.

July 15th   Receives credit note from Carson's Furniture Co. allowance for goods needing polishing £10·00.

July 16th   Pays for security guard on day off £7·50 cash.

July 17th   Pays office expenses £3·25 cash.

July 19th   Cash sales for week £525·50; banks £1 000·00 from till.

July 23rd   Sells goods on credit to A. Rotemeyer £64·50.

July 24th   Purchases goods at auction £275·00 cash.

July 25th   Pays wages £32·75 in cash.

July 26th   Cash sales for week £638·50; banks £400·00 from till.

July 29th   Pays fire-insurance premium £24·00 in cash.

July 30th   Sells goods on credit to R. Cartier £48·50.

July 31st   Cash sales for week £1 252·50; drawings by cheque £120·00.

5. On January 1st 19.. Paul Dombey's financial position was as follows: cash in hand £27·50; cash at bank £1 056·50; stock £500·00; land and buildings £13 800·00; furniture and fittings £425·00; plant and machinery £3 250·50. Debtors M. Wyatt £72·80 and C. Dobson £116·50. Creditors C. Dickens £175·60. Open the books with an opening Journal entry, enter the following transactions in the correct books of original entry, post them to the ledger and extract a Trial Balance as at January 31st 19.. Then draw up a full set of Final Accounts, bearing in mind that closing stock was £650·00 on that date.

January 1st   Buys a second-hand motor van on credit from Royal Motors Ltd. for £725·00.

January 2nd   Buys goods for resale at auction £53·50, by cheque.

January 2nd   Cash sales £76·50.

January 3rd   M. Wyatt returns goods valued at £15·50.

January 4th   Buys goods from C. Dickens on credit, £72·75.

January 5th   Pays cash for stationery £7·55, postage £3·25 and motor-vehicle expenses £12·55.

January 6th   M. Culver sold Dombey goods, value £48·50 on credit.

January 7th   Pays C. Dickens's account as at January 1st, less 5 per cent cash discount, by cheque.

January 9th   M. Wyatt pays his account as at January 1st, less discount 5 per cent, by cheque.

January 10th   Cash sales £89·50; banks £100·00 for safe keeping.

January 13th   Purchases desks and chairs for office use £68·00 by cheque.

January 17th   Buys goods from C. Dickens on credit £85·50.

January 19th   C. Dobson pays his account of £116·50 in full by cheque.

January 22nd   Pays motor-vehicle expenses £15·50 in cash.

January 24th   C. Dobson's cheque is returned dishonoured.

January 29th   Pays salaries by cheque £85·00.

January 31st   Drawings by cheque £120·00; sells M. Wyatt goods on credit £45·60.

6. On January 1st 19.. Gerard Eliasson's financial position was as follows:

cash in hand £75·00; cash at bank £1 534·50; stock £1 525·00; land and buildings £7 500·00; furniture and fittings £850·00; plant and machinery £2 250·00. Debtors J. Van Eyck £296·00 and M. Wittenhagen £350·00. Creditors G. Van Swieten £1 550·00. Open the books with an opening Journal entry, enter the following transactions in the correct books of original entry, post them to the ledger and extract a Trial Balance as at January 31st 19.. Then draw up a full set of Final Accounts, bearing in mind that closing stock was £1 750·00.

January 1st Buys a second-hand motor vehicle RTW 176 on credit from Hague Motors Ltd. £850·00.

January 2nd Buys goods for re-sale at auction £175·00 by cheque.

January 3rd Eliasson returns goods valued at £150·00 to G. Van Swieten, receiving a credit note from him for this amount.

January 4th Buys goods from G. Van Swieten on credit £240·00.

January 5th Pays cash for stationery £17·50, postage £3·50 and repairs £4·25.

January 6th J. Denys sells Eliasson goods value £100·00 on credit.

January 7th Loan arranged with Mercantile Bank Ltd. £1 000·00 (interest to be charged later); pays Van Swieten's account as at January 1st less 5 per cent cash discount.

January 9th J. Van Eyck pays his account in full, less discount 5 per cent, by cheque.

January 10th Cash sales £480·00; banks £400·00.

January 13th Sells goods to M. Wittenhagen valued at £425·00 on credit.

January 17th Wittenhagen pays his account by cheque as at January 1st, less 5 per cent discount.

January 19th Cash sales £236·50; banks £200·00.

January 22nd Pays sundry expenses £1·25 cash.

January 24th Pays cash for goods for resale £14·50.

January 29th Pays salaries by cheque £95·00.

January 31st Drawings for personal use £60·00 by cheque.

Unit Eighteen

Limitations of the Trial Balance

18.1 Errors not Disclosed by the Trial Balance

One of the chief reasons for drawing up a Trial Balance of the accounts is to discover whether there are any mistakes of double entry in the month's work. When the Trial Balance does balance, we usually assume that the accounts have been carefully prepared, and we can go on to the next month's work without any problems. If it is the end of the financial year, we prepare a set of Final Accounts from the Trial Balance, and determine the profit for the period.

In fact there are five classes of error which, as will be shown, do not show up on a Trial Balance, either because they affect both sides in the same way or because they affect the same side in opposite ways, so that—for example—the debit column is increased by £5·00 by one error and decreased by £5·00 by the other error. As a result the errors are not revealed. They pass unnoticed, and yet mistakes definitely exist and will be revealed later—possibly by angry letters from customers or sarcastic letters from business associates. A correct Trial Balance is therefore often said by accountants to give only a *prima facie* proof of accuracy. *Prima facie* means 'at a first look'. A second look, later, may reveal one of these five errors.

The five classes of errors are:

(1) original errors,
(2) errors of omission,
(3) errors of commission,
(4) compensating errors,
(5) errors of principle.

(1) Original Errors

These are errors in the original documents, or errors made in copying those documents into the book of original entry. In each of these cases an incorrect figure may be copied from, say, the invoice to the Purchases Day Book, and from there, posted to the credit side of the ledger account of the supplier and to the debit side of the Purchases Account. Clearly it will not show up on the Trial Balance. Both sides will be wrong, by the same amount. A good way to reduce original errors is to take each day's bundle of invoices, or credit notes, or whatever the document is, and pre-list them with an adding-listing machine. Then, when the total entries have been made in the Day Book, the increase in the Day-Book total should be the same as the pre-list. If not, an error in copying may have occurred. It is particularly helpful if different people do the pre-listing and the entering into the Day Books.

(2) Errors of Omission

Sometimes a document is left out altogether, omitted completely from the accounting records. It may blow out of the window one blustery day. Clearly it does not reach any account at all. The Trial Balance balances, and everyone feels pleased—but when the creditor who is waiting to be paid finally rings the accountant to know why the debt has not been settled, the accountant will not be pleased at all.

(3) Errors of Commission

The word 'commission' means 'authority to do something'. An error of commission is a faulty performance of one's duty, and they are very common errors. Most of the errors by junior members of the accounting staff are errors of commission. For example where two debtors have the same name and initials it is quite easy to post a debt to the wrong account. Mr D. Smith of Harrow is debited with goods supplied to Mr D. Smith of Henlow. The Trial Balance does not distinguish between these two gentlemen, the total of 'debtors' is correct; but Mr D. Smith of Harrow will write a sarcastic letter when he is requested to pay the account, and Mr D. Smith of Henlow will wonder if he is ever going to be asked to pay for the goods he has already enjoyed.

(4) Compensating Errors

Sometimes the Trial Balance agrees, but in fact two quite separate errors of the same amount exist. This is often true of addition errors, say £1 or £10, or £100 errors. If two similar slips in addition are made, one affecting an account on the debit side and one affecting an account on the credit side, the Trial Balance will be wrong twice over, but it will appear—*prima facie*—to be correct.

(5) Errors of Principle

This type of error is caused by a failure to appreciate the *principles of accounting* which this book is designed to outline. It amounts to a misconception of the double-entry system, and it most commonly occurs as a failure to appreciate the difference between *capital* and *revenue expenditure*. A full discussion of this is given later, in Unit Twenty-one, but a simple example would be as follows.

Mr A.'s clerk receives an invoice for the purchase of an asset and, instead of doing a Journal entry in the Journal Proper, enters it in the Purchases Day Book. It follows that the asset is not recorded on the debit side of an asset account, but instead is recorded on the debit side of Purchases Account. The credit entry of course would be in the creditor's account and would be correct. The Trial Balance would agree, and appear to be correct, but in fact a serious error of principle has occurred. In due course the error on Purchases Account will increase the cost of goods sold in the Trading Account and thus reduce the profits. Mr A. will therefore be given a false impression of the profitability of the business. Also, since the asset is understated, the Balance Sheet will give a false view of the position of the business.

Errors of principle therefore offend against two fundamental rules of accounting.

(a) The accountant should always bring out a true net profit of the business.

(b) The accountant should always display a true and fair view of the business in the Balance Sheet.

These two rules are dealt with more fully later (see Section 26.2). The point here is that an error of principle is not revealed by a Trial Balance.

18.2 A Trial Balance that Does Not Agree—The Procedure to be Followed

When a Trial Balance does not agree, how shall we resolve the difficulty? Clearly there must be some mistake in the double entries. The question is, where? The following procedure will help to discover it fairly quickly.

(a) Add up the Trial Balance again—it may be just an addition error. If this does not solve the problem then proceed to (b).

(b) Take one side from the other to discover the amount of the error. Of course this may be the result of twenty different mistakes, but there is just the chance that only one error is present. Suppose it is an error of £45·50. Someone may recall 'Ah, now that is the valuation we placed upon the motor vehicle sold to the caretaker as surplus to requirements. We agreed to deduct it from his wages over the next six months. Have we forgotten to make him a debtor?' And of course we have! If no one can recall an item of this amount we proceed to (c).

(c) Divide the error in half. Half of £45·50 is £22·75. Is there an item of £22·75 which has been put on the wrong side of the Trial Balance? If so it will make one side £22·75 too large and the other side £22·75 too small. The result will be an apparent error of twice the amount concerned. If there does not seem to be a figure of this amount proceed to (d).

(d) In certain accounting systems it is usual to keep *control accounts*, or *total accounts*, which check up on certain parts of the ledger. This is quite a complex idea, and the whole of Unit Thirty-four is given to explaining control accounts. If a control-account system is in use, or if one can be built up quickly from the total figures, it will eliminate areas where no mistake exists, and bring out areas where there are mistakes. This reduces the total amount of checking necessary.

(e) The only remaining thing to do is to check every entry that has been made throughout the month to ensure that a correct double entry has taken place. This is a long and laborious process. Now you can see why a Trial Balance is extracted at least once a month. It is bad enough to have to look through a whole month's entries. To go through a whole year's entries would be altogether too time-consuming.

18.3 Suspense Accounts

Suppose that it proves impossible to get the books correct, even though hours of work have been devoted to the task. The only solution is to open up a *Suspense Account*. This is a general name for any account where we hold a balance until we decide what to do with it. In this case we have a Suspense Account holding a 'difference on books' figure. Clearly the mistake will be explained sooner or later, probably as a result of some letter of complaint.

Some firms take the view that it is a waste of time looking for an error on the Trial Balance—whatever the mistake, it will turn up one day. Therefore, they argue, it is simpler just to enter the difference in a Suspense Account and carry on with next month's work. The only difficulty here is that if it is the end of the year, the balance must appear on the Balance Sheet as 'difference on books'. That is not a happy thing for any accountant to have to admit.

The creation of a Suspense Account is quite simple. Suppose the debit side of the Trial Balance is greater than the credit side by £50·00. A Suspense Account opened as shown in Fig. 18.1 will immediately put the Trial Balance right. Of course it is a complete invention, but in due course we shall be able to remove it from the books as the mistakes that caused it are discovered.

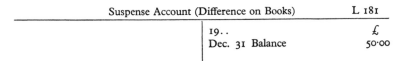

Suspense Account (Difference on Books)		L 181
	19..	£
	Dec. 31 Balance	50·00

Fig. 18.1 Correcting a Trial Balance that will not agree

18.4 The Correction of Errors

One of the commonest types of question in examinations concerns the correction of errors. This may or may not involve work where a Suspense Account has been opened. For example, if an error has been made on the books, and it is reported or discovered within a few days, we shall be able to get it right without having to open a Suspense Account. If the error has existed for some time, so that the end of a month arrives and the error is not discovered, we may have to open up a Suspense Account. This will mean that any eventual correction which we make will now involve the Suspense Account as well as the account containing the error.

When correcting errors there is no simple rule. We must discover the nature of the error, and do whatever it is necessary to do to put the matter right. A few examples will illustrate the problems.

Example 1: An Error of Commission

On January 1st 19.. we discover that T. Smith has been debited in error with goods sold to E. Smith, valued at £50·00. To correct this error we must remove the £50·00 from T. Smith's Account and enter it where it really belongs, in E. Smith's Account.

The Journal entry will be as in Fig. 18.2 and the ledger accounts as in Fig. 18.3.

19..						£	£ J 11
Jan.	1	E. Smith	Dr.	L	56	50·00	
		T. Smith		L	57		50·00
		Being correction of error whereby £50 was debited in T. Smith's account in error					

Fig. 18.2 An error of commission

		E. Smith				L 56
19..				£		
Jan.	1 T. Smith	J 11	50·00			

		T. Smith						L 57
19..				£	19..			£
Jan. 1 Balance		B/d	50·00		Jan.	1 E. Smith	J 11	50·00

Fig. 18.3 The ledger accounts corrected

Example 2: An Error of Principle

Thomas Hudson's book-keeper has entered an invoice for the purchase of office furniture from Times Furnishing Co. in the Purchases Day Book, and has posted the entry to the ledger accounts. Correct this error with a Journal entry and show the ledger postings. The amount concerned was £240·00 and the mistake was discovered on July 12th 19...

Here the situation is as follows:

(a) The Purchases Account has been debited with the total of the Purchases Day Book which includes this £240·00—in other words it is overstated by £240·00.

(b) The account of Times Furnishing Co. has been credited with £240·00. This entry is of course correct.

The error of principle is that the Purchases Account has been debited with £240·00 when it ought to be the asset account that is debited, i.e. Furniture and Fittings Account.

To correct the error we must debit Furniture and Fittings Account and credit Purchases Account. The Journal entry reads as shown in Fig. 18.4 and the ledger accounts as in Fig. 18.5.

19..						£	£ J 8
July	12	Furniture and Fittings A/c Dr.	L	21		240·00	
		Purchases A/c	L	31			240·00
		Being correction of error of					
		principle in which the purchase					
		of an asset was treated as					
		purchases of goods for resale					

Fig. 18.4 An error of principle

		Purchases A/c			L 21
19..		£	19..		£
June 30 Sundry			July 12 Furniture and		
Purchases PDB 1	4 075·25		Fittings A/c J 8	240·00	

		Furniture and Fittings A/c		L 31
19..		£		
Jan. 1 Balance	B/d	2 800·00		
July 12 Purchases A/c	J 8	240·00		

Fig. 18.5 The accounts corrected

Example 3: An Arithmetic Error

It often happens that a slip in arithmetic results in a difference on the books, and it is nearly always a single-sided error. For example, a careless addition of the Sales Day Book which results in a total which is wrong by £50·00, will not necessarily affect any other account than the Sales Account, to which this total is posted. It is most unlikely that the same error would be made elsewhere, and if it was it would be quite separate, even if it resulted in a compensating error. (See Section 18.1.)

The problem arises as to how we should correct a single-sided error of this sort. Two solutions are as follows:

(a) We can physically cross out the incorrect total posted to Sales Account, and replace it by the correct figure. In such circumstances it is wise to initial the error, or better still, to sign your full name against it. This explains the untidiness in the book-keeping and allocates responsibility for the error, or for its correction. Clearly this sort of physical correction of an error should not be carried out by an office junior without the approval of the accountant or chief clerk. Such an error would be corrected as in Fig. 18.6.

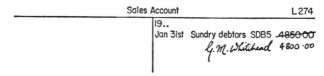

Fig. 18.6 An error corrected by deletion and substitution of the correct figure

(*b*) We can do a single-sided Journal entry. This is rather unusual but it is the only way to put the matter right, since only one account is affected. The Journal entry and account would be as shown in Fig. 18.7.

19.. Feb.	6	Sales A/c Dr.	L 274	£ 50·00	£ J 5
		Being a single-sided correction of an arithmetical error			

Sales A/c					L 274
19.. Feb.	6 Correction of error	J 5	£ 50·00	19.. Jan. 31 Sundry Debtors	£ SDB 5 4 850·00

Fig. 18.7 A single-sided Journal entry

18.5 Clearing a Suspense Account

When a Suspense Account has been opened, the errors which caused it to be made out will gradually come to light as the business receives complaints from aggrieved persons who have been over or undercharged. When these errors are corrected, it will usually be possible to remove some, or all, of the Suspense-Account balance. Consider the following example.

(1) Example

An accountant finds his Trial Balance on January 31st 19.. to be £43·50 in excess on the debit side. A Suspense Account is opened to correct the Trial Balance, but later is cleared by the following discoveries:

(*a*) Furniture purchased for £85·00 was entered properly in the cash book but posted to Furniture Account as £58·00.

(*b*) A balance due to R. Tomlinson for £79·00 had been omitted from the Trial Balance, although Tomlinson's account was perfectly correct.

(*c*) Bank charges of £8·50 had been entered in the Cash Book, but not posted to the Nominal Account.

Make the Journal entries and show the Suspense Account as it will finally appear.

The explanation is as follows. The Trial Balance had to be corrected by putting a balance of £43·50 on the credit side, as in Fig. 18.8.

Suspense A/c		L 272
	19.. Jan. 31 Balance	£ 43·50

Fig. 18.8 A Suspense Account opened

Item (a) Here the Furniture Account has been under-debited by £27·00 (£85·00 − £58·00). We must debit Furniture Account with £27·00 and credit Suspense Account with £27·00. Fig. 18.9 illustrates this.

19.. Feb.	27	Furniture A/c Dr.	L 5	£ 27·00	£ J 6
		Suspense A/c	L 272		27·00
		Being correction of an error where furniture purchased for £85·00 was entered as £58·00			

Furniture A/c   L 5

19..				£
Jan. 28	Bank	CB 7	58·00	
Feb. 27	Suspense A/c J	6	27·00	

Suspense A/c   L 272

			£
19..			
Jan. 31	Balance		43·50
Feb. 27	Furniture A/c J 6		27·00

Fig. 18.9 Correcting a mis-posting

Item (b) Here we have a single-sided correction. There is nothing wrong with Tomlinson's Account, but it has not been entered on the Trial Balance, where it would have been in the credit column. Its omission has resulted in the Suspense Account being £79·00 bigger on the credit side than necessary. But there isn't as much as £79·00 on the Suspense Account anyway, so how can we say it is £79·00 too big? The only explanation must be that a further undiscovered error has still to be revealed. Fig. 18.10 shows the correction for item (b), which is to debit Suspense Account with £79·00.

19.. Feb.	28	Suspense A/c Dr.	L 272	£ 79·00	J 6
		Being correction of Suspense A/c due to an omission from the Trial Balance			

(contd. on page 182)

		Suspense A/c				L 272

19..			£	19..		£
Feb.	28	Correction of		Jan. 31 Balance		43·50
		error J 6	79·00	Feb. 27 Furniture A/c J 6		27·00

Fig. 18.10 Correcting an omission from the Trial Balance

Item (c) Here Bank-Charges Account has not been debited with £8·50. If we debit it with £8·50 and credit Suspense Account, we shall finally clear the Suspense Account. This tells us that the errors have now all been discovered. Fig. 18.11 illustrates this final correction. Note that as this error was not discovered until March 4th, the Suspense Account would have been balanced off and tidied up at the end of February when the February Trial Balance was prepared.

19..					£	£ J 7
Mar.	4	Bank-Charges A/c Dr.	L 42	8·50		
		Suspense A/c	L 272			8·50
		Being correction of error in				
		which bank charges were not				
		posted to Bank-Charges A/c				

		Bank-Charges A/c		L 42

19..			£	
Mar.	4 Suspense A/c J 7		8·50	

		Suspense A/c				L 272

19..			£	19..		£
Feb.	28 Correction			Jan. 31 Balance		43·50
	of error J 6	79·00		Feb. 27 Furniture A/c J 6		27·00
				Feb. 28 Balance c/d		8·50
			£79·00			£79·00
19..				19..		
Mar.	1 Balance B/d		£8·50	Mar. 4 Bank Charges J 7		£8·50

Fig. 18.11 Clearing the Suspense Account

18.6 Exercises Set 24: Limitations of the Trial Balance

1. There are several types of error not disclosed by the Trial Balance. List them, and give an example of two different types.

2. 'An agreed Trial Balance is only *prima facie* proof of accurate accounting records.' Explain this statement fully.

3. What procedures should be followed if a Trial Balance fails to agree? List the measures you would take in logical order, and explain them.

4. 'If an item is placed on the wrong side of a Trial Balance it causes an error of twice its value.' Explain this statement, using an actual example of a Trial Balance which had the Discount-Allowed Account listed as a credit balance of £14·98. Invent suitable totals for the Trial Balance to demonstrate your reasoning.

5. Correct, by Journal entries, the following entries which have been made in the ledger of R. Taylor. Date the entries September 30th 19. .
   (a) £18·00 received from P. Dark had been posted to the account of D. Park.
   (b) £40·00 expended by the trader on his own expenses had been posted to the Office-Expenses Account.
   (c) £10·00 received in respect of the sale of some book-cases from the office had been posted to the Sales Account. The book value of the book-cases was exactly £10·00.   (RSA 1, COS)

6. Correct by Journal entries, the following entries which have been made in the ledger of A. Trader. Date the entries May 31st 19. .
   (a) £28·00 paid to D. Montgomery had been posted to the account of D. Montmorency.
   (b) £65·00 expended by the trader on office furniture had been posted to the Office-Expenses Account.
   (c) £10·00 discount allowed has been posted to the credit side of the Discount Account.

7. Show, by means of Journal entries, how the following errors would be corrected in the books of M. Bines. Date all items June 30th 19. .
   (a) Machinery valued at £1 600 purchased on credit from Machinery Ltd. had been debited to Purchases Account.
   (b) When paying A. Rosner, a creditor, Bines had deducted £7·50 as discount. Rosner had disallowed this discount.
   (c) Depreciation of £80·00 on machinery had been credited to Fixtures and Fittings Account.

8. Correct by Journal entries the following errors:
   (a) A purchase of furniture valued at £120·00 was debited in Furnishing Co. Ltd.'s account instead of in Furniture and Fittings Account. The mistake was discovered on July 5th 19. .
   (b) A lorry recorded in the books of R. Lamperter was valued at £220·00. It was sold on August 4th 19. . by Lamperter to R. Gould and Co. for £175·00, but the Motor-Vehicles Account was only credited with £175·00 instead of the full book value. The error was discovered on August 8th 19. .

(c) A machine was purchased for £2 000·00 from Lucas Engineering Ltd., but the invoice was not passed through the books at all. On July 12th 19.., six months later, it was agreed with the managing director of Lucas Engineering Ltd. that a cheque would be sent in full at once, and with 5 per cent interest *per annum* added.

9. (a) What is a Suspense Account? (b) on April 30th 19.. R. Whistler decides to open a Suspense Account with a debit balance of £45·00, because he cannot discover the error on his books. On May 17th it is found to be due to a failure to post a cheque for £45·00 paid to a creditor R. Lawson from the cash book to his account. Show the Journal entry clearing the Suspense Account and the Suspense Account itself.

10. On August 31st 19.. R. Hull's Trial Balance failed to agree, the debit side being £42·50 greater than the credit side and consequently he opened a Suspense Account. The errors proved to be as follows:
   (a) The total of discount allowed for one week £8·50 had not been posted to the appropriate account.
   (b) A debtor R. Day had paid his account, £51·00 in full, but this had not been credited to his account.
   Show (i) the Journal entries to correct these errors, and (ii) the Suspense Account after the corrections had been completed. Invent sensible dates in September for these corrections.

11. On September 30th 19.. R. T. Crafty extracted a Trial Balance. The debit side of the Trial Balance totalled £18 150·85, and the credit side £17 887·80. Crafty opened a Suspense Account for the difference. During October he discovered the following errors, which accounted for the difference:
   (a) The total of the Purchases Book for the month of September, £5 479·00 had been posted to the Purchases Account as £5 749·00.
   (b) The discount-received column in the cash book had been wrongly totalled and posted to the Discount-Received Account as £55·14 instead of £57·19.
   (c) A cheque £76·42 paid for light and heat had been posted to the Light and Heat Account as £67·42.
   (d) A credit note sent to S. Gilbert for £16·50 had been entered in the Sales-Returns Book at £15·60 and posted to Gilbert's Account at that figure.
   Draw up the Suspense Account, inventing suitable dates in October.

12. On October 31st 19.. R. Lyons failed to balance his Trial Balance and after spending a considerable time looking for errors decided to open a Suspense Account for the balance. The debits exceeded the credits by £93·30. Errors were discovered as follows:
   November 7th It was found that a cash payment of £81·69 made by

T. White had been entered in the cash book but had not been posted to the debtor's account.

November 11th A credit balance of Commission-Received Account of £38·50 had been entered in the accounts correctly, but on extracting it to the Trial Balance it had been written as £30·85, in the *debit* column.

November 17th A debit of £50·00 payable by H. Herron had been entered in H. Hair's Account in error.

November 19th The total of discount allowed for one week in October, £28·87, had been credited to Discount Account.

Draw up the Suspense Account showing how the correction of these errors cleared the difference of £93·30.

Unit Nineteen

Simultaneous Records

19.1 The Idea of Simultaneous Records

Whenever entries are made in one book, and are then posted to another book, two main criticisms arise: first that the work is being duplicated unnecessarily, and second that there is a chance that errors will be made.

These criticisms can be met by using one of the modern 'simultaneous-records' systems which have been designed and marketed by a number of firms specializing in this field.

The principle of these systems, which depend upon the use of carbon paper to produce the simultaneous records required, is that any group of documents and records which are related, and carry the same information, might as well be produced at the same time. Since carbon paper is a little tiresome to interleave, and the more copies you make, the fainter they become, it is usual to limit the system to three or four related sets of records. There are many such related groups of documents required in business. Some of the most necessary are listed below and described in the pages that follow.

  (a) The Sales-Ledger system.
       (i) The statement placed on top of
       (ii) the ledger card placed on top of
       (iii) the Sales Day-Book sheet.
  (b) The Purchases-Ledger system.
       (i) The remittance advice note placed on top of
       (ii) the ledger card placed on top of
       (iii) the Purchases Day-Book sheet.
  (c) Payments by credit transfer.
       (i) The credit transfer slip, placed on top of
       (ii) the bank list placed on top of
       (iii) the payments cash book.
  (d) Wages and salaries systems.
       (i) The employee's tax and earnings card, placed on top of
       (ii) the payroll sheet and
       (iii) the employee's pay slip.
  (e) The stock-records system.
       (i) The stock-record card placed on top of
       (ii) the stock-control sheet.
  (f) Income-tax records system.
       (i) The P11 form (tax deducted in year) placed on top of
       (ii) the P60 form (certificate of tax deducted) placed on top of
       (iii) the P35 form (total tax deducted from all employees).

In each case the system used provides a plastic posting board sufficiently large to take the largest of the documents conveniently, with a row of studs or other mechanical or magnetic devices to hold the sheets in position. The magnetic posting boards illustrated in this section are by courtesy of George Anson and Co. Ltd. of Ilford.

19.2 A Sales-Ledger System with Simultaneous Entries

Here the important record is the *ledger card* of the customer, which is kept in a posting tray designed so that a particular ledger card can be found quickly by the posting clerk, who is said to 'pull' them from the system.

Kept with the ledger card is the monthly statement, which is renewed every month as the previous month's statement is dispatched to the customer. The posting clerk 'pulls' the statement with the ledger card and assembles them on the magnetic posting board.

The third record is the Sales Day Book, in loose-leaf sheet form.

(1) Advantages of the System

(*a*) All three records—statement, ledger card and Day Book—are prepared simultaneously.

(*b*) No posting errors can be made since the entries in all three records are carbon copies of one another.

(*c*) Errors that might not show up until the Trial-Balance stage are revealed on the day they occur if the checks and controls devised by the system planners are implemented.

(*d*) By careful use of the analysis columns provided, an efficient control of business trends can be achieved. For example, sales in a particular department which handles seasonal goods can be encouraged at appropriate times by increasing the floor space or shelf space allocated to the department.

(*e*) Statements are ready for dispatch at the end of the month without any work other than the actual mailing activities.

(2) Procedure

(*a*) The Sales Day-Book form is laid on the plastic magnetic posting board, its left-hand margin held to the board by two projecting studs.

(*b*) The posting clerk 'pulls' the ledger card and statement on which she has to make an entry from the posting tray, and positions them, with carbon, so that the next clean line of each is against the next clean line of the Sales Day-Book form. The statement is on top.

(*c*) Details of the invoice are then entered on the statement and simultaneously carbon-copied on to the ledger card and Day Book below them.

(*d*) The updated ledger card and statement are then returned to the posting tray, and the posting clerk selects the next card and statement to be updated.

(*e*) There are many different rulings of such Day-Book forms, but the one shown here is helpful in providing control-account records and departmental records in the analysis columns at the end of the Day-Book sheet.

SALES/PURCHASES   DAY/CASH BOOK   Control account records   SHEET No. 45
                                                                               DATE 3.4.19.
Invoice numbers   Departmental Information

DATE	REF	DETAIL	DEBIT	CREDIT	BALANCE	A/c No	OLD BALANCE	NAME	A—E 1	F—M 2	N—S 3	T—Z 4	Furniture 5	Glass Chino 6	Electrical 7	Art 8
3.4.19.	DL321	7051	23 70		69 90	46	20	J.Marshall & Sons	23 70	23 70			23 70			
		PL569 7052	184 54		240 24	55	70	Kellohers Ltd.	184 54	184 54	184 54					
						49	66	R.Maw & Son	273 72	273 72	273 72		273 72			
						12	15	R.T.Loughlin		14 75				14 75	61 50	
						37	40	P.Quire Co.		14 75	61 50		81 45			
						42	20	M.Martin Ltd.	28 50	28 50	61 45					28 50
						61	15	Laver and Co.	67 20	67 20					67 20	38 66
						197	12	B.Broadbent & Sons	38 45							
						286	94	R.Sheldroke Ltd.		27 72	27 72		27 72			
						163	86	R.Reeve Ltd.		68 55	68 55		68 55			
						148	77	M.Timpson				12 84				12 84
						51	15	R.Brood Bros.	11 75	11 75			11 75			
						10	20	M.Lanark Ltd.	44 90	19 70					19 70	
						—	—	R.Hills*		44 90			-4 90			

LEDGER CARD

STATEMENT/REMITTANCE ADVICE

A/c No.

⌐ R.Hills,
  21 High Street,
  Newtown,
  Essex.   ⌐   ⌐ DATE

DATE	REF	DETAIL	DEBIT	CREDIT	BALANCE
		A/c RENDERED			49 90
3.4.19.	50845	17055	44 90		44 90

The monthly sales to
the customer's may be
compared here

ANSON FORM NO. SP13

These analysis columns may be used
in any way the accountant desires.

Here they have been used to provide Control
Account figures (see index) and
departmental figures (see index.)

The last figure shown in the
final (shaded) column represents the balance of
your account in our books.

ANSON

PAT. PEND.

Fig. 19.1 Simultaneous records—the Sales Ledger

(f) At the end of the page a check can be made on the entries in the follow-ing ways. Take Fig. 19.1 as an example, where invoices are being posted.

   (i) The total of the debit column should be the same as the total of the invoice pre-list (an adding-machine total pinned to the batch of invoices to be posted).

  (ii) The total of the old balances, added to the total of the debits entered, should equal the total of the new balances.

 (iii) The control-account columns should cross-tot to the total of the debits entered.

 (iv) The departmental columns should cross-tot to the total of the debits entered.

19.3 Wage System—A Simple Wages Book

In most countries today the employer is not only expected to pay the wages of his workers, but to act as an agent for the Government in the collection of various forms of tax. The modern social system now provides such extensive welfare and social-security services that it is quite impossible to finance them all by taxation on a few luxury goods, as in former times. Today every employee must pay contributions to National Health and Insurance schemes, and many must also pay income tax and pension contributions. Many employ-ers also help employees to save in National Savings schemes, or collect for charitable organizations such as Dr Barnardo's orphanages. These deductions are removed from the employee's gross wages, leaving a net figure, in many cases considerably below the gross earnings. The amounts deducted are collected together into totals and paid over to the various bodies entitled to receive them, for example the collection offices of the Income Tax authorities, the Department of Health and Social Security, etc.

A simple wages book is illustrated in Fig. 19.2. It is suitable for an employer of up to twenty staff.

Name 1	Gross Pay 2		Deductions – Employee			Total Deductions 6		Net Wage 7		Employer's		
			Tax 3	Grad. Pension 4	N H I 5					Grad. Pension 8	N H I 9	10
J. Jacobs	20	00	3 50	– 51	– 88	4	89	15	11	– 51	– 89	
W. Fielding (Mrs)	7	50	– 25	– –	– 75	1	00	6	50	– –	– 76	
K. Knight	12	50	2 20 (Credit)	– 18	– 88	1 14 (Rebate)		13	64	– 18	– 89	
Totals	40	00	1 55	– 69	2 51	4	75	35	25	– 69	2 54	

Grad. Pension	Employee (Col. 4)	–	69		N H Insurance	Employee (Col. 5)	2	51
	Employer (Col. 8)	–	69			Employer (Col. 9)	2	54
	Total	1	38			Total	5	05

Fig. 19.2 A simple wages book (by courtesy of George Vyner Ltd.)

More advanced wages systems are usually prepared by means of the simultaneous-records system. This is illustrated and discussed below.

(1) The Taxation of Wages—PAYE

As far as employees are concerned, the British tax system is a *pay-as-you-earn* system, which is abbreviated to PAYE. This is by far the most convenient system for the ordinary employee, since there is no need to save money in order to pay income tax. Instead, the tax and various other deductions are removed before the pay packet is prepared and the 'net pay' taken home is the residue which is available for the employee's own use. There are suggestions that this PAYE system will be ended shortly, but over the years it has proved an efficient, cheap method of collection. It is based upon the following arrangements.

(*a*) **Code numbers.** Every employee is given a *code number*, which is calculated on the allowances to which an employee is entitled. These include *personal allowances* (for single and married persons), *child allowances, dependent-relatives allowances, sons' and daughters' services, housekeeper services, small-income relief* and other small allowances for hardship cases such as *blindness.* From these allowances a code number is calculated: a person with heavy responsibilities has large allowances and hence a high code number, a person with few responsibilities has a low code number and is taxed more heavily. A change in circumstances, for instance the birth of a child, results in a change of code number as soon as it is reported.

(*b*) **Tax tables.** These are prepared by the Inland Revenue and issued to employers. By consulting the tax table, the employer can determine exactly how much tax should have been deducted by that week in the year. He can then compare this difference with the total tax paid already up to the previous week. The difference must be the amount that is to be deducted from this week's pay packet. If a change of circumstances has resulted in a change of code number, the tables may indicate that less tax is due altogether this week than the employee has already paid. This means that an immediate refund is due to the employee, and it is put at once into the pay packet.

The total sums deducted from pay for taxation are payable each month by the employer to the Inland-Revenue authorities.

(*c*) **Other important tax records.** The P45 is a form which is given to employees who change employment. The new employer can only deduct the correct tax if information is supplied by the old employer about the amount deducted to date and the total earned in the old employment. This information is supplied by the old employer on a P45 given to the employee when leaving the job.

The P60 is a form given to all employees at the end of the tax year. It shows the total pay received, the tax deducted, the National Insurance and other payments made and the net pay. It is widely used as part of the social-security system, and should be kept by the employee in case he, or his family, wish to claim benefits such as student grants, etc.

DATE	HRS	RATE	BASIC	A	B	C	GROSS PAY FOR WK/MTH	GROSS PAY TO DATE	TAX FREE PAY	TAXABLE PAY TO DATE	INCOME TAX DUE	TAX WK/MTH	REFUND	GRAD. PENS.	NAT. INSCE	1	2	3	4	TOTAL DEDUCTIONS	NET PAY	PAYROLL NO.	NAME
19·· 17·5	42	0·61	24 40	3 00	1 83		29 23	240 34	180 00	60 34	16 00	2 34	– –	1 20	0 88	0 05				4 47	24 76	1712	M. Thatcher

PAY ROLL

WEEK/MONTH ENDING 17·5·19·· SHEET No. 3

DATE	HRS	RATE	EARNINGS: BASIC	PROD A	OVERTIME B	C	GROSS PAY FOR WK/MTH	GROSS PAY TO DATE	INCOME TAX: TAX FREE PAY	TAXABLE PAY TO DATE	INCOME TAX DUE	TAX WK /MTH	REFUND	DEDUCTIONS: GRAD. PENS.	NAT INSCE	DR BARNARDO 1	2	3	4	TOTAL DEDUCTION	NET PAY	PAYROLL NO.	NAME	EMPLOYERS CONTRIBUTIONS: NAT INSCE
19·· 17·5	42	0·61	24 40	3 00	1 83		29 23	240 34	180 00	60 34	16 00	2 34	– –	1 20	0 88	0 05				4 47	24 76	1712	M. Thatcher	0 89
17·5	47	0·55	22 00	3 00	5 77		30 77	202 50	156 80	45 70	11 20	1 20	– –	1 20	0 88	0 05				3 33	27 44	1713	T. Larkins	0 89
																							R. Grainger	
																							G. Wright	
																							P. Suckling	
																							M. Thomas	
																							G. M. Whiteside	

ADDRESS 13 Hill Road, Newtown, Essex. TAX DISTRICT Gateshead 3 TAX REF. No. 530/1 NAME WHITESIDE G. M.

DATE OF BIRTH 31·7·1921 DATE STARTED 9·9·54 DATE LEFT ______ OCCUPATION Turner DEPT. Prod control

EARNINGS: DATE		RATE	BASIC	PROD	OVERTIME		GROSS WK/MONTH
1·1·19··		55p	22 00	3 00	0 77½		25 00

INCOME TAX: DATE APPLIED	CODE
1·1·19··	852

COMPANY'S PENSION SCHEME IN/OUT

NAT. INSCE No. TW | 60 | 15 | 78 | B

DATE	DEDUCTIONS: NAT. INSCE	UNION					TOTAL DEDUCTION
1·1·19··	03	0 17					20

COYS CONTRIBUTION: DATE	NAT. INSC
1·1·19··	

WK NO. / MTH NO.	DATE	HRS.	RATE	BASIC	A	B	C	GROSS PAY FOR WK/MTH	GROSS PAY TO DATE	TAX FREE PAY	TAXABLE PAY TO DATE	INCOME TAX DUE	TAX WK/MTH	REFUND	GRAD. PENS.	NAT. INSCE	1	2	3	4	TOTAL DEDUCTION	NET PAY	PAYROLL NO.
27																							
1 1																							
2 2 28																							
3 3 29																							
4 4 30																							
5 5 31																							
6 6 32																							
7 7 33																							
8 8 34																							

K5868L

LESS PAY AND TAX IN PREVIOUS EMPLOYMENT

PAY AND TAX IN PREVIOUS EMPLOYMENT

GPS

4	TOTAL DEDUCTIONS	NET PAY	PAYROLL NO.	NAME

Fig. 19.3 Simultaneous wage systems

(2) Simultaneous Wages Records

The wages records necessary for any firm are as follows:

(a) **An individual record card**, showing the wages paid to the employee, week by week, or month by month, so that at any time an employee's card may be produced and discussed with him if he complains about the payments made.

(b) **A payroll**, showing the amounts paid to all the employees in any given week, or month, and the amounts deducted, etc.

(c) **A pay slip**, to be put into the wage packet, or given in an envelope to any employee who is paid by credit transfer direct into his bank account.

These three records all need exactly the same information, and may be prepared simultaneously, as shown in Fig. 19.3 on the posting board already described in Section 19.2 on the Sales Ledger. The procedure is as follows:

(a) A sheet of sixteen wage slips—perforated to make separation easy after the slips have been written out—is placed on to the magnetic posting board and secured with two pegs.

(b) A sheet of carbon is placed over these pay slips and the payroll sheet is superimposed upon it, exactly covering the wage slips. It, too, has sixteen lines of records. This is covered by another carbon sheet as wide as the record card.

(c) The employee's record card is taken from the posting tray and is placed with its next clean line exactly covering the next clean line on the pay roll. It is held in position by the magnetic card holder. Details of the gross pay, tax and other deductions, and the net pay are then written in, and simultaneous copies appear on the pay roll and wages slip below. The record card is returned to the posting tray and the next card is selected.

(d) At the completion of each page of payroll, the wage slips are torn up along the perforations, and are used to prepare the wage packets. The payroll sheet is totalled to give total figures for net pay, tax payable, voluntary savings, etc. and these totals are used to draw money from the bank, and to make cheques payable to the Inland Revenue authorities, etc.

19.4   Conclusion: The Use of Simultaneous Records

Business has become very competitive these days and the use of computers and other electronic equipment has intensified this competition. However, computer time and programming are expensive and the tendency is therefore towards amalgamation, since only large firms can afford these heavy accounting expenses. For smaller firms to resist this tendency, they must adopt accounting techniques which increase efficiency and are inexpensive. Simultaneous-record systems are certainly part of the answer to this problem.

A general textbook of this sort cannot possibly do justice to the variety of systems provided by the specialist firms in this field, many of them adaptable to suit most trades or professions. If you have a particular accounting problem, you should take it, without obligation, to one of these specialist firms.

Apart from those whose systems are illustrated in this book, other names may be obtained from the Business Equipment Trade Association, 109 Kingsway, London WC2B 6PU.

19.5 Exercises Set 25: Simultaneous Records

1. What is the meaning of the term 'simultaneous records'?

2. What are the advantages of keeping a record of sales by simultaneous-records methods?

3. Write a few lines about the following income-tax matters:
   (a) Code numbers.　　　　(c) Gross pay, taxable pay and net pay.
   (b) Form P45.　　　　　　(d) Form P60.

Unit Twenty

Bank Reconciliation Statements

20.1 Introduction

The word 'reconcile' means 'to make compatible'. It frequently happens in business that two sets of figures which should agree, for some reason do not. For example we might estimate that a certain profit should be made in a given period, but in fact we fail to achieve this expected profit. A good accountant would seek to reconcile the two sets of figures, examining the reasons for the discrepancy.

Perhaps the commonest of all such situations is the reconciliation of the Bank Account, as shown in our ledger, with the Bank Account in the Bank's ledger, as shown when the bank sends us a computerized *bank statement*. This is a computer printout showing the various transactions which have taken place between the bank and ourselves. We may have banked cheques, or made withdrawals during recent weeks or months. The bank may have undertaken certain payments or collections on our behalf. The printout shows the bank's view of these matters, but we may need to reconcile its view with our own.

20.2 Practical Banking

When a bank agrees to permit a customer to open a current account by paying in an initial sum of money, and gives him a cheque book so that he may make any payments through the cheque system, it does not undertake to correspond with the customer every time a transaction takes place. Some banks hardly ever write to their customers at all, except when the customer fails to keep enough funds in his account to ensure that the bank will always be able to honour any cheques presented. Similarly the customer never writes to the bank to tell them he is making out a cheque. Every now and then the customer may ask for a bank statement, or the bank. feeling that a sufficiently large collection of paid cheques has accumulated on its files, will render a statement to the customer.

There are several reasons why the bank statement may differ from the Bank Account in our three-column cash book, and in practice it will rarely be the case that the two accounts show the same balance. The differences are always due to a lack of knowledge of what the other person has been doing. The reasons may be divided into three groups:

(a) Differences arising from the bank's actions, about which we have not been notified.

(b) Differences arising from the time-lag which is inevitable whenever cheques are sent in payment of debts, or are received and paid into the bank for clearing through the bankers' clearing house.

(c) Errors, either by the bank, or by our own cashier.

Such errors are unlikely to occur frequently, because the banks usually institute careful checks on their figures, and a cashier is usually a responsible member of the staff. Inevitably though, mistakes do occur from time to time. Fuller explanations of the first two causes of difference are desirable at this point.

(1) Differences Arising due to a Lack of Knowledge of the Bank's Actions

There are many circumstances when the bank does not bother to inform us that it has taken money from, or has credited money to, our account. It expects us to ask for a statement at regular intervals, usually on the last day of the calendar month, and when we receive this statement we shall discover that the bank has taken certain actions. The most common are:

(a) The removal of sums for bank charges, or for interest on overdrafts.

(b) The payment of standing orders which we may have instructed the bank to pay. Most people remember to deduct these sums from the Bank Account if they are monthly payments, for example mortgage payments or payments for rates. The less regular ones may be overlooked, such as annual contributions to bodies like the Automobile Association, or to professional bodies.

(c) The receipt of sums by credit transfer, either from debtors or, more usually, from investments. For example, the Bank of England, which manages the gilt-edged security market on behalf of the Treasury, prefers to pay interest on securities directly into the investor's bank account, rather than send him a cheque for the amount due. This credit transfer will appear on the Bank Statement as a deposit, increasing the balance on the account.

When such items are discovered on a Bank Statement they must at once be entered in the Bank Account in the three-column cash book. They will increase the balance on the Bank Account (i.e. debit it) if they are receipts, and decrease the balance (i.e. credit the account) if they are sums paid away by the bank, or taken by the bank for services rendered.

The correct procedure for items of this type discovered in the bank statement is: enter them in the Bank Account in the three-column cash book, thus updating that account now that the customer is aware of the bank's actions.

(2) Differences Arising due to Inevitable Delays in the Cheque System

(a) Imagine that we send a cheque for £50·00 to Angus McDowall who lives in the Highlands of Scotland. Before we post the letter containing the cheque, we shall credit the item in the Bank Account, which has given value, £50·00. It will probably be at least two days before that letter arrives, and when it does arrive Mr McDowall may find it difficult to get to the bank and pay it in. There will then be a further delay while the cheque is passed through head office in London, or through the clearing house if he banks with a different bank from ours. During this time-lag, our Bank Account will show that we have deducted the cheque from our available funds, but the bank will think that we still have this money. Sometimes, when a creditor puts a cheque in his pocket and forgets to pay it in, several months may pass before the two accounts agree on this point. *Neither of them is wrong*, and it would be a mistake to 'correct' them or take any action—we must simply wait for Mr McDowall to put the matter right by getting down to the bank in his local town and paying the cheque into his account. *Such a situation would be explained in the bank reconciliation statement*, which, as its name implies is a written statement explaining a difference between the two accounts.

(*b*) Now imagine it is the last day of the month, and we are going to the bank to collect a bank statement which the bank has already promised to prepare for us. Incidentally, while we are down there we will pay in those cheques that arrived this morning in the mail from customers. Before setting off we record these cheques in the Bank Account, on the debit side, and list them in the paying-in book. On arrival at the bank we greet the cashier, pay in the cheques and collect the bank statement. This bank statement however will not be completely up to date, because the cheques just paid in will not appear upon it. The cashier cannot stop work to update our bank statement, because a queue of people is waiting for attention. *Instead we shall have to explain the difference between the Bank Account and the bank statement by a sentence or two in the bank reconciliation statement.*

20.3 How to Prepare a Bank Reconciliation Statement

Consider the cash book (bank columns only) and the bank statement shown in Fig. 20.1.

The following points are of interest:

(*a*) Note that the items which appear as debits on A. Ryder's cash book are credits on the bank statement. This appears confusing, but in fact it is only sensible, because the bank keeps its account with Ryder from its point of view and not Ryder's point of view. If Ryder has more cash in the bank (a debit entry in Ryder's cash book) it means the bank owes him more money, i.e. he is a creditor for a greater amount (a credit entry in Ryder's account in the bank).

(*b*) Note that on January 1st the two accounts were different, Ryder thought he had £494·24 while the bank thought he had £508·40. Where there was a discrepancy to start with like this, it was clearly due to a time-lag on the account, and we should expect it to be cleared up at some time in the month under consideration. As we can see, in this case, the outstanding cheque was cleared up on January 3rd when someone (a creditor) presented a cheque for £14·16 for payment. This made the two accounts agree.

(*c*) Ryder must now compare the two accounts to see which items are different. Looking down Ryder's debit column (and the bank statement credit column) we can see that there are two differences. These are:

(i) £14·94 from R. Loring was paid into the bank on the last day of the month. Clearly the bank have not yet credited Ryder with the value of this cheque. It is a 'time-lag' item and must be explained on the bank reconciliation statement.

A. Ryder—Cash Book (Bank columns only)

19..			£	19..			£
Jan. 1	Balance	B/d	494·24	Jan. 2	T. Wilson	L 72	71·65
5	Sales	L 21	62·80	13	UDC	L 33	30·50
12	Sales	L 21	75·00	15	Cash	C	60·00
14	T. Bainbridge	L 44	12·56	29	R. Long	L 56	48·00
19	Sales	L 21	35·00	31	Anne Employee	L 5	120·00
26	Sales	L 21	85·00	31	Balance	c/d	449·39
31	R. Loring	L 57	14·94				
			£779·54				£779·54
Jan. 31	Balance	B/d	449·39				

A. Ryder—Bank Statement
In account with Barclays Bank PLC

Date	Details	Dr.	Cr.	Balance
		£	£	£
1.1.19..	Bal. c/fwd			508·40
3.1.19..	Cheque	14·16		494·24
5.1.19..	Sundries		62·80	557·04
12.1.19..	Sundries		75·00	632·04
14.1.19..	Cheque	30·50		601·54
14.1.19..	Sundries		12·56	614·10
15.1.19..	Cheque	60·00		554·10
19.1.19..	Sundries		35·00	589·10
26.1.19..	Sundries		85·00	674·10
29.1.19..	Cheque	48·00		626·10
30.1.19..	Charges	4·55		621·55
30.1.19..	International Investors (transfer)		12·80	634·35

Fig. 20.1 A Bank Account and a bank statement

(ii) £12·80 has been transferred by a firm called International Investors to Ryder's account. This must be a dividend on his investments and needs to be entered in his cash book—he was not aware that the bank had collected this money on his account.

Running our eyes down the credit side of Ryder's account (and down the debit column on the bank statement) we see that there are four further differences, of which one has already been referred to in (b) above. This leaves three further outstanding points. They are:

(iii) The cheque for £71·65 paid to T. Wilson on January 2nd has not yet been presented by him for collection through the bankers' clearing house. This is a 'time-lag' item and will need to be explained on the bank reconciliation statement.

(iv) On January 30th the bank deducted £4·55 bank charges from Ryder's account. This needs to be entered in the cash book, since it is the first Ryder has heard about the bank's actions.

(v) On January 31st the cheque paid to Anne Employee, £120·00, has not yet been presented for payment. This is similar to Wilson's cheque in (iii) above.

The first thing to do is to bring the Bank Account up to date by including items (ii) and (iv) above (see Fig. 20.2).

A. Ryder—Cash Book (Bank columns only)

19..			£	19..			£
Jan. 31	Balance	B/d	449·39	Jan. 31	Bank Charges		4·55
31	Dividends				Balance	c/d	457·64
	Received		12·80				
			£462·19				£462·19
Feb. 1	Balance	B/d	457·64				

Fig. 20.2 Updating the cash book

We are now ready to draw up the bank reconciliation statement. This requires us to start either with the cash-book balance or the bank-statement balance, and explain why it is in fact a perfectly good figure if the outstanding items are taken into account. We do this by working towards the other figure. Careful reading of the example in Fig. 20.3 will make this explanation clear.

Bank Reconciliation Statement
(as at January 31st 19..)

		£
Balance as per cash book =		457·64
Deduct cheque paid in, not yet cleared		
R. Loring		14·94
(*because the bank does not regard us as*		
having yet received the money)		442·70
Add back cheques drawn but		
not yet presented for payment		
T. Wilson	71·65	
Anne Employee	120·00	
(*because the bank regards us as*		191·65
still having this money)		
Balance as per bank statement		£634·35

Fig. 20.3 Reconciling the cash book and the bank statement

This statement satisfactorily reconciles the Bank Account with the bank statement, and we may therefore feel content that no errors on the bank's or cashier's part have occurred.

A neat copy of the bank reconciliation statement will be typed and filed away for reference purposes.

20.4 Exercises Set 26: Bank Reconciliation Statements

1. Enter in the Bank Account of R. Lawrence, starting with the balance shown below, any item that needs to be entered. Then prepare a bank reconciliation statement from the following particulars:

	£
Cash at bank as per bank statement on March 31st 19. .	254·36
Cheques received and paid into the bank but not yet entered in bank statement	126·55
Cheques drawn and entered in the cash book but not yet presented to the bank	187·10
Interest charged by the bank but not yet entered in the cash book	15·40
On March 31st the bank column of the cash book showed a debit balance of	209·21

2. On April 30th 19. . B. Grant's cash book showed a balance at the bank of £404·24 but at the same date the monthly statement from his bank showed a balance of £425·50.

The difference between the two balances was found to be due to the following:

(a) On April 10th a charge of £1·45 for foreign-exchange commission had been made by the bank. Grant had forgotten to deduct this on his cash book.

(b) An annual subscription of £5·25 had been paid by standing order on April 25th. This had also been overlooked by Grant.

(c) Cheques for £25·30 and £42·45 drawn in favour of D. Jones and T. Fortescue had not been presented for payment by them.

(d) A cheque for £39·79 from R. Sterling paid into the bank on April 15th had been returned marked 'Refer to Drawer—No Account'. No entry of this dishonour had been made in the cash book.

You are asked to open Grant's cash book (bank columns only) on April 30th with the balance of £404·24; to enter such items as need to be entered; to balance off the cash book again, and then, using this new balance, prepare a bank reconciliation statement as at April 30th 19. . for any remaining items.

3. On March 31st 19. . the balance in the bank account as shown in the cash book of C. Roper was £485·00. On checking the cash book with the bank statement, he discovered the following differences:

(a) Cheques credited in the cash book but not yet presented for payment—£142·00.

(b) The bank statement did not include cheques paid into the bank on March 31st, and debited in the cash book on that day, worth £137·50.

(c) The bank had charged his account with £8·25 charges, and had credited his account with £18·50, being a dividend received by the bank on his behalf. Neither of these items had been entered in the cash book.

(d) The bank statement balance was £499·75.

You are required

    (i) to adjust the cash-book balance, and

    (ii) to reconcile the adjusted balance with the balance on the bank statement at March 31st 19. .

4. Here are the Bank Account and bank statement of L. Roberts for the last week of June 19. .

Cash Book (Bank columns only)

			£				£		
June 25	Balance	B/d	284·50	June 29	Knight		34·90		
26	Jones		50·00	29	Harvey		72·60		
28	Brown		110·25	29	Roach		5·55		
29	Smith		35·45	30	Rudolfo		4·72		
				30	Balance	c/d	362·43		
			£480·20				£480·20		
30	Balance	B/d	362·43						

Bank Statements (as at June 30th 19. .)

Date	Details	Dr.	Cr.	Balance
		£	£	£
June 25	Balance			284·50
26	Cheque		5·00	289·50
28	Cheque		110·25	399·75
29	Cheque	34·90		364·85
29	Charges	4·30		360·55
30	Credit transfer (H. Neale)		42·60	403·15

You are asked

(a) to correct the cash book, bearing in mind that the cheque from Jones was really only £5·00.

(b) to reconcile the new cash balance with the bank-statement balance.

5. (a) Your cash book shows a balance of £350·00. Cheques drawn but not presented total £135·00. What should be the balance according to your bank?

(b) A standing order for £20·00 has not been entered in your cash book. If your bank statement shows a balance of £450·00, what should be the balance in your cash book before the standing order is recorded?

(c) Your bank statement shows a balance of £700·00. Cheques drawn but not presented total £140·00. What should be the balance in your cash book?

(d) A traveller paid £150·00 into your account. His notification was lost in the post. If your bank statement shows a balance of £780·00, what should be the balance in your cash book?

6. Below are given the cash book and bank statement of a trader D. Stevenson. You are required

   (a) to bring the cash book up to date, starting with the balance brought down on July 1st, and then

   (b) to prepare a statement reconciling the corrected cash book balance with the balance shown by the bank statement.

Cash Book (Bank columns only)

			£				£
June 24	Balance	B/d	600·00	June 25	Neil and Son		40·00
27	Cash		50·00	27	Riley		15·00
28	Lucas		8·15	28	Morris		10·12
30	Smithers		22·10	28	White		41·13
30	Jones		15·15	30	Balance	c/d	589·15
			£695·40				£695·40
July 1	Balance	B/d	£589·15				

Bank Statement

		Dr. £	Cr. £	£
June 24	Balance			617·04
25	Neil and Son	40·00		577·04
26	Cash		50·00	627·04
26	Grey	17·04		610·00
27	Riley	15·00		595·00
28	Lucas		8·15	603·15
	Brown (Credit transfer)		10·00	613·15
30	Charges	5·25		607·90

7. At close of business on February 28th 19.., A. Trader's cash book showed a balance of £1 017·12, which did not agree with his bank statement, the following being sources of disagreement:

   (a) Cheques issued but not presented: Green £115·10; Riley £237·50; Stokes £38·00.

   (b) Lodgement February 28th not credited by bank: £185·15.

   (c) Traders' credits not entered in cash book: Boxer £5·75; Striker £16·60.

   (d) A standing order for £10·50, being subscription to a trade association, had been paid by the bank but not entered in the cash book.

   (e) A charge of £4·22 had been made by the bank for operating the account, but had not been entered in the cash book.

You are required to
(i) make such entries in the cash book as will result in the correct balance being shown;
(ii) prepare a statement accounting for the difference between your corrected cash book and the bank statement balance;
(iii) show on the statement required in (ii) the balance per the bank statement. (COS)

8. The balance at the bank on March 31st 19.. according to R. Green's cash book was £1 318·52. Checking against his bank statement revealed the following discrepancies:
(a) Cheques drawn but not presented
Abbott   £111·74
Moser   £83·88
Raven   £201·95
(b) Amount deposited but not credited by bank: £538·22.
(c) Traders' credits received by bank but not entered in Green's cash book
Blanche   £4·42
Peters   £103·08
(d) Standing order paid by bank but not entered in cash book by Green in favour of Trade Protection Society   £10·50
(e) Bank charges not entered in cash book   £4·46.
You are required to
(i) reopen the cash book, making such entries as are necessary;
(ii) prepare a statement reconciling your revised cash-book balance with the balance shown by the bank statement.

(COS)

9. Set out below are the cash book (bank columns only) and bank statement of E. Hemingway for the month of January 19.. You are asked to
(a) reopen the cash book with the balance of £1 192·13 and enter such items as have clearly not yet been entered (this will enable you to find a new balance as per cash book);
(b) draw up a bank reconciliation statement as at January 31st, which reconciles your new cash balance with the bank statement balance.

Cash Book (Bank columns only)

19..				£	19..				£
Jan.	1	To Balance	B/d	1 027·16	Jan.	5	By R. Palmer		14·18
	13	,, Smith		16·18		7	,, Wages		18·10
	13	,, Cash		54·10		19	,, T. Burton		7·12
	27	,, Lovell		7·12		21	,, Wages		18·10
	27	,, Cash		42·01		28	,, L. Mannheim		10·99
	31	,, Whiteley		114·05		31	,, Balance	c/d	1 192·13
				£1 260·62					£1 260·62
Jan.	31	,, Balance	B/d	1 192·13					

Bank Statement (as at January 31st 19..)

Date		Details	Dr. £	Cr. £	Balance £
Jan.	1	—			1 027·16
	7	Drawings	18·10		1 009·06
	9	R. Palmer	14·18		994·88
	13	Sundries		70·28	1 065·16
	21	Drawings	18·10		1 047·06
	21	H.M. Treasury Interest		12·15	1 059·21
	24	Bank Charges	5·55		1 053·66
	27	Sundries		49·13	1 102·79
	28	L. Mannheim	10·99		1 091·80

10. The following statement was received from the bank, indicating M. Lowe's position during the month of January.

Bank Statement (as at January 31st 19..)

			Dr. £	Cr. £	Balance £
Jan.	1	Balance			402·55
	4	Sundries		74·50	477·05
	5	Credit transfer (R. Johnson)		168·50	645·55
	9	Drawings	140·00		505·55
	10	Sundries		186·50	692·05
	12	Dividend (Bank of England)		25·00	717·05
	17	Sundries		195·40	912·45
	20	Charges	8·50		903·95
	23	Drawings	146·00		757·95
	24	Sundries		227·25	985·20
	30	Drawings	138·50		846·70
	30	Sundries		242·60	1089·30

Checked against the Cash Book, the following discrepancies were revealed:

(a) The sundries item paid in on January 10th had been accidentally omitted altogether from Lowe's cash book.

(b) Three cheques drawn in the last few days of the month had not yet been presented by

      A. Nicholls   £42·50
      B. Lamb   £1·55
      C. Forrester   £108·20

(c) Johnson's credit transfer, the Dividend and the Bank charges had not previously been notified to Lowe.

(d) Cash paid in on January 31st does not appear on the bank statement, £150·55.

(e) The foreign-exchange department of his local bank had requested Lowe by post to authorize an automatic debit transfer connected with his subscription to an American magazine. Lowe had deducted this year's £10·50 from his cash book but the debit transfer had not yet reached his bank.

You are required

(i) to state which of the above items need to be entered in Lowe's cash book;

(ii) to draw up a bank reconciliation statement starting with the balance shown above, and bring out the final cash-book balance.

Capital and Revenue Expenditure and Receipts

21.1 The Distinction Between Capital and Revenue Items

Years ago, the distinctions between capital and revenue expenditure, and capital and revenue receipts were not matters of much concern. Recently these distinctions have acquired great importance, because of high taxation. Tax systems are chiefly based upon the taxation of income. A businessman's income can only be determined if we calculate what he has received each year by way of fees, commissions and other business receipts, and set against these earnings the costs of achieving them. It becomes necessary to sort out what he has received this year from what he already had—the accumulated capital of an earlier period. A study of taxation is not required in a book which is about the principles of accounting, but the concepts of capital and revenue expenditure, and capital and revenue receipts are of fundamental importance to the determination of profits, and are necessary if 'correct' profit figures are to be found. You may wonder why the word 'correct' is written in quotation marks. The reason is that there is no one way of determining profit—there are many areas which are debatable, and businessmen often go to law with the Inland-Revenue authorities, to determine the 'correct' way of determining profits. In many such disputes the distinction between capital and revenue expenditure is at the centre of the discussion.

21.2 Capital and Revenue Expenditure

Whenever we spend money we receive something in return. These items may be classified as follows:

(a) Items which last a long time, and are used in the business over a period of years. These are called *capital assets* or capital expenditure. Examples are land and buildings, plant and machinery, fixtures and fittings, motor vehicles, leases on property, patent rights.

(b) Items which do not last a long time, but are quickly used for the benefit of the business and are then lost for all time. Examples would be postage stamps, telephone calls, petrol and oil for motor vehicles. These are called *revenue items*, or revenue expenditure.

(c) Items which are purchased for resale, or purchased for manufacture before being resold. In many cases the whole purpose of the business is to manufacture a finished product from certain raw materials. Moreover the intention is to do so in the minimum possible time, without taking years over the matter, so that all such items may be regarded as *revenue items.*

(d) Services, which are obtained in return for the money paid. These services are usually the result of contracts of service (employees) or contracts for services (outside contractors). Whichever they are, they may usually be regarded as relatively short term, and therefore be counted as *revenue items*.

It follows that the duration of use of an item—how long it lasts—is crucial in deciding whether it is capital or revenue expenditure. The dividing line chosen is one year, because the Government claims its share of the rewards of any enterprise annually. Therefore the following definitions are appropriate.

Capital expenditure *is expenditure on items which last longer than a year, and which therefore have an enduring influence on the profit-making capacity of the business.*

Revenue expenditure *is expenditure on consumable items, on services and on goods for re-sale. They last less than one year, and therefore only temporarily influence the profit-making capacity of the business.*

In fact, at the end of any given year, there will be some revenue items which are still in hand and which will pass over to the new year, even though they were purchased in the previous year. These items have to be the subject of *adjustments* and are dealt with fully in Section 26.3—7.

Using the definitions above to determine whether expenditures are capital or revenue, you should look at the examples given below, quoted from an imaginary manufacturing firm.

   (i) Purchase of a new factory: capital expenditure.
  (ii) Plant and machinery to equip the factory: capital expenditure.
 (iii) Wages for employees: revenue expenditure.
 (iv) Salary of factory manager: revenue expenditure.
  (v) Interest on money borrowed from bank: revenue expenditure.
 (vi) Raw material purchases: revenue expenditure.
(vii) Office equipment (typewriters, etc.): capital expenditure.
(viii) Office software (stationery, documents, etc.): revenue expenditure.
 (ix) Repairs and redecorations: (*prima facie*) revenue expenditure, but the management may decide to spread the payment over several years.
  (x) Goodwill payment on purchase of a marketing area to assist disposal of new product: capital expenditure.

21.3   Capital and Revenue Receipts

When a business receives money it may be a contribution by the proprietor, partners or shareholders towards the capital of the firm, in other words a *capital receipt*. Alternatively it may be a result of the firm's activity in the current period, part of its rewards for offering goods or services to the public. Such items would include payments received from customers and debtors for goods supplied, or fees received for services rendered. All such items are *revenue receipts*, and must be set against the revenue expenses in order to determine the profitability of the business for the period under discussion.

The only other kind of receipt is a receipt of money when a loan or a mortgage on property is arranged. This is like a contribution of capital to the business by someone outside the business, not the proprietor. It is regarded as a capital item, but the interest charged for the use of the money will be a revenue expense of the period in which it becomes due.

21.4 The Calculation of Profits—Revenue Accounts

We have already seen that capital expenditure and capital receipts do not enter into the calculation of a businessman's profit for taxation purposes. It is only the revenue expenditure and revenue receipts which are set against one another to discover the profit or loss on the period concerned. This, we already know, is done in the Trading Account and Profit and Loss Account of a business enterprise. However some businesses find the terms Profit and Loss distasteful or inappropriate. Thus doctors do not like to say 'We made a profit of £25·50 out of Farmer Brown's broken leg', and organizations like the Royal Automobile Club would not speak of 'making a profit out of the members'.

For these reasons, the following names have been devised over the years:

(a) *Revenue Account*—for a professional partnership of lawyers, doctors, dentists, etc. This is the account where revenue expenditure will be set against revenue receipts to discover the excess of fees over expenses.

(b) *Trading and Profit and Loss Accounts*—the accounts used by business enterprises to discover profits over a period by setting revenue expenditure against revenue receipts.

(c) *Income and Expenditure Accounts*—the name given to the accounts of a non-profit-making body to determine the surplus, or deficit, contributed by the members.

These three names all refer to very similar accounts.

(1) Capital Receipts and Profits—a Possible Error

Clearly, if a businessman brings in extra capital, this will be a capital receipt and should not be counted as profit. There are certain types of business where there might be some danger of the income-tax authorities making this mistake. These are businesses where no proper books of account are kept, i.e. businesses with *incomplete records* (see Section 30.2). If a petty trader does not keep records of his receipts and expenses the tax authorities usually adopt a simple system for discovering the profit. They value the business each year at the beginning and end of the year. Suppose A. Trader's business is worth £100·00 at the start of the year and £2 100·00 at the end of the year. Clearly the extra wealth must have come from the profitable nature of his business. Not only this, but he has also lived through the year. The tax authorities will take the increased wealth £2 000·00 and add on the trader's estimate of drawings for the year. Suppose he gave his wife £30·00 per week and had £15·00 for his own pocket. This makes £2 340·00 per year. Thus they would levy tax on earnings of £4 340·00—clearly a profitable business. However if A. Trader points out that because of a legacy from a relation he actually contributed £1 500·00 extra capital, then this must be deducted from the £4 340·00 and reduces the taxable earnings to £2 840·00.

To arrive at a true earnings figure for any business we must set the revenue expenditure against the revenue receipts only, and find the difference between them.

21.5 Arriving at a 'True' Profit Figure

In order to arrive at a true profit figure we must obey the following rules:

(a) *Revenue expenditure*—ensure that the period under consideration carries every penny of loss that it should carry, but not a penny more.

(b) *Revenue receipts*—ensure that the period under consideration is credited with every penny earned in the period, but not a penny more.

To ensure these two things, we become involved in a number of adjustments. These adjustments are concerned with two ideas, the capitalization (even if only for a short while) of revenue expenditure and the *revenue-ization* of capital expenditure. Revenue-ization is an awkward word, but it is used to convey the idea of converting a capital item into a revenue item.

(1) The Capitalization of Revenue Expenditure

Sometimes we pay out money (revenue expenditure) for something which eventually becomes a capital asset. Thus we might employ our workmen to extend the factory canteen, or to erect machinery and shelving, belting systems, etc. If we were to charge these expenses as a loss in the Profit and Loss Account, we should be making this year bear the entire loss for an asset that will last several years. To overcome this difficulty we capitalize the revenue expenditure, removing it from the 'loss' account and transferring it to an asset account.

Consider the following example:

A. Shopkeeper is a builder's merchant. He also undertakes small contracts for householders in the area, employing six members of staff for the purpose. In February there is little work about, and he decides to use this labour force to redesign the shop premises and redecorate. The labour cost involved, (that is, wages) is £245·00, and materials are used from stock at a cost of £450·00. The premises are calculated to increase in value by £1 000·00 as a result. Make the entries as at February 28th to capitalize this revenue expenditure.

How should Shopkeeper record these matters in his account? Clearly the wages will already have been debited in Wages Account and the materials will be debited in Purchases Account. What he has to do is to capitalize the revenue expenditure, changing it to a capital asset—premises—instead of two revenue losses—wages and purchases. In addition he has made a profit out of the work, since the premises are now believed to be worth £1 000·00 extra. This profit is to be treated as a capital profit, not a revenue profit, and will be credited to Appreciation of Buildings Account. The Journal entry will be as shown in Fig. 21.1.

19.. Feb. 28				£	£ J 111
	Premises A/c Dr.	L 1		1 000·00	
	Wages A/c	L 25			245·00
	Purchases A/c	L 38			450·00
	Appreciation of Buildings A/c	L 152			305·00
	Being capitalization of revenue expenditure incurred in improving shop layout				

Fig. 21.1 Capitalizing revenue expenditure

The Journal entries, assuming some imaginary figures already existing on the accounts, would be as shown in Fig. 21.2.

Premises A/c   L 1

19..			£	
Jan. 1 Balance	B/d		6 000·00	
Feb. 28 Wages etc.	J 111		1 000·00	

Wages A/c   L 25

19..			£	19..			£
Jan. 31 Cash	CB	5	280·00	Feb. 28 Premises A/c	J 111		245·00
Feb. 28 Cash	CB	17	330·00				

Purchases A/c   L 38

19..			£	19..			£
Jan. 31 Sundry Creditors	PDB	11	4 875·00	Feb. 28 Premises A/c	J 111		450·00
Feb. 28 Sundry Creditors	PDB	16	3 850·00				

Appreciation of Buildings A/c   L 152

				19..			£
				Feb. 28 Premises A/c	J 111		305·00

Fig. 21.2 Ledger accounts affected by capitalization of revenue expenditure

(2) The 'Revenue-ization' of Capital Expenditure

There is of course no such word as 'revenue-ization', but it is used here to convey the idea that all capital assets do eventually get written off to Profit and Loss Account over the years of their useful life. The proper term for this process is *depreciation*, and it is discussed in Unit Twenty-two. Here it is only necessary to say that where we are attempting to calculate the profits of a trading period we must ensure that the Profit and Loss Account is debited with every penny of loss that it ought really to carry. If the trading period has used up some of the life of an asset; whether it is machinery, furniture, loose tools, patent rights, royalties owned or any other asset that is slowly consumed in the service of the business, then that asset must be depreciated by a 'fair' amount for the use made during the year, or other period concerned.

21.6 Doubtful Cases—Capital or Revenue Expenditure

Sometimes it is difficult to decide whether an item should be treated as capital or revenue expenditure. Capital expenditure lasts longer than a year, and gives us something of permanent benefit to the firm. There are some expenses which seem to do the first part, without doing the second. For example, repainting the premises usually lasts several years, but it only gives

Repairs and Decorations Suspense A/c					L 77
19..		£	19..		£
May 31 Bank A/c	J 15	600·00	Dec. 31 Profit and Loss		
			A/c	J 29	150·00
			31 Balance	c/d	450·00
		£600·00			£600·00
Next year			Next year		
Jan. 1 Balance	B/d	450·00	Dec. 31 Profit and Loss		
			A/c	J 58	150·00
			31 Balance	c/d	300·00
		£450·00			£450·00
Year 3			Year 3		
Jan. 1 Balance	B/d	300·00	Dec. 31 Profit and Loss		
			A/c	J 98	150·00
			31 Balance	c/d	150·00
		£300·00			£300·00
Year 4			Year 4		
Jan. 1 Balance	B/d		Dec. 31 Profit and Loss		
		£150·00	A/c	J 145 £150·00

Fig. 21.3 Temporary capitalization of a revenue expense

us a property that is restored to its original new condition—no extra value is really added—though the deterioration of the premises may be avoided. In such cases it is up to the accountant to make up his mind what to do. Most accountants would probably feel that the considerable expenditure involved should be spread over more than one year—otherwise this year's profits will take a serious knock. Probably a decision to capitalize the revenue expenditure and spread it out over this year and the next three years would be a sound idea. To do this we could open a Repairs and Decorations Suspense Account, and write it off in four instalments. This account is shown in Fig. 21.3.

21.7 Stock Losses

Some expenses need *not* be written off as losses of the business, because they will automatically be taken account of when we take stock. For example if we suffer losses of stock due to accidental damage, or even due to pilfering by the staff or shop-lifting by the customers, these losses need not be entered as losses in the Profit and Loss Account. They will automatically be picked up as losses when we count stock. When the stock is counted, they will not be there to count and so the stocktaking figure will be correspondingly lower than it should be. To enter such items a second time as losses would be to reduce the profits twice for the same loss.

Another example that has the same effect is losses of stock caused by perishable items which go bad. The spoiled items are disposed of and stocks reduced. There is no point in writing these off as losses; they will automatically reduce the stock figure. What we should do, though, is find out why the buyer concerned overbought—clearly it is bad buying to purchase perishable goods which are then left unsold. If you go to any supermarket on a Saturday afternoon you will hear the loudspeakers pushing the sales of perishable items like lettuces, tomatoes and bananas. Prices are reduced to dispose of goods likely to spoil over the week-end.

Some firms do run *perpetual inventory procedures*. These are systems where a team of specialist stock-takers is at work all the year round. Such firms deal with stock losses in rather a different way from smaller firms, and may not disregard the losses as explained above. For ordinary firms not using *perpetual inventory* there is no need to write off stock losses; they are automatically accounted for when stock is counted.

21.8 Exercises Set 27: Capital and Revenue Expenditure

1. Define capital expenditure and revenue expenditure. What is the importance of the distinction?

2. What is a capital receipt? What is a revenue receipt? The Inspector of Taxes for Alfred Jones' area tells him that as his business was worth only £1 500·00 on January 1st of last year, and by December 31st it was worth

£6 500·00, he must have made £5 000·00 profit in the year. Jones had expanded his business by selling £4 000·00 of investments which were his personal property purchased many years earlier. He used the proceeds to retool and re-equip the business. He now asks you to write a letter for him rejecting the tax inspector's suggestion. What would you say?

3. (a) Writing about four or five lines on each, explain what is meant by
     (i) capital expenditure;
     (ii) revenue expenditure.
   (b) Give *two* examples of each type of expenditure.
   (c) A monkey escapes from the pet shop next door and rushes in to A. Chinaseller's shop. It breaks
     (i) a display of china valued at £16·00, part of the stock to be sold;
     (ii) the shop window, worth £25·00 which was unfortunately not insured.
   Explain whether it would be necessary to write these items off as losses at the end of the financial year and give your reasons. The pet-shop owner is insolvent and cannot pay any compensation.

(East Anglian Examination Board)

4. State whether the following transactions of a sports club should be classified as capital expenditure or revenue expenditure.
   (a) The redecoration of the club premises.
   (b) The installation of a new wine bar.
   (c) The building of an extension to the club dressing rooms.
   (d) The purchase of wines and spirits.
   (e) The purchase of a record player for use in the club lounge.

(RSA 1)

5. Explain briefly the distinction between capital and revenue expenditure. State, with reasons, how you would classify each of the following two items:
   (a) Wages of own workmen on building an extension to a firm's factory, and
   (b) Cost of rebuilding the wall of a factory.

6. The Newtown Players have recently enjoyed such success in their dramatic activities that they have been able to make purchases to improve their organization. As specified in the club rules, the treasurer regards all consumable and breakable items as revenue expenditure. Which of the following items would you regard as capital and which as revenue expenditure?
   (a) Erection of a theatre for club use.
   (b) Make-up for the next presentation.
   (c) Membership fee for the British Drama League.
   (d) Stage fittings, wings and pillars.
   (e) Flash powder for special effects.

(f) Purchase of spotlights and dimmers.

(g) A club minibus for outside presentations.

(h) Crockery for refreshment service.

(i) Bar stocks.

(j) Tickets for next performance.

7. M. Larkin has the following items of expenditure on his books for the year.

(a) Wages paid to employees in warehouse—£5 800·00.

(b) Wages paid to these same workers who agreed to assist in redesigning the warehouse layout during the firm's annual fortnight holiday closure £360·00.

(c) Shelving and structural materials purchased for the redesigning programme £750·00.

(d) Fork-lift trucks £850·00.

(e) Purchases of goods for resale to stock warehouse after capacity had been increased £3 500·00.

Consider each of these items and state whether in your view it is capital expenditure or revenue expenditure. Then state whether the item would appear in the Trading Account, Profit and Loss Account or Balance Sheet.

8. The Linden Manufacturing Organization is setting up its own reprographic department. Write down the letters (a) to (j) to correspond with the items below, and write against them your opinion as to whether the item is capital or revenue expenditure.

(a) The purchase of a dyeline copying machine.

(b) Diazo copying paper for the above.

(c) A line-selection spirit duplicator.

(d) A hand-operated spirit duplicator.

(e) Transfer sheets and run-off paper for the above.

(f) Electricity bill for department.

(g) Salary of the reprographic manager.

(h) Supply of ink for offset litho machine.

(i) Hiring charge for an electrostatic copier.

(j) Guillotine for trimming copies.

9. Your employer A. Decorator asks you to explain why a stock of wallpaper, which was thrown away as useless, has not been entered on the Profit and Loss Account as a loss. Justify your failure to write this item off. It had been damaged by rainwater after a skylight was accidentally left open.

10. A motor-vehicle manufacturer is retooling a section which produces batches of components for use on the main assembly line. It means closing the section for two weeks. To avoid laying-off the men involved, he asks them to agree to act as labourers in the installation and

construction work going on. The following payments result from the re-equipment:

(a) Purchase of machines £16 000·00 on credit from Power Tools Ltd.

(b) Purchase of materials £450·00 on credit from Leigh Building Co.

(c) Wages of departmental staff for the fortnight £300·00.

(d) Wages of craftsmen, electricians, builders, etc., employed on installation (these men are specialists employed in the plant) £580·00.

All these items including the revenue items are to be capitalized as part of the Machinery Account. Show the Journal entry required on July 30th 19. .

11. Plastics Ltd. employ their own maintenance staff on the extension of their canteen premises. The labour involved is £580·00 and the materials cost £650·00. The value of the premises is increased by £2 000·00 as a result of the extension, the balance to be regarded as a capital profit and recorded in Appreciation on Buildings Account. Make the Journal entries necessary to record the above items in Plastics Ltd.'s records on July 14th 19. .

12. (a) Give three examples of capital expenditure that might be undertaken by a restaurant proprietor, and three examples of revenue expenditure that might be incurred by a garage owner.

(b) Smart Wear Ltd. spend £1 000·00 on redecorating their premises. They decide to regard this as lasting for five years, and to record it in a Decorations Suspense Account. At present £600·00 of it, which was paid as wages, is debited in Wages Account. The other £400·00, spent on materials, is included in Purchases Account after being posted there from the cash book. Do the Journal entry to capitalize this revenue expenditure at August 31st 19. .

Unit Twenty-Two
Depreciation

22.1 The Principles of Depreciation

Every capital asset, that is every purchase resulting from capital expenditure, wears out as the years go by. This is usually referred to as 'fair wear and tear', a decline in value of the asset as it renders service to the business. People who own motor vehicles know how lucky they are if they last longer than five years of steady wear and tear. By the end of that time repair bills begin to increase and breakdowns are more frequent. Sooner or later the inconvenience arising from the vehicle's uncertain behaviour leads to a decision to replace it.

The accounting term for this declining value of assets is *depreciation*. The principles that underlie depreciation may be listed as follows.

(*a*) *The idea that every year should carry a proper share of the burden of business expenses.* We have already mentioned this idea when discussing revenue expenditure (see Section 21.2). It is only a short step to extend the idea to include a fair share of the burden of capital losses incurred through fair wear and tear. Only if a year carries its full share of the losses of the business shall we arrive at a correct profit figure.

(*b*) *These losses should be spread evenly over the lifetime of the asset, unless there are very good reasons for not doing so.* Thus where a machine was only utilized in the manufacture of a particular article, and the number of articles made varied from year to year, there might be some case for depreciating the machine according to the use made of it in a particular year. Otherwise we try to equalize the charges made.

(*c*) *The assets must be correctly valued on the Balance Sheet.* If we do otherwise, the Balance Sheet does not give a 'true and fair view' of the assets of the business as required by law for limited companies. Although there is no actual legal requirement for sole traders and partnerships, it is still desirable that assets should be accurately valued on their Balance Sheets as well.

22.2 The Methods of Depreciation

There are several different methods of depreciation used in business, some of which are very sophisticated and difficult to calculate. Here we will consider the three commonest methods in use. These are:

(*a*) The 'equal-instalment' method, or 'straight-line' method.

(*b*) The diminishing-balance method.

(*c*) The revaluation-method.

22.3   The Equal-Instalment Method

With this method, the asset is written down in value each year by the same amount, the sum being calculated by the use of a formula, as follows:

$$Depreciation\ charge = \frac{Cost\ price\ of\ the\ asset - residual\ value}{Estimated\ lifetime\ in\ years}$$

Imagine that a machine costs £10000·00, and a further £2 500·00 is needed to erect it into position and install access features for the product it is to process. It is estimated to have a working life of ten years, and at the end of the time it will fetch £1 500·00 on sale to scrap dealers. The depreciation charge on the basis of the formula given above will be

$$\frac{£12\ 500 - £1\ 500}{10} = £1\ 100\ per\ annum$$

The asset will appear on the books as shown in Fig. 22.1.

	Machinery A/c				L 167
19.. (Year 1)		£	19..		£
Jan. 1 New Machine		10 000·00	Dec. 31 Depreciation A/c		1 100·00
1 Installation etc.		2 500·00	31 Balance c/d		11 400·00
		£12 500·00			£12 500·00
19.. (Year 2)			19..		
Jan. 1 Balance	B/d	11 400·00	Dec. 31 Depreciation A/c		1 100·00
			31 Balance c/d		10 300·00
		£11 400·00			£11 400·00
19.. (Year 3)					
Jan. 1 Balance	B/d	10 300·00			
	and so on over the years until				
19.. (Year 10)			19..		
Jan. 1 Balance	B/d	2 600·00	Dec. 31 Depreciation A/c		1 100·00
			31 Balance c/d		1 500·00
		£2 600·00			£2 600·00
19.. (Year 11)					
Jan. 1 Balance	B/d	1 500·00			

at this point steps will be taken to dispose of the machine

Fig. 22.1 Depreciation by the equal-instalment method

Advantages and Disadvantages of the Equal-Instalment Method
(a) *Advantages.*

(i) It is easy to understand, and the calculations are simple.

(ii) The valuation of the asset appearing on the balance sheet each year is reasonably fair, and complies with the Companies Acts in the vast majority of cases.

(b) *Disadvantages.*

(i) If a further machine was purchased, the amount now required to be written off needs to be recalculated (with a percentage method of depreciation such as the diminishing-balance method this is not necessary).

(ii) The charge to the Profit and Loss Account increases over the years, for in the first year or two repairs will be uncommon, but as the machine gets older it will require more frequent attention. Suppose that in Year 1 the repairs cost £80·00, and in Year 8 they cost £650·00. The charge against the Profit and Loss Account in Year 1 totals £1 180·00 and in Year 8 it is £1 750·00.

Both these criticisms are overcome by the use of the diminishing-balance method.

22.4   The Diminishing-Balance Method

Under the diminishing-balance method a fixed percentage of the diminishing value of the asset is written off each year. Thus the depreciation percentage

	Machinery A/c			L 167
19.. Year 1	£	19..		£
Jan. 1 New Machine	10 000·00	Dec. 31 Depreciation A/c		
1 Installation, etc.	2 500·00	(20%)		2 500·00
		31 Balance	c/d	10 000·00
	£12 500·00			£12 500·00
19.. Year 2		19..		
Jan. 1 Balance B/d	10 000·00	Dec. 31 Depreciation A/c		2 000·00
		31 Balance	c/d	8 000·00
	£10 000·00			£10 000·00
19.. Year 3		19..		
Jan. 1 Balance B/d	8 000·00	Dec. 31 Depreciation A/c		1 600·00
		31 Balance	c/d	6 400·00
	£ 8 000·00			£ 8 000·00
19.. Year 4				
Jan. 1 Balance B/d	6 400·00			
	and so on over the years until			
19.. Year 10		19..		
Jan. 1 Balance B/d	1 678·00	Dec. 31 Depreciation A/c		336·00
		31 Balance	c/d	1 342·00
	£ 1 678·00			£ 1 678·00
19.. Year 11				
Jan. 1 Balance B/d	1 342·00			

(Note that the balance has come down lower than the residual value of £1 500·00. This is because 20 per cent was deducted instead of 19 per cent.)

Fig. 22.2 Depreciation by the diminishing-balance method

might be agreed at 20 per cent and one-fifth of the value at the start of the year be written off each year. The calculations involved in deciding the correct percentage are outside the range of our study here, but in the Machinery Account just considered they work out to about 19 per cent. Taking 20 per cent as a more convenient figure, you will see that this is one-fifth of the diminishing value of the asset, a much larger percentage than was written off under the equal-instalment method. The actual deductions, however, only come to about the same figure over the full lifetime of the asset, because the percentage deduction is being made only on the diminishing balance, and consequently the actual amount written off gets less every year. Figure 22.2 shows the figures over the ten-year period.

Advantages and Disadvantages of the Diminishing-Balance Method

(a) *Advantages.*

(i) It gives a more even charge against the profits, since the decreasing charges for depreciation each year cancel out the increasing charges for repairs. Thus the charges shown in Fig. 22.2 in ten years might be as follows:

		£
Year 1	Depreciation	2 500·00
	Repairs (say)	80·00
	Charge to Profit and Loss Account	£2 580·00

		£
Year 10	Depreciation	336·00
	Repairs (say)	2 200·00
	Charge to Profit and Loss Account	£2 536·00

Of course this is only a very 'rough and ready' way of equalizing the charge to Profit and Loss Account, but it is better than the previous method from this point of view.

(ii) No recalculation is necessary when further assets are purchased.

(b) *Disadvantages.*

(i) The percentage figure to be deducted each year is difficult to calculate.

(ii) For assets with a very short life, the percentage figure is so high that it becomes ridiculous. Thus, an asset with a life of two years only, would need to be written off by 99 per cent to remove it from the books in two years. Thus a £1 000 machine would be reduced by £990 in the first year—leaving a £10 balance, and 99 per cent of that, £9·90, would be written off in Year 2. Clearly this is not a very sensible percentage, and in particular it gives an unsatisfactory Balance-Sheet value at the end of Year 1. The asset would appear on the books after half its useful life at one-hundredth of its original value. This hardly gives a 'true and fair view' of the asset as required by the **Companies Acts.**

22.5   The Revaluation Method

Sometimes it is impossible to treat a particular kind of asset in the ways outlined. For example a Herd Account in farm accounting cannot be depreciated in a regular way at all. Animals are maturing, bearing young, changing and declining as the years go by. It is ridiculous to say that a cow has depreciated 10 per cent in the year, especially if she has borne two calves. Similarly even in engineering there are certain tools which are very expensive to make, whose value cannot be said to decline in use, and indeed they may even appreciate in value. Such items could be the very expensive presses for stamping out plastic articles. These may cost £5 000·00 or £10 000·00 to produce, but if well cared for will have very long lives indeed.

When it comes to the end of a year the best solution to the problem of whether these items have, or have not depreciated, is to revalue them. An independent valuer, preferably, is asked to appraise them and give a figure for their value. The difference in value can then be taken into account, or the better method is to write off the whole of the old value to Profit and Loss Account and bring in the whole of the new value as a profit. The accounting effect of these entries is shown below, in Journal-entry form. Consider the following example.

Example

Farmer Giles's Herd Account shows a value on his books at January 1st, 19.. of £12 785·00. On December 31st the herd is valued at £13 980·00. Record these matters in his Journal and post to the appropriate accounts.

19.. Dec.	31	Profit and Loss A/c Dr. Herd A/c Being valuation of herd at start of year transferred to Profit and Loss A/c at this date	L 192 L 73	£ 12 785·00	J 27 £ 12 785·00
Dec.	31	Herd A/c Dr. Profit and Loss A/c Being new valuation of herd at close of year brought on to books as an asset at this date	L 73 L 192	13 980·00	13 980·00

Herd A/c

19..			£	19.. Dec. 31 Profit and			£
Jan.	1 Balance	J 1	12 785·00	Loss A/c	J 27	12 785·00
Jan.	1 Profit and Loss A/c	J 27	13 980·00			

(contd. on page 220)

	Profit and Loss A/c		L 192
19.. Dec. 31 Herd A/c	£12 785·00	19.. Dec. 31 Herd A/c	£13 980·00

Fig. 22.3 Changing asset valuation directly entered into the Profit and Loss Account (by-passing Depreciation Account)

An alternative method would have been to find the increased value—in this case £1 195·00—and enter it to the debit of Herd Account and the credit of Profit and Loss Account.

22.6 The Amortization of Leases

When a lease on property is obtained, it is usually granted for a term of years. This phrase includes fractions of a year, so that some leases may only be weekly or monthly leases. Special considerations enter into the use of property in this way. Therefore if a lease is for ten years when it is obtained, usually on payment of a lump sum, it will only have nine years to run one year after purchase, eight years to run two years after purchase, etc. The final year the tenant must either move out, or renew the lease. The old leasehold rights are said to have died, and can only be brought to life by a new agreement. Clearly we ought to recognize the gradual dying away of the leasehold rights over the course of the lifetime of the lease and this is called *amortization* (from the French word *mort*—dead).

Amortization is simply a special case of the straight-line method, there being no residual value on the lease. The amortization charge is found by the formula

$$\frac{\text{Original cost of lease}}{\text{Lifetime of the lease}} = \text{Amortization charge}$$

It would simply be entered into Depreciation Account, after a simple Journal entry, as shown in Fig. 22.4.

						J 25
19.. Dec.	31	Depreciation A/c Dr. Lease A/c Being amortization of one year's life of a twenty-year lease	L 86 L 155	£ 250·00		£ 250·00

	Depreciation A/c		L 86
19.. Dec. 31 Lease A/c J 25	£ 250·00		

(contd. on page 221)

Lease A/c			L 155		
19..		£	19..		£
Jan. 1 Bank A/c (Lease			Dec. 31 Depreciation		
Purchase) J 5		5 000·00	A/c	J 25	250·00
			31 Balance	c/d	4 750·00
		£5 000·00			£5 000·00
Dec. 31 Balance B/d		4 750·00			

Fig. 22.4 Amortization of a lease

(1) Lease Dilapidations and Lease Renewals

One clause inserted in most leases is a dilapidations clause. Such a clause requires the leaseholder to return the property to the owner in the same condition as it was when he originally received it. This usually requires a sum of money to be paid for any repairs required to the property to restore it to its original condition.

A wise leaseholder will set aside sums of money to meet this contingency, and also to meet the cost of renewing the lease or purchasing another one when the present lease expires. The best thing to do is to invest this money, either in some institution like a building society or in a balanced portfolio of shares. This means that the leaseholder buys shares and debentures on the stock exchange, but reduces his risks by buying a variety of shares, so that if one firm gets into difficulties, it will be unlikely to represent a serious loss to the investor. Such investments are called *sinking funds* and they ensure that when the time comes to renew the lease the funds can be obtained by selling or realizing the investment. A typical double entry is shown in Fig. 22.5.

Cash Book (*Bank Columns Only*)			CB 17	
		19..		£
		Dec. 31 Investment		
		A/c	L 124	500·00

Investment Account			L 124
19..		£	
Dec. 31 Bank A/c CB 17		500·00	

Fig. 22.5 A Sinking Fund to meet future needs

(2) Machinery-replacement Sinking Funds

Exactly similar sinking funds may also be set up to provide the necessary funds to retool and re-equip a factory when its present equipment ceases to be economic. The sinking fund ensures that cash will be available from an outside source.

22.7   Depreciation and the Companies Acts 1948–1981

These Acts attempt to ensure that an investor, considering whether to invest in a company, shall have available all the information necessary to ensure that he makes a wise decision. One unsatisfactory aspect of company accounts before 1948 was that there was no need to show whether the assets listed were new, or old and worn-out. The Acts now require that assets are shown 'at cost—less the total depreciation to date'. Thus the plant and machinery shown below reveals to the investor that it is largely obsolete equipment.

Fixed Assets	*At Cost*	*Less Depreciation*	*Present Value*
Plant and Machinery	£100 000·00	£96 000·00	£4 000·00

To assist in making these figures available, it is usual, instead of writing down the asset on the asset account each year, to leave it on the asset account at its original cost. The depreciation deducted is collected in a Provision for Depreciation Account, and is only deducted from the asset account when it is finally disposed of. Fig. 22.6 illustrates the accounts referred to above.

	Plant and Machinery A/c			L 2
19..			£	
Jan. 1 Bank A/c	CB 5		100 000·00	

	Provision for Depreciation on Plant and Machinery A/c			L 73
				£
	Yr. 1	Depreciation A/c	J5	16 000·00
	Yr. 2	Depreciation A/c	J9	16 000·00
	Yr. 3	Depreciation A/c	J16	16 000·00
	Yr. 4	Depreciation A/c	J25	16 000·00
	Yr. 5	Depreciation A/c	J33	16 000·00
	Yr. 6	Depreciation A/c	J38	16 000·00

Fig. 22.6 Collecting depreciation in a Provision Account

You should now attempt some of the exercises in depreciation which follow.

Note:

From here on in the book '·oo' will be left off all round figures. It will only appear in displayed text where fractions of £1 need to be shown (i.e. pence).

22.8   Exercises Set 28: More about Depreciation

1. Mills Ltd. purchased a machine by cheque for £1 500 on January 1st 19.. Its probable working life was estimated at ten years and its probable scrap value at the end of that time as £200. It was decided to write off

depreciation by equal annual instalments over the ten years. Show the Machinery Account for the first two years.

2. A. Thompson purchased a machine by cheque for £2 800 on January 1st 19. . Its probable working life was estimated at eight years and its probable scrap value at the end of that time as £400. It was decided to write off depreciation by equal annual instalments over the years. Show the Machinery Account for the first three years.

3. T. Brown started business on January 1st 19. . and on that date purchased machinery by cheque for £3 000. He decided to close his books each year at December 31st and to depreciate machinery by 10 per cent of the original cost for each year of use, assuming a scrap value of nil at the end of the life of the machines.

    On July 1st of the following year he purchased by cheque another machine for £600.

    You are required to show:
    (a) the Machinery Account as it would appear in the ledger from January 1st year 1 to December 31st year 3 inclusive, and
    (b) how this asset would appear in the Balance Sheet at December 31st, Year 3.

4. On January 1st 19. . a firm, Marshall Bros., bought furniture and fittings for £1 200 cash and on April 1st 19. ., one year later, bought additional furniture for £400 cash. At the end of each year depreciation is provided for at the rate of 5 per cent *per annum* by the diminishing balance (i.e. reducing instalment) method. Show the Furniture and Fittings Account for the first two financial years.

5. On January 1st 19. . Peter Walker bought a machine for £1 800 by cheque. It was decided to write off depreciation by the diminishing balance method, at 25 per cent *per annum*. Show the Machinery Account for the first two years.

6. John Mainway started business as a haulage contractor on January 1st 19. . He bought one new lorry for £2 000 by cheque. His business expanded, and on July 1st 19. . of the following year he purchased lorry number 2 for £2 000. On October 1st of the next year he purchased lorry number 3, also for £2 000.

    At the end of year 4, he engaged an accountant to prepare Final Accounts for each of his four years in business. You are required to write up his Motor-Lorries Account allowing for depreciation at the rate of 20 per cent of original cost *per annum* (i.e. on the fixed-instalment method).

    Your calculations, showing how the figure for depreciation each year is reached, must be shown separately underneath the account.

7. On January 1st year 1 Tom Smith, a haulage contractor, purchased four motor lorries for £2 400 each by cheque. At the end of each year

depreciation is provided for at the rate of 20 per cent *per annum* on the straight-line method, this depreciation being recorded in a separate Provision Account.

One of these vehicles was sold on January 1st year 4 for £1 500 paid by cheque and on the same date a new lorry was purchased for £2 700. Show the appropriate ledger accounts for the years 1, 2, 3 and 4.

8. The balance on A. Trader's Delivery-Vans Account at January 1st 19.. was £1 240. On March 1st, a second-hand van was purchased for cash, the cost being £630 and on September 1st a further van was bought on credit from Van Sales Ltd. for £720.

You are required

(*a*) to prepare a statement showing the depreciation for the year, the annual rate being 20 per cent diminishing balance method, your calculations in respect of the new vans to be made in months; and

(*b*) to write up the Delivery-Vans Account showing the written-down value of the vans at December 31st of that year.

9. Marketing Ltd. provides for depreciation of its machinery, at 10 per cent *per annum* on the diminishing-balance system. This depreciation is calculated by reference to the number of months during which the machines are in use.

On December 31st 19.. the machinery consisted of three items, purchased as under:

	£
On January 1st, year 1	Cost 3 000
On July 1st, year 2	Cost 2 400
On October 1st, year 3	Cost 1 400

Show the entry in the firm's Journal for depreciation for year 3 to December 31st, and show your calculations in the narration.

10. A. Manufacturer had the following machines in his factory at January 1st 19..

	Cost	Depreciation written off to date
	£	£
Machine No. 1	600	240
Machine No. 2	400	160
Machine No. 3	500	135

During the year he bought the following machines on the dates indicated

		Cost
		£
Machine No. 4	Feb. 1	700
Machine No. 5	Apr. 1	800
Machine No. 6	Aug. 1	1 000
Machine No. 7	Dec. 1	1 200

Depreciation is written off at the rate of 12 per cent *per annum* on cost, new machines being depreciated from the date of purchase and any machines disposed of are depreciated to the date of sale. On July 1st, Machine No. 3 was sold for £300.

You are required to prepare a statement showing the depreciation on each machine for the year ended December 31st and to calculate:

(*a*) The total depreciation for the year;

(*b*) The profit or loss on the disposal of Machine No. 3.

Note: Your calculations should be made in months.

Unit Twenty-Three
Columnar Books

23.1   Controlling a Business

At one time business competition was chiefly exercised in manufacturing, and men like Henry Ford, who developed new methods of working, planning factory layout, became world famous. More recently warehousing, distribution and retailing have come under careful scrutiny as businessmen seek economies of operation in all these fields. Management itself has had to examine office practices to streamline documentation, and costing, financial and departmental controls have been instituted.

The basis of all control activities is the evaluation of figures collected about the activities of different departments and functions in the enterprise. Very often, estimates are prepared beforehand so that actual performances can be compared with estimated performances and any differences (known by the technical name 'variances') can be investigated. *Variance analysis* is one of the really important control techniques.

The collection of the figures required is a simple matter, provided management is prepared to adapt procedures and systems. The simplest adaptations are the addition of analysis columns to Day Books, cash books, etc., to bring out the figures required. For example, in retail trade an analysis of sales made over different counters in variety chain stores reveals which lines are móst worth shelf space. Seasonal variation patterns are quickly established and adjustments to marketing capacity can be planned to anticipate changes and ensure the greatest volume of sales.

23.2   Columnar Sales and Purchases Day Books

A businessman having a variety of lines which he markets simultaneously will find it interesting to analyse his sales on a product basis. This will reveal which lines sell best and can even lead to the preparation of Trading and Profit and Loss Accounts on each product. Thus he may discover that one product does not yield a profit at all, and should be discontinued, or raised in price.

Fig. 23.1 illustrates a columnar Day Book of this sort. The following points are of interest:

(*a*) The end two columns have not changed their function, and the end column still provides the figures to be posted to each customer's ledger account.

(*b*) The extra analysis columns must cross-tot to give the same total as the figure shown in the end column. These columns may be totalled by data-processing methods, or by registers on the accounting machine. Alter-

Date	Details	Groceries £	Green Groceries £	Bread and Cakes £	Wines £	Folio	Details £	Total £
19.. Jan. 1	*Roebuck and Co.* 6 cases tomatoes 4 crates white wine		18·50		16·50	L 27	18·50 16·50	35·00
2	*Lamont Ltd.* 5 sides bacon 5 crates beans Loaves etc.	32·80 7·50		17·50		L 13	32·80 7·50 17·50	57·80
2	*Frobisher Ltd.* 6 cases tomatoes		18·50			L 8		18·50
	and so on throughout the month until							
31	*Lucas and Co.* Loaves etc.			35·25		L 91		35·25
		£3 856·25	£725·55	£495·25	£866·25	L 272		£5 943·30

Fig. 23.1 A columnar Sales Day Book

natively they may be added on an adding-listing machine or a calculator.

(c) When posted to the ledger, the total figures may either be posted to separate accounts, for example a Sales of Groceries, Sales of Greengroceries, etc., or may be posted to a special columnar account using analysis ledger paper as shown in Fig. 23.2.

Page
centre

	Date		Details	Groceries	Green-groceries	Bread and cakes	Wines	F	L 272 Total
	19.. Jan.	31	Sundry debtors	3856·25	725·55	495·25	866·25	SDB9	5943·30

Fig. 23.2 A columnar Sales Account (credit side only)

23.3 Columnar Cash Books

For control-account purposes it is often convenient to know the total cash payments made by customers with names in a certain section of the alphabet. For example, a young clerk may be in charge of the A–E debtors' ledger. A mistake may be made, perhaps several mistakes in the course of a month, and as a result the Trial Balance will fail to agree. If we can prepare an A–E Debtors' Ledger Control Account, telling us what this section of the ledger should total at the end of the month, any error the clerk has made will be revealed before the figures are passed to the Trial-Balance clerk. Part of the work of preparing such a Control Account is to draw up the figures of total cash paid by this group of debtors. This can be done if columnar 'Cash-Received' Books are kept, as part of, or as memorandum books related to, the three-column cash book. (A memorandum book is one that gives additional details of a particular group of transactions but is not itself part of the double-entry system.) Fig. 23.3 illustrates such a columnar ruling, giving control account figures for each sub-division of the ledger.

23.4 Exercises Set 29: Columnar Books

1. Rule up a suitable Purchases Day Book in columnar form giving columns for furniture, soft furnishings, electrical goods and carpets. Insert three invoices, each having three items on the invoice. Total the columns and cross-tot to check your entries. Invent appropriate folio numbers.

2. Rule up a suitable analysis cash book for cash payments made, in which the payments made are analysed into two sections, the A–K and the L–Z creditors. Enter five items, at least two from each sub-division. Total and cross-tot the book to check its accuracy. All the creditors are to be paid by cheque and we receive cash discount of 5 per cent on all payments.

		A-E	F-L	M-S	T-Z	F	Discount	Cash	Bank
		£	£	£	£		£	£	£
19..									
Jan. 1	R. Marks			30·00			1·50		28·50
1	M. Evans	45·50					2·27		43·23
2	P. Peters			46·50			2·32		44·18
2	L. Toff				27·90			27·90	
2	S. Marshall			13·25				13·25	
2	R. Bones	14·65							14·65
3	B. Wyvern				15·75		0·79		14·96
3	S. Potter			46·00					46·00
		etc.	etc.	etc.	etc.		etc.	etc.	etc.
31	T. Helga		149·90				7·49		142·41
		£957·28	£1 056·42	£1 279·30	£820·70		£72·56	£184·72	£3 856·42

Fig. 23.3 A columnar Cash-Received Book

3. Give the ruling of a columnar Sales Book suitable for a businessman dealing in three classes of goods: cigarettes and tobacco, confectionery, and gifts for smokers. Insert three suitable entries, supplying your own dates, names, etc. Total and cross-tot the three entries.

4. G. Jenkins is in business as a wholesale nurseryman. He deals in four main classes of goods: roses, trees, shrubs and bulbs. Record the following invoices in a suitable Sales Day Book—analysed for these four departments:

£

19..

June 13th	B. Lobley purchases goods as follows:		
	100 assorted rose bushes	=	22·00
	100 assorted shrubs	=	28·80
	10 sacks bulk narcissi	=	15·00
June 18th	R. Brown purchases goods as follows:		
	6 boxes crocus bulbs	=	4·50
	12 roses (standards)	=	9·25
	3 boxes iris bulbs	=	2·25
June 27th	B. Grant purchases goods as follows:		
	100 trees (cypresses)	=	17·50
	2 000 rose bushes	=	400·00
	2 000 assorted shrubs	=	500·00
June 30th	G. Wakeman purchases goods as follows:		
	6 boxes crocus bulbs	=	4·50
	100 shrubs (assorted)	=	28·80
	100 rose bushes	=	22·00

5. Rule up a special sheet of Day-Book analysis paper, and record the following invoices in the columnar Purchases Day Book of the Pop Musical Co. This firm has four departments: (a) sheet music and records (b) record players (c) hi-fi equipment (d) musical instruments. You should head the analysis columns accordingly. Rule off the Day Book on April 30th, inventing suitable folio numbers as if you had posted the Day Book to the ledger.

19..

April 1st   Bought from Musical Instruments Co. Ltd. 6 guitars @ £8·50 each.

April 11th   Bought from R. T. Lamb (Electrical) Ltd. 12 record players @ £15·25 each, and batteries to fit, value £25·50.

April 19th   Bought from Recording Ltd. 200 L.P. discs @ £1 each and 4 violins @ £3·75 each.

April 25th   Bought from A. Dealer two-saxophones @ £29 each.

April 30th   Bought from R. K. Radios 10 Hi-Fi control panels @ £5·75 each.

Unit Twenty-Four

The Bank Cash Book

24.1 Introduction

The idea behind the bank cash book is the establishment of control over the movement of cash. Cash is easy to misappropriate, and a system which requires that all the cash received is paid at once into the bank, reduces the chances of misappropriation. The sums paid in must agree exactly with the sums collected on the till rolls, etc., and any difference will be the subject of rigorous investigation. If any disbursement of cash is required it will be arranged through the imprest system, that is, through the petty-cash system. Sometimes, where businesses are open at hours when the banks have shut, it is necessary to pay the remainder of the day's takings in by the 'night-safe' system. Managements adopting this policy regard the small charge made for the night-safe service as well worth while in view of the extra control given to them over the cash received. The manager who has to bank the evening's takings before going home is less likely to be tempted to use them for his own ends, while premises which are known to have no cash in the tills are less likely to be burgled.

In these circumstances the cash column on the three-column cash book is not required. It may be used instead for an addition column, where the items collected may be totalled into a sub-total of daily payments into the bank. This sub-total is useful when doing bank reconciliation statements, since these daily banking sub-totals are the figures that appear on the bank statement.

Fig. 24.1 shows a typical bank cash book.

24.2 Notes on the Bank Cash Book

(a) The Cash Account is not needed. No payments are made in cash except through the petty-cash book on the imprest system, and all cash received is treated as if it was cheques and paid straight into the bank. It follows that the Cash Account columns can be used as details columns to show the daily totals of transactions. These daily totals are particularly useful on the debit side, since the total entered daily will appear on the bank statement at a later date as 'sundries' paid in. It is very useful to have this sundries figure in one total on the cash book.

(b) Daily takings are cashed up at the end of the day and paid in at the end of the day.

Apart from these differences, the bank cash book is exactly like the three-column cash book.

Debit side:

Date	Details	Folio	Discount Allowed £	Details £	Bank £
19.. March 1	Balance	B/d			1 747·50
1	M. Smith	L 15	1·50	24·50	
1	T. Grover	L 27		36·25	
1	Cash Sales	L 59		72·80	133·55
2	T. Lark	L 18	2·10	93·90	
2	R. Parsons	L 22	3·20	6·80	
2	Cash Sales	L 59		48·50	149·20
3	R. Jones	L 7	2·50	47·50	
3	P. White	L 11		38·20	
3	E. Tucker	L 28		14·95	
3	Cash Sales	L 59		63·60	164·25
			£ 9·30		£ 2 194·50
			L 27		
4	Balance	B/d			£1 946·25

Credit side:

Date	Details	Folio	Discount Received £	Details £	Bank £
19.. March 2	Urban Dist. Council	L 77			46·50
3	Lee and Co.	L 13	5·00	95·00	
3	Millward Ltd.	L 57		72·50	
3	T. Harper	L 53	0·75	14·25	
3	Petty Cash	PCB 7		20·00	
3	Balance	c/d			201·75
					1 946·25
			£ 5·75		£2 194·50
			L 29		

Fig. 24.1 The bank cash book

24.3   Exercises Set 30: The Bank Cash Book

1. Write up A. Trader's bank cash book from the following information:
   (a) His balance at the bank at the close of business on May 27th 19..
   according to his cash book was £872·80.
   (b) The counterfoils of his paying-in book give the following details:
   May 28th Total paid in £203·30—consisting of cash from sales
   £45·80, a cheque from B. Bath for £60, and a cheque from
   L. Poole for £97·50. Poole's cheque was accepted in full
   settlement of £100 owed by him.
   May 30th Total paid in £44·15—consisting entirely of cash from
   sales.
   May 31st Total paid in £80·50—consisting of cash from sales £39
   and a cheque from H. Winton for £41·50.
   (c) The counterfoils of his cheque book show:

		£
May 28th	J. Battle and Co. Ltd.	290·13
May 30th	W. Thorley and Co.	195·00
May 31st	Petty Cash	26·15
	Self	50·00
	Elton's Garage	17·11

   The cheque to Elton's Garage was for petrol, oil and maintenance of
   the delivery van for the previous month, and no previous record of this
   transaction had gone through the books.
   The details columns of the cash book should indicate clearly which
   ledger account is to be debited or credited in respect of each entry. Rule
   off and balance the cash book as at the close of business on May 31st 19..
   (RSA 1)

2. George Vyner, the proprietor of a trading business, banks all the business
   receipts daily and meets all but petty-cash expenditure by cheque. You
   are required to write up his bank cash book from the following information:
   (a) The balance at the bank at the close of business on May 3rd 19..,
   according to the cash book, was £375·40.
   (b) He drew four cheques in the remaining days of the week; the counterfoils of the business cheque book show:

	£
May 4th H. Moore and Sons	172·11
W. Blake and Co.	95·00
May 5th Eastern Electricity	19·10
May 6th Cash (Self £20; Petty Cash £8·66)	28·66

   Note: The cheque to W. Blake and Co. was in full settlement of £100
   owing to them, and the payment to Eastern Electricity was in prompt
   payment of their account for the last quarter's consumption of
   electricity.

(c) The counterfoils of his paying-in book gives the following details:

May 4th Total paid in £96·77—consisting of shop takings £31·17; a cheque from J. Hart for £18·10 and a cheque from G. Farley for £47·50 (accepted in full settlement of £50 owed by him).

May 5th Total paid in £51·17—consisting entirely of shop takings.

May 6th Total paid in £90·45—consisting of shop takings £48 and a cheque from R. Nelson for £42·45.

In drawing up the cash book, see that the details column contains the name of the ledger account to which the posting is to be made in respect of each entry. Rule off and balance the cash book as at the close of business on May 6th 19.. (RSA 1)

3. Write up D. Lobley's bank cash book from the following particulars:

(a) His balance at the bank at the close of business on May 27th 19.. according to his Cash Book, was £893.

(b) The counterfoils of his paying-in book give the following details:

May 28th Total paid in £196—consisting of cash from sales £49, a cheque from A. Plum for £50 and a cheque from B. Berry for £97. Berry's cheque was accepted in full settlement of £100 owed by him.

May 29th Total paid in £48—consisting entirely of cash from sales.

May 30th Total paid in £75—consisting of cash from sales £40 and a cheque from C. Flower for £35.

(c) The counterfoils of his cheque book show:

May 28th Orchard and Co. Ltd. £327.

May 29th Hedges and Co. £195.

May 30th Petty Cash £29 and Self £50—one cheque for £79.

May 31st Wood's Garage £18.

The cheque to Hedges and Co. was accepted in full settlement of £200 owing to them. The cheque to Wood's Garage was for petrol, oil and servicing for the previous month and no previous record of this had gone through the books.

The particulars columns of the cash book should show clearly the name of the ledger account which is to be debited or credited in respect of each entry.

Rule off and balance the cash book at the close of business on May 30th (RSA 1)

4. Write up A. Heathcliff's bank cash book from the following information:

(a) His balance at the bank at the close of business on July 4th 19.. according to his cash book, was £676·50.

(b) The counterfoils of his paying-in book give the following details:

July 5th Total paid in £293—consisting of cash from sales £135·50, a cheque from R. Loosely for £60, and a cheque from L. Driver for £97·50. Driver's cheque was accepted in full settlement of £100 owed by him.

July 7th Total paid in £57·50—consisting entirely of cash from sales.

July 8th Total paid in £80·50—consisting of cash from sales £39 and a cheque from R. Windsor for £41·50.

(c) The counterfoils of his cheque book show:

	£
July 5th J. Ranch and Co. Ltd.	256·00
July 7th W. Thorpe and Co.	195·00
July 8th Petty Cash	26·75
Self	50·00
Romax Garage	17·50

The cheque to Thorpe and Co. was accepted in full settlement of £200 owing to them.

The cheque to Romax Garage was for petrol, oil and maintenance of the delivery van for the previous month, and no previous record of this transaction had gone through the books.

The details columns of the cash book should indicate clearly which ledger account is to be debited or credited in respect of each entry. Rule off and balance the cash book as at the close of business on July 8th 19. .

5. Write up M. Tyler's bank cash book from the following particulars:

(a) His balance at the bank at the close of business on June 8th 19. . according to his cash book, was £893.

(b) The counterfoils of his paying-in book give the following details:

June 9th Total paid in £296—consisting of cash from sales £48, a cheque from R. Thomas for £150 and a cheque from B. Brown for £98. Brown's cheque was accepted in full settlement of £100 owed by him.

June 10th Total paid in £40—consisting entirely of cash from sales.

June 11th Total paid in £85—consisting of cash from sales £40 and a cheque from R. Maitland for £45.

(c) The counterfoils of his cheque book show:

	£
June 9th Trihard and Co. Ltd.	287
June 10th Bloom and Co.	185
June 11th Petty Cash £39 and Self £50—	
one cheque	89
Peter's Garage	28

The cheque to Bloom and Co. was accepted in full settlement of £190 owing to them. The cheque to Peter's Garage was for petrol, oil and servicing for the previous month and no previous record of this had gone through the books.

The particulars columns of the cash book should show clearly the name of the ledger account which is to be debited or credited in respect of each entry.

Rule off and balance the cash book at the close of business on June 11th 19. .

Unit Twenty-Five

Stock Valuation

25.1 The Valuation of Stock

At the end of any financial period it is necessary to value the stock in hand, *which will be handed on by the current period to the next period at the agreed valuation.* The purchase of stock during the year is a revenue expense, because it is the purchase of goods for resale, but at the end of the year the balance in hand has, for a few hours, to be capitalized, and handed on to the next year as an asset of the business. As soon as the business commences on the first day of the new period, the customers start once again to purchase the goods and the revenue activities of selling goods and replacing them with new stock begins again, for a further trading period.

The process of valuing stock is one of the *adjustments* which have to be taken into account at the end of the financial year. These are dealt with more fully in Unit 26, but it is more convenient to treat stock as a special case.

To value stock the following activities must be carried out.

(a) *The counting of the stock—physically checking it to discover how many units remain on the shelves.* Ideally it is best to have this activity performed by special 'stock-takers'. A dishonest manager, who has been misappropriating cash or stock, can cover his activities by exaggerating the stock in hand. Stock-taking by specialist staff frequently uncovers *defalcations.*

(b) *The valuation of the units.* This is a most important point. How shall we value stock? If we value it at the price at which it is marked on the shelves, i.e. the selling price, we shall in effect be valuing it with the profit 'mark-up' on it, and shall be overstating its value. If we value it at cost price, this will be better, but sometimes the item may have depreciated in value and it is worth less now than we paid for it. Even to state it at cost price in these circumstances would overstate the value. The rule is *Stock is valued at cost price, or net realizable value, whichever is lower.* This rule is laid down in *Statements of Standard Accounting Practice No. 9.* The effect of Statement No. 9 is to make firms value stock at cost price, unless the goods have actually deteriorated below cost price so that they can only be disposed of at a lower figure. You are advised to learn the above rule by heart and also the name of the Accounting Standard (published by the accounting bodies) in which it is laid down.

(c) *The multiplication of the unit value by the number of units in hand, and the addition of all these items into a grand 'closing-stock' figure.* Thus where we have 136 tins of baked beans at 4p per tin (valued at cost price) the value of this item of stock would be

$$136 \times 4p = £5.44$$

When added to the other items of stock, a grand total of several thousand pounds may well result.

25.2 Stock-taking Sales

The labour of counting and valuing stock, and calculating the total closing stock figure can be very great. It may be reduced if a stock-taking sale is held just before the stock-taking period, and large sections of the stock are disposed of. This is an excellent opportunity to review the stock, and consider those items which appear to be slow-moving. Who purchased these items? The buyer concerned may be consistently buying lines which do not sell, perhaps because of bad judgement on his part, perhaps because of a strong personal interest in a particular subject. Thus a photography enthusiast may over-buy cameras, or a racing-car enthusiast may over-buy gadgets for fast cars. The buyer may actually be accepting bribes from a particular supplier, or may be under 'undue influence' or duress in some respect. Corrective action to restrain the buyer will have a salutary effect.

The Effect of Stock-taking Sales on Profit Margins

If sales are held, the reduction of prices involved necessarily results in a fall in profit margins. The slow-moving items disposed of at cut prices will reduce the total profit earned from the expected profit margin to something rather lower. We shall see (in Section 32.3) that these margins—called *gross-profit percentages*—are used to control business activities. A fall in gross-profit percentage is always investigated by an astute management. Clearly the necessity to sell goods at cut prices indicates bad buying, and it will be a cause of a fall in gross-profit percentage achieved during the trading period.

25.3 Importance of Correct Stock-taking

Where stock is incorrectly valued the effects are as follows:

(a) The gross profit is affected. An overvalued stock exaggerates the profit made, and an undervalued stock understates the profit made.

(b) As stock is also a Balance-Sheet item, the Balance Sheet will not give a 'true and fair view of the affairs of the business', stock being either overstated or understated in the current assets.

For these reasons it is very important to have accurate stock-taking figures, so that an honest profit figure and an honest Balance Sheet are produced.

Stock-taking in Inflationary Times

In periods of rapidly changing prices the method used to value stock can have a very important effect on the accounts. For example, suppose I have a stock of ten motor car components—five of which cost me £25 each, while the other five were purchased later at £30 each. If I use four of them to repair a customer's car, what is the value of the six which I have left in stock? The problem is often referred to as the *FIFO/LIFO problem*—should the stock be valued on a First In First Out basis (stock would be 1 @ £25 and 5 @ £30, i.e. £175) or a Last In First Out basis (stock would be 1 @ £30 and 5 @ £25, i.e. £155)? Alternatively the stock could be valued on an average cost basis (AVCO). These systems are all discussed in Section 38.9.

25.4   A Stock-valuation Example

A firm has the following information about its stock position.

Ladies' Cardigans

19. .		Cost Price £	Quantity
Opening Balance January 1st 19. .		2·50	1 400
Purchases January		2·60	4 000
"	February	2·65	3 500
"	March	2·55	2 800
Sales	January	3·20	3 000
"	February	3·50	3 800
"	March	3·90	3 900
Closing Stock		?	?

Current selling price of the articles is now £3·95. All goods are sold in strict rotation, first in first out.

Calculate
(a)   The value of the closing stock.
(b)   The gross profit for the three months shown.

Calculation: (a).

Total stock purchased = 1 400 + 4 000 + 3 500 + 2 800 = 11 700
Total sales = 10 700

Therefore stock left in hand = 1 000

This stock was clearly all part of the purchases made in March.
These cost £2·55 and are now being sold for £3·95.

Therefore closing stock is worth 1 000 × £2·55 = £2 550

Calculation: (b) To calculate the gross profit we shall need to draw up a Trading Account. The necessary figures are as follows:

Opening stock = £2·50 × 1400 = £3 500

Purchases   = (4 000 × £2·60) + (3 500 × £2·65) + (2 800 × £2·55)
= £10 400 + £9 275 + £7 140
= £26 815

Sales   = (3 000 × £3·20) + (3 800 × £3·50) + (3 900 × £3·90)
= £9 600 + £13 300 + £15 210
= £38 110

Closing stock = £2 550 (Calculated in section (a) above)
The Trading Account would therefore be drawn up as shown below.

	£		£
		Trading Account	L 169
		(for three-month period ending March 31st 19..)	
Opening Stock	3 500	**Sales**	38 110
Purchases	26 815		
Total Stock available	30 315		
Less Closing Stock	2 550		
Cost of Sales	27 765		
Gross Profit	10 345		
	£38 110		£38 110

You should now try this sort of calculation for yourself, using the exercises which follow.

25.5   Exercises Set 31: The Valuation of Closing Stock

1. At stock-taking, a firm found that it had 420 of a certain article in stock. Of these, 200 had been purchased at £1·50 each, 100 at £1·70 each and the remainder at £2 each. The current price of these articles is £2·25 each. Some 20 of the items purchased at £1·50 have become discoloured due to bad storage, and are valued as only likely to sell at £1 each by the manager. The firm usually sells at 50 per cent above cost. Calculate the stock-taking valuation placed upon this item on the stock sheets.

2. Badbuyers Ltd. find that on taking stock at December 31st one year they have 84 units of a certain article in stock. Four of these originally cost £32 each, but are now damaged and offered for sale at only £20 each. 16 of the rest cost £39·50 each, and the remainder were bought at £45·50 each. Current price of such goods from their usual supplier is now only £41·50, but a competitor is offering them at £40. The firm usually adds 50 per cent to cost price to find its selling prices. Value these articles in accordance with sound accounting practice.

3. (a) On what basis is stock valued at the end of the financial year?
   (b) Peter Lawson had, on January 1st 19.., a stock of 4 000 pairs of shoes valued at cost price (£2 each). During January he sold 1 800 pairs and bought 2 500 pairs at £2·30 each. In February he bought a further 2 500 at £2·20 each and sold 3 000 pairs. At the end of February he still has 100 pairs of the January 1st stock unsold and the shoes bought in February have not yet been offered to his customers. Calculate the value of his stock if the current selling price of these shoes is £3·25 per pair on February 28th 19..

4. (a) What is the usual basis for stock valuation at the end of the financial year?

(b) John Richards, a sugar merchant, prepared his Trading Account at December 31st 19. . His stock consisted of 200 tonnes purchased at the following prices.

> 40 tonnes @ £28·50 per tonne
> 60 tonnes @ £29·50 „ „
> 100 tonnes @ £27·00 „ „

On December 31st the price of sugar on the market was £28·00. Richards always sells sugar at 25 per cent above current market price.

Draw up a statement showing the value of Richards' stock of sugar for Trading-Account purposes at December 31st 19. .

5. A trader had in stock on March 1st 8 000 articles at £0·15 each. During March he purchased a further 16 000 costing £0·17 each, but was given an allowance of £0·05 each on 2 000 of these, as they arrived in a damp condition. His sales during the month were 14 000 articles at £0·25 each and 1 400 of the damaged articles at £0·18 each. Goods are disposed of under the 'first in first out' rule. The current replacement price of similar articles was £0·18 on March 31st. In view of this he intends to sell in future at £0·26 each, but will dispose of the rest of the damaged items at only £0·10 since they are the more seriously damaged of the batch. Show the Trading Account of the trader for the month ended March 31st.

6. The following information is available from the records of a small manufacturer of plumbing ware. He makes three products A, B and C.

January 1st 19. .

Stocks in hand	A=186 units	B=94 units	C=100 units
Value (manufacturing cost)	A=£2·50	B=£1·50	C=£0·50
Manufactures during year	A=2 350 units	B=1 800 units	C=1 500 units
Sales during year	A=2 500 units	B=1 600 units	C=1 550 units
Average sales prices	A=£15·25	B=£3·20	C=£0·95

Calculate:

(a) The total closing stock figure, bearing in mind that manufacturing costs have not changed.

(b) His trading profit for the year.

25.6 Practical Difficulties in Stock-taking

The owner of a small business often finds it difficult to take stock for the purposes of his Final Accounts, since the end of a financial year often falls on a week-day when he has customers to serve and staff to supervise. A sole trader may therefore decide to do his stock-taking on the Sunday, or on his half-day closing, even though this does not fall on the last day of the financial year. He then calculates his true closing-stock figure by taking into account the changes in the stock position that have occurred in the two or three days between the stock-taking date and the end of the financial year. The following simple example will illustrate the method.

Example

Tom Smith's financial year ends on March 31st. He decides to postpone his stock-taking figure until Sunday April 5th. He values the stock at that date at a figure of £6 700. In the first five days of April the following events had occurred:

  (i) Takings at the tills totalled £455
 (ii) Goods were also sold on credit £160
(iii) Goods were delivered by suppliers £480
(iv) A customer returned goods originally sold to him for £30.

Tom has always added 25 per cent to his cost prices to give his selling prices. What was his true closing-stock fiigure on March 31st?

We must think very clearly about these figures. In logical sequence these points must be taken into account:

  (i) Stock valuation at April 5th = £6 700
 (ii) Sales during the first five days of April = £455 + £160
                                               = £615

Since these were not sold on March 31st they would still have been in stock at that date and must be added back, *but this adding back must be at cost price, not selling price.*

To find out what the cost price was we must deduct one-fifth from £615
$$£615 - £123 = £492$$
Valued at cost price these items were worth £492

Therefore stock in hand must be increased by £492 to give the true March 31st figure.

Arithmetical Note: If you cannot follow the calculation of this 'cost of stock sold' figure, you should note that when 25 per cent is added to cost price, it is the same as 20 per cent off the selling price.

$$\text{Cost Price} + \text{profit} = \text{selling price}$$
$$100\% \quad +25\% = 125\%$$

If we know the selling price, and the mark-up on cost, but wish to calculate the cost we have the following situation.

$$\text{Cost Price} + \text{profit} = \text{selling price}$$
$$100\% \quad +25\% = 125\% = £615$$

To deduct the 25% added on, we only need $\frac{1}{5}$ of £615·00. (There are 5 × 25% in 125%.)

$$\tfrac{1}{5} \text{ of } £615 = £123$$

Therefore cost price = £615 − £123 = £492

The arithmetic of this type of problem is best illustrated by the table
$$\tfrac{1}{2} \text{ on CP} = \tfrac{1}{3} \text{ off SP}$$
$$\tfrac{1}{3} \text{ on CP} = \tfrac{1}{4} \text{ off SP}$$
$$\tfrac{1}{4} \text{ on CP} = \tfrac{1}{5} \text{ off SP, etc.}$$

Sometimes the margin added to cost price is not a simple fraction, like $\frac{1}{2}, \frac{1}{3}, \frac{1}{4}$, etc., but is a percentage like 40 per cent. The cost price is then found most easily by saying

$$\text{SP} = \text{CP} + 40\%$$
$$\text{i.e. } 140\% = 100\% + 40\%$$

Therefore to find the cost price from any given selling price requires $\frac{100}{140}$ of the selling price. For example goods sold at £280 after a 40 per cent mark-up must have cost

$$280 \times \tfrac{100}{140} = £200$$

To return to our problem:

(iii) Goods delivered by the suppliers in the first five days of April were clearly not in stock on March 31st and may be deducted from the stock figure.

(iv) Goods returned by the customer in early April (£30 at selling price) must be deducted from the stock figure since they were not in stock at March 31st. This deduction must be made at cost price, i.e. £30 − $\frac{1}{5}$ of £30 = £24.

Therefore closing stock on April 5th	=	£6 700
Add sales made in early April, but at cost price	=	492
		7 192
Deduct		
(*a*) Goods taken into stock in early April	£480	
(*b*) Returns in the same period at cost price	24	
	—	504
Closing stock at March 31st		£6 688

Note:

If Tom Smith had valued his stock on Sunday, March 29th, the adjustments would have been made the opposite way. Sales made in the last two days of March would have been deducted from the March 29th figure (since they were lost to Stock before the end of the year). Stock received and returns by customers would have been added in to give the true end-of-the-year position.

25.7   Exercises Set 32: Stock-taking Problems

1. R. and T. Traders are retailers whose financial year ended on Thursday, December 31st. They took stock on the following Saturday after closing their premises for the day, and then presented the accountant with the following figures.

	£
Stock at cost on Saturday January 2nd	3 180
Cost price of goods taken into stock from suppliers delivering on January 1st and 2nd	340
Sales on January 1st and 2nd (cash takings)	88
Credit sales on these days	108
Credit note to customer for goods returned on January 1st	32

R. and T. Traders add 33$\frac{1}{3}$ per cent to 'cost prices' to fix their 'selling prices'. Calculate the correct stock figure for December 21st 19. .

2. A. Trader began stock-taking for the year ended June 30th 19. . on that date. He did not complete the stock-taking until the close of business on

July 4th 19.., when he ascertained the value of stock at cost price as
£7 250.

The following information is available for the period July 1st–4th 19..:

Purchases included in stock figure   £460
Sales of goods not included in stock figure £725

Goods invoiced to a customer on June 30th 19.. at £120 but held
in the factory pending instructions as to delivery, were included in the
stock figure. Percentage of gross profit on sales is 25%.

Draw up a statement to show the correct value of stock at cost price
on June 30th 19..

3. R. Marshall did his stock-taking on Sunday, December 27th, although the
financial year did not end until December 31st. He valued his stock at that
date at £12 725.

Records for the end of December were as follows:

December 28th–31st	£
Sales in cash	895
Stock received from suppliers at cost	1 055
Sales on credit	585
Returns by customers (at selling price)	60
Returns to suppliers (at cost price)	48
A 50-gallon drum of paraffin oil leaked in a shed where dried goods were also stored. This stock had to be thrown away. Value (at cost)	128
The proprietor took home stock (cost price)	12

Marshall adds 50 per cent to cost prices to find his selling prices. Calculate the stock figure as at December 31st (to the nearest £1).

4. In a burglary at the warehouse of J. Cook and Son on the night of September 30th 19.. part of the stock was stolen.

From the following particulars show in account form the estimated
value of the loss of stock.

	£
Stock at cost July 1st 19..	7 840
Purchases from July 1st to September 30th 19..	15 600
Sales from July 1st to September 30th 19..	18 400
Stock remaining after the burglary was valued at	2 420

J. Cook and Son's usual gross profit is 25 per cent of selling price.

(RSA 1)

5. During the year 19.. R. Green bought goods value £8 400 and his sales,
on which he made a gross profit of 25 per cent, were £11 600. The value
of his stock at the beginning of the year was £1 600. What was the value
of his stock at the end of the year? Show details of your calculations.

(RSA 1)

6. From the following information calculate the value of R. Butler's stock
on September 30th 19..

	£
September 1st 19.. stock (at cost)	1 300
Purchases during month	15 000
Sales during month	20 000
Sales returns during month	800
Goods taken by Butler (selling price)	400

Gross profit is 20 per cent on turnover.

7. A. Draper began to take stock at 5 p.m. on Saturday, December 28th 19.. He used cost price as the most suitable valuation. By the time the shop re-opened on Monday, December 30th, he knew that the value of the stock in hand was £7 280.

On that day and the next day new stock arrived (cost price = £240), and a customer also returned goods sold to him in early December (invoice value = £300). Cash sales for the two days were £100 and £80 respectively, and credit sales were £200 and £220 respectively.

Draper always adds 20 per cent to cost price to fix his selling prices.

Adjust the stock-taking figure of £7 280 to allow for the movements of stock on the last two days of the year, and thus arrive at the closing-stock figure for December 31st 19..

All working is to be clearly shown.

8. R. Mortimer sells on both cash and credit terms, adding 33⅓ per cent to the purchase price of his goods to obtain his selling price. His stock, at cost, on May 27th 19.. amounted to £6 650. During the remaining four working days of the month the following transactions took place:

Goods were purchased at a cost of £530

Sales were as follows: cash £156; credit £152

Goods which had been sold to a customer for £16 were returned by him and taken back into stock.

You are required to draw up a statement of account showing the value of the trader's stock as at May 31st 19..   (RSA 1)

9. P. Larkins sells his goods for cash and on credit, and adds 33⅓ per cent to purchase prices to obtain the selling prices.

The stock of the concern, at cost, on December 27th 19.. amounted to £5 320. In the remaining three working days of the financial year the following transactions took place:

	£
Purchases at cost	424
Credit sales at selling prices	124
Cash sales at selling prices	120
Goods previously sold to a customer for £12 were returned by him, undamaged, and taken back into stock.	

Prepare a statement showing the value of the firm's stock at December 31st 19..   (RSA 1)

Adjustments in Final Accounts

26.1 Recapitulation

You have now reached a point in your studies where you are about to leave behind the more routine aspects of accounting, and move on to a slightly higher level of activity, interpreting and controlling the business's situation. It is helpful at this point to recapitulate the stages covered. We have considered the following aspects:

(a) The basic idea of double-entry accounting.

(b) The recording of original documents in the books of original entry, i.e. the Day Books, the cash book and the petty-cash book.

(c) The posting of these original entries into the ledger, which is the main book of account.

(d) The extraction of a Trial Balance from the ledger.

(e) The preparation from this Trial Balance of Trading Accounts, Profit and Loss Accounts and Balance Sheets.

We must now move on to consider the finer points of accounting, and we begin with the examination of what are called 'adjustments'.

26.2 Adjustments in Final Accounts

There are two guiding principles in the preparation of Final Accounts. These are:

(a) Every Trading Account and every Profit and Loss Account must be prepared accurately, so that the correct profit for the period is obtained. This can only be achieved if the accounts carry every penny of the losses for the year, and include every penny of the profits earned.

(b) Every Balance Sheet must give a 'true and fair view' of the affairs of the business, showing the assets and the liabilities at their 'true' values.

In order to achieve these two aims, the accountant must take into account many matters which require adjustment. For example the Wages Account may include some wages given in advance for next year to an employee who has requested an advance of salary to help him meet some domestic difficulty. This amount must be removed from the wages bill to be charged to the Trading Account; if it is not removed the Trading Account for this year will be carrying next year's losses. Similarly, a commission earned for selling a piece of property for a client may not have been paid yet although it is definitely due from the customer. If it is omitted from the Profit and Loss Account this year's profits will be understated and next year's profits will be exaggerated. A full list of adjustments includes:

(a) Payments in advance by the firm.

(b) Payments in advance to the firm.
(c) Payments accrued due by the firm.
(d) Payments accrued due to the firm.
(e) Bad debts and provisions for bad debts.
(f) Provisions for discounts.
(g) Closing-stock adjustments.
(h) Depreciation of assets.
(i) Appreciation of assets.
(j) Amortization of leases.
(k) Depreciation of goodwill.
Each of these will be considered in turn in Sections 26.3—26.11.

26.3   Payments in Advance by the Firm

Certain payments are always made in advance. The best example is insurance payments, for, until the first premium is paid, the insurance company will not offer any cover. It follows that whenever we make out the Final Accounts of the business there is usually some balance of insurance cover due, which has been paid for already but the protection afforded will carry over into the next year. Consider the Insurance Account shown in Fig. 26.1.

Insurance A/c		L 175
19..	£	
Jan. 1 Motor Vehicle A (Bank A/c)	175·50	
April 1 Motor Vehicle B (Bank A/c)	66·00	
June 30 Motor Vehicle C (Bank A/c)	156·00	
Sept. 30 Fire insurance (Bank A/c)	25·00	

Fig. 26.1 An insurance account

Clearly the premium paid on January 1st has given cover for a whole year by December 31st and its protection has been fully enjoyed. The whole of this £175·50 is a loss chargeable to this year's Profit and Loss Account. The other items are not fully used: one-quarter of the April 1st payment has still to be enjoyed and it will give protection until March 31st next year. Half of the June payment and three-quarters of the September payment similarly represent unexpired benefits to be enjoyed in the coming year. It follows that the true charge to the Profit and Loss Account for insurance this year is as follows:

		£
(a) The whole of the January payment	=	175·50
(b) Three-quarters of the April payment	=	49·50
(c) Half the June payment	=	78·00
(d) One-quarter of the September payment	=	6·25
Charge to Profit and Loss Account	=	£309·25

The transfer of this charge to Profit and Loss Account is shown in the Journal entry of Fig. 26.2 and the balance on the account in Fig. 26.3. This balance is a debit balance, an asset, and will appear in the Balance Sheet as an asset—payment in advance. This is shown in Fig. 26.4.

19..					£	£ J 27
Dec.	31	Profit and Loss A/c	Dr.	L 206	309·25	
		Insurance A/c		L 175		309·25
		Being transfer of correct portion				
		of insurance paid to Profit and				
		Loss Account				

Fig. 26.2 The correct charge for insurance for the year

Insurance A/c   L 175

19..			£	19..			£
Jan.	1	Motor Vehicle A		Dec.	31	Transfer to Profit and	
		(Bank A/c)	175·50			Loss A/c J 27	309·25
April	1	Motor Vehicle B		Dec.	31	Balance c/d	113·25
		(Bank A/c)	66·00				
June	30	Motor Vehicle C					
		(Bank A/c)	156·00				
Sept.	30	Fire insurance					
		(Bank A/c)	25·00				
			£422·50				£422·50
Dec.	31	Balance B/d	113·25				

Fig. 26.3 A nominal account that has temporarily become an asset account

Balance Sheet
(as at December 31st 19..)

	£	
Current Asset		
Premiums in Advance	113·25	

Fig. 26.4 The temporary asset on the Balance Sheet

Payments in advance are also commonly made for rates, for advertising and occasionally for wages when an employee, for some domestic reason, seeks an advance of salary. Very often, too, there will be a balance of postage stamps, advertising brochures and stationery in stock. All these should be carried forward to the next year.

26.4   Payments in Advance to the Firm

If payments can be made in advance by firms then clearly some other firms will be receiving them in advance. The insurance premiums referred to in the last section will be part of a mass of premium revenue received by the insurance companies, much of which represents a liability for cover in the new year. Where an insurance company still owes clients protection in the early months of the year ahead, it will not be able to treat these sums as revenue income for the year that has passed. It will instead carry them forward as a liability for the coming year. Some typical entries are shown below.

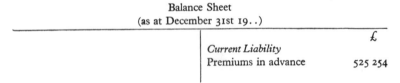

	Premiums-Received A/c		L 121
19..	£	19..	£
Dec. 31 Profit and Loss		Jan.—Dec. Sundry Cash	
A/c	850 000	items	1 375 254
31 Balance c/d	525 254		
	£1 375 254		£1 375 254
		19..	
		Jan. 1 Balance B/d	525 254

Fig. 26.5 Payments in advance to the firm

Balance Sheet
(as at December 31st 19..)

	£
Current Liability	
Premiums in advance	525 254

Fig. 26.6 A temporary liability on the Balance Sheet

However, the accounts of insurance companies present special difficulties and are not within the range of discussion of this book.

26.5   Payments Accrued Due by the Firm

At the end of a financial year there are invariably some payments due, which will not be paid until the next financial period. These are often called 'accruals', that is, debts which have collected and are due for payment.

A common case of accrued expenses is the unpaid part of the wages for the year which is left unpaid when the financial year does not end on pay day, which is usually a Friday. Clearly only once every five or six years will December 31st be a Friday; on other years the last Friday of the year will be some other day. If Friday is pay day, and wages are only paid on that day, then clearly a few remaining days of wages in most years will have 'accrued due' by the last day of the year. This amount of wages should be added to the wages paid to give a complete picture of the expense for the year.

Entries would appear as shown in Figs. 26.7 and 26.8.

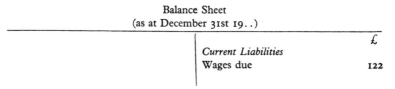

	Wages A/c			L 162
19..	£	19..		£
Jan.—Dec. 27 Cash payments	17 246	Dec. 31 Transfer to Trading		
Dec. 31 Wages due c/d	122	A/c		17 368
	£17 368			£17 368
		Jan. 1 Balance	B/d	122

	Trading A/c		L 177
19..	£		
Dec. 31 Opening Stock, etc.	—		
31 Wages	17 368		

Fig. 26.7 Transferring wages for the full year, including wages accrued due

Balance Sheet
(as at December 31st 19..)

		£
	Current Liabilities	
	Wages due	122

Fig. 26.8 Accrued expenses on the Balance Sheet

Other common accrued expenses are such items as rent due, light and heat bills due, advertising expenses due, etc.

What is the Effect of the Credit Balance?

As shown in Fig. 26.7, any expense due appears as a credit balance on the account. What is the effect of this credit balance? Consider the first wages payment of the new year, made, let us say, in this case on January 5th. Clearly this payment will be credited on the cash book and debited in the Wages Account as a revenue expense for the new year. This is shown in Fig. 26.9.

	Wages A/c			L 162
19..	£	19..		£
Jan. 5 Cash A/c	CB 19	368·50	Jan. 1 Balance	B/d 122·00

Fig. 26.9 The first wage payment of the new year

Clearly this payment of £368·50 is not all a revenue expense for the new year. That part of it (£122) which was taken into account as a loss of the previous year will not be also a loss for the new year. The effect of the balance on the credit side of the Wages Account is therefore to reduce the revenue expense for the new year to the proper figure of £246·50.

26.6   Payments Accrued Due to the Firm

Just as debts can collect which are due for payment by the firm, it is also possible for items to collect due to the firm. Often a sub-tenant will be behind with his rent, or a firm will delay paying commission to which we are entitled. In such circumstances the profit earned from these transactions will be taken into account even if it has not been paid. What is needed is to arrive at a true profit figure for the year, even though some of this profit has not yet been collected from those who owe it to us. Figs. 26.10 and 26.11 illustrate the treatment.

			Rent-Received A/c			L 134
19..			£	19..		£
Dec. 31	Transfer to			Mar. 31 Cash	CB 5	150
	Profit and Loss			June 29 Cash	CB 11	150
	A/c	L 178	600	Sept. 27 Cash	CB 19	150
				Dec. 31 Balance	c/d	150
			£600			£600
19..						
Jan. 1	Balance	B/d	150			

		Profit and Loss A/c		L 178
		19..		£
		Dec. 31 Rent Received		600

Fig. 26.10 Taking the correct profit figure for the year into account

Balance Sheet
(as at December 31st 19..)

	£	
Current Assets		
Rent due from sub-tenant	150	

Fig. 26.11 An asset (rent due to the business)

You should now attempt some exercises on payments in advance and accrued expenses.

26.7   Exercises Set 33: Payments in Advance and Accrued Expenses

1   The Trial Balance extracted from the books of J. Cakebread at December 31st 19.. includes the following debit balances:

	£
Rent paid	750
Rates	500
Wages	36 000
Interest on loan	100
Insurance	120

The following adjustments have to be made before the preparation of the Final Accounts:

	£
Rent outstanding	250
Rates paid in advance	125
Wages accrued due	500
Interest on loan unpaid	100
Insurance paid in advance	30

Show the ledger accounts from which the Trial Balance was prepared, give the closing entries and bring down all balances.   (RSA I)

2. Goodsell commenced trading on January 1st 19.. on which date he took over a showroom suite at an annual rental of £1 700.

On August 1st 19.. a section of the premises was sub-let at an annual rental of £300.

During the year ended December 31st 19.. at which date Goodsell ends his financial year, the following payments had been made in respect of rent:

March 25th, £425; June 24th, £425; September 29th, £425
and the following amounts had been received from the sub-tenant:
August 2nd, £75; November 1st, £75.

Write up separate accounts for rent payable and rent receivable and balance them at the financial year end, showing the appropriate transfers to Profit and Loss Account.   (RSA I)

3. From the following particulars write up P. Mugleston's Electricity Account for the year ending December 31st 19.. Show the amount transferred to the Profit and Loss Account.

		£
January 1st	Electricity used since last reading and already	
	charged to Profit and Loss Account	20
February 8th	Paid Electricity Board cash	38
May 13th	,, ,, ,, ,,	36
August 11th	,, ,, ,, ,,	27
November 12th	,, ,, ,, ,,	31

On December 31st P. Mugleston read his meter and found he had used 1 680 units since his meter was last read for the account in November. He is charged £0·01 per unit, and wishes to bring this charge into account for the year just ended.

4. At January 1st 19.. D. Bird, a grocer, owed £150 for rent and his rates were paid in advance to the extent of £22. During the year he made the following payments:
Rent: March 27th, £300; September 29th, £320.
Rates: April 4th, £44; October 8th, £46.
  You are required to write up Bird's combined Rent and Rates Account for the year, taking into consideration the following matters outstanding at December 31st.
Rent accrued £160
Rates prepaid £23
and showing the transfer to Profit and Loss Account for the year ended December 31st 19..

5. A. Retailer sub-lets the flat over his shop at an annual rental of £312, payable quarterly in arrear. During 19.. the tenant paid the rent due from him on March 25th, June 30th and September 29th, but at December 31st he had not yet paid the quarter's rent due. Show the rent account in the retailer's ledger, as it would appear after the preparation of his Profit and Loss Account for the year.

(RSA 1)

6. The Unworthy Wholesaling Co. Ltd., pays its wages on the system of keeping a week in hand. On January 1st 19.. the company held £7 000 in hand. During the year they paid £360 000 in wages and held £6 500 on December 31st 19..
  Of the wages paid, it was calculated that £12 000 should be charged to warehouse maintenance.
  Write up the Wages Account for the year ended December 31st 19.. and show the amount transferred to the Trading Account.

7. Here is the trial balance of H. Hollow as at March 31st 19.. Prepare his Trading Account, Profit and Loss Account and Balance Sheet.

	Dr. £	Cr. £
Capital (H. Hollow)		5 000·00
Cash	125·00	
Bank	6 975·00	
Premises	4 000·00	
Motor Vehicles	850·00	
Plant and Machinery	1 270·00	
Office Furniture	866·50	
Office Salaries	2 735·25	
Factory Wages	1 624·00	
Office Light and Heat	38·00	
Commission Received		594·00
Loan from M. Long		4 406·00
Office Expenses	28·25	
Advertising	164·00	
Discount Allowed and Received	27·00	36·75
Purchases and Sales	5 246·00	18 294·75
Sales Returns and Purchases Returns	124·00	196·75
Drawings (H. Hollow)	4 600·00	
Stock at March 1st 19..	1 320·00	
Debtors and Creditors	686·50	2 339·75
Carriage In	160·00	
Carriage Out	28·50	
	£30 868·00	30 868·00

Stock at the end of March was valued at £1 800. £48·50 is owing for factory wages and is to be included in the above accounts. Commission amounting to £26 has not yet been received, but is to be included as part of the year's profits.

8. On January 1st 19.. R. Green, a wholesale tobacconist, owed £15 for stationery and had in his office stationery valued at £18. During the three months ended March 31st he made the following payments to his stationery suppliers (for whom personal accounts are not kept):
January 28th, £43; February 26th, £17; March 29th, £57.
At March 31st Green had unpaid bills for stationery amounting to £8 and he estimated the value of his stationery stock at £32.
Write up Green's Stationery Account, balancing it at March 31st 19.. at which date Green prepares his quarterly Profit and Loss Account.
(RSA 1)

9. On January 1st 19.. P. Green, who owns his premises, lets the flat over his shop for an annual rent of £420, payable in cash monthly in advance. During the first six months of his tenancy the tenant paid the rent due on

January 1st, February 3rd, March 2nd, April 9th, and May 14th; but the rent due for June had not been paid when the Profit and Loss Account for the six months was prepared on June 30th. Show the Rent Account as it would appear in P. Green's ledger as at that date.   (RSA I)

10. From the following Trial Balance prepare a Trading Account and Profit and Loss Account for the year ended December 31st 19.. and a Balance Sheet as at that date. The adjustments given below the Trial Balance are to be taken into account.

F. Grosvenor's Books
Trial Balance (as at December 31st 19..)

	Dr.	Cr.
	£	£
Postage	385	
Printing and Stationery	525	
Capital (F. Grosvenor)		4 735
Cash in Hand	25	
Cash at Bank	1 560	
Opening Stock	1 250	
Purchases and Sales	24 750	46 650
Returns In and Out	150	650
Carriage In	250	
Carriage Out	190	
Wages (Trading Account)	2 500	
Office Salaries	3 100	
Rent Received from Sub-tenant		355
Bad Debt Recovered		25
Rent and Rates	800	
Premises	5 500	
Plant and Machinery	3 250	
Drawings (F. Grosvenor)	1 000	
Insurance	250	
Discount Allowed and Received	150	20
Debtors and Creditors	4 250	5 750
Advertising	3 300	
Distribution Expenses	6 700	
Loan from P. Carr		4 000
Furniture and Fittings	800	
Motor Vehicles	1 500	
	£62 185	£62 185

Closing Stock on December 31st 19.. = £1 000
Rates Paid in Advance = £20
Wages Due = £50.   (East Anglian Examinations Board)

26.8 Adjustments for Bad Debts and Provisions for Bad Debts

At the end of any financial year the accountant should appraise his list of debtors to consider whether there are any bad debtors among them. If there are any such bad debtors they should be written off at once, the loss being charged to Profit and Loss Account for the year. (See Section 13.2.)

Even when such bad debtors have been eliminated the accounts do not represent a 'true and fair view' of the debtors, since every accountant knows that he will suffer a certain percentage of bad debts. This percentage varies with the type of trade, the locality, etc. How shall the accountant provide for these bad debts, which cannot be written off at once, because we have no idea which debtor will eventually fail to pay. The answer lies in setting aside an agreed percentage of the total debtors' figure in a special account called the Provision for Bad Debts Account. This account represents some of the owner's profits, tucked away in the Provision for Bad Debts Account instead of being made available to the proprietor as profit for the year. The Journal entry and accounts are shown in Figs. 26.12 and 26.13.

				£	J 1 £
19.. Dec.	31	Profit and Loss A/c Dr. Provision for Bad Debts A/c Being profits set aside equal to 5 per cent of the debtors' figure at this date	L 178 L 163	240	240

Fig. 26.12 Providing for future bad debts

Profit and Loss A/c				L 178
19.. Dec. 31 Provision for Bad Debts J 1	£ 240			

Provision for Bad Debts A/c				L 163
	19.. Dec. 31 Profit and Loss A/c J 1	£ 240		

Fig. 26.13 The Provision for Bad Debts Account

(1) Displaying the Debtors on the Balance Sheet
The Provision for Bad Debts Account is an account with a credit balance—a liability of the business. To whom is it owed? The answer is that it is owed

to the proprietor; it is some of this year's profit tucked away in a special account, since we have an uneasy feeling that it is not really profit at all, but will be lost as some of the debts become bad debts. How shall we show it on the Balance Sheet? Clearly it should be on the liabilities side, *but it is much better to show it as a deduction from the assets* side in order to bring out the estimated true value of the debtors. This is demonstrated in Fig. 26.14.

Balance Sheet
(as at December 31st 19..)

	£	£
Current Assets		
Debtors	4 800	
Less Provision for bad debts	240	
	———	4 560

Fig. 26.14 Displaying debtors at a truer valuation

(2) The Provision for Bad Debts Account in Subsequent Years

In the next year, three possible situations could arise:

(*a*) The bad debts could prove to be exactly the same as the provision made for them, i.e. £240 in the example given. This is so extremely unlikely that we will disregard it.

(*b*) The bad debts could be less than the sum set aside. In this case there will be a balance left on the Provision Account which will reduce the charge for bad debts in the coming year.

(*c*) The bad debts could exceed the sum set aside. This would be the most likely case, for not only would bad debts be expected on the debts outstanding on January 1st, but also on new debts incurred during the year as it proceeded.

The best thing to do in both these cases is to charge the Bad Debts Account, not to the Profit and Loss Account, but to the Provision for Bad Debts Account, and adjust any outstanding balance as the provision for the new year is made.

The effects of cases (*b*) and (*c*) are shown in Figs. 26.15 and 26.16.

Provision for Bad Debts A/c   L 163

19..			£	19..				£
Dec. 31 Bad Debts for				Jan. 1 Balance		B/d	240
year	J 1	139	Dec. 31 Profit and Loss J 5			99
31 Balance	c/d	200				
		£339				£339

				19..				
				Jan. 1 Balance		B/d	200·00
				(*Note*: Being 5% of debtors at end of year)			

Fig. 26.15 A good year—not too many bad debts

			Provision for Bad Debts A/c			L 163
19..			£	19..		£
Dec. 31 Bad Debts for				Jan. 1 Balance B/d		200
year	J 11	396		Dec. 31 Profit and Loss J 11		446
31 Balance	c/d	250				
		£646				£646

19..					
Jan. 1 Balance		B/d	250		
(*Note:* Being 5% of debtors at end of year)					

Fig. 26.16 A bad year—many bad debts

26.9 Provisions for Discounts

(1) Discount to be Allowed

If it is correct to reduce the debtors' figure by the amount of the expected bad debts, it could equally be argued that it is also desirable to reduce the debtors' figure by the amount of expected discount that the debtors will claim as they pay their accounts. In Fig. 26.14 the debtors of £4 700 have been reduced by £240 for expected bad debts. The remainder of the debtors are expected to pay, but will they pay the figure of £4 560 shown on the Balance Sheet. Almost certainly not, for they will probably claim discount. We ought therefore to prepare a Provision for Discount Account very similar to the Provision for Bad Debts. Fig. 26.17 and 26.18 illustrate these points. Note that the Provision for Discount is only calculated on the *remaining* debtors' figure.

19..					£	£ J15
Dec.	31	Profit and Loss A/c Dr.	L 154		228	
		Provision for Discounts A/c	L 155			228
		Being discount provided at 5% on the balance of debtors deemed to be good				

Fig. 26.17 Providing for discount allowed

The entries in the accounts will result in a reduction of the profits for the year by the amount provided £228, and this would be balanced on the Balance Sheet by the following entries.

Balance Sheet
(as at December 31st 19..)

	£	£
Current Assets		
Debtors	4 800	
Less Provision for Bad		
Debts	240	
	4 560	
Less Provision for		
Discounts	228	
		4 332

Fig. 26.18 A 'true and fair' view of the debtors

(2) Discounts to be Received

If it is fair to provide for possible losses, such as bad debts or discounts to be allowed, is it also fair to take account of the discount to be received? Clearly the creditors we must pay will not be as great as appears on the Trial Balance if discount is to be earned by early payment. This is one of those debatable points which some accountants would be prepared to consider, while others would reject the idea. Since it offends against that important rule that we should always accept a loss when it is likely to occur, but should never take a profit until we actually make it, it is better not to anticipate a profit in this way.

You should now try some exercises on the treatment of provisions for bad debts.

26.10   Exercises Set 34: Bad Debts and Provision for Bad Debts

1. At December 31st 19.. a firm's debtors totalled £2 670 and its Provision for Bad Debts Account from January 1st 19.. amounted to £140. It was decided to write off as irrecoverable debts of £130 and to carry forward a provision of 5 per cent of the debtors.

   Prepare the Provision for Bad and Doubtful Debts Account, the entries in the Profit and Loss Account, and the entry for debtors on the Balance Sheet at December 31st 19..   (RSA 1 adapted)

2. At January 1st 19.. a firm's debtors amounted to £24 240 and at December 31st 19.. £26 360. It is the firm's practice to have a bad debt provision of 5 per cent of the debtors at the end of each year.

   During the year, a debt amounting to £132 was written off, and a debt of £24, previously written off, was paid in full.

   Draw up a statement showing the amount of the charge to Profit and Loss Account for the year 19.. in respect of bad debts (including adjustment of the bad debt provision).

3. At April 1st 19.. a firm's debtors amounted to £18 750 and at March 31st a year later to £11 500. It is the firm's practice to have a bad debt provision of 5 per cent of the debtors at the end of each year.

During the year, a debt amounting to £380 was written off, and a debt of £46 previously written off, was paid in full.

Draw up a statement showing the amount of the charge to Profit and Loss Account if any for the financial year in respect of bad debts (including adjustment of the bad debt provision).

4. N. Thorn maintains a bad and doubtful debts provision equal in amount to 5 per cent of the debts outstanding at the end of each financial year.

From the following information prepare the Provision for Bad and Doubtful Debts Account for the year 19..

		£
Total debtors on January 1st 19..		4 500
Total debtors on December 31st 19..		5 360
Debts written off as irrecoverable:		
On May 31st 19..	T. Tomkins	26
On May 31st 19..	S. Carter	145
On July 31st 19..	P. Lane	40
On November 30th 19..	N. Lucas	57

On October 1st a first and final dividend of £0·15 in the pound was received in respect of the debt from P. Lane written off on July 31st. On November 17th 19.. £30 was received in respect of a debt due from K. Jones which had been written off in a previous year.

Balance the account as on December 31st 19.. and show the amount charged to the Profit and Loss Account for the year.

5. The Balance Sheet of J. Wilson, dated January 1st 19.. gave his total debtors as £5 500 and there was a provision of 8 per cent against bad debts. During the following year the bad debts written off amounted to £350, but a debt of £72 written off in the previous year was paid in full.

At December 31st 19.. Wilson's debtors were £6 500 and he decided to increase his provision to 10 per cent of that amount.

You are to prepare the Bad Debts and Provision Accounts for the year 19.. and to show the relevant entries in the Profit and Loss Account for 19.. and in the Balance Sheet dated December 31st 19..

6. On January 1st 19.. the Sales Ledger of Roberts and Brown Ltd., showed the following debtors:

	£
Hall	480
Smith	260
Stevens	320
Peterson	150
Johannsen	56

The firm had a Bad Debt Provision equal to 10 per cent of the total debts outstanding. Trading continued during the year 19.. with these and other customers, except that there were no sales to Peterson or Johannsen, the former made no payment in respect of the amount due from him, while Johannsen paid only £30 during the year. On December 31st 19.. (a) it was found that the Sales Ledger debit balances, including those due from Peterson and Johannsen, totalled £876; (b) it was decided to write off as bad debts the amounts then due from Peterson and Johannsen, and (c) it was decided to adjust the bad debts provision to 20 per cent of the remaining debts.

You are asked to show the entries recording the above in the appropriate impersonal Ledger Accounts for the financial year ended December 31st 19.., including the entries in the firm's Profit and Loss Account for the year.

7. The Balance Sheet of C. Bolton, dated January 1st 19.., gave his total debtors as £8 500 and there was a provision of 5 per cent against bad debts. During the following year the bad debts written off amounted to £500, but a debt of £150 written off in a previous year was paid in full.

At December 31st, a year later, Bolton's debtors were £9 000 and he decided to increase his provision to 10 per cent of that amount.

You are to prepare the Bad Debts and Bad Debts Provision Accounts for the year 19.. and to show the relevant entries in the Profit and Loss Account and in the Balance Sheet dated December 31st 19..

(RSA 1 adapted)

8. M. Rooselar's Trial Balance was as follows on December 31st 19.. Prepare his Trading Account, Profit and Loss Account and Balance Sheet. The following adjustments are to be taken into account:

Stock at December 31st 19.. was £3 000.

Debts worth £50 are considered completely bad and are to be written off.

A provision for bad debts of £200 is to be created.

Trial Balance
(as at December 31st 19. .)

	Dr.	Cr.
	£	£
Opening Stock	1 950	
Capital		6 377
Carriage Out	26	
Sundry Expenses	300	
Purchases and Sales	25 000	34 000
Returns In and Out	86	36
Salaries	2 350	
Cash	25	
Land and Buildings	3 500	
Plant and Machinery	1 500	
Office Furniture	1 850	
Discount Allowed and Received	26	125
Debtors and Creditors	1 534	3 676
Light and Heat	190	
Commission Paid to Travellers	760	
Cash at Bank	2 875	
Rent and Rates	242	
Drawings	2 000	
	£44 214	£44 214

(East Anglian Examinations Board)

9. Here is the Trial Balance of Gerard Eliasson on December 31st 19. .
You are asked to prepare his Trading Account and Profit and Loss
Account for the year, and his Balance Sheet, as at this date, bearing in
mind the adjustments given below the Trial Balance.

Trial Balance
(as at December 31st 19. .)

	Dr.	Cr.
	£	£
Cash in Hand	27	
Cash at Bank	2 465	
Purchases and Sales	8 248	13 612
Returns In and Out	112	48
Stock (at January 1st 19. .)	780	
Wages (Trading Account)	450	
Salaries	580	
Light and Heat	420	
Commission Received		650
Rent Received		100
Telephone Expenses	120	
Insurance	250	
Motor Vehicles	250	
Land and Buildings	4 000	
Plant and Machinery	1 400	
Loan from Southern Bank		2 000
Interest Paid	150	
Capital		2 812
Debtors and Creditors	3 250	4 280
Drawings	1 000	
	£23 502	£23 502

Notes:

1. At December 31st 19. . stock was valued at £1 250.
2. Debtors include one debt of £150 which is regarded as definitely bad.
3. It is decided to provide for future bad debts at 10 per cent of the *remaining* debtors, and then to provide for discount at 5 per cent on the outstanding balance. (To nearest £1.)

(East Anglian Examinations Board)

26.11   Other Adjustments

To return to our list of adjustments to Final Accounts (Section 26.2), we will now look at the last five items on that list.

Closing stock. Closing stock has been fully discussed in Unit Twenty-five, and in the Unit on the Trading Account, Section 5.4.

Depreciation of assets. This has been fully discussed in Unit Twenty-two.

The appreciation of assets. It has been said already that one of the important principles of accounting is that one should never anticipate a profit; one should leave it to be enjoyed in the period when it is actually realized. There is one exception to this rule. It is the appreciation (increase in value) of land, which is the result of the pressure of population and higher living standards on available housing and property. It is a matter of some concern to limited companies, whose shares may be purchased on the stock exchange. These firms may find that unrealized appreciations in the values of the sites they occupy may lead to take-over bids by speculators anxious to take over the company, not to continue it as a going concern, but to close it down and realize the very considerable sums of money to be obtained by selling the site for redevelopment.

If it is decided to recognize the increase in site values and raise the value of land and buildings above its original cost, the resulting profit, which is of a capital nature, should be credited to Capital Account, or a Capital Reserve Account, and not be treated as a revenue profit, since it would then be taxable. The increase in value, if caught by tax at all, would only be caught for taxation purposes at a later date. The recognition of the true site value in this way will be reflected in the price of shares on the market and will reduce the profitability of a take-over bid. The presence of a 'secret reserve' of which other investors are not aware is the situation which gives the speculator his opportunity. The Journal entry, etc., would be as shown in Figs. 26.19 and 26.20.

19..					£	£ J27
Dec.	31	Land and Buildings Dr.	L 1		3 000	
		Capital A/c (or Revaluation				
		of Premises A/c)	L 2			3 000
		Being revaluation of premises to				
		take account of changing site				
		values				

Fig. 26.19 Appreciation of site values

Balance Sheet
(as at December 31st 19..)

	£	£		£
Fixed Assets			*Capital at Start*	17 500
Land and Buildings	20 000		*Add* capital appreciation	3 000
Revaluation	3 000			————
	————	23 000		20 500
				etc.

Fig. 26.20 Assets revalued to give a 'true and fair' view

Amortization of leases. This subject has been adequately described in the Unit on depreciation, Section 22.6.

Goodwill—an unusual asset. When a businessman purchases a going concern, he nearly always has to pay an additional sum for the *goodwill* of the business. This is a payment to compensate the previous owner for his hard work in the past, since that hard work will continue to earn profits for the new owner in the future. One judge defined goodwill as 'a payment for the probability that the old customers will return to the old place'. It is often referred to as an *intangible asset*, in that the payment purchases an asset which does exist, but only in the minds of local people. It cannot be physically touched like other assets taken over.

(*a*) *The paradox of goodwill.* Accountants sometimes talk of the paradox of goodwill. A paradox is something which is self contradictory. The paradox of goodwill arises because of the practice of depreciating goodwill. We will examine the paradox by considering a simple example.

Mr A. buys a grocery retail business paying £5 000 for the premises, etc., and £3 000 extra for goodwill. He does not know anyone in the district and no one knows him. On the commencement of business, say January 1st 19.., no one bears him any goodwill at all, despite the balance on his Goodwill Account which reads '£3 000'. Clearly this goodwill is not born to him— but to the previous owner. It is an untrue statement really, and should be written off. Mr A. decides to write the goodwill off over three years at £1 000 per annum. As he does so, the Goodwill Account first diminishes on the Balance Sheet, and finally vanishes from it. Yet at the same time the goodwill actually borne to Mr A. is increasing. He is now the life and soul of the local Chamber of Trade, perhaps, and is a popular and respected trader in the district. *The paradox of goodwill is that when valued on the books at a high figure it is really worth nothing, and when valued on the books at nothing it is really worth a high figure.*

(*b*) *Writing-off goodwill—an appropriation of profit.* The important point about writing off goodwill is that it is not a revenue expense, not a charge against the profits, but an appropriation of profit towards the reduction of capital.

The difference between a *charge against the profits* and an *appropriation of profit* is an important one. A charge against the profits is a revenue expense, which reduces the profit for the year. It is admissible by the Inland-Revenue authorities as a legitimate cost incurred in earning the incomes received, and reduces tax payable. An appropriation of profit is quite different. It is a voluntary decision by the owner of a business to appropriate the profit earned, after tax has been paid, in a particular way, which results in the writing off of an intangible or fictitious asset. A *fictitious asset* is one for which there is nothing real to show at all. The best example is *Preliminary Expenses Account* of a limited company, where legal and other expenses have been paid just to get the company organized and under way. Appropriations of profit only take place after the profit has been assessed for the year—they do not determine the profit made. It follows that the Journal entry for the depreciation of goodwill charges the reduction to Capital Account, not Profit and Loss Account. This is shown in Figs. 26.21 and 26.22.

19.. Dec.	31	Capital Account Dr. Goodwill Account Being appropriation of profit to reduce Goodwill at this date	L 2 L 3	£ 1 000	£ J27 1 000

Fig. 26.21 Appropriating profit to reduce Goodwill Account

Balance Sheet
(as at December 31st 19..)

	£	£		£	£
Fixed Assets			Capital At start		8 000
Goodwill	3 000		Net Profit	2 850	
Less Appropriation	1 000		Less Drawings	850	
		2 000		2 000	
			Less Goodwill		
etc.			reduction	1 000	
					1 000
					9 000

Fig. 26.22 Goodwill reduced on the Balance Sheet

You should now attempt some of the Final Accounts exercises shown below, designed to contain every type of adjustment possible.

26.12   Exercises Set 35: Difficult Final-Accounts Exercises

1. The following Trial Balance was extracted from the books of J. March, a wholesale merchant, on December 31st 19. .

	£	£
Capital		17 800
Drawings	1 000	
Leasehold Premises (Lease to run 10 years from January 1st of this year)	5 000	
Advertising	138	
Motor Vans	938	
Purchases and Sales	68 496	73 572
Stock at January 1st 19. .	2 036	
Debtors and Creditors	14 898	9 570
Insurance	203	
Bad Debts	37	
Returns Inwards	67	
Returns Outwards		403
Furniture and Fittings	1 110	
Telephone Expenses	45	
Rates and Water	112	
Wages (Trading Account)	2 848	
Lighting and Heating	102	
Postage	149	
Cash in Hand	363	
Balance at Bank	3 803	
	£101 345	£101 345

Prepare the Trading and Profit and Loss Accounts for the year ended December 31st 19. . and the Balance Sheet at that date. In preparing the accounts, the following matters should be taken into consideration:

(a) The stock at December 31st 19. . was valued at £9 645.

(b) An appropriate rate of amortization should be written off the leasehold premises.

(c) 20 per cent *per annum* on cost (£1 500) should be written off motor vans.

(d) 10 per cent *per annum* should be written off furniture and fittings.

(e) Wages accrued amounted to £34.

(f) A provision for bad debts of £230 is to be created.   (RSA II)

2. From the following information prepare the Light and Heat Account in the ledger of R. Smart, showing the entries in correct date order and

the sum finally transferred to the Profit and Loss Account, at December 31st 19. .

	£
January 1st Debit Balance—Stock of fuel oil	42·50
January 1st Credit Balance—Electricity bill due	62·50
Payments for electricity during year to Eastern Electricity Board	
January 16th	62·50
April 20th	55·75
July 18th	45·25
October 16th (Repairs)	0·90
October 17th	52·50
Payments for fuel oil to Morgan Ltd.	
March 31st	96·50
September 30th	100·20

The bill for electricity supplied up to December 31st was £80·60. This was not paid until January 4th, 19. . On December 31st the stock of fuel oil carried forward to the next year was valued at £51·40.

(East Anglian Examinations Board)

3. The following trial balance was extracted from the books of Saul, a trader, on December 31st 19. .

Trial Balance

	£	£
Capital Account		25 000
Freehold Land and Buildings	9 000	
Furniture and Fittings	1 340	
Stock in Trade January 1st 19. .	11 400	
Lighting and Heating	178	
Drawings	5 800	
Purchases	78 600	
Sales		105 200
General Expenses	3 602	
Balance at Bank	824	
Motor Van	240	
Discounts Received		1 764
Discounts Allowed	2 228	
Trade Debtors	9 500	
Trade Creditors		7 650
Rates and Insurance	192	
Wages and Salaries (Profit and Loss Account)	14 970	
Goodwill	1 200	
Bad Debts written off	860	
Provision for Bad Debts January 1st 19. .		320
	£139 934	£139 934

The following matters are to be taken into account:

(a) Stock in trade December 31st 19.. £15 800.

(b) Rates and insurance paid in advance December 31st 19.. £50.

(c) The motor van shown in the trial balance was sold on December 31st 19.. for £80 cash, which Saul retained for private use. No entry for this transaction had been made in the books.

(e) Goodwill is to be reduced by £300.

(f) Lighting and heating outstanding on December 31st 19.. was £28.

(g) The provision for doubtful debts is to be increased to £460.

(h) Provide for depreciation of furniture and fittings £134.

You are required to prepare a Trading and Profit and Loss Account for the year 19.. and a Balance Sheet as on December 31st 19.. (RSA II)

4. The following balances were extracted from the books of S. Smith at December 31st 19..

	£
Capital—Smith	10 059
Stock in Trade, January 1st 19..	2 720
Petty Cash	55
Bank Overdraft	2 522
Sundry Debtors	7 009
Sundry Creditors	6 735
Motor Vans (cost £2 000)	1 500
Drawings	2 459
Fixtures and Fittings (cost £4 000)	3 800
Purchases	33 436
Provision for Bad Debts	162
Sales	50 261
Purchase Returns	120
Carriage Inwards	546
Rent and Rates	626
Salaries and Wages (Profit and Loss Account)	5 226
General Expenses	920
Interest on Bank Overdraft and Bank Charges	56
Carriage Outwards	720
Discounts Allowed	65
Discounts Received	59
Returns Inwards	240
Freehold Buildings	10 300
Bad Debts	240

You are given the following information:

(a) The stock in trade at December 31st 19.. was valued at £4 270.

(b) Wages and salaries outstanding at 31st December 19.. were £426.

(c) Rates paid in advance at December 31st 19.. amounted to £100.

(*d*) The provision for bad debts is to be increased to £260.

(*e*) Depreciation is to be charged as follows:
>   Motor vans, 25 per cent *per annum* on cost;
>   Fixtures and fittings, 5 per cent *per annum* on cost.

Now prepare a Trading and Profit and Loss Account for the year 19.. and a Balance Sheet at December 31st 19..   (RSA II)

5. The Trial Balance extracted from the books of Wormley, a trader, as at December 31st 19.. was as follows:

Trial Balance

	£	£
Capital		11 219
Furniture and Equipment (cost £2 100)	1 640	
Motor Vans (cost £1 700)	1 120	
Purchases	36 291	
Rent and Rates	800	
Salaries	3 969	
Bad Debts	281	
General Expenses	1 062	
Bank Balance	308	
Sales		45 622
Provision for Doubtful Debts as at January 1st 19..		269
Stock in Trade as at January 1st, 19..	8 726	
Debtors	4 289	
Creditors		3 164
Drawings	1 788	
	£60 274	£60 274

You are given the following additional information:

(*a*) Stock in trade December 31st 19.. £9 428.

(*b*) Rates paid in advance at December 31st 19.. £60.

(*c*) General expenses unpaid at December 31st 19.. £166.

(*d*) Provision for doubtful debts is to be adjusted to £241.

(*e*) A motor van purchased on January 1st of this year at a cost of £800 was traded in for £350 on December 31st 19.. and a new van purchased at a cost of £1 000 on the same day. The amount due on the new van was payable on January 1st 19.. No entries had been made in the books in respect of this transaction when the Trial Balance at December 31st 19.. was extracted.

(*f*) Depreciation is to be charged on furniture and equipment at the rate of 5 per cent *per annum* on cost and on the vans at the rate of 25 per cent *per annum* on cost.

You are asked to prepare Wormley's Trading and Profit and Loss Account for 19.. and his Balance Sheet as at December 31st 19..

(RSA II)

6. M. Smith is the owner of a large retail store. He lets a small part of the premises to an independent tobacconist. The Trading and Profit and Loss Account for the year ending December 31st 19.. and a Balance Sheet as at that date, are being prepared.

In respect of each group (i to iv) show:

(a) The entry which should appear in the Profit and Loss Account.

(b) The entry which should appear in the Balance Sheet.

(c) The final amount or amounts on the ledger accounts.

(i) January 1st 19.. rent received in advance £20.
Rent received during year ending December 31st 19.. £120.
Rent due on December 31st 19.. £10.

(ii) January 1st 19.. shop furniture and fittings £2 400.
Furniture purchased during year ending December 31st 19.. £600.
December 31st 19.. depreciation written off £400.

(iii) January 1st 19.. provision for bad and doubtful debts £250.
December 31st 19.. total trade debtors £4 800.
December 31st 19.. provision adjusted to 5 per cent of debtors.

(iv) January 1st 19.. rates paid in advance £45.
Rates paid during year ending December 31st 19.. £90.
December 31st 19.. rates due and unpaid £45.

(RSA 1)

7. C. Violet carries on business as a retailer and the balances on his books at 30th September 19.. were as follows:

	£	£
Capital Account		4 496
Drawings	1 200	
Bad Debts and Provision	106	126
Bank Overdraft		567
Carriage Inwards	286	
Carriage Outwards	59	
Equipment of Shop at cost	550	
General Expenses	211	
Insurance	130	
Lighting and Heating	118	
Motor Van at cost	720	
Provision for Depreciation of Motor Van		144
Purchases	43 694	
Rent	360	
Sales		48 699
Stock (at 1st October, previous year)	3 972	
Trade Debtors	2 838	
Trade Creditors		1 693
Salaries	1 762	
Upkeep of Premises	50	
Sales Returns and Purchases Returns	195	987
Van Running Expenses	397	
Cash in Hand	64	
	£56 712	£56 712

Prepare the Trading and Profit and Loss Account for the year ending September 30th 19.. and the Balance Sheet at that date taking the following into consideration:

(a) The stock on hand at September 30th 19.. was valued at £4 196.

(b) The rent paid includes only nine months' rent to June 30th 19..

(c) The provision for bad debts is to be made up to £138, and a provision for discount is to be created of 5 per cent of the remaining debtors.

(d) Insurance in advance at September 30th 19.. amounted to £30.

(e) An account due for repairs to the roof of the premises amounting to £28 had been omitted from the books.

(f) Depreciation of the motor van is to be provided at the rate of 20 per cent *per annum* of cost.

(g) Provide the sum of £100 in respect of the depreciation of the equipment of the shop.

Unit Twenty-Seven
Partnership Accounts

27.1 Partnerships

There are many situations in business life when a partnership seems to be the best type of business unit. For example, in family businesses it is sometimes helpful to recognize the merits of various interested parties by designating them as partners in the business. Names such as Harrison Bros., Sorrell and Son, and Scammell and Nephew are common. In professional businesses the partnership is often the only satisfactory form of business unit, for limited companies are often not permitted by professional bodies, and a single person rarely has all the expertise required for a sophisticated professional service in medicine, dentistry, the law or management consultancy.

The chief reasons for forming partnerships may be listed as follows:

(a) In order to obtain increased capital for an enterprise, so that improved machinery, equipment and buildings may be obtained.

(b) In order to broaden the knowledge and experience available, and thus to offer a more comprehensive service to the public. Thus lawyers who specialize respectively in divorce, motor accident, criminal and conveyancing law may form a partnership to pool their knowledge and experience in these fields.

(c) In order to unite wisdom and experience with youth and vitality. A doctor of mature years who is finding all the calls he is required to make too great a strain upon his health may seek a young and lively partner who will take on the more active part of the practice in exchange for consultations with his senior colleague on tricky cases where a second opinion is desirable.

(d) In order to reduce the onerous responsibilities of a one-man business, where it is impossible to take time off, and where sickness can endanger the very existence of the business. Partners are free to take annual vacations, days and week-ends off, and in times of sickness they can cover the absence of the partner who is not well.

27.2 Agreements Between Partners

Two people can hardly work together at all unless they are in agreement about most things, though such agreements are often not reduced to written form. A mere handshake is sufficient to inaugurate a partnership, and early partnerships were often called 'common ventures' or 'joint ventures'—phrases which include the idea that all business is to some extent an adventure in the way of trade.

Partnerships may be held to have existed by the courts if either partner can prove (*a*) an oral agreement (proved by witnesses), or

(*b*) a systematic course of dealing together by way of trade or professional services, or

(*c*) a written agreement, either formal (drawn up by a solicitor in deed form) or informal (a mere undertaking in writing to be associated with one another). Clearly the formal *partnership deed* is most desirable, since a lawyer experienced in these matters will bring to the partners' attention many points that have caused controversy between partners in the past. Even where people agree to work together at the start of a partnership it does not follow that disagreement will not arise at a later date.

Matters to be Included in a Partnership Deed

The following major points should be included in any partnership agreement.

(*a*) The amount of capital to be contributed by each partner.

(*b*) Whether this capital is to earn interest for the partner, and if so at what rate per cent. Usually it is desirable to give interest on capital if the amounts contributed are unequal. This prevents the partner contributing the greater sum from developing a sense of grievance.

(*c*) Whether any partner is to receive a salary, and if so how much.

It often happens that a young man contributes very little to a partnership in capital, but a great deal in health, strength and energy. While his older partner sits and thinks, the young man is actively engaged on the routine but diverse requirements of the firm's day-to-day activities. The older man should recognize this contribution as one entitling the young man to a reward in the form of a basic salary.

(*d*) The ratio for sharing profits and losses. Simple fractions are usually adopted, i.e. $\frac{1}{2}$ and $\frac{1}{2}$, $\frac{3}{5}$ and $\frac{2}{5}$, $\frac{2}{3}$ and $\frac{1}{3}$, etc.

(*e*) The date the partnership shall commence, and the duration of the partnership. If the duration is to be 'at will', i.e. indefinitely so long as they are in agreement, then it is also wise to specify what arrangements are to be made in the event of the death of a partner. Imagine a partner whose share in the business is £10 000. At his death the heirs to his wealth, and even the Inland-Revenue authorities, will be interested in obtaining their share of the estate. This may result in the collapse of the whole enterprise if assets have to be sold to realize the funds required. It is a wise policy to insure your partner's life, so that if he or she dies you will receive a sum of money which may be used to pay the heirs their share of the inheritance.

(*f*) How much each partner is permitted to draw as 'drawings' each month, or week. Is it desired to charge interest on these drawings?

(*g*) In the event of disputes how shall the dispute be resolved. Some partners specify a particular person to act as arbitrator. Others suggest a formula for choosing an arbitrator, such as a bank manager for financial matters and a solicitor for legal points.

27.3   The Partnership Act of 1890

Partnership law was codified in 1890, that is to say the legal cases on which the law had formerly depended were enacted as a formal set of rules by Parliament, and modified in line with modern thought at that time. It was an age when legislators still believed that controls in business affairs were largely undesirable. The Act therefore established rules to which reference could be made as a last resort, when partners failed to agree on how certain specific points were to be settled. The points enumerated below are not observed by the vast majority of partnerships. An original agreement, however informal, to behave differently from the way suggested in the Act will always be upheld by the Courts. The rules stated below are residual only, that is to say they are used in the few remaining cases where partners entered into no clear arrangements with one another on the point concerned.

These accounting rules are as follows.

(a) All partners are entitled to contribute equally to the capital of the firm. Partners must share equally in the profits and contribute equally to the losses.

(b) No partner may have a salary.

(c) No partner may have interest on capital.

(d) A partner lending money to the firm, over and above his capital contribution is entitled to interest at 5 per cent *per annum*. This interest is a charge against the profits, i.e. it will appear in the Profit and Loss Account as one of the expenses of the business. We shall see below that it is credited to the partner in his Current Account.

(e) Any partner may see and copy the books of the firm, which must be kept at the ordinary place of business.

(f) No new partner may be introduced without the general consent of all the partners.

27.4   The Partnership Capital and the Partners' Accounts

It is usual to keep the original capital contributions of the partners recorded unchanged in their Capital Accounts. That is to say, the Capital Account is not varied from year to year as profit is ploughed into the business or drawings are made from time to time. The Capital Accounts remain at the original figure for the duration of the partnership.

Since it is essential to have some account to which profits may be credited, and from which drawings may be deducted (in this case debited) each partner has a Current Account (i.e. a running account) where these adjustments may be made. Each partner therefore has three accounts.

(a) A Capital Account, credited with the original capital contributed by the partner, and remaining unchanged during the life of the partnership.

(b) A Current Account, credited with all profits earned and debited at the end of the year with all drawings, whether in cash or in kind. (Many partners take home goods for personal use which are charged as drawings although not drawn in cash. These are called *drawings in kind*.)

(*c*) A Drawings Account, into which cash drawings are accumulated as the months go by. This account is cleared at the end of the financial year into the Current Account of the partner.

Typical partnership accounts are illustrated below. For privacy they are often recorded in a separate ledger, called the Private Ledger, and kept by the partners separate from the ordinary books of account.

Capital A/c (A. Partner)				L 1
		19..		£
		Jan. 1 Bank A/c	J 1	3 000·00

Current A/c (A. Partner)						L 2
19..			£	19..		£
June 30 Typewriters A/c	J 4		25·00	Dec. 31 Salary	J 8	1 200·00
Dec. 31 Drawings A/c	J 8	1	550·00	Dec. 31 Interest on		
Dec. 31 Balance	c/d		232·50	Capital	J 8	180·00
				Dec. 31 Share of Residue		
				of Profit	J 8	427·50
		£1	807·50		£1	807·50
				19..		
				Jan. 1 Balance	B/d	232·50

Drawings A/c (A. Partner)						L 3
19..			£	19..		£
Mar. 31 Bank	CB 5		400·00	Dec. 31 Current A/c	J 8	1 550·00
June 30 Bank	CB 12		400·00			
Sept. 30 Bank	CB 19		400·00			
Dec. 31 Bank	CB 27		350·00			
		£1	550·00		£1	550·00

Fig. 27.1 A partner's accounts

27.5 Partnership Final Accounts—the Appropriation Account

The accounts of partnerships are identical with the accounts of sole traders, as to routine books of original entry, the ledger and the Final Accounts, the Trading and Profit and Loss Accounts. Where they differ from the accounts of sole traders is in the allocation of the profits between the partners. This requires a special account, called the Appropriation Account, though some accountants regard it merely as a section of the Profit and Loss Account and called it the Appropriation Section of the Profit and Loss Account.

In the Appropriation Account the net profit achieved, instead of being credited to the Capital Account as with a sole trader, is appropriated between the partners in accordance with the partnership agreement. The chief matters entering into the calculations are as follows, and they are entered in the order shown below.

(a) There may be goodwill to be written off.

(b) A partner, or partners, may be entitled to a partnership salary.

(c) A partner, or partners, may be entitled to interest on capital.

(d) The residue of the profit will then be shared up between the partners in the agreed manner.

It also sometimes happens that partners may be charged interest on drawings, which appear as a credit item on the Appropriation Account. The Appropriation Account shown in Fig. 27.2 illustrates these matters. It refers to the partnership of Hills and Hobbs in the example given below:

Example

Hills and Hobbs are in partnership with capitals of £5 000 and £3 000 respectively. The partnership agreement provides that

(a) profits shall be shared $\frac{5}{8}$ and $\frac{3}{8}$ after giving

(b) Hobbs a salary of £800 and giving

(c) both partners interest on capital at 6 per cent *per annum*.

(d) partners are also to pay interest on drawings calculated at 6 per cent *per annum*.

Draw up the Appropriation Account of the partnership, given that Hills' Drawings were £1 500, drawn in two halves on June 30th and December 31st, while Hobbs had drawn £1 400, in four equal amounts on March 31st, June 30th, September 30th and December 31st. The net profit for the year was £4 800. £500 is to be written off the Goodwill Account.

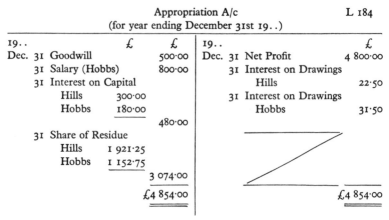

		Appropriation A/c				L 184
		(for year ending December 31st 19..)				
19..		£	£	19..		£
Dec. 31	Goodwill		500·00	Dec. 31 Net Profit		4 800·00
31	Salary (Hobbs)		800·00	31 Interest on Drawings		
31	Interest on Capital			Hills		22·50
	Hills	300·00		31 Interest on Drawings		
	Hobbs	180·00		Hobbs		31·50
			480·00			
31	Share of Residue					
	Hills	1 921·25				
	Hobbs	1 152·75				
			3 074·00			
			£4 854·00			£4 854·00

Fig. 27.2 An Appropriation Account of a partnership

Notes:

(*a*) Goodwill is an intangible asset—it exists in the minds of the people in the area around the business premises. It is best to write off such assets, and disregard their value until the business comes to be sold again. Such sums written off are not regarded as losses that can be deducted from profits—they are *appropriations of profit*, and as such are not deductible for tax purposes.

(*b*) Hobbs' salary is credited to his Current Account.

(*c*) The interest to which each partner is entitled is credited to his Current Account.

(*d*) The interest payable on Drawings is an unusual item. Since the partner is receiving interest on capital it is sometimes felt desirable to charge him interest if he draws out any of his capital. The simplest way to do this is to add an extra column to the Drawings Account, into which the interest can be added. It is calculated on the period outstanding until the end of the year. Two illustrations of such accounts are shown in Fig. 27.3. The interest charged to Drawings Account is credited in the Appropriation Account, and is shared between the partners.

(*e*) The residue of the profit is then shared in the proper proportions.

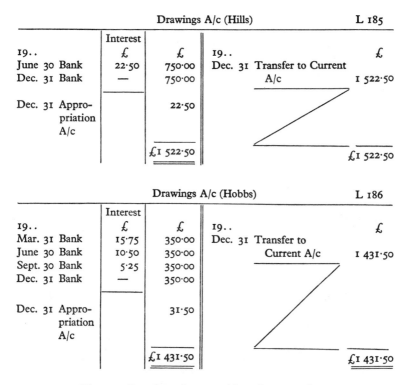

Fig. 27.3 *Drawings Account with an interest column*

27.6 Appropriating a Loss

Sometimes it happens that there is a net loss on the year's activities. This might appear to give some difficulty, but in fact it presents no problems. The various items of salary, interest on capital, etc., are still given to the partners entitled to them. Of course this increases the loss, but the final sharing of the residue appropriates this loss in a proper manner. Fig. 27.4 illustrates the situation, using similar figures to those in Fig. 27.2.

		£	£				£
						Appropriation A/c	L 184

Appropriation A/c   L 184
(for year ending December 31st 19..)

19..		£	£	19..			£
Dec. 31	Net Loss		1 560·00	Dec. 31	Interest on Drawings		
31	Salary (Hobbs)		800·00		Hills		22·50
31	Interest on Capital				Hobbs		31·50
	Hills	300·00		31	Share of Loss		
	Hobbs	180·00			Hills		1 741·25
			480·00		Hobbs		1 044·75
			£2 840·00				£2 840·00

Fig. 27.4 Appropriating a loss

27.7 Exercises Set 36: Partnership Appropriation Accounts

1. Sybrandt and Cornelis are in partnership. They have a written agreement which says:
   (a) Partnership capitals shall carry interest at 10 per cent.
   (b) Cornelis shall have a salary of £750 *per annum*.
   (c) Goodwill shall be reduced each year by 20 per cent.
   (d) Profits over and above those required for the first three clauses shall be shared two-thirds to Sybrandt and one-third to Cornelis.
   Capitals are Sybrandt £5 000; Cornelis £1 000. Goodwill is valued at £2 000. Show the Appropriation Account (i.e. the Appropriation Section of the Profits and Loss Account) for the year if the profits for the year to December 31st 19.. were £4 000.

2. Wheel and Barrow are in partnership under an agreement which provides that profits and losses shall be shared three-fifths and two-fifths respectively, and that, before this division is made, Barrow shall be entitled to a salary of £1 200 *per annum* and partners shall be credited with 8 per cent *per annum* interest on their capitals which are as follows: Wheel—£10 000, Barrow—£4 000.
   The profit for the year ended December 31st 19.., before making any of these adjustments, amounted to £8 820.
   Write up the Profit and Loss Appropriation Account for the year.

3. The Partnership Agreement of Able, Baker and Charles contains the following provisions:

  (a) The partners fixed capital shall be: Able £10 000, Baker £8 000, Charles £6 000.

  (b) Able and Baker are each to receive a salary of £600 per year;

  (c) Interest on capital to be calculated at 5 per cent *per annum*;

  (d) Able, Baker and Charles are to share profits and losses in the ratios 3:2:1.

  The Profit and Loss Account for the year showed a profit of £4 500 before charging interest on capital or partners' salaries.

  Show the Profit and Loss Appropriation Account for the year ended December 31st 19. .

4. At January 1st 19. . R. Hawtrey owned a business in which he had £8 000 capital. As from July 1st 19. . W. Grigg came in as a partner on the following terms:

  (a) The capital to be brought in by Grigg would be £2 000. Hawtrey's capital would remain at £8 000.

  (b) Grigg should have a salary of £1 500 *per annum*.

  (c) Interest at 8 per cent *per annum* to be allowed on both partners' capitals from the start of the partnership.

  (d) After charging both salary and interest on capital any further profit should be shared $\frac{3}{4}$:$\frac{1}{4}$, Hawtrey taking the larger share.

  You are asked to show the Appropriation Section of the Profit and Loss Account at December 31st 19. . for the half year ended on that date. The net profit available for division between the partners was £3 650.

5. Melville and Ahab entered into partnership on April 1st 19. . with capitals of £4 000 and £1 000 respectively.

  The Partnership Agreement provided as follows:

  (a) Ahab to draw a salary of £650 *per annum*;

  (b) interest on capitals to be given at 6 per cent *per annum*;

  (c) residue of profit to be shared two-thirds to Melville and one-third to Ahab.

  On December 31st 19. . they prepared Final Accounts for the nine-month period, showing that the profits were £2 799.

  You are to show the Appropriation Account which shares these profits between the partners.

27.8 The Current Accounts of the Partners

Every partner has three private accounts: a Capital Account to record the original contribution of capital; a Drawings Account, as shown in Fig. 27.3 to record cash drawings; and a Current Account which records the fluctuating part of the partner's relationship with the business. Here are recorded the profits accumulated and the drawings made in cash (transferred from the

Drawings Account) and in kind (transferred by means of Journal entries—see below).

The result of any year's activities results in either a credit balance on the Current Account of a partner, or a debit balance. Imaginary Current Accounts for two partners, B. Careful and A. Spendthrift are shown below in Fig. 27.5.

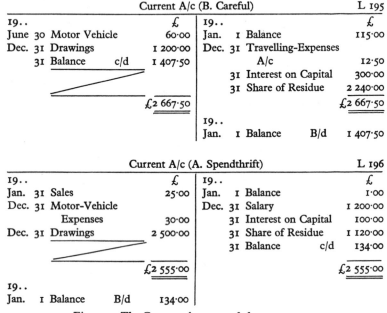

Current A/c (B. Careful)			L 195
19..		19..	£
June 30 Motor Vehicle	60·00	Jan. 1 Balance	115·00
Dec. 31 Drawings	1 200·00	Dec. 31 Travelling-Expenses	
31 Balance c/d	1 407·50	A/c	12·50
		31 Interest on Capital	300·00
		31 Share of Residue	2 240·00
	£2 667·50		£2 667·50
		19..	
		Jan. 1 Balance B/d	1 407·50

Current A/c (A. Spendthrift)			L 196
19..	£	19..	£
Jan. 31 Sales	25·00	Jan. 1 Balance	1·00
Dec. 31 Motor-Vehicle		Dec. 31 Salary	1 200·00
Expenses	30·00	31 Interest on Capital	100·00
Dec. 31 Drawings	2 500·00	31 Share of Residue	1 120·00
		31 Balance c/d	134·00
	£2 555·00		£2 555·00
19..			
Jan. 1 Balance B/d	134·00		

Fig. 27.5 The Current Accounts of the two partners

Notes on these Current Accounts

(a) *The opening balances.* Usually a current account will have an opening balance. In both cases these accounts open with a credit balance, showing that the business owes the balance to the partner—it is a liability for profit made by the partner and not withdrawn.

(b) *The profits earned.* The profits appropriated to the partners in the Appropriation Account have been credited in the partners' current accounts. These items are: (i) Spendthrift's salary, (ii) interest on capital to both partners, (iii) both partners shares of the residue of the profit—in this case shared up two-thirds to Careful and one-third to Spendthrift.

(c) *Drawings in kind. Drawings in kind* are drawings made in the form of goods, furniture, etc., taken from the business by the partner. The most usual item here is the removal for personal use of goods purchased for resale. Following the rule in Sharkey v. Wernher (1953) these must be regarded as sold to the partner at selling price, even though it would be more sensible to regard him as having bought them at cost price. The ruling means that he is forced to make a profit out of himself, which is contrary to common sense. To comply with the law on this point we must debit the partner's Current Account (he has received goods) and credit Sales Account which has given value. This requires a Journal entry as shown below in Fig. 27.6.

19.. Jan.	31	Current A/c (Spendthrift) Dr. Sales A/c Being goods taken home for partner's private use	L 196 L 36	£ 25·00	£ J 19 25·00

Fig. 27.6 Drawings in kind (goods for resale)

Another example of the same sort of charge to Current Account is where a partner takes a vehicle, or other asset of the business, at an agreed valuation, because it is surplus to the requirements of the business. Similarly he may agree to pay some portion of motor vehicle expenses because he has used the firm's vehicles for private purposes. All such matters lead to a debit entry in the Current Account, and a credit entry in the asset account or expense account.

Conversely, where a partner is to be recompensed for some payment out of his own pocket for the business, he would be credited in his Current Account and the loss or asset account would be debited. Typical Journal entries are shown below.

19.. June	30	Current A/c (Careful) Dr. Depreciation A/c Dr. Motor-Vehicles A/c Being sale of motor vehicle valued at £100·00 on book for £60·00 to a partner (Careful)	L 195 L 37 L 52	£ 60·00 40·00	£ J 19 100·00
Dec.	31	Current A/c (Spendthrift) Dr. Motor-Vehicles Expense A/c Being portion of motor vehicle expenses agreed to be chargeable to Spendthrift for private use of the firm's motor vehicle.	L 196 L 55	30·00	 30·00
Dec.	31	Travelling Expenses A/c Dr. Current A/c (Careful) Being fares to Exeter paid by Careful out of his own pocket for business purposes.	L 56 L 195	12·50	 12·50

Fig. 27.7 Drawings in kind and payments by the partner

(d) *The balance at the close of the year*. The balances of the two accounts shown illustrate that the final result of any Current Account may be either a credit or a debit. The credit balance represents a liability of the business to the partner; it is the part of his profit for the year which the partner has not withdrawn, but has left in the business. A debit balance represents an excess of drawings over profits earned, and leaves the partner a debtor for the sum. It is a current asset of the business, but it is unlikely that the partner will pay the balance in. It will more likely remain as a debit balance to be set against next year's profits.

You should now attempt some of the exercises given below.

27.9   Exercises Set 37: Current Accounts of Partners

1. Salt and Pepper are in partnership with capitals of £5 000 and £1 000 respectively. The partnership deed provides that:
   (a) Pepper is entitled to a salary of £750 *per annum*.
   (b) Each gets 6 per cent interest on capital *per annum*.
   (c) The remaining profits are shared three-quarters to Salt, one-quarter to Pepper.

   Each partner has a Current Account to which all items of personal income arising from the firm are posted, and against which any drawings, either of cash or goods, are charged.

   Show Pepper's Current Account for the year 19. . On January 1st 19. ., he had a credit balance of £180. During the year he drew £1 040 in cash and took home goods valued at £78. Profits for the year were £5 240.

2. Jackson is a partner in a business and is entitled to one-third of the net profit of the firm. From the following particulars write up the Capital and Current accounts of Jackson for the year to December 31st 19. . as they would appear in the ledger of the partnership.

19. .			£
January	1st	Balance on Jackson's Capital Account (credit)	3 000
January	1st	Balance on Jackson's Current Account (credit)	450
May	1st	Additional capital brought in by Jackson	600
December	31st	Jackson's drawings for the year	1 600
December	31st	Interest allowed on Jackson's capital	170
December	31st	Jackson's salary	800
December	31st	Net profit for the year (after adjustment of partners' salaries and interest) divisible between the partners	6 300
December	31st	Amount transferred from Jackson's Current Account to his Capital Account	1 400

   (RSA 1)

3. Messrs Wilson and Brown are in partnership, sharing profits and losses; Wilson three-fifths, Brown two-fifths. Their fixed capitals are: Wilson

£8 000, Brown £5 000. The partnership agreement provides that interest of 5 per cent *per annum* shall be paid on fixed capital and that Brown is to receive a salary of £400 *per annum* and 2 per cent commission on the balance of trading profit after charging his salary, but before charging interest on capital.

The balances of the Current Accounts at January 1st 19.. are: Wilson credit £420, Brown credit £350.

Drawings during the year: Wilson £2 000, Brown £1 800.

The trading profit for the year ended December 31st 19.. was £5 400.

Prepare the Current Account of each partner for the year ended December 31st 19.. (RSA 1)

4. (a) What are the reasons for keeping a Current Account as well as a Capital Account for each partner?
   (b) A Capital Account can show only a credit balance. Do you agree with this statement?
   (c) In what circumstances would a Current Account show a debit balance?

5. Smith and Edwards are in partnership sharing profits and losses in the ratio 2:1. Their accounts are made up for the year ending December 31st 19.. From the following information write up the Profit and Loss Appropriation Account of the partnership, and the Current Accounts of Smith and Edwards as they would appear in their private ledger.

January 1st 19..	Current-Account balance	
	Smith	£400 Cr.
	Edwards	£350 Dr.
December 31st 19..	Drawings during year	
	Smith	£3 500
	Edwards	£2 000
Interest on Capital:	Smith 5 per cent of £13 000	
	Edwards 5 per cent of £7 000	

Salary—Edwards £1 000.

Net Profit to be divided *after* charging interest on capital and paying Edwards' salary £5 400.

27.10 The Balance Sheet of a Partnership Enterprise

The Final Accounts of a partnership consist therefore of a Trading Account, a Profit and Loss Account, an Appropriation Account, two Current Accounts and a final Balance Sheet. This Balance Sheet is only different from the sole trader's Balance Sheet in that it has two entries for the Capital Account, which are merely added together. The Current Account balances appear in appropriate places either as liabilities to the partners or, if they have debit balances, as current assets of the business, as shown in Fig. 27.8 below.

Balance Sheet of Brighton and Hove
(as at December 31st 19 . .)

Fixed Assets	£	£	Capital	£	£
Land and Buildings		5 000	At Start Brighton		6 000
Plant and Machinery		4 000	Hove		4 000
Furniture and Fittings		1 000			
Motor Vehicles		1 750			10 000
		———	Current Account		
		11 750	Brighton		55
Current Assets			Long Term Liability		
Current A/c Hove	160		Mortgage		3 500
Stock	1 800		Current Liabilities		
Debtors	1 520		Creditors	2 350	
Cash at Bank	900		Wages due	350	
Cash in Hand	125			———	2 700
	———	4 505			
		£16 255			£16 255

Fig. 27.8 A partnership Balance Sheet

27.11   Exercises Set 38 : Final Accounts of Partnerships

1. From the following list of balances you are required to prepare the Profit
and Loss Appropriation Account and the Current Accounts of the partnership of Lester and Payne for the year ended December 31st 19 . . and
their Balance Sheet as at that date.

	£
Profit and Loss Account (net profit)	4 012
Cash in Hand	35
Cash at Bank	630
Trade Debtors	938
Trade Creditors	416
Provision for Bad Debts	70
Insurance Prepaid	25
Rent Owing	40
Furniture, Fittings and Equipment (Cost £2 200)	1 880
Stock	2 840
Motor Van	490
Loan (Lester)	600
Capital Accounts (January 1st):	
Lester	2 000
Payne	1 500
Drawing Accounts:	
Lester	1 210
Payne	920
Current Accounts (Cr.): (January 1st)	
Lester	208
Payne	122

Notes:
(*a*) The motor van had been purchased for £600 on January 1st 19. .
(*b*) Lester's loan—for the purchase of the van—is for five years and bears interest at 6 per cent *per annum*; this has not been provided for. (Make it the first Appropriation Account item.)
(*c*) Payne is entitled to be credited with a partnership salary of £600.
(*d*) The partners share profits and losses in the proportions: Lester three-quarters, Payne one-quarter. (RSA II)

2. A. Bull has been having a quarrel with his partner T. Cow over the distribution of the profits made last year (£5 800). Bull and Cow are agreed on one thing, that it never entered the heads of either to discuss the question of how profits should be shared as they were more concerned with avoiding losses. Bull is now claiming 10 per cent interest on capital (Bull £10 000, Cow £500) and a salary for his work (he does 60 per cent of the work to Cow's 40 per cent). Advise the partners.

3. Baker and Grocer are in partnership sharing profits and losses equally. Interest on capital is allowed at 5 per cent *per annum*. From the following Trial Balance (extracted after the Trading, and Profit and Loss Accounts had been completed) prepare the partners' Profit and Loss Appropriation Account, and Current Accounts for the year ended December 31st 19. . and a Balance Sheet on that date.

	£	£
Capital Accounts (January 1st 19. .)		
Baker		7 000
Grocer		5 000
Current Accounts (January 1st 19. .)		
Baker		275
Grocer	125	
Net profit (year ended December 31st) 19. .		3 600
Drawings during year ended December 31st 19. .		
Baker	1 400	
Grocer	1 700	
Creditors		450
Rates due		50
Premises	8 000	
Vans	2 000	
Shop Fittings	900	
Stock	1 700	
Debtors	30	
Bank Balance	400	
Cash in Hand	60	
Insurance in advance	60	
	£16 375	16 375

(contd. on page 286)

During the year ended December 31st 19.. the following depreciation had been written off: Motor Vans—£500, Shop Fittings—£100.

(RSA 1)

4. At January 1st 19.. G. Wilson owned a business in which he had £10 000 capital. As from July 1st 19.. W. Gibbs came in as a partner on the following terms:
   (a) Wilson's capital was to remain unchanged and Gibbs was to bring in £2 300 of which £500 was to be credited to his current account.
   (b) Interest at 5 per cent was to be allowed on both capitals from the start of the partnership.
   (c) Gibbs was to be credited with a salary of £700 *per annum*.
   (d) Profits, after charging interest and salary, were to be divided Wilson two-thirds and Gibbs one-third.

   Gibbs withdrew £450 on August 1st, £325 on September 30th and on November 30th £325. At December 31st 19.. the net profit available for division before charging the partnership interest and salary was £1 485.

   You are required to prepare the partnership's Appropriation Account and the Current Account of W. Gibbs.

(RSA 1)

5. Ross and Glass were in partnership sharing profits equally. The following Trial Balance was extracted from their books as at December 31st 19. .

Trial Balance
(as at December 31st 19. .)

		£	£
Capital:	Ross (as at January 1st 19. .)		8 507
	Glass (,, ,, ,, ,, ,,)		6 894
Drawings:	Ross	2 060	
	Glass	1 980	
Building at Cost		6 000	
Plant at Cost *less* Depreciation		2 800	
Motor Vans at Cost *less* Depreciation		400	
Stock in Trade January 1st 19. .		2 476	
Debtors		3 938	
Creditors			2 840
Purchases		32 496	
Sales			47 389
Rates and Insurances		1 450	
Wages (Profit and Loss Account)		8 210	
Bad Debts		430	
Provision for Doubtful Debts			315
Discounts Received			612
Discounts Allowed		838	
Bank Balance		2 334	
General Expenses		897	
Van Running Expenses		248	
		£66 557	£66 557

Stock in trade at December 31st 19. . amounted to £2 984.

The provision for bad debts is to be changed to £395.

You are required to prepare a Trading Account, Profit and Loss Account, Appropriation Account and two Current Accounts for the year ending December 31st 19. ., and a Balance Sheet as at that date.

6. Brown and Marshall are in partnership sharing profits and losses in the ratio of 2 to 1. They have agreed to keep their drawings in that ratio. At the end of their financial year they have attempted to draw up a Balance Sheet, and produced the following:

Balance Sheet as at December 31st 19. .

	£		£	£
Premises	8 000	Capital invested		
Machinery	3 200	Brown	10 000	
Motor Vehicles	2 800	Marshall	4 000	
Fixtures and Fittings	1 000		——	14 000
Stock	4 600	Profit for the First Year		9 600
Debtors	4 300	Creditors		3 400
Bank	1 640	Depreciation		
Cash	100	Motor Vehicles	700	
Drawings	3 000	Fixtures	240	
			——	940
		Provision for Bad Debts		700
	£28 640			£28 640

Set out the Balance Sheet in acceptable form, with fixed Capital Accounts and Current Accounts for each partner.

7. Bennett and Clark are in partnership, sharing profits and loss in the ratio of 3:2. Their abridged Trial Balance at the close of business on December 31st 19.. was:

		Dr. £	Cr. £
Gross Profit			8 660
Salaries		785	
Heating and Lighting		490	
Rates		435	
Bad Debts		515	
Provision for Bad Debts			640
Discounts		240	200
Carriage Outward		610	
Vehicle Expenses		725	
Building Repairs		250	
Loan Interest, 7 per cent		70	
Advertising		600	
Cash in Hand		165	
Cash at Bank		1 125	
Debtors and Creditors		5 120	2 250
Stock		6 995	
Motor Vehicles		4 000	
Land and Buildings		9 500	
Goodwill		2 100	
Current Account Balances:	Bennett		175
	Clark	105	
Drawings:	Bennett	1 500	
	Clark	1 395	
Bank Loan			2 000
Capital Accounts	Bennett		12 800
	Clark		10 000
		£36 725	£36 725

You are required to draw up the Profit and Loss Account, Appropriation Account, etc., of the partnership for the year ending 31st December 19.. and a Balance Sheet as at that date, taking into account the following additional information:

(a) Depreciate the motor vehicles 10 per cent.

(b) Carry forward £200 of the advertising costs.

(c) The loan was made to the partnership on January 1st 19..

(d) Clark is entitled to a salary of £500.

(e) Interest at 5 per cent *per annum* is to be allowed on the capitals of the partners. Bennett brought in £1 800 of his capital on June 30th 19..

8. State where in the Profit and Loss Account and/or Balance Sheet of a partnership you would place the following amounts:
   (a) The cost of installing a new machine.
   (b) The credit balance of an account in the Sales Ledger.
   (c) A loan to one of the partners by the firm.
   (d) Interest which was owing on the loan to the partner.
   (e) Sums written off the firm's goodwill.
   (f) The debit balance of an account in the Purchases Ledger.
   (g) Goods unsold at the end of the financial year.

9. Knowle and Sentry were partners sharing profits and losses in the proportion Knowle two-thirds and Sentry one-third. The following trial balance was extracted from their books as at December 31st 19..

Trial Balance
(as at December 31st 19..)

		£	£
Capital:	Knowle		12 509
	Sentry		8 791
Drawings:	Knowle	2 420	
	Sentry	1 790	
Purchases		44 720	
Sales			57 690
Repairs to Buildings		763	
Stock in Trade January 1st 19..		6 144	
General Expenses		1 494	
Motor Car		900	
Car Expenses		297	
Trade Debtors		5 178	
Trade Creditors			3 987
Freehold Land and Buildings		8 500	
Furniture and Fittings		1 380	
Wages and Salaries		8 416	
Discounts Allowed		1 038	
Discounts Received			801
Rates and Insurances		236	
Bad Debts		347	
Provision for Bad Debts January 1st 19..			128
Balance at Bank		283	
		£83 906	£83 906

The following matters are to be taken into account:
(a) Stock in trade December 31st 19.. amounted to £8 451.
(b) Wages and salaries outstanding at December 31st 19.. £249.
(c) The provision for bad debts to be increased to £164.

(d) The item 'repairs to buildings £763' includes £480 in respect of alterations and improvements to the buildings.

(e) Rates and insurances paid in advance at December 31st 19.. £56.

(f) During the year Knowle withdrew goods valued at £190 (sale price) for his own use and Sentry paid car expenses for the firm's car out of his own pocket amounting to £79. No entries had been made in the books for either of these matters.

You are required to prepare a Trading and Profit and Loss Account, etc., for the year to December 31st 19.. and a Balance Sheet as on that date.

Note:

Ignore depreciation of fixed assets.   (RSA II)

10. Richard and Stanley Bridges formed a partnership on January 1st 19.. in which they invested £4 500 and £2 250 respectively. At the same time they obtained a twenty-year lease on a property valued at £4 000.

They agreed that interest should be allowed on their capitals at 6 per cent *per annum* and that profits and losses should be divided as follows: Richard three-fifths and Stanley two-fifths.

Prepare the Journal entries at the year ending December 31st 19.. to deal with the two following items:

(i) The charge against revenue in respect of the lease at the end of the year.

(ii) It was discovered after the preparation of the Balance Sheet dated December 31st 19.. that the entries for interest on capital had been omitted from the Profit and Loss Appropriation Account.

11. Rathlin and Lambay were partners sharing profits and losses in the ratio of 3:2. The following Trial Balance was extracted from their books as on December 31st 19..

Trial Balance
(as at December 31st 19..)

	£	£
Capital account balances January 1st 19..		
Rathlin		28 000
Lambay		14 000
Drawings: Rathlin	6 800	
Lambay	4 400	
Furniture and Fittings (cost £1 700)	1 360	
Stock in Trade January 1st 19..	21 000	
Trade Debtors and Trade Creditors	16 328	12 750
Purchases	152 000	
Sales		206 000
Freehold Properties at Cost	18 500	
Wages and Salaries	25 454	
Rates	300	
General Expenses	9 832	
Balance at Bank	2 408	
Discounts Allowed	4 154	
Discounts Received		1 630
Rents Received		156
	£262 536	£262 536

You are given the following additional information:

(a) Stock-in-Trade December 31st 19.. £23 500.

(b) Wages and salaries outstanding December 31st 19.. £304.

(c) Rates paid in advance at December 31st 19.. £60.

(d) Rent received £156 includes £12 for the month of January 19..

(e) Depreciation on furniture and fittings is to be provided at the rate of 10 per cent *per annum* on cost.

(f) The partners are to be credited with interest at the rate of 5 per cent *per annum* on the balances on their capital account as at January 1st 19.. They are also to be charged with interest on their drawings: Rathlin is to bear £170 and Lambay £110.

You are required to prepare a Trading and Profit and Loss Account, etc., for the year 19.. and a Balance Sheet as on December 31st 19..

12. The following Trial Balance was extracted from the books of Messrs Bristol and Avon, wholesale merchants, who share profits and losses three-quarters and one-quarter respectively. From it you are required to prepare their Trading and Profit and Loss Account, etc., for the year ended December 31st 19.. and Balance Sheet as at that date.

Trial Balance
(as at December 31st 19..)

	£	£
Capital Accounts—January 1st 19..		
Bristol		12 000
Avon		4 000
Drawings: Bristol	1 950	
Avon	1 250	
Current Accounts—January 1st 19..		
Bristol		1 105
Avon		863
Trade Debtors and Creditors	5 500	3 400
Purchases and Sales	10 402	24 232
Warehouse Wages	3 200	
Office Salaries	1 800	
Returns	362	302
Stock—January 1st 19..	6 332	
Cash in Hand	43	
Balance at Bank	1 744	
Freehold Premises	8 500	
Furniture and Equipment	1 640	
Motor Vehicles	1 400	
Bad Debts	75	
Stationery	166	
Advertising	377	
Lighting and Heating	572	
Rates	248	
Postage and Telephone	130	
Insurance	60	
Discounts	246	418
Motor Vehicles Expenses	394	
Sundry Expenses	54	
Provision for Bad Debts		125
	£46 445	£46 445

Attention must be paid to the following matters which have not yet been put into effect in the books:

(a) The stock at December 31st 19.. was valued at £4 429.

(b) Three-quarters of the expenses for rates and lighting and heating is to be charged to the warehouse and the remainder to the office.

(c) The furniture and equipment is to be depreciated by 10 per cent and the motor vehicles by 20 per cent.

(d) Insurance unexpired amounts to £10.

(e) The provision for bad debts at December 31st 19.. is to stand at 2 per cent of the trade debtors at that date.

13. Bush and Mill are partners sharing profits in the ratio of 3:2. The following trial balance is extracted from their books as at December 31st 19..

Trial Balance
(as at December 31st 19..)

		£	£
Capital:	Bush		8 823
	Mill		6 132
Drawings:	Bush	1 800	
	Mill	1 420	
Debtors and Creditors		2 401	1 869
Sales			22 718
Purchases		15 226	
Discounts Received			249
Discounts Allowed		418	
Motor Expenses		326	
Rent and Rates		940	
Salaries		2 461	
Lighting and Heating		322	
Bad Debts		298	
Provision for Doubtful Debts			450
General Expenses		649	
Balance at Bank		492	
Stock in Trade January 1st 19..		4 288	
Delivery Vans at Cost *less* Depreciation		2 500	
Freehold Building at Cost		6 700	
		£40 241	£40 241

You are given the following additional information:

(a) Stock in trade December 31st 19.. amounts to £5 263.

(b) Rent due at December 31st 19.. amounted to £200. A bill for £160 for rates for the half-year to the following March 31st was paid on November 1st 19..

(c) Lighting and heating due at December 31st 19.. amounted to £39.

(d) The balance on Delivery Vans Account represents three vans each costing £1 000; two were purchased on January 1st the previous year and the third on July 1st of that year. Depreciation has been charged at the rate of 20 per cent *per annum* on cost and the same rate is to be continued for 19..

(e) Provision for doubtful debts is to be increased to £500.

(f) Bank charges, £28, were debited by the bank on December 30th 19.. but have not yet been entered in the books.

You are asked to prepare a Trading and Profit and Loss Account, etc., for the year ended December 31st 19.. and a Balance Sheet as at that date.

14. Ross and Cromarty carry on business in partnership and the following are the balances on the books of the firm as at March 31st 19..

	£	£
Ross Capital Account		7 000
Cromarty Capital Account		3 000
Ross Drawings Account	2 040	
Cromarty Drawings Account	1 020	
Purchases	70 835	
Sales		81 213
Purchases Returns		915
Sales Returns	581	
Stock at April 1st previous year	4 969	
Salaries	3 251	
Rent and Rates	660	
Insurance	136	
Carriage Inwards	1 638	
General Expenses	804	
Debtors and Creditors	6 179	3 736
Discounts Allowed and Received	165	185
Office Furniture and Fittings—cost	760	
Provision for Depreciation of Office Furniture and Fittings at start of year		302
Balance at Bank	3 272	
Provision for Bad Debts at start of year		80
Bad Debts written off	121	
	£96 431	£96 431

Prepare the Trading and Profit and Loss Account, etc., for the year ending March 31st 19.. and the Balance Sheet at that date, making such adjustments as are required by the following:

(a) The partners' capital accounts are to remain constant and to carry interest at the rate of 5 per cent *per annum.*

(b) Profits and losses are to be divided in the proportions of two-thirds to Ross and one-third to Cromarty.

(c) The stock on hand at March 31st 19.. was valued at £5 395.

(d) Rent owing at March 31st 19.. was £60.

(e) Insurance paid in advance at March 31st 19.. was £49.

(f) Depreciation of office furniture to be charged at the rate of 5 per cent *per annum* on the cost.

(g) The provision for bad debts is to be made up to £179.

15. Copeland and Bangor were partners sharing profits and losses in the ratio of 2:1. The following trial balance was extracted from their books on December 31st 19..

Trial Balance
(as at December 31st 19..)

	£	£
Capital Accounts as at January 1st 19..		
Copeland		26 500
Bangor		14 200
Drawings: Copeland	6 450	
Bangor	4 200	
Sales		237 864
Purchases	179 465	
Salaries	26 192	
Rates	500	
Discounts Allowed	4 264	
Discounts Received		2 146
General Expenses	10 261	
Balance at Bank	2 694	
Freehold Properties at Cost	17 500	
Trade Debtors	17 042	
Trade Creditors		13 149
Furniture and Equipment (cost £2 500)	1 650	
Stock in Trade January 1st 19..	23 641	
	£293 859	£293 859

You are given the following additional information:

(a) Stock in trade December 31st 19.. £24 780.

(b) Rates paid in advance at December 31st 19.. £120.

(c) After the preparation of the trial balance it was decided that debtors amounting to £478 were bad.

(d) Salaries outstanding at December 31st 19.. amounted to £514.

(e) Depreciation on furniture and equipment is to be provided at the rate of 10 per cent *per annum* on cost.

(f) The partners are to be credited with interest at the rate of 5 per cent *per annum* on the balances on their capital accounts as at January 1st 19.. They are to be charged with interest on their drawings. Copeland is to bear £204 and Bangor £162 for this item.

You are required to prepare a Trading and Profit and Loss Account and Appropriation Account and two Current Accounts for the year 19.. and a Balance Sheet as at December 31st 19..

Non-profit-making Organizations

28.1 Non-profit-making Institutions

Most enterprises are run for private profit. The proprietor, as a sole trader, earns his living by his activities in the business, or two or more partners may work together for their mutual benefit. However there are many institutions in society where the aims are not to make profits but to provide useful services to other people, or to promote activities which interest or amuse them. Such institutions are called *non-profit-making* bodies, or more commonly 'clubs'. They exist wherever a body of interested persons comes together as *members*, elects a *committee*, subscribes *funds* and proceeds to conduct affairs. Local hockey clubs and cricket clubs, football supporters' clubs and even world-famous clubs like the United Nations Association or the International Red Cross, are examples.

In this Unit we shall study the accounting principles behind all such activities. It does not follow that these organizations are small; for example many co-operative organizations are enormous. In the United Kingdom co-operative trade totalled £3 500 million last year, and over ten million members took part in the activities of this non-profit making organization.

The important feature of clubs from the legal point of view is that they have no separate legal status. In the eyes of the law they are nothing but a mere collection of individuals. These individuals are totally responsible for all the things done in the club, and those individuals who volunteer to become chairman, secretary, treasurer, etc., are personally liable for the actions they take, the contracts they make, etc.

The *treasurer* is the committee member responsible for the collection of funds, and will often also be concerned with paying bills, rent of premises, etc. It is often considered desirable that more than one person shall be concerned with these payments, to prevent the treasurer misappropriating funds, and in these cases it will often be laid down in the club rules that the chairman and the treasurer must both sign cheques. Any misappropriation of funds in such circumstances must involve a criminal conspiracy, or forgery, both of which are more severely punished than mere theft.

The chief functions of the treasurer are the collecting of subscriptions and other funds and the paying of any bills that arise. He must also prepare and submit to the committee at the *annual general meeting* of the club suitable Final Accounts for the year that has just passed. These accounts may be very simple, in which case they are called *Receipts and Payments Accounts*. For large clubs, especially those with substantial assets, they take the form of an Income and Expenditure Account, followed by a Balance Sheet as at the last day of the year—or season if it is a seasonal activity.

Both these types of 'Final Accounts' are prepared from the cash book of the club.

28.2 Keeping the Cash Record of a Club

The chief concern of the treasurer is to collect subscriptions and other income and to pay such bills as are presented. These are mainly cash activities, though most clubs would also have Bank Accounts, where club funds can be deposited, or at least safeguarded in a current account. A simple cash record can be kept in a cheap cash notebook obtainable at any stationers. The treasurer goes to the club on the evening of the meetings, prepared to accept any subscriptions offered to him. He may also collect donations for special occasions, help organize raffles and other fund-raising activities, and empty the boxes where members pay for the use of such facilities as billiard tables, pin-ball machines, etc. Probably each evening he will also collect the balance of the proceeds of the sale of refreshments—after the social secretary or other person has deducted the expenses they have paid out for the purchases of sandwich materials, tea, milk, sugar, etc.

This cash record, which is a simple Cash Account, might appear as follows.

The Merry Players' Drama Society
Cash A/c

19..		£	19..		£
Sept. 7	Balance in Hand	14·25	Sept. 7	Hire of Hall	0·25
7	Subs—Mrs Dillon	2·00	7	Refreshment Expenses	1·00
7	Subs—Mr Metcalfe	2·00	7	Raffle Prize	0·25
7	Refreshments	1·37	14	Hire of Hall	0·25
7	Raffle Proceeds	1·05	14	Raffle Prize	0·45
14	Subs—Miss Latymer	2·00	14	Leaflet Printing	2·40
14	Subs—Mr Lidyard	2·00	14	Refreshment Expenses	1·42
14	Subs—Rev. P. Stacey	2·00			
14	Refreshments	2·13			
14	Raffle Proceeds	1·46			

Fig. 28.1 A simple club Cash Account

Analysing Receipts and Payments
One of the chief disadvantages of such a club cash book is that the transactions recorded day by day are not analysed under various headings, but simply appear in date order. To analyse these items, it is necessary to go through the figures collecting together similar items. For example we have in Fig. 28.1 the items listed on page 300.

The Merry Players' Drama Society

Date	Details	Sub-scrip-tions £	Com-peti-tions £	Ref-resh-ments £	Sun-dry R'pts £	Total £
19.. May 1	Balance in Hand				14·25	14·25
Sept. 7	Sub—Mrs Dillon	2·00				2·00
7	Sub—Mr Metcalfe	2·00				2·00
7	Refreshments			1·37		1·37
7	Raffle		1·05			1·05
14	Sub—Miss Latymer	2·00				2·00
14	Sub—Mr Lidyard	2·00				2·00
14	Sub—Rev. P. Stacey	2·00				2·00
14	Refreshments			2·13		2·13
14	Raffle		1·46			1·46
14	Sub—Mr Darby	2·00				2·00
	and so on throughout the season until					
Apr. 29	Sub—Mr Way	2·00				2·00
29	Raffle		1·14			1·14
29	Refreshments			1·45		1·45
30	Donation				5·50	5·50
30	Refreshments			1·10		1·10
		68·00	38·54	53·24	26·22	186·00
May 1	Balance in Hand				40·56	40·56

Date	Details	Equip-ment £	Com-peti-tions £	Ref-resh-ments £	Gen. Exp-enses £	Total £
19.. Sept. 7	Hire of Hall				0·25	0·25
7	Refresh. Expenses			1·00		1·00
7	Raffle Prize		0·25			0·25
14	Hire of Hall				0·25	0·25
14	Raffle Prize		0·45			0·45
14	Leaflet Printing				2·40	2·40
14	Refresh. Expenses			1·42		1·42
21	Hire of Hall				0·25	0·25
21	Cups	5·50				5·50
21	Postage				0·50	0·50
21	Raffle		0·60			0·60
	and so on throughout the season until					
Apr. 29	Hall Charge				0·25	0·25
29	Refreshments			0·30		0·30
30	Hall Charge				0·25	0·25
30	Refreshments			0·56		0·56
30	Balance in Hand				40·56	40·56
		28·50	41·50	24·30	91·70	186·00

Fig. 28.2 The analysed cash book of a club

Receipts		£
Subscriptions £2 + £2 + £2 + £2 + £2	=	10·00
Refreshments £1·37 + £2·13	=	3·50
Raffle proceeds £1·05 + £1·46	=	2·51
		£16·01

Payments		£
Hire of hall £0·25 + £0·25	=	0·50
Refreshment expenses £1·00 + £1·42	=	2·42
Raffle prizes £0·25 + £0·45	=	0·70
Printing	=	2·40
		£6·02

This type of analysis work is laborious, especially if a busy treasurer has a whole year's takings to analyse. A better system is to keep an analysed cash book, which can be purchased from most reputable stationers. (A good ruling is the *Simplex School Fund and Club Accounts Book*, obtainable from George Vyner Ltd., Holmfirth, Huddersfield, designed by Geoffrey Whitehead.) The entries would then be as shown in Fig. 28.2.

28.3 Simple Club Accounts—The Receipts and Payments Account

At the annual general meeting (AGM) of a club, the treasurer will present to the members a statement of the club's financial position. The simplest type of statement that can be presented is a Receipts and Payments Account, prepared from the analysis figures revealed either by a physical analysis of the club's cash book as shown above, or from the analysis columns of the type of cash book shown in Fig. 28.2. When the members arrive for the meeting a duplicated copy of the Receipts and Payments Account will be distributed to all members present. They then listen to the treasurer's account of the year's proceedings and criticize the conduct of the club and its affairs.

Using the figures shown in Fig. 28.2, the Receipts and Payments Account would be as shown in Fig. 28·3.

The Merry Players' Drama Society
Receipts and Payments Account
(for Winter Season 19. .—19. .)

19. .		£	19. .		£
May 1	Balance from last season	14·25	Sept.—	Purchase of Equipment	28·50
Sept.—	Subscriptions	68·00	April	Competitions and	
April	Competitions and			Raffle Expenses	41·50
	Raffles	38·54		Refreshment Expenses	24·30
	Refreshment Sales	53·24		General Expenses	51·14
	Sundry Receipts	11·97	Apr.30	Balance in Hand	40·56
		£186·00			£186·00
19. .					
May 1	Balance in hand	40·56			

Fig. 28.3 A simple Receipts and Payments Account

Note that the figures are not exactly the same as those in the analysis columns of the cash book. The figure for sundry receipts does not correspond, since in fact it also includes the opening cash figure. You might say that on the receipts side of the cash book the opening cash balance is received by this season from last season. Similarly on the payments side the 'general expenses' item is reduced by the amount of the closing balance of cash in hand, which is not really an expense of the season but is handed on to the next season by the present season.

The Receipts and Payments Account may be defined as the analysed cash book of a club listing the receipts and payments for the year and revealing any cash balance in hand.

You should now prepare several Receipts and Payments Accounts from the information given in Exercise 39 below.

28.4   Exercises Set 39: Simple Receipts and Payments Accounts

1. Prepare a Receipts and Payments Account from the following information drawn from the cash book of the treasurer of the Newtown Football Club, at the end of the season, May 30th 19. .

   Cash in hand at start £48; earnings from gate £778; payments for goal posts £15; for players' kits £23·50; for a deposit on the Club House £500; earnings from refreshments £1 026·54; payments for refreshment materials £827·78 and for annual dinner £86·25; donation from Supporters' Club £326·62; payments for postage £17·62; wages of secretarial help £256·50; balance of cash in hand £2·51; balance at bank £450.

2. Prepare the Receipts and Payments Account of the Jolly Wanderers Rambling Club for the year ended December 31st 19. .

   Balance in hand at start of year, cash £57·50, bank £120; sales at bar

£5 085; subscriptions received £955; dividends on club investment received £105; purchases of bar stocks £3 600; wages £713; purchase of new furniture £25; rent and rates £290; repairs to premises £120; general expenses paid £401; cash in hand at end of year £55; cash at bank £1 118·50.

3. Prepare the Receipts and Payments Account of the Roman Camp Archaeological Society from the following information, for the season ended October 31st 19. .

Balance in hand at January 1st 19. . £27·50; subscriptions collected £276; cost of new digging equipment £45·40; weather-protection material £16; sale of surplus finds from digs £132·75; earnings from conducted tours of digs £585·50; cost of printing brochures and reports £47·20; contribution to local museum fund £100; expense of labourers £285; transport £84·50.

4. Prepare the Robert Burns Society's Receipts and Payments Account for the year ended December 31st 19. . given that
   (a) Balance in hand at start was £175·50.
   (b) Expenses by cheque were as follows: transport to outings £25·50; refreshments £31·50; hire of musicians £33.
   (c) Expenses in cash were: wages £48; stationery £7·50; postage £12·25; repairs to dresses and outfits £17·55.
   (d) Subscriptions of £3·15 each were paid by 47 members.
   (e) Entrance fees paid to festivals totalled £147·50.

5. The Kingswood Community Association was formed some years ago and on January 1st 19. . had a balance of cash in hand of £33·81. Its receipts and payments for the year were as follows: subscriptions received £275·35; donations from past presidents £20. Payments: for use of hall £60; for refreshments £128·30; for Christmas party £37·35; for summer outing £28·25. The treasurer and secretary had been given £10 each as an honorarium and the Christmas bazaar had raised £73·35 for the funds of the club.

(a) Prepare the Receipts and Payments Account of the club for the year bringing out the balance of cash in hand.

(b) This balance is kept at the treasurer's home. What change in this arrangement would you suggest?

28.5 Defects of the Receipts and Payments Account as a Record of Club Activities

The Receipts and Payments Account is an unsatisfactory record of the club's activities, for a number of reasons. These may be listed as follows:

(a) The record shows no assets of the club other than the cash balance and assets purchased during the year. This is very unsatisfactory where a club has considerable assets worth, perhaps, thousands of pounds.

(b) There is no record of liabilities, so that members cannot tell whether the club is in debt or not. They may of course ask the Treasurer to clarify this point, but it may not occur to members to ask.

(c) Members do not know whether the club's activities for the year resulted in a profit or loss for the year. This information, if available, would tell them whether the subscription was too high, or too low.

For these reasons it is usual to present a more sophisticated set of final accounts where a club has valuable assets which should be accounted for. These more sophisticated accounts are an Income and Expenditure Account, and a Balance Sheet. Before discussing these records one or two special points must first be made.

28.6 Profits and Non-profit-making Organizations

All clubs make profits on such activities as bazaars, raffles, etc., which are designed to raise funds for various club purposes. Such profits will appear in the accounts, but it is not usual to regard the final profit on the year's activities as 'profit' in the normal meaning of that word. A non-profit-making organization does not make 'profits'. If there is any extra money it must represent a surplus contribution by the members over and above what it was really necessary for them to contribute in view of the activities they enjoyed. The better term therefore is *surplus for year*. If the result of the year's activities is a loss, this is described as a *'deficit for the year'*, the members' contributions being insufficient for the functions they held.

28.7 Capital and Non-profit-making Organizations

When a club starts its activities it usually begins by collecting the first year's subscriptions from the members, which are payable in advance. Sometimes a fee is charged on joining, besides the annual subscription. These sums are not quite the same as the capital of a sole trader or partnership enterprise, but clearly a club which eventually owns valuable assets must have some sort of capital to record on the balance sheet. Capital is not a particularly good word to describe the liability the club owes to its members who have contributed or raised funds for its activities. It is usual to call this liability an *accumulated fund*, since this name aptly describes the way the fund is built up. Any surplus in the first year which is carried over to the second year may be said to have been 'accumulated'. Therefore the Balance Sheet of a club records on one side the club's assets, and on the other side its liabilities, including the Accumulated Fund.

At the start of any given year the club will have an opening balance on this Accumulated Fund. How is it to be calculated? The answer is given by the formula.

Accumulated Fund = assets owned at the date named — liabilities

Consider the following example. The Marco Polo Society has the following assets and liabilities at January 1st 19...

Assets

	£	
Furniture	240	
Projector and other visual aids	120	
Various Chinese artifacts	150	
Library of reference books	200	£710

Liabilities

	£	
Printing bill due	25	
Members subs in advance	20	£45

Using the formula given above we have:

$$\text{Accumulated Fund} = £710 \quad - \quad £45$$
$$= £665$$

28.8   Trading by Non-profit-making Organizations

Where a club carries out a considerable amount of trading it is sometimes deemed desirable to prepare one or more Trading Accounts. Thus where the club operates a bar for members it is usual to prepare a Bar Trading Account. Some sub-committees might similarly present a Trading Account, for example a Dances and Socials Committee Trading Account, or a Publications Committee Trading Account. These would be no different from the normal Trading Accounts of a sole trader or partnership, and any closing stocks of wine, spirits, etc., or unsold books and pamphlets would be brought on to the Balance Sheet as assets of the club.

28.9   The Income and Expenditure Account of a Non-profit-making Organization

Sole traders prepare profit and loss accounts. The comparable account for a club is an *Income and Expenditure Account*. The income is entered on the credit side, like the profits of a sole trader. The expenditure is entered on the debit side, like the losses of a sole trader. The surplus (if any) is transferred to the Accumulated Fund, to increase the Fund, in the same way as the net profit increases the sole trader's capital when he ploughs it back into the firm. The deficit (if any) is transferred to the Accumulated Fund and reduces the fund, indicating that members have been 'consuming capital' during the year, by enjoying more facilities than they paid for.

The two starting points for the preparation of an Income and Expenditure Account, and the Balance Sheet, of a club are the Accumulated Fund calculation and the Receipts and Payments Account. It is now time to prepare one of these more sophisticated sets of 'Final Accounts' for a club, and the example which follows illustrates all the points mentioned.

Example
The Harrison's Rocks Mountaineering Club was formed some years ago and on January 1st 19.. had assets and liabilities as follows:

Club premises and gymnasium £2 000; equipment £500; motor van £450; cash at bank £360 (on deposit); cash in hand £32·50. £30 is owed to the Snowdonia Instruction Club for the services of visiting lecturers and £5 for a printer's bill.

During the year it was resolved to obtain and sell to members at a small profit any climbing gear or camping equipment they might need, and a special sub-committee called the Climbing-Gear Committee agreed to supervise this activity.

At December 31st a Receipts and Payments Account was prepared as follows:

Receipts and Payments Account
(for the year ending December 31st 19..)

Receipts	£	Payments	£
Cash in Hand	32·50	Snowdonia Instruction Club	30·00
Subscriptions	124·00	Refreshment materials	22·50
Sale of gear to members	158·00	Printing, etc.	12·25
Sale of refreshments	36·50	Club gear for club house	48·50
Donation from Anne		Purchase of gear for resale	200·00
Enthusiast	25·00	Ambulance expenses	5·50
Insurance claim paid	20·00	Medical expenses (injured	
		member)	25·00
		Insurance premium	10·00
		Motor van expenses	35·00
		Balance of Cash in Hand c/d	7·25
	£396·00		£396·00
Balance in Hand B/d	7·25		

You are required:

(a) to calculate the Accumulated Fund at the start of the year,

(b) to draw up a Trading Account for the Climbing Gear Committee,

(c) to prepare an Income and Expenditure Account for the year ending December 31st 19.. and

(d) to prepare a Balance Sheet as at December 31st 19..

Notes:

On December 31st stocks of gear for resale were valued at £52, and £4 of the subscriptions listed as receipts were payments in advance for the coming year. The motor van is to be depreciated by 20 per cent and equipment in hand at December 31st 19.. by 10 per cent.

The accounts would be prepared as follows:

(a) **Calculation of Accumulated Fund at start of year**

Assets	£	Liabilities	£
Premises	2 000·00	Snowdonia Club	30·00
Equipment	500·00	Printer	5·00
Motor Van	450·00		£35·00
Cash at Bank	360·00		
Cash in Hand	32·50		
	£3 342·50		

Accumulated Fund = £3 342·50 − £35·00
                 = £3 307·50

Notes:

(a) When the Accumulated Fund has been calculated in this way it is carried straight to the Balance Sheet where it occupies the position usually taken by the Capital Account in a sole trader's accounts (page 308).

(b) When this figure is entered on the liabilities side of the Balance Sheet it must clearly be balanced by an equal and opposite figure. This means that *every figure that gave rise to it, i.e. the assets and liabilities above, must also be carried to the Balance Sheet, either unchanged or in a modified form.* If the assets or liability will still be in existence at the end of the season, i.e. premises, equipment, motor van and bank deposit in the case above, they are entered unchanged on the Balance Sheet. Those that would not be still in existence at the end of the season are entered in the Cash Account, or are taken into account as we prepare the Income and Expenditure Account. They therefore play their part in deciding what modified cash figure, or surplus or deficiency figure, eventually appears on the Balance Sheet.

(b) **Trading Account**

Climbing-Gear Committee Trading A/c
(for the year ending December 31st 19..)

19..		£	19..		£
Dec. 31	Purchases	200	Dec. 31	Sales	158
	Less Closing Stock	52			
	Cost of Sales	148			
	Profit on Sales of				
	gear	10			
		£158			£158

Fig. 28.4 A Trading Account of a club

Notes:

(i) As this club activity only began in the current year there was no opening stock.

(ii) The profit on trading is taken to the Income and Expenditure Account, like the Gross Profit of a sole trader being transferred to Profit and Loss Account.

(c) Income and Expenditure Account

Income and Expenditure A/c
(for the year ending December 31st 19..)

19..		£	19..		£
Dec. 31	Refreshment materials	22·50	Dec. 31	Subscriptions 124·00	
	Printing (for year)	7·25		*Less* Subs	
	Ambulance expenses	5·50		in advance 4·00	
	Medical expenses	25·00			120·00
	Insurance premium	10·00		Refreshment sales	36·50
	Motor van expenses	35·00		Donation	25·00
	Depreciation			Insurance claim	20·00
	Equipment 54·85			Profit on sales of	
	Motor Vans 90·00			gear	10·00
		144·85			211·50
				Deficiency for year	
				(transferred to	
				Accumulated Fund)	38·60
		£250·10			£250·10

Fig. 28.5 The Income and Expenditure Account of a club

Notes:

(i) You may be confused by the fact that items appearing on the Receipts and Payments Account have crossed over sides as they enter the Income and Expenditure Account. For example 'refreshment sales' appears on the debit side of Receipts and Payments Account, and on the credit side of the Income and Expenditure Account above. The explanation is that the Receipts and Payments Account is a cash book, not a Trial Balance. It has never been posted to any account, for most clubs do not have any accounts. It follows that the profit items are on the debit side of the cash book (receipts) and the losses are on the credit side (payments).

(ii) The subscriptions figure has been adjusted to take account of the subscriptions paid in advance—which therefore appear on the Balance Sheet as a liability—we owe the members concerned a year's entertainment.

(iii) The payments to Snowdonia Instruction Club and for printing due do not appear in this year's account since they refer to last year's expenses.

(iv) The club gear purchased was a capital item and therefore does not appear on the Income and Expenditure Account, but goes straight to the Balance Sheet.

(v) The deficiency for the year is carried to the Balance Sheet and deducted from the Accumulated Fund.

Balance Sheet
(as at December 31st 19..)

Fixed Assets	£	£	Accumulated Fund	£	£
Premises		2 000·00	At Start	3 307·50	
Equipment	500·00		Less Deficiency	38·60	
+Additions	48·50				3 268·90
	548·50		Current Liabilities		
Less Depreciation	54·85		Subs. in advance		4·00
		493·65			
Motor Vans	450·00				
Less Depreciation	90·00				
		360·00			
		2 853·65			
Current Assets					
Stock of gear for					
re-sale	52·00				
Cash at Bank					
(deposit)	360·00				
Cash in Hand	7·25				
		419·25			
		£3 272·90			£3 272·90

Fig. 28.6 The Balance Sheet of a club

Notes: The presentation is similar to sole traders' accounts and may be presented either in the order of liquidity or in the order of permanence as shown above.

You should now try some of the exercises given in 28.10.

28.10   Exercises Set 40: Final Accounts of Non-profit-making Organizations

1. Choose from the items shown below those necessary to prepare the Income and Expenditure Account of the 'Snowdonia Young Climbers' Club' for the summer season ended October 31st 19.. A Balance Sheet is not required.

	£
Subscriptions for current year	240·00
Subscriptions for previous year	5·50
Refreshment profits	25·00
Accumulated fund of club at start	1 225·00
Purchases of magazines for Club House	10·25
Purchase of climbing ropes and other gear (expected to last only two years)	160·50
Payments to farmer for camping fees	25·00
Printing and stationery	15·00
Charges to visiting parents	65·50
Train fares—accident victim	12·50
Ambulance charges	3·15
Donation by Club to Mountain Rescue Service	20·00
Purchase and erection of mountain hut	100·00

(East Anglian Examination Board)

2. The following figures were supplied to you by the treasurer of the Forsyth Tennis Club. They refer to the year ended December 31st 19..

	£
January 1st 19.. Balance in bank and in hand	300
Rates due and unpaid	10
Subscriptions owing to the club	5

Receipts and Payments for the year ended December 31st 19.. were as follows:

	£
Subscriptions (including £5 arrears)	350
Tournament (entrance fees received)	70
Tournament (cost of prizes)	40
Postages and Stationery	10
Light and Heat (Club House)	30
Rates (including arrears for previous year £10)	60
Cost of new roller, bought for cash	40
Repairs to netting	10
Club House decorations (expected to last 5 years)	50
Wages of part-time groundsman	250

On December 31st 19.. subscriptions £15 due for the year had not been paid, but were certain to be received.

The rates paid included £10 for the first quarter of the next year.

The Club's furniture and fittings are depreciated by £20 every year.

You are asked to prepare the Forsyth Tennis Club's Receipts and Payments Account and Income and Expenditure Account for the year ended December 31st 19.. A Balance Sheet is not required.

(RSA I)

3. From the following information prepare a Cash Account and an 'Income and Expenditure Account' for the year ended March 31st 19.. of the Brownridge Town Band.

19..

April	1st	The Band treasurer held £29 in the band account.
April	23rd	The council paid a grant of £50.
October	3rd	The council paid a further grant of £50.

Paid engagements during the year were as follows:

			£
May	28th	Brownbank Park	10
June	3rd	Tolverton Park	25
June	10th	St John's Church Fête	5
June	24th	Brownbank Park	10
July	1st	Little Barr Park	20
July	8th	Brownbank Flower Show	30
July	29th	Little Barr Horse Show	20
September	1st	Tolverton Labour Club	5
September	15th	Brownbank Conservative Club	25

All cash was received on the day of the engagement

Payments made during the year were as follows:

			£
May	28th	Two guest instrumentalists @ £1 each	2
June	30th	Payment for performing rights	2
July	8th	One guest instrumentalist	1
October	23rd	Music	2
February	20th	Music	2

During the year the band entered for one contest. This was held on March 11th 19.. at Nottingham. In connexion with this event the following payments were made:

February	17th	Entrance fee	2
February	21st	Hire of rehearsal room	2
March	11th	Hire of coach	15

A charge for friends on the coach brought in £3.

The band won the second prize which included £7 in cash.

On March 31st 19.. the following accounts were due and unpaid:

| Repairs to tenor trombone | 2 |
| Two new uniforms (treated as a revenue expense) | 24 |

(RSA II)

4. The treasurer of the Good Companions Sports Club provided the following analysis of his receipts and payments during the year ended December 31st 19... From it and the notes given below, draw up the club's Income and Expenditure Account as it should have been presented to the members on December 31st.

Receipts	£
Subscriptions:	
Current year	272
Previous year	12
Profit on refreshments	35
Competition fees	18

Payments:	
New games equipment	24
Printing, postages and stationery	13
Periodicals	18
Competition prizes	12
Sundry expenses	20
Wages	78
Rent	120
Rates	49

Notes:

(a) Subscriptions due but unpaid for current year amount to £18.

(b) The club furniture and games equipment at the beginning of the year was valued at £80. It is to be written down—ignoring additions during the year—by 20 per cent.

(c) At January 1st, rates paid in advance amounted to £12, and of the rates payment made during the year £13 was in respect of the following year.

(RSA II)

5. On January 1st 19.. the financial position of the Mid-Sussex Gun-dog Society was:

Assets	£	Liabilities	£
Equipment	125	Accumulated Fund	220
Subscriptions due	35	Trainer's fees accrued	10
Cash at Bank	70		
	£230		£230

During the year ended December 31st 19.. receipts and payments were as follows:

Receipts		£	Payments		£
1 January 19..			Printing		80
Balance at Bank		70	Stationery and postage		23
Subscriptions for previous			New equipment		18
year		20	Hire of training ground		50
Subscriptions for current			Trainer's fees (including £10		
year		140	for previous year)		40
Subscriptions in advance for			General expenses		15
following year		25	Field Trials:		
Field Trials entrance fees		144	Judges fees		100
Receipts from advertise-			Expenses		21
ments in Society Year Book		55	December 31st 19..		
			Balance at Bank		107
		£454			£454

The following items must also be taken into account:

(a) £18 is owing for subscriptions for current year.

(b) The balance of subscriptions for previous year still outstanding is to be written off as a bad debt.

(c) The balance of equipment at January 1st 19.. was to be depreciated by 20 per cent.

(d) There is an amount of £12 owing for printing expenses.

You are required to prepare the Income and Expenditure Account for the year ended December 31st 19.. and a Balance Sheet as at that date. All calculations to be shown in detail.   (RSA II)

6. In preparing the Income and Expenditure Account of a tennis club you find:

(a) Rent owing at beginning of the year £18, paid during the year £80, owing at the end of the year £28.

(b) Members' subscriptions overdue at the beginning of the year £10; received during year £340; payments in advance included in receipts £6.

(c) Rates prepaid at the beginning of the year £4; paid during the year £19 which sum includes £3 in respect of the following year.

You are required to calculate (showing details of your workings) the amounts which would be shown in the Income and Expenditure Account for the year in respect of (i) Rent; (ii) Subscriptions; (iii) Rates.

Note:

You are not required to present the accounts.   (RSA I)

7. The accounts of a social club are made up annually as at December 31st. At December 31st Year 1, subscriptions in arrears amounted to £69 and subscriptions received in advance for Year 2 amounted to £43. During Year 2 £837 was received in respect of subscriptions; this included the

£69 arrears for Year 1 and £29 in advance for Year 3. At December 31st subscriptions in arrears amounted to £76.

The annual income and expenditure account is credited with all subscriptions in respect of the year to which the account relates, on the basis that all arrears will afterwards be collected.

Show the Subscriptions Account for Year 2.

Note: There are no separate accounts for subscriptions in arrear or for subscriptions in advance.

8. (*a*) The Daleshire Social Club was founded on January 1st 19.. with one hundred members; the annual subscription per member being two pounds. By the end of that year two members had not paid their subscriptions but nine had paid for a year in advance.

Prepare the Club's Subscription Account as it would appear after the closing of the Income and Expenditure Account at December 31st 19..

(*b*) A trader uses the term 'net profit'. What is the comparable term used by the treasurer of a non-profit-making club?

9. The New Social Club was founded on January 1st 19.. On the same day, ten life members subscribed £5·25 each and it was agreed that this revenue should be spread evenly over five years. The annual subscription for each ordinary member was fixed at £1·05.

At January 1st four years later seven of the hundred ordinary members still owed their subscriptions for the previous year. During this year twelve new members were enrolled and paid their subscriptions. By the end of the year all dues except those of three members for the current year had been received.

Prepare the Life Members' Subscription Account and also one for the ordinary members as they would appear after the Income and Expenditure Account for the year ending December 31st had been closed.

10. The following is the Trial Balance of the Greensward Cricket and Social Club on December 31st 19..

	Dr. £	Cr. £
Accumulated Fund at January 1st 19..		2 136
Club house	2 000	
Club-room equipment	420	
Sports equipment	270	
Sale of refreshments		243
Purchase of refreshments	185	
Interest-free loan from a member		500
Subscriptions received for current year		370
Subscriptions outstanding for previous year	5	
Receipts from club-room games		182
Maintenance of games and sports equipment	42	
Postages	76	
Insurance	18	
Sundry expenses	48	
Printing and stationery	84	
Wages	208	
Cash at Bank	62	
Cash in Hand	13	
	£3 431	£3 431

Prepare:

(a) an account to show the profit or loss on sale of refreshments and

(b) the Income and Expenditure Account for the year ended December 31st 19.. and a Balance Sheet at that date.

The following to be taken into consideration:

(i) Sports equipment to be depreciated at 20 per cent *per annum* and club-room equipment at 10 per cent *per annum*.

(ii) Subscriptions due for current year and not yet paid £15.

(iii) There is an unpaid account for provisions (refreshments purchased) amounting to £12.

(iv) The stock of provisions (refreshments) on hand at December 31st 19.. was £16.

(v) The subscriptions still outstanding from the previous year are to be written off as a bad debt.

11. The following information was extracted from the books and records of the Herring Bone Club:

Bank A/c for 19..

	£		£
Balance January 1st 19..	762	Bar supplies	17 146
Subscriptions for 19..	1 864	Cost of social events	722
Subscriptions in advance for		Wages	2 468
next year	21	General expenses	1 962
Bar takings	22 184	Repairs and decorations	
Receipts from social events	794	to premises	1 400
Balance December 31st 19..	573	New furniture purchased	
		July 1st 19..	2 500
	£26 198		£26 198

Note :

All bar takings and other receipts are banked intact.

The buildings belonging to the club were valued on January 1st at £15 000. The written-down value of the furniture at that date was £1 600. Subscriptions in advance amounting to £26 were received in the previous year.

Depreciation on furniture is to be provided at the rate of 10 per cent *per annum* on the written-down value of the old furniture and on the cost of the new purchases.

The following additional details are given:

	January 1st 19..	December 31st 19..
	£	£
Bar stock	861	928
Creditors for bar supplies	1 241	1 266

You are asked to give the club's Bar-Trading Account and Income and Expenditure Account for 19.. together with the Balance Sheet as at December 31st 19.. (RSA II)

12. (*a*) How does a Receipts and Payments Account differ from an Income and Expenditure Account?

(*b*) On April 1st 19.. the start of the financial year the XYZ Recreation Club's records showed cash in hand and at savings bank £210; furnishings and equipment £370; subscriptions outstanding for the previous year £8.

From the following information relating to the year ended March 31st one year later, prepare:

(*a*) the Receipts and Payments Account,
(*b*) the Income and Expenditure Account of the club for the year and
(*c*) the Balance Sheet of the club as at that date.

Payments: £
   Rent and rates   160
   Light and heat   42
   New darts boards   7
   Repairs to billiard table   9
   Sundry expenses   12
Receipts:
   Subscriptions (including those outstanding at April 1st 19..)   196
   Darts and billiards   72
   Savings-bank interest   5

Bring the following matters into account:

(i) Subscriptions £6 were outstanding for the year ended March 31st.

(ii) Equipment is to be depreciated by £27.

(iii) An account for £14 is outstanding for light and heat.

(iv) One month's rent £10 is paid in advance.

(University of London O level)

Manufacturing Accounts

29.1 Manufacturing

Manufacturing is the process of taking raw materials which Nature, or some primary industry like agriculture, has provided, and turning them into more sophisticated and useful products. Thus the steel industry converts iron to steel, and the oil industry converts crude oil to petrol, and other products. The cotton industry takes raw cotton, an agricultural product, and converts it into cloth and clothing. These activities are at the root of much of our national wealth, and the accounting activities connected with them are of great importance. Much of these accounting activities are in the specialized field of *cost accounting*, which is chiefly concerned with controlling costs to eliminate wasteful activities and keep our goods competitive in price on world markets. Cost accounting can only be introduced in this Unit. For a full discussion see *Success in Accounting and Costing* and its companion volume, *Success in Accounting and Costing: Problems and Projects*, by Geoffrey Whitehead and Arthur Upson.

29.2 Types of Cost in Manufacturing Accounts

In the preparation of Manufacturing Accounts it is necessary to discover the total cost of manufacturing goods. The costs met with come into two main groups, each of which has several alternative names.

The first group of costs is concerned with those costs which are directly embodied in the product. Raw materials are typical costs in this first group, as are wages of workers employed in the actual manufacturing process. This first group are often called *prime costs*—prime meaning 'first'. Another name is *direct costs*, since these costs are embodied directly in the product. A third name is *variable costs*, since these costs vary fairly directly with the output. For example if we double the output of cars on a production line we shall double the quantity of sheet steel used. We may list the names of these costs therefore as:

(a) *Prime* or *direct costs* or *variable costs*.

The second group of costs are not directly embodied in the product, but are necessary to the production process just the same. For example, the rent of a factory cannot be said to be embodied in the goods manufactured, but it will still have to be borne by the product when we price it to recover total costs. If 10 000 suits are made per week in a clothing factory, we must add on one-tenthousandth part of the week's rent to each suit, and hence the word *'oncosts'* is sometimes used to describe this type of cost. Other names are *indirect costs*, since they are indirectly embodied in the price of the articles produced, and *fixed costs*, since they do not vary with output. Thus a manager's salary will not be doubled just because output is doubled; he will be expected to supervise the factory activities whatever the output may be. The names of these costs may be listed as follows. All these names are commonly used, and are interchangeable.

(*b*) *Secondary costs* or *indirect costs* or *fixed costs* or *oncosts* or *supplementary costs* or *overheads*.

The commonest costs of this type are factory rent and rates, light and heating, insurance, supervisory-staff salaries, repairs of machinery, oil and lubricants, etc.

In order to separate these two groups of costs the Manufacturing Account is built up in two parts, as shown below:

Manufacturing Account

(for year ended December 31st 19. .)

Prime-Cost Section

(Here are listed raw materials, wages of operatives and all other variable costs)

Cost of Manufactured Goods Section

(The total of the prime costs is brought down to this section and the overheads, or fixed costs, are added)

29.3   Stocks in Manufacturing

Manufacturing stocks can present a problem. Not only will there be *stocks of raw materials* at the start of the process, and *stocks of finished goods* at the end, but there will also be *stocks of work in progress* or partly-finished goods going through the production lines as well.

Imagine a furniture manufacturer who is about to prepare his Final Accounts for the year, and arranges for stock to be taken at noon on December 31st. The stock-taking will involve not only the counting and valuation of all the finished furniture that is in stock, but also of all the raw materials and components in stock too. Not only this, but between the start of the production line and the finish there will be many partly-finished units of output, ranging from sawn planks at one end, which have barely started the production process, to nearly-finished articles needing merely labelling and packaging at the other end. Clearly it will require some calculation to decide the value of this work in progress. The accountant will have to decide what value to place upon it and whether to include overhead charges as well as prime costs in the calculations. It is probably most common to value the work in progress at 'factory cost', that is to say at prime cost (raw materials, labour and other variable costs) plus overheads (a proportion of total overhead costs being added). If this procedure is adopted, the work in progress will appear in the second part of the Manufacturing Account, i.e. in the Cost of Manufactured Goods Section.

29.4 The Final Accounts of a Manufacturer

A manufacturer's Final Accounts include the following sections of work:

(a) A Manufacturing Account in two parts, a Prime-cost Section and a Cost of Manufactured Goods Section.

(b) A Trading Account.

(c) A Profit and Loss Account.

(d) If the firm is a partnership or a limited company there will then be an Appropriation Account.

(e) Finally the firm's Balance Sheet must be prepared.

This is a fairly lengthy series of activities and for text-book and examination purposes it is usual to produce only the Manufacturing Account and Trading Account. You have, in any case, mastered the preparation of the other accounts. In Fig. 29.1 a manufacturer's accounts are prepared in this way. Do try and work through them carefully and make sure that you understand the preparation of each part.

Example

R. Wilkinson is a manufacturer. Prepare his Manufacturing Account and Trading Account for the year ending December 31st 19.. and carry the gross profit to the Profit and Loss Account.

	£
Stocks at January 1st 19..	
Raw Materials	1 900
Work in Progress	3 300
Finished Goods	6 850
Purchase of Raw Materials	27 550
Sales	66 345
Returns In	305
Factory	
Wages (variable)	7 910
Power (fixed)	710
Salaries (fixed)	2 949
Rent and Rates (fixed)	350
Stocks at December 31st	
Raw Materials	3 000
Work in Progress	5 550
Finished Goods	2 376
Factory	
Lighting (fixed)	400
Repairs (fixed)	1 600
Depreciation (fixed)	2 275
Warehouse	
Wages	3 710
Rates	740

Manufacturing Account
(for year ending December 31st 19..)
(*Prime-Cost Section*)

Raw Materials	£	Prime Cost	c/d	£
Opening Stock at		Prime Cost	c/d	34 360
January 1st	1 900			
Purchases	27 550			
	29 450			
Less Closing Stock	3 000			
Cost of Raw Materials used	26 450			
Wages	7 910			
	£34 360			£34 360

(*Cost of Manufactured Goods Section*)

	£	£		£
Prime cost	B/d	34 360	Cost of Finished Goods	
Overheads			(transferred to Trading	
Factory Power	710		Account)	40 394
Factory Salaries	2 949			
Factory Rent and Rates	350			
Factory Lighting	400			
Factory Repairs	1 600			
Factory Depreciation	2 275			
		8 284		
		42 644		
Work in Progress				
Stock at January 1st	3 300			
Less Stock at Dec. 31st	5 550			
		−2 250		
		£40 394		£40 394

Trading A/c
(for year ending December 31st 19..)

Finished Goods		£			£
Opening Stock at January 1st		6 850	Sales		66 345
Cost of Finished Goods		40 394	*Less* Returns		305
		47 244	Net Turnover		66 040
Less Closing Stock		2 376			
Cost of Goods Sold		44 868			
Wages	3 710				
Rates	740				
		4 450			
Cost of Sales		49 318			
Gross Profit		16 722			
		£66 040			£66 040

Profit and Loss A/c
(for year ending December 31st 19..)

		£
	Gross Profit	16 722

Fig. 29.1 A manufacturer's accounts

Notes:

(a) In the prime-cost section it is for the accountant to decide which costs he will regard as prime costs. It is always the case that raw materials and wages are embodied in the finished product. Some accountants would regard *power for machines* as a prime cost.

(b) Work in progress presents some difficulties. If the opening stock of work in progress is bigger than the closing stock the effect will be an increase in the cost of manufactured goods. If the closing stock of work in progress is greater than the opening stock there will be a decrease in the total cost of finished goods. It really means that more work in progress has been held back —to be passed on to next year's accounts—than was handed on to this year by the previous year, on January 1st.

You will see that the total cost of the manufactured goods is found by the formula:

Prime costs + overheads + or − net work in progress

(c) In the Trading Account, the manufacturer does not have 'purchases' in the usual way. He purchases raw materials, which appear in the Manufacturing Account. Instead the 'finished goods' manufactured are transferred to the warehouse, in this case at their manufactured cost, and the gross profit is the difference between this cost price and the sales figure.

29.5   Finding a 'Manufacturing Profit'

As described in (c) above, where the manufacturer transfers his goods to
the warehouse at 'factory cost price' the gross profit is found by deducting
this cost price, or rather the cost of sales based upon it, from the selling price.
Unfortunately this is not entirely satisfactory, because it does not give any
indication of the profitability of the factory. The gross profit achieved is the
result of two processes: the manufacturing process and the trading process.
If the results of these two activities can be separated to show their respective
results we improve our control of the business. Suppose the factory is very
efficient, but the sales manager is lax, and negotiates sales at too low a price?
The profit made from the factory will be lost by his weakness. In contrast
a very efficient sales manager, striking good bargains with customers, will
bring us no benefit if the factory is inefficient and running at high cost. Where
it is possible to bring out a manufacturing profit it is desirable that we do so.
This can be achieved by comparing the 'factory cost' with the current market
price at which goods like the ones we manufacture can be purchased on the
open market. Where such a figure can be obtained, a revised Manufacturing
Account can be prepared with the cost of manufactured goods section showing
a manufacturing profit. Fig. 29.2 below illustrates the effect of this on the
profit figures calculated in Fig. 29.1. The market value of the goods
manufactured, i.e. the total we would have to pay to buy them from an
outside firm, is taken as £50 000.

Cost of Manufactured Goods Section

	£	£		£
Prime Cost	B/d	34 360	Market value of Finished Goods	
Overheads			(transferred to Trading A/c)	50 000
Factory Power	710			
Factory Salaries	2 949			
Factory Rent and Rates	350			
Factory Lighting	400			
Factory Repairs	1 600			
Factory Depreciation	2 275			
	———	8 284		
		42 644		
Work in Progress				
Stock at January 1st	3 300			
Less Stock at Dec. 31st	5 550			
	———	−2 250		
		40 394		
Manufacturing Profit		9 606		
		£50 000		£50 000

Trading A/c
(for year ending December 31st 19..)

Finished Goods	£	£			£
Opening Stock		6 850	Sales		66 345
Market Value of Goods			Less Returns		305
Manufactured		50 000			66 040
		56 850			
Less Closing Stock		2 376			
Cost of Goods Sold		54 474			
Wages	3 710				
Rates	740				
		4 450			
Cost of Sales		58 924			
Gross Profit		7 116			
		£66 040			£66 040

Profit and Loss A/c
(for year ending December 31st 19..)

	£
Manufacturing Profit	9 606
Gross Profit	7 116
	16 722

Fig. 29.2 Bringing out a manufacturing profit

Notes:

(a) It will be seen that the total profit is unchanged, but now the proportion attributable to the factory can be seen. It leads us to conclude that the factory is earning profits and is therefore worthwhile.

(b) Imagine that the market value had only been £30 000. This would have meant that a manufacturing loss of £10 394 would have been suffered. This would have been completely hidden, because the Trading Account, which was making a £27 116 profit, would have obscured it. The factory should be shut down, in these circumstances, and the goods purchased from our (obviously more efficient) competitors.

You should now prepare some Manufacturing Accounts from the exercises given below.

29.6   Exercises Set 41: Manufacturing Accounts

1. R. Rayner is a manufacturer. From the following details prepare:
   (a) A Manufacturing Account, in the usual two sections, a prime-cost section and a cost of manufactured goods section;
   (b) A Trading Account
   for the year ended December 31st 19..

	£
Stocks at January 1st 19.. (valued at cost)	
Raw Materials	7 250
Finished Goods	19 275
Stocks at December 31st 19.. (valued at cost)	
Raw Materials	8 500
Finished Goods	16 375

Purchases of Raw Materials	18 250
Carriage on Raw Materials	550
Sales of Finished Goods	49 500
Factory Wages (prime cost)	7 300
Factory Expenses	4 700

Work in Progress (valued at factory cost)	
January 1st 19..	2 755
December 31st 19..	3 900

2. M. Lockhart Ltd. is a manufacturing company and the following details for the year 19.. are extracted from their books:

	£
Stock of Raw Materials January 1st 19..	5 275
Stock of Raw Materials December 31st 19..	4 385
Stock of Manufactured Goods January 1st 19..	17 350
Stock of Manufactured Goods December 31st 19..	16 000
Work in Progress January 1st 19.. (valued at factory cost)	3 800
Work in Progress December 31st 19.. (valued at factory cost)	3 250

Purchases of Raw Materials	13 850
Manufacturing Wages	12 725
Sales	48 000
Factory Expenses	2 500
Rent, Rates of Factory	1 500
Rent, Rates of Office	500

General Administration Expenses	3 250
Salesmen's Salaries	1 750
Motor Expenses (for delivery to customers)	550
Other Selling Expenses	340
Depreciation: Plant and Machinery (Manufacturing Account)	500
Motor Vans	400

Prepare the firm's Manufacturing Account, Trading Account and Profit and Loss Account for the year ending December 31st 19...

3. Robespierre Ltd. is a manufacturing company and the following details for the year 19.. are extracted from their books:

Stock of Raw Materials January 1st 19..	3 585
Stock of Raw Materials December 31st 19..	3 400
Stock of Manufactured Goods January 1st 19..	12 725

	£
Stock of Manufactured Goods December 31st 19..	11 855
Work in Progress (valued at factory cost) January 1 19..	2 725
Work in Progress (valued at factory cost) December 31st 19..	3 000
Purchases of Raw Materials	5 850
Manufacturing Wages	7 000
Sales	27 000
Factory Expenses	4 000
Rent, Rates of Factory	620
Rent, Rates of Office	280
General Administration Expenses	2 200
Motor Expenses (for delivery to customers)	480
Salesmen's Salaries	1 550
Other Selling Expenses	350
Depreciation: Plant and Machinery (Manufacturing Account)	800
Motor Vans	400

Robespierre Ltd. valued the goods manufactured at £20 000, and 'sold' them to the Trading Account at this price so as to reveal the profitability (or otherwise) of the factory. Draw up the Manufacturing Account, Trading Account and Profit and Loss Account of Robespierre Ltd. for the year ending December 31st 19...

4. Sudbury Ltd. is a manufacturing company and the following details for the year 19.. were extracted from its books:

	£
Stock of Raw Materials January 1st 19..	16 249
Stock of Raw Materials December 31st 19..	18 216
Stock of Manufactured Goods January 1st 19..	19 241
Stock of Manufactured Goods December 31st 19..	17 485
Work in Progress January 1st 19..	22 706
Work in Progress December 31st 19..	23 298
Purchases of Raw Materials	144 252
Manufacturing Wages	88 264
Sales	366 487
Factory Expenses	21 826
Rent, Rates of Factory	10 000
Rent, Rates of Office	4 500
General Administration Expenses	24 269
Salesmen's Salaries	7 836
Motor Expenses (for delivery to customers)	4 367
Other Selling Expenses	7 602
Depreciation of Plant (Manufacturing Account)	9 000
Depreciation of Motor Vans	2 200

You are asked to prepare Sudbury's manufacturing account and a Trading and Profit and Loss Account for the year 19..   (RSA II)

5. Rymer and Ross Ltd. is a manufacturing company and the following details for the year 19.. are extracted from their books:

	£
Stock of Raw Materials January 1st 19..	3 854
Stock of Raw Materials December 31st 19..	3 600
Stock of Manufactured Goods January 1st 19..	12 724
Stock of Manufactured Goods December 31st 19..	10 500
Work in Progress January 1st 19..	1 816
Work in Progress December 31st 19..	1 450
Purchase of Raw Materials	17 275
Manufacturing Wages	8 425
Sales	49 258
Factory Expenses	1 100
Rent, Rates of Factory	750
Salary of Factory Manager	2 850
Repairs to Factory	650
Repairs to Warehouse	880
Depreciation: Plant and Machiney (Manufacturing Account)	600
Warehouse Fittings	580

It is decided to value the factory output at a market value of £40 000. Prepare:

(a) A Manufacturing Account which brings out clearly
    (i) The prime cost
    (ii) The cost of goods manufactured
    (iii) The manufacturing profit
(b) A Trading Account bringing out the gross profit.
Transfer both these profits to the Profit and Loss Account.

6. Tradescantia Ltd. manufactures one product only. The following data refer to the year 19..

	£
Stock Raw Materials January 1st 19..	12 491
Stock Raw Materials December 31st 19..	14 292
Stock Manufactured Goods January 1st 19..	15 428
Stock Manufactured Goods December 31st 19..	16 140
Work in Progress January 1st 19..	17 289
Work in Progress December 31st 19..	22 140
Purchases of Raw Materials	128 294
Administration Expenses	31 228
Factory Expenses	13 480
Salesmen's Salaries	6 298
Sundry Selling Expenses	8 449
Depreciation on Plant	8 920
Carriage Outwards	4 200
Factory Rent and Rates	7 000

	£
Office Rent and Rates	2 980
Manufacturing Wages	102 989
Sales	322 243

You are required to prepare Manufacturing, Trading and Profit and Loss Accounts for the year 19.. The goods manufactured are valued at a notional value of £280 000, for the purpose of calculating the manufacturing profit (or loss). (RSA 11 adapted)

7. Suffolk Ltd. is a manufacturing company and the following details for the year 19.. were extracted from its books:

	£
Stock of Raw Materials January 1st 19..	32 330
Stock of Raw Materials December 31st 19..	36 480
Stock of Manufactured Goods January 1st 19..	38 550
Stock of Manufactured Goods December 31st 19..	34 000
Work in Progress January 1st 19..	25 500
Work in Progress December 31st 19..	26 750
Purchases of Raw Materials	279 800
Manufacturing Wages	166 900
Sales	735 500
Factory Expenses	42 550
Rent, Rates of Factory	20 000
Rent, Rates of Office	9 050
General Administration Expenses	45 250
Salesmen's Salaries	14 924
Motor Expenses (for delivery to customers)	8 725
Other Selling Expenses	15 717
Depreciation of Plant (Manufacturing Account)	16 850
Depreciation of Motor Vans	3 400

(a) You are asked to prepare Suffolk's Manufacturing Account and a Trading and Profit and Loss account for the year 19.. The goods are valued at a notional figure of £480 000 for the purpose of determining the profitability of the factory.

(b) During the year 500 000 units were manufactured. Another manufacturer who has excess capacity in his workshops offers to supply these at a cost of £1 per unit. What arguments would you put forward for accepting this offer? What arguments are there against acceptance?

Unit Thirty
Incomplete Records

30.1 The Accounts of a Petty Trader

There are many businesses which are very small-scale enterprises. Their proprietors are untrained in accounting and yet succeed in making profits year after year. Such petty traders often deal exclusively in cash, buying at wholesale produce markets and selling from local market stalls, or hawking their produce from house to house in vans adapted for the purpose. To such a trader there is really no need for written records; he conducts his entire affairs from his trouser pocket or his wallet. The few debtors he might allow to have goods on credit are personally known to him, and he will make sure no serious debts build up. In earlier years such businesses would only have a Balance Sheet taken out once in a lifetime, when the trader died and his heirs succeeded to the business.

Today things are not quite so simple. The government requires its share of the profits of every enterprise to pay for social services, and the Inland-Revenue authorities require at least an annual assessment of profits. To achieve this assessment they have devised a system, known as *the increased-net-worth method of finding profits*. It is very simple, and from the information it provides a trained accountant can often build up a complete set of accounts.

30.2 'Single-Entry' Records

The term *single entry* is given to any type of book-keeping record which is not double entry. There are many such records kept, which often help the accountant in preparing a full set of final accounts from *incomplete records*. For example, a trader who uses a cash register will often have a *till roll* which shows his total cash sales for the period. A small retailer will often keep a book in which he records the names of debtors, and the amounts owed. When the debtor calls in to pay the debt the trader will cross it out on the book, the debtors gradually being deleted until a few 'slowpayers' only are left. All such records are known as *single-entry records* as distinct from proper accounting records which are always *double entries*.

30.3 The Increased-net-worth Method of Finding Profits

The method used to find what profits a petty trader has made is the increased-net-worth method. It requires the preparation of two *statements of affairs*. A statement of affairs is a Balance Sheet drawn up at a particular moment of time, showing the assets and liabilities of a small trader. 'Statement of affairs' is a better name than 'Balance Sheet', since the latter implies that there are accounts with balances on them. Since this type of trader keeps no accounts, but only at best single-entry records, the title Balance Sheet is inappropriate.

Consider the following statement of affairs.

A. Stallholder
Statement of Affairs
(as at January 1st 19..)

Fixed Assets	£	Capital	£
Motor Van	180	Net Worth	380
Current Assets			
Cash in Hand	200		
	£380		£380

Fig. 30.1 A simple statement of affairs

Notes:

(a) The trader has only a sum of money in cash at the commencement of the year, and an old motor van.

(b) The 'net worth' of the business, to the owner of the business, is £380. The exact meaning of net worth cannot be explained here—since there are no external liabilities. It is explained in the notes below the next statement of affairs. At the end of the year a second statement of affairs is drawn up. Here it is:

A. Stallholder
Statement of Affairs
(as at January 1st 19..)

Fixed Assets	£	£	Capital	£
Motor Vehicles		850	Net Worth	1 329
Scales and Cash Registers		165	Current Liability	
		1 015	A. Supplier	350
Current Assets				
Stock	58			
Bank Balance	480			
Cash in Hand	126			
		664		
		£1 679		£1 679

Notes:

(a) There has been a considerable increase in the value of the assets. Clearly Stallholder has bought a new van, or vans, and also other equipment. He has saved money and has a certain amount of stock.

(b) The total value of the business—its 'worth'—is £1 679. However some of this value is owned by the external creditor A. Supplier, who has supplied goods but not been paid. The balance is the 'net worth' of the business to the owner of the business. The word 'net' here, as usual, means clean worth or clear worth (clear of any debts to outsiders).

The profit in this case is calculated in the following way:

(i) Calculate the increase in net worth. Clearly the extra wealth must have come from somewhere, and it can only be from the success of Stallholder's trading activities.

(ii) Adjust this figure to take account of drawings. Let us suppose that Stallholder admits taking £30 per week to give to his wife for housekeeping money, while he himself takes £15 per week for personal use.

(iii) Take into account any extra capital supplied during the year. Suppose Stallholder declares that £500, won on the football pools, was paid into the business during the year. Clearly this is responsible for some of the increase in value of the assets.

The calculations will be as follows:

	£
Final Net Worth	1 329
Less Original Net Worth	− 380
Increase in Net Worth	949
Add Drawings (since if they had not been extracted from the business the increase in net worth would have been greater) £45 × 52 weeks	= 2 340
	3 289
Deduct new capital paid in (since without it the increase in Net Worth would have been smaller)	500
	£2 789

Clearly this is the sum Stallholder has earned as a result of his business and on this figure he would pay an appropriate level of taxation.

It might be thought that this method of assessing profits is wide open to abuse by the petty trader, who might not truthfully reveal the value of the business assets when drawing up his statement of affairs. While it is conceivable that some petty traders might attempt minor tax evasions, these are made less easy by the statistics available to the Inland Revenue authorities, who have been accumulating tax records for well over a century. They are able to compare Stallholder's profits with those of many similar enterprises all over the country. If Stallholder proves to be the least profitable petty trader in his area they will probably re-examine the assessment, and increase it.

You should now attempt some questions from the set of exercises given below. In most cases the simplest approach is to draw up two statements of affairs, thus revealing the capital (net worth) at the beginning and the end of the period. It will then be an easy matter to calculate the increased net worth etc.

30.4 Exercises Set 42: Simple Incomplete Records

1. John Brown's Balance Sheet at December 31st 19. . showed the value of his assets as £21 000, and amounts owing to creditors £9 000.

   At 1st January 19. . his assets had been £15 000 and amounts owing to creditors £8 000.

   During the year Brown had introduced £2 000 as additional capital, and had drawn £20 per week for personal use.

   Calculate the amount of Brown's profit for the year.

2. H. Cook owns a store. His records are incomplete and you have been called in to prepare his accounts.

   You ascertain the following:

At January 1st 19. .	Stock	£2 100	Debtors	£1 300
	Creditors	£960	Rates in advance	£80
	Motor Vehicles	£1 200	Cash at Bank	£900
At December 31st 19. .	Stock	£2 240	Debtors	£1 040
	Creditors	£1 000	Rates in advance	£96
	Motor Vehicles	£1 000	Cash at Bank	£2 344

   Drawings during the year were £1 200 and a legacy of £400 received on March 1st 19. . had been paid into the bank.

   You are required:

   (a) To draw up two statements showing (i) Net Worth at January 1st 19. . (ii) Net worth at December 31st 19. .

   (b) To compile a statement showing the profit for the year ended December 31st 19. .   (RSA I)

3. The following are summaries of the assets and liabilities of John Smith, a retail trader, at the dates stated:

	January 1st 19. .	December 31st 19. .
	£	£
Debtors	4 186	5 319
Creditors	2 918	2 184
Stock	3 750	4 100
Loan from J. Green (repayable at the end of 5 years)	3 000	3 000
Cash in hand	175	125
Bank balance	1 273	
Bank overdraft		628
Plant and Machinery	4 500	5 000
Land and Buildings	15 000	15 000
Fixtures and Fittings	800	700

   During the year, Smith had drawn £200 per month on account of profits. Required:

   (a) a statement showing Smith's Capital at January 1st 19. .

(b) a statement showing the profit/loss for the year.

(c) a statement of affairs at December 31st 19.. showing the Capital Account in detail. (RSA 1)

4. From the following figures calculate M. Law's profit or loss for the year ended June 30th 19..

	At start £	At close £
Fixed Assets	3 250	3 000
Stock	1 860	2 140
Debtors	620	950
Creditors	490	350
Balance at Bank	1 100	1 730

Law's drawings totalled £800, and he had also taken home goods valued at £125.

5. On October 1st 19.. C. Cropper started a business. His assets then were: bank balance £350; debtors £120; a van worth £600 and stock valued at £300. His only liability was £75 for van repairs. Three months later he owed £1 009 to his creditors. His assets were: bank balance £264; debtors £488; stock £628 and the van now estimated to be worth £500. There were prepayments amounting to £20 for the van licence and insurance.

During the quarter Cropper brought in no fresh capital, but he had withdrawn £104 for personal expenses.

Calculate the profit or loss made by Cropper during the period, showing clearly the method you adopt to obtain your result. (RSA 1)

6. T. Newman started business on January 1st 19.. with a balance at the bank of £4 000, of which he had borrowed £1 000 from V. Trusting. Newman did not keep a complete set of records but at December 31st 19.. a valuation showed the following assets and liabilities:

	£
Furniture and Fittings	1 200
Motor Van	900
Stock in Hand	1 700
Trade Debtors	540
Cash at Bank	1 300
Trade Creditors	1 240

The loan from Trusting was still outstanding and interest at 5 per cent *per annum* was due to him on this loan. During the year, Newman had drawn £16 per week in anticipation of profits.

From the above information draw up a statement showing the profit or loss for the year ended December 31st 19.. and a Balance Sheet at that date. (RSA 1)

7. On July 1st 19.. I. Gamble started in business as a sole trader, his only asset being £1 300 with which he opened the business Bank Account. He

had no business training and for the next six months the only book he kept was a cash book, though he kept a note of all his credit sales and purchases.

At December 31st 19.. he had £26 cash in hand and the bank balance amounted to £158. His customers owed him £230 and there were outstanding amounts due to his suppliers which totalled £640. He had a business car which was worth £380, and his stock, valued at cost prices, amounted to £416. During the half-year he had withdrawn £710 from the business for his personal expenses.

Draw up a statement, in as clear a form as you can, to show Gamble—as far as the information will allow—the result of his six months' trading.

(RSA 1)

30.5 Deriving a Full Set of Final Accounts from Incomplete Records

Sometimes it is necessary to build up a complete picture of the profits of a business from incomplete records. Usually it is possible to start from the statement of affairs at the beginning of the year, and to know the cash and cheque payments during the year. The outstanding debts can be found by adding up the entries in the debtors' records book, and the creditors can be found by adding the invoices unpaid. With this kind of detail an attempt can be made to draw up the Trading, Profit and Loss Account and Balance Sheet. The following plan of attack upon this type of problem will help the reader.

(a) Draw up the opening Statement of Affairs if it is not available already and hence calculate the capital (net worth) of the business.

(b) Draw up a Receipts and Payments Cash Account, if the trader deals in cash during the year. Hence discover the balance of cash in hand.

(c) Draw up a Receipts and Payments Bank Account, of receipts and payments by cheque, and hence discover the bank balance.

(d) Draw up a Total Debtors' Account and hence find the sales for the year.

(e) Draw up a Total Creditors' Account and hence find the purchases for the year.

(f) From the figures now available draw up a Trading Account, Profit and Loss Account and Balance Sheet.

The following example will help you follow this type of difficult exercise.

Example
The Balance Sheet of R. Trevor, a trader, on January 1st 19.. was as follows:

Balance Sheet January 1st 19..

	£		£
Furniture	1 790	Capital	5 992
Stock in Trade	2 836	Trade Creditors	2 126
Trade Debtors	2 464	Creditors for Expenses	54
Balance at Bank	1 082		
	£8 172		£8 172

Trevor pays all his takings into his bank account and draws cheques for all business payments.

The following figures relating to the year 19.. have been taken from his books:

	£
Receipts from customers	42 144
Payments to suppliers	33 646
General expenses paid	1 832
Drawn from bank for private purposes	4 600
Discounts Allowed	760
Discounts Received	280
Salaries and Wages Paid	4 300

At December 31st 19.. trade debtors amounted to £2 712 and trade creditors amounted to £2 204. General expenses paid in advance were £30 and the stock in trade was valued at £3 246.

During 19.. Trevor incurred travelling expenses for business purposes amounting to £184 which he paid in cash from his own pocket.

There were no transactions other than those which can be ascertained from the information given above.

Depreciation on Furniture is to be charged at the rate of 10 per cent *per annum* on the value at January 1st in each year.

You are required to prepare:

(a) A summary of Trevor's Bank Account for 19..

(b) Total accounts for debtors and for creditors for 19..

(c) A Trading and Profit and Loss Account for 19.. and

(d) A Balance Sheet at December 31st 19..   (RSA II)

The solution is as follows:

(i) The opening Balance Sheet is given so that it need not be prepared.

(ii) Trevor does not deal in cash, paying in all his takings as received into the Bank Account. A Cash Account is therefore not required.

(iii) The Bank Account is prepared as shown below.

Receipts and Payments Bank A/c

		£				£
Jan.	1 Balance	1 082	Dec.	31 Creditors		33 646
Dec.	31 Debtors	42 144		31 General Expenses		1 832
	31 Balance (overdraft)			31 Drawings		4 600
	c/d	1 152		31 Salaries and Wages		4 300
		£44 378				£44 378
			Dec.	31 Balance	B/d	1 152

(iv) The Total Debtors' Account is drawn up from the figures given as follows. The closing balance of Debtors is the difficult item. Since it must be a debit balance *after* being brought down it must be a credit entry *before* being carried down. From this it is possible to calculate the Sales figure.

Total Debtors' A/c

		£				£
Jan.	1 Balance	2 464	Dec.	31 Bank		42 144
Dec.	31 Sales	43 152		31 Discount		760
				31 Balance	c/d	2 712
		£45 616				£45 616
Dec.	31 Balance	B/d	2 712			

(v) Similarly the Total Creditors' Account enables us to calculate the Purchases figure for the year.

Total Creditors' A/c

		£				£
Dec.	31 Bank	33 646	Jan.	1 Balance		2 126
	31 Discount	280	Dec.	31 Purchases		34 004
	31 Balance	c/d	2 204			
		£36 130				£36 130
			Dec.	31 Balance	B/d	2 204

(vi) Finally the Trading Account, Profit and Loss Account and Balance Sheet of the trader would be like this:

Trading A/c
(for year ending December 31st 19..)

19..	£	19..	£
Opening Stock	2 836	Sales	43 152
Purchases	34 004		
	36 840		
Less Closing Stock	3 246		
Cost of Stock sold	33 594		
Gross Profit	9 558		
	£43 152		£43 152

Profit and Loss Account
(for year ending 31st December 19..)

19..	£	£	19..	£
General Expenses	1 832		Gross Profit	9 558
Less Amount for			Discount Received	280
Previous year	54			9 838
	1 778			
Less Amount for				
next year	30			
		1 748		
Discount Allowed		760		
Salaries and Wages		4 300		
Travelling expenses		184		
Depreciation		179		
		7 171		
Net Profit		2 667		
		£9 838		£9 838

Balance Sheet
(as at December 31st 19..)

Fixed Assets	£	£	Capital	£	£	£
Furniture	1 790		At Start			5 992
Less Depreciation	179		Add Net Profit		2 667	
	——	1 611	Less Drawings	4 600		
Current Assets			—Travelling			
Stock	3 246		Expenses	184		
Debtors	2 712			——		
General expenses	30				−4 416	
	——	5 988	Excess of drawings over profit		−1 749	
						4 243
			Current Liabilities			
			Creditors		2 204	
			Bank Overdraft		1 152	
					——	3 356
		£7 599				£7 599

You should now attempt some of these more difficult exercises.

30.6   Exercises Set 43: Building up a Full Set of Final Accounts from Incomplete Records

1. C. Monger, a wholesaler, does not keep proper books of account. The following information was obtained from his records on December 31st 19..

	£
January 1st 19..	
Stock	7 400
Trade debtors	6 000
Trade creditors	2 100
January 1st to December 31st 19..	
Receipts from trade debtors	55 530
Payments to trade creditors	46 320
Warehouse wages	2 000
Carriage on purchases	1 570
December 31st 19..	
Stock	8 200
Trade debtors	5 750
Trade creditors	2 740

From the above information you are required to:
(a) Calculate Monger's Purchases and Sales, showing your workings.
(b) Draw up his Trading Account for the year ended December 31st 19..   (RSA 1)

2. F.K. started business on January 1st 19.. by renting a shop at £900 *per annum* and opening a business bank account into which he paid £400.

He sells all goods for cash.

He uses some of this cash for running expenses and for his private expenses, paying the remainder into the bank.

He does not keep proper books of account but the following information is available at December 31st 19..

(a) Business Bank Account

	£
Receipts —Cash sales paid in	14 200
Payments—Rates	360
Shop fittings	300
Rent	975
Delivery van	800
Trade creditors	11 740
Insurance	40

(b) F. K. paid bills for light and heat £105 out of cash takings and estimates that he also paid sundry expenses £65 out of these takings.

(c) F.K. retained £1 500 of cash takings for his private use.

(d) On December 31st 19..

    (i) Rates £240 for the half-year October 19.. to March 31st following had not been paid.

    (ii) There was an outstanding bill for electricity £35.

    (iii) Trade creditors amounted to £1 210.

    (iv) Stock-in-trade was valued at £1 150.

    (v) One month's rent was paid in advance.

    (vi) Shop fittings were depreciated by 5 per cent and the delivery van by 20 per cent.

    (vii) F.K. had cash takings in hand £130.

Prepare F.K.'s Trading and Profit and Loss Accounts for the year ending December 19.. and a Balance Sheet as at that date.

(University of London O level)

3. F. L. Winter did not keep proper books of account. The following information relates to his business for the year ended December 31st 19..

Assets and liabilities at January 1st 19..

Cash in hand and balance at bank £541; sundry trade debtors £194; stock £989; furniture and fittings £250; motor van £600; sundry trade creditors £1 240.

Cash book summary for the year ended December 31st 19..

Receipts	£	Payments	£
Cash sales	6 943	Payments to trade creditors	5 988
Receipts from trade debtors	1 236	Drawings	700
		Rent, rates and insurance	540

£

Payments (continued)

	£
Light and heat	42
Motor van expenses	226
Repairs and renewals	17
New shop fittings	50
Refunds to customers on cash sales	3
General expenses	84

Prepare Winter's Trading and Profit and Loss Account for the year ended December 31st 19.. and a Balance Sheet as at that date taking the following into account.

On December 31st 19..

(*a*) Stock was valued at cost £910; sundry trade debtors were £136 and sundry trade creditors £1 570.

(*b*) Light and heat outstanding was £11.

(*c*) Rates and insurance prepaid were £30.

(*d*) Ten per cent depreciation is to be written off the balance of furniture and fittings at December 31st 19.. and 20 per cent off the value of the motor van at January 1st 19..

Note : All calculations must be clearly shown immediately before or after the accounts.

4. On January 1st 19.. G. Smith started business as a building decorator and repairer with £3 000 in the bank. He kept no books but banked all receipts and paid all accounts by cheque. His bank statement disclosed the following information for the year ended December 31st 19..

	£
Receipts for work done	4 000
Cost of second-hand motor van	1 000
Cost of materials purchased	1 750
Motor van expenses	270
Insurance	20
Cost of new equipment	1 300
Drawings for private expenses	1 000
Payments to Building Society for private house	400
Rent of yard	100

On December 31st 19.. stock was valued at £250, and debtors amounted to £150. G. Smith decided to write 20 per cent depreciation off his motor van, and 10 per cent off his equipment.

Prepare G. Smith's Trading and Profit and Loss Account for the year ended December 31st and a Balance Sheet on that date.

Note : You will find it useful to calculate his balance in bank on December 31st 19.. before attempting the Balance Sheet. (RSA II adapted)

5. W. Davis is the proprietor of a small café. His sales are strictly cash, and he banks all takings every night. All purchases are paid for by cheque on delivery. He lives on the premises with his family.

A statement of affairs on January 1st 19.. showed his position to be as follows:

	£		£
Premises	3 000	Capital	4 670
Furniture	1 000		
Stock	150		
Bank	500		
Cash	20		
	£4 670		£4 670

A study of his cash book provides the following information:

		£
Takings during year ended December 31st 19..		10 000
Purchases	,,	7 400
Personal expenses	,,	1 500
Light and heat	,,	200
Cleaning	,,	30
Wages	,,	500
New furniture bought during year		200
Cash in Hand (December 31st 19..)		30
Bank Balance (December 31st 19..)		660

You are asked to prepare a statement showing W. Davis's profit or loss for the year ended December 31st 19.. and a Balance Sheet on that date.

The following are to be taken into consideration:

(a) Valuation of stock on December 31st 19.. £150.

(b) £100 of the Light and Heat was allocated to his private accommodation.

6. R.T. started business on January 1st 19.. by renting a shop at £800 *per annum* and opening a business bank account into which he paid £500.

He sells all goods for cash.

He uses some of this cash for running expenses and for his private expenses, paying the remainder into bank.

He does not keep proper books of account but the following information is available at December 31st 19..

(a) Business Bank Account

		£
Receipts —Cash sales paid in		15 700
Payments—Rates		420
	Shop fittings	400
	Rent	866
	Delivery van	700
	Trade creditors	12 340
	Insurance	50

(b) R.T. paid bills for light and heat £124 out of cash takings and estimates that he also paid sundry expenses £72 out of these takings.

(c) R.T. retained £1 600 of cash takings for his private use.

(d) On December 31st 19..

  (i) Rates £300 for the half-year October 1st 19.. to March 31st next had not been paid.

 (ii) There was an outstanding bill for electricity £42.

(iii) Trade creditors amounted to £1 670.

(iv) Stock-in-trade was valued at £1 280.

 (v) One month's rent was paid in advance £66.

(vi) Shop fittings were depreciated by 5 per cent and the delivery van by 20 per cent.

(vii) R.T. had cash takings in hand £165.

Prepare R.T.'s Trading and Profit and Loss Accounts for the year ended December 31st 19.. and a Balance Sheet as at that date.

The Accounts of Companies

31.1 The Limited-Liability Company

Limited companies are the commonest business units today. There are over half a million *private limited companies*, and about eight thousand *public limited companies* in the United Kingdom alone. Between them limited companies carry out the vast majority of business activities in the United Kingdom, and in almost all the free-enterprise countries of the world. The popularity of companies is explained by the *limited liability* which the shareholder has. Whereas a sole trader, or a partner, is liable to the full extent of his personal wealth for all the obligations of the business, the liability of the shareholder is limited to the value of his shareholding. He cannot be held personally liable for the debts of the business in excess of the nominal value of the shares he has purchased, or agreed to purchase. This concession to shareholders was originally made by Parliament in order to reduce the hardships suffered by early shareholders, whose liability was unlimited. As a result, when their company collapsed, they were held fully liable for the debts of the company, *even though they were not directors of the company and had no chance of influencing personally the conduct of its affairs.* Many small investors, in the early canal and railway companies for example, found themselves thrown into the debtors' prisons just because they owned a share in a company which had failed.

When the shareholders were thus freed from liability, a new group, the *creditors*, was placed in difficulties. If the shareholders could not be held liable for the debts of the business, who could be? The answer is 'no one'. The creditors must look to the contributed capital as the sole source of repayment. This places them in a difficult position. To warn them of this possibility Parliament has enacted that company names must have the word *Limited* or the words *Public Limited Company* to warn suppliers to check on the financial soundness of a company before doing business with it. You may think that a limited company is a sound and reliable organization. Of course many are, but many have only £100 or less as the capital to which creditors may look should the company get into difficulties. It is unwise to supply goods in large quantities to companies where the capital is insufficient to cover the order. You should inspect the affairs of a few companies by visiting Company House in London or Cardiff and examining their records.

31.2 The Accounts of Limited Companies

There are many unusual features of company accounts, and a complete explanation is impossible in a Unit of this size. Auditors must be prepared to report that the accounts give 'a true and fair view' of the company's affairs.

(1) The Capital of Companies

The capital of companies is subscribed not by an individual or even a few individuals but by many people, known as *shareholders*. There are many different types of shares but the two major classes of shareholders are *ordinary shareholders* and *preference shareholders*. Ordinary shares, often called *equity shares*, take an equal share of any profit that is available, but give way to preference shareholders who, as their name implies, have preferential rights to dividends. It might be thought that a preferential right to a dividend is so desirable that everyone would buy preference shares, but in fact preference shares only take an agreed percentage of dividend, often perhaps 5 per cent or 7 per cent. This would not be attractive to a wealthy investor who hoped to earn perhaps a 20 per cent or 25 per cent dividend, even if there was a risk that in a bad year he might receive no dividend at all. Small investors, seeking security and a regular dividend, may buy preference shares, which besides their fixed dividend often have a prior right to repayment when a company is dissolved. When applying to form a company the founders must state what they consider to be the desirable sum for capital, and if this is approved by the Department of Trade and Industry it becomes the *Authorized Capital*. This sum must be shown on the Balance Sheet.

(2) The Profits of Companies

After all charges against the profit have been met, the net profit is available to be appropriated among the various classes of shareholders. This does not mean that it will necessarily be shared up to the last penny. It is for the directors to recommend a dividend. They usually do recommend that the preference-share dividend shall be paid in full, but even this is not obligatory, and they may pass it over, arguing that it is better for the company to do so. Indeed a special class of *cumulative preference shares* has been specially created to take account of this possibility. Such shares are allowed to claim, in a subsequent year when good profits are made, any dividends passed over in earlier bad years; the dividends-due accumulate. *Non-cumulative preference shares* do not have any right to claim back-dividends, which are lost for all time. Naturally, shareholders who do not receive a dividend may be disgruntled about the conduct of the company's affairs, but the only redress of their grievances is to remove the *board of directors* at the *annual general meeting*. It does not follow that they will be able to do so, since voting is arranged 'one vote for each share'. If the chairman of the board, or the directors between them, own 51 per cent of the voting shares it will be impossible to remove the board. Under the Companies Acts 1948–1981, it is possible for the *minority shareholders* to complain to the Department of Trade and Industry about unfair treatment. In practice, such complaints have not been numerous and although the Department of Trade and Industry is alive to the problem, actual investigations of companies from this point of view are rare events.

Generally speaking, the directors will pay the agreed preference dividend, and will also pay a reasonable ordinary dividend, depending upon the position of the company and their plans for its future development. What is a *reasonable* dividend is discussed later (see Section 32.9). For the purpose of this Unit it is sufficient to enumerate the reasons why it is often undesirable to pay out the full profit earned. These are:

(*a*) When dividends are paid, actual cash has to be available to pay them. It may be that there are not sufficient liquid funds to pay out, and the directors will be forced to pass the dividend.

(*b*) Profits are not usually steady over the years, and it is wise to *equalize the dividend* by building up a *general reserve* of profits. Consider a shareholder who receives a 75 per cent dividend one year and a 1 per cent dividend the next. 'Marvellous company, mine,' he says the first year. 'What have the stupid fools been up to?' he says the second year. The average shareholder would be happier if he received, say 30 per cent dividend each year. He is actually worse off yet he feels contented. For this reason directors appropriate profits to general reserves in good years, which can be transferred back from reserves in bad years to equalize the dividend. Remember that this does not automatically mean that cash will be available to pay the dividend, and the directors must ensure that cash is available.

(*c*) It is often necessary to build up reserves of profits to meet eventualities such as plant replacement, lease renewal, etc. In inflationary times such as we live in today, a machine may double in price over ten years. It is necessary to avoid paying out dividends at too high a rate so that funds are available to meet these charges when renewal becomes inevitable. In industries where the pace of technology is advancing rapidly, such as the computer industry, the possibility of obsolescence requiring premature replacement of assets must also be borne in mind.

(3) Debentures

Sometimes companies raise funds for the expansion of the enterprise in the form of loans secured on the assets of the company. This type of money is sometimes loosely referred to as loan capital, but this is a bad term since it is not in any way capital of the business. The security issued is called a *debenture*, or *debenture bond*. A bond is a *written promise*, and a debenture bond is a promise to repay. Debenture holders are not shareholders in the company, but *secured creditors* of the company. This means that they are able to seize the assets which form their security and sell them in order to regain the funds they have loaned to the company. They are able to exert this right in preference to the unsecured creditors of the company, so that a company which has many debentures on issue is a less satisfactory firm to deal with for ordinary suppliers of goods and services. Debentures must be recorded on a separate schedule of charges registered with the company registrar at Company House.

Debentures may be:

(i) *Fixed debentures*, secured on the fixed assets,

(ii) *Floating debentures*, secured on the floating assets, i.e. the stock. The difference between these two lies in the nature of the assets forming the security. A fixed debenture, secured on plant and machinery, prevents the company from selling the assets concerned without the debenture holders' permission. A floating debenture, secured on the stock, does not prevent the company selling the stock—that would be ridiculous—but at the least sign of financial difficulty it *crystallizes* over the stock in hand, preventing its sale except for the benefit of the debenture holders.

(iii) *Naked debentures.* These are not secured on any assets; hence their name (the holder is rather exposed). They do constitute a formal acknowledgment of the debt and can sometimes be issued by very reputable companies.

Debentures are very safe, and are therefore desirable investments to timid small-scale investors whose chief concern is to avoid losing their capital. To exert the rights of the debenture holders a *debenture trustee* is appointed, usually a bank, or firm of accountants. Debentures like most secure investments, do not receive a high return, say 7–9 per cent. *This is a payment of interest to creditors, not a dividend (which is a payment to shareholders).*

(4) Preliminary Expenses

When a company is formed, it is obliged to meet certain preliminary (or formation) expenses. For example it is required to pay a tax of £0·50 per £100 of capital, and may be involved in legal and other expenses. It will need to publish its *prospectus* if it is a public company which is appealing to the public for shares, and it may be necessary to *underwrite the issue* if there is any chance that the public will not take up the shares. In this case the underwriters will buy all the shares not subscribed for, so that the project is certain to proceed. Where the company does not underwrite the issue, and the public response is so poor that the *minimum capital* is not subscribed, all the money must by law be returned to those who did apply. The minimum capital is that sum agreed by the Department of Trade and Industry to be the very least that the company requires to establish a sound enterprise.

These preliminary expenses are quite unavoidable, yet they result in little more than a *certificate of incorporation*, which is like the birth certificate of the company, and a *certificate of trading* which permits the company to commence trading. Several thousand pounds may have been spent, yet the only assets obtained are these two documents. Such assets are rather like that intangible asset 'goodwill' (see Section 26.17). Perhaps the best name for preliminary expenses, or formation expenses, is to classify them as *fictitious assets*, since there is nothing real to show for them. These are dealt with in a special way on the Balance Sheet, and must be written off within a few years. The number of years allowed must be stated in a note.

(5) Classes of Assets and their Depreciation

The Companies Act 1981 requires assets to be displayed in two main classes—fixed assets and current assets. Fixed assets are then sub-divided into three groups—intangible assets, tangible assets and trade investments.

Intangible assets are assets which have no physical existence, but exist as legal rights which may be enjoyed. Thus an inventor's rights to payment for the use of patents, or an author's rights to royalties on his books or the proprietor's right to goodwill (see Section 26.11) are intangible assets. *Tangible assets* you are already familiar with. They are assets which do have a physical existence and can actually be touched (tangible). Examples are land and buildings, plant and machinery, office equipment and motor vehicles. Trade investments require some explanation.

It often happens that a company wishes to gain effective control of other companies. In such cases the parent company is known as a *holding company*, the company that is controlled is a *subsidiary*, and the whole enterprise is called a *group*. The parent company keeps control of its subsidiaries by securing 51 per cent of the voting shares. These shares are known as *trade investments*, that is to say investments in other companies in the same trade as the parent company. A holding company does not hold trade investments in order to sell them again, but in order to retain control of the subsidiary. It therefore will not sell them, and they are fixed assets. The requirement to show trade investments as a separate item is useful to investors thinking of investing in a company, since it helps them to judge the financial position of the company. Trade investments are displayed on the Balance Sheet as the third class of fixed assets.

Other *investments*, which are often held by companies as a method of earning temporary profits on funds not yet required for the company's affairs, are shown as current assets because they can be turned into cash very easily when required.

The Companies Acts require that fixed assets shall be shown 'at cost, less the total depreciation to date'. This is a very useful requirement to those investing in companies, since it enables them to judge how modern the firm's assets are. It has led to the new method of recording depreciation in separate provisions for depreciation (see Section 22.7).

(6) Reserves of Companies—Revenue Reserves and Capital Reserves

(a) *Revenue reserves*. Where a company sets aside sums out of profits for particular purposes, such as to equalize dividends over the years, or to replace plant when it wears out, these are known as revenue reserves. All such reserves are required to be shown on the Balance Sheet at the end of the year, with an indication of any increases in the reserves made during the last trading period. Three points are of interest with regard to these revenue reserves.

(i) Revenue reserves, since they have been set aside out of profits, are the property of the ordinary shareholders only, and not of the preference shareholders. This is because the preference shareholders always take the full dividend to which they are entitled, and never plough any profits back into the business. Many companies, in their balance sheets, muddle up the ordinary share capital with the preference share capital, following this mixture with the reserve figures. This is highly undesirable, because it obscures from view exactly 'who' owns 'what'. The best way, as illustrated in Fig. 31.4 is to separate the ordinary shareholders' interest in the company from the preference shareholders' interest in the company.

(ii) Revenue reserves may always be recouped as profits for distribution purposes, whether they have been set aside for more permanent use, say as *plant replacement* reserves, or for general use—as *general reserves*. *Capital reserves*, which are explained below, may *never* be distributed as dividends (though they may be given away as *bonus shares*).

(iii) The last revenue reserve which will be shown on every balance sheet is the final balance left on the Appropriation Account. Unlike partnerships, where the residue of the profit can usually be shared up to the very last penny, a company can rarely share up its profits exactly. For example, if a company has 100000 shares and makes a profit of £35 751 it can only pay out £0·35 in the £1 (making a total distribution of £35 000). There will be £751 on the Appropriation Account undistributed. This is inevitable. It is more likely that the directors will pay out a simple round figure—say £0·20 per share, and leave £15 751 as a balance on the Appropriation Account.

(b) *Capital Reserves.* These are quite different types of reserve. They have not been set aside out of profits like the revenue reserves just described, but instead have been earned in unusual ways, which are of a capital nature. The four chief types of capital reserve are explained below.

(i) *Profits prior to incorporation.* Sometimes a limited company which is only in the process of formation takes over and commences to operate an existing business. It may be that the proprietor has died, or is too ill to conduct the business himself. In selling to a company, formed especially to take over the business, the sheer necessity of continuing its affairs may result in profits being earned before the company registrar issues the Certificate of Incorporation. Since one cannot make profits before one is 'born' (for legal capacity only commences on issue of the Certificate of Incorporation) the profits are not regarded as revenue profits, but form part of the capital transaction on take-over. These are capital reserves, and may not be distributed as dividend to the ordinary shareholder.

(ii) *Share premiums and debenture premiums.* Sometimes shares or debentures are issued at a premium, that is to say at a price over the face value (or par value) of the shares. This might be possible where a company was a particularly prosperous and profitable firm. Shareholders might be prepared to pay a premium on entry. If they do, the premium is a capital profit and belongs to the ordinary shareholders. It is a reward for their hard work and self denial in building up the company.

(iii) *Revaluation of assets.* It often happens that assets, especially land and buildings, instead of depreciating over the years grow more valuable as the years go by. If these assets are left on the books at their cost price, they may represent hidden assets which constitute an attraction to speculators interested in realizing the hidden profits by taking-over the company and disposing of the valuable sites. It is wise to revalue such assets, which means that the assets side of the balance sheet will increase in total value. The revaluation will be balanced by the creation of a capital reserve, part of the ordinary shareholders' interest in the company.

31.3 The Appropriation Account of a Limited Company

Just as the profits of a partnership must be shared between the partners, the profits of a limited company must be appropriated among the various classes of shareholders. A typical Appropriation Account, with notes, is given in Fig. 31.1.

Appropriation A/c   L 170
(for year ending December 31st 19..)

19..		£	19..		£
Dec. 31	Reserve for		Jan. 1 Balance		1 475
	Corporation Tax	10 800	Dec. 31 Net Profit		27 284
	Preliminary Expenses	500			
	Plant Replacement				28 759
	Reserve	2 000			
	General Reserve	5 000			
	Preference Dividend	1 400			
	Ordinary Dividend	6 000			
	Balance c/d	3 059			
		£28 759			£28 759
			19..		
			Jan. 1 Balance .. B/d		3 059

Fig. 31.1 The Appropriation Account of a company

Notes:

(a) The opening balance on the Appropriation Account is that part of the profit that was not distributed or placed to a reserve account in the previous year.

(b) The net profit was transferred in from the Profit and Loss Account.

(c) Corporation Tax, roughly calculated at about 40 per cent, but still awaiting proper assessment was placed to a Corporation Tax Reserve Account.

(d) Preliminary expenses have been written down by £500.

(e) £2 000 has been set aside in plant-replacement reserve, and £5 000 in general reserve, to provide for plant replacement and the equalization of dividend in future years respectively.

(f) Preference dividends and ordinary dividends have been appropriated for the year, and will in due course be paid.

(*g*) The balance on the Appropriation Account, which is to be retained as a further reserve, is carried down to the credit side of the account.

The double entries for these items are shown in Fig. 31.2.

		Corporation-Tax Reserve		L 171
		19..		£
		Dec. 31 Appropriation A/c	L 170	10 800

			Preliminary-Expenses A/c		L 172
19..		£	19..		£
Jan. 1 Balance		1 500	Dec. 31 Appropriation A/c	L 170	500

		Plant-Replacement Reserve A/c		L 173
		19..		£
		Jan. 1 Balance	B/d	4 000
		Dec. 31 Appropriation A/c	L 170	2 000

		General-Reserve A/c		L 174
		19..		£
		Jan. 1 Balance	B/d	6 500
		Dec. 31 Appropriation A/c	L 170	5 000

		Preference Dividend A/c		L 175
		19..		£
		Dec. 31 Appropriation A/c	L 170	1 400

		Ordinary Dividend A/c		L 176
		19..		£
		Dec. 31 Appropriation A/c	L 170	6 000

Fig. 31.2 Appropriations of profit at the end of a year

Special Note—The Difference Between Provisions and Reserves

It will be noted that all the accounts named in Fig. 31.2 except the fictitious asset preliminary expenses and the accounts for payment of dividends are designated 'reserve' accounts. You should remember that *reserves are appropriations of profit made after the profits have been calculated*. Provisions, like provisions for bad debts and provisions for discounts, *are charges against the profits and appear in the Profit and Loss Account where they assist in the calculation of a correct profit*.

Clearview Ltd. Balance Sheet
(as at December 31st 19..)

Fixed Assets	£	£		Ordinary Shareholders' Interest in the Co.	£ Authorized	£ Issued
Tangible Assets						
Land and Buildings (at cost)		28 000		£1 Ordinary Shares (fully paid)	100 000	50 000
Plant etc., (at cost)	33 000					
Less Depreciation	25 000					
		8 000		*Capital Reserves*		
				Profits prior to incorporation	3 421	
				Premium on Pref. Shares	1 000	
Furniture and Fittings at cost	7 000				—	4 421
Less Depreciation	1 500					
		5 500		*Revenue Reserves*		
				Plant Replacement		
Patent Rights Owned at cost	3 000			Reserve	4 000	
Less Depreciation	1 000			+ Additions	2 000	
		2 000			6 000	
Motor Vehicles at cost	8 500			General Reserve	6 500	
Less Depreciation	2 500			+ Additions	5 000	
		6 000			11 500	
		49 500				
Trade Investments						
Shareholdings in Subsidiaries at cost		27 500				
(valued by directors at £33 500)						

Current Assets
Other investments 15 000
(Market Value £18 500)

Stock (cost) 18 000
Debtors 7 250
Cash at Bank 4 250
Cash in Hand 1 050
                       45 550

Less
Current Liabilities
Ord. Dividend 6 000
Pref. Dividend 1 400
Creditors 8 215
Wages due   155
                       15 770

Net Current Assets 29 780

Net Assets £106 780

Balance on
Appropriation A/c 3 059

Less Fictitious Assets
Preliminary Expenses 1 500
Less Amount written off 500
                              1 000
                                              2 059
                                             19 559

Ordinary Shareholders' Equity 73 980

Preference Shareholders' Interest in the Co.   Authorized

7% Preference Shares of £1 .... 20 000   20 000

Long-term Liabilities
6% Debentures of £100 .... 2 000
Reserve for Corporation Tax 10 800
                                           £106 780

Fig. 31.3 The Balance Sheet of a limited company

31.4   The Balance Sheet of a Limited Company

The Companies Act 1981, which incorporates the requirements of the European Economic Community's Fourth Directive on the harmonization of company law, gives two alternative formats for the Balance Sheet, one of which must be followed by all companies. One format shows the Balance Sheet in traditional double-sided style, with the assets stated first, on the left-hand side, and the liabilities stated second, on the right-hand side (Fig. 31.3). The other format shows the Balance Sheet in vertical style (Fig. 31.4). The following points are important in considering these balance sheets.

(*a*) In this example one requirement of the Companies Acts cannot be complied with because of the page sizes of this book. This is the requirement to show the previous year's figures alongside the current year's figures for purposes of comparison. However, in examinations at this stage it is not usual for these figures to be given anyway.

(*b*) The ordinary shareholders' interest in the company has been kept separate from the preference shareholders' interest in the company so that a clear indication is given of the value of their holding. This enables prospective investors to judge how much they should pay for a share.

(*c*) The assets have been separated into fixed assets and current assets, and the fixed assets have been further sub-divided into tangible assets and trade investments.

(*d*) The current liabilities have been taken over to the assets side, and deducted from the current assets. This brings out the net working capital (also called the net current assets) position. This presentation also shows the 'net assets' position. In the final total of the Balance Sheet the net worth of the business to the shareholders (and debenture holders) can clearly be seen.

The order for current liabilities is now laid down in the format given in the 1981 Companies Act. It is in the order of permanence, with the most permanent items shown first and the most liquid item last.

(*e*) The fictitious assets have been taken over to the liabilities side and deducted from the balance on the Appropriation Account. This is required by the 1981 Act and recognizes that there is nothing 'real' about these assets, which are in the process of being written off anyway.

(*f*) The Companies Acts require that the book value of investments shown on a Balance Sheet must also be accompanied by the current market value (i.e. the value on the stock exchange at the end of the financial year of the company's holding). If the shares are in a private company the directors must give their considered opinion of the value of the investment if it should be sold privately.

(*g*) Where debentures are redeemable, the date of redemption must be shown.

Clearview Ltd.
Balance Sheet
(as at December 31st 19..)

Fixed Assets	£	£	£
Tangible Assets	*At Cost*	*Less Depreciation to date*	*Present Value*
Land and Buildings	28 000	—	28 000
Plant and Machinery	33 000	25 000	8 000
Furniture and Fittings	7 000	1 500	5 500
Patent Rights Owned	3 000	1 000	2 000
Motor Vehicles	8 500	2 500	6 000
	79 500	30 000	49 500

Trade Investments	(valued by directors at £33 500)		27 500
Current Assets			
Other investments	15 000 (market value £18 500)		
Stock	18 000		
Debtors	7 250		
Cash at Bank	4 250		
Cash in Hand	1 050		
		45 550	
Less			
Current Liabilities			
Ordinary Dividend	6 000		
Preference Dividend	1 400		
Creditors	8 215		
Wages Due	155		
		15 770	
		Net Current Assets	29 780
		Net Assets	£106 780

Financed by:

	£	£	£
Debentures			
6% Debentures			2 000
Reserve for Corporation Tax			10 800

		Authorized	
Preference Shareholders' Interest in the Company			
7% Preference Shares of £1		20 000	20 000
Ordinary Shareholders' Interest in the Company			

	Authorized	Issued	
£1 Ordinary Shares fully paid	100 000	50 000	
	c/fwd	£50 000	£32 800

(contd. on page 354)

	b/fwd	£50 000	£32 800
Capital Reserves	£		
Profits prior to incorporation	3 421		
Premium on Preference Shares	1 000		
		4 421	
Revenue Reserves			
General Reserve	6 500		
Plus additions	5 000		
	11 500		
Plant Replacement Reserve	4 000		
Plus additions	2 000		
	6 000		
Balance on Appropriation A/c	3 059		
Less Fictitious Assets			
Preliminary Expenses 1 500			
Less amounts written off 500			
	1 000		
	2 059		
		19 559	

Ordinary Shareholders' Equity   73 980

£106 780

Fig. 31.4 A Balance Sheet in vertical style

31.5   The Published Accounts of Limited Companies

Until you have actually looked at the published final accounts of a range of companies you cannot really consider your knowledge of Final Accounts of companies complete. These are available on request from public companies or they may be inspected at Companies House, London, EC1 (Registrar of Companies and Ltd. Partnerships, Department of Trade and Industry), or at Cardiff. In legislating for the publication of companies' accounts Parliament wished to ensure that the fullest information should be disclosed. This would enable investors and creditors to judge a company's performance and financial stability before investing, or supplying goods.

It is not possible to enter into a full account of the requirements of the Companies Acts with regard to the publication of accounts, but emphasis is placed on the following points, among others.

(*a*) The authorized capital must be shown on the Balance Sheet, as well as the issued capital.

(*b*) The 1981 Companies Act defines special classes of companies as 'small' companies and 'medium' companies. Small companies are those whose turnover is less than £1 400 000, whose Balance Sheet totals are less than £700 000 and who employ less than 50 people. Such companies need not publish a Profit and Loss Account and need only provide a very abbreviated Balance Sheet to the Registrar of Companies each year. The Bolton Committee, in its report on the 'Small Firm', recommended that these companies should be able to keep turnover secret, since takeover bids could be made by bigger firms who were able to find out all the details from Company House. Medium companies are those whose turnover is less than £5·75 million, whose total assets are less than £2·8 million and who employ less than 250 people. These firms must submit a Profit and Loss Account, but need not reveal turnover.

All other companies must publish accounts which follow the formats given in the Companies Act 1981.

(c) The fees and salaries earned by directors must now be published, but only if the aggregate of the Board's emoluments exceeds £40 000. Originally this was £7 500, but again the Bolton-Report recommendation has been accepted that the figure be raised to a point where the small firm is not embarrassed.

(d) Assets must be shown at cost less total depreciation to date.

(e) Reserves must be shown in such a way that the source of additions made in the current financial year can be seen.

(f) Corresponding figures for the previous year must be shown.

(g) Contingent liabilities, i.e. liabilities that may arise due to some unfortunate event must be stated by way of note. Examples are the possible dishonour of bills bearing the firm's endorsement, and adverse decisions in law suits pending.

(h) Capital commitments entered into, but not yet actual liabilities, must similarly be noted.

(i) The present value of investments must be shown, although they usually appear on the books at their original cost. The directors add a note to the published accounts showing, for 'quoted' shares, their market value. For unquoted shares in private companies, the directors' estimate of their value is the best that can be provided.

Elementary examinations in the principles of accounts do not usually require this degree of knowledge, and the reader is reminded that this whole subject must eventually be pursued in much greater detail by the student seeking a full professional understanding of company accounting.

Inflation Accounting. The effects of inflation on accounting are such that it is necessary to examine existing accounting practices to discover whether accounts based on historical cost (i.e. the cost of things at the time they were purchased) can give a 'true and fair view' of the profits of a business, or its 'value' as stated on the Balance Sheet. *Statement of Standard Accounting Practice No. 16*, prepared by the accountancy bodies, requires very large companies to prepare *Inflation Accounts* as well as *Historical Cost Accounts*. (A detailed discussion of the subject is not within the scope of this book.)

You should now attempt the preparation of some sets of limited company Final Accounts, although not in the form required for publication. All that is necessary is that you should be able to prepare Trading and Profit and Loss Accounts, Appropriation Accounts and Balance Sheets, in both horizontal and vertical styles. Details of the preparation of more advanced accounts for limited companies are given in the companion volume, *Success in Accounting and Costing*.

31.6 Exercises Set 44: Company Final Accounts

1. The following Trial Balance was extracted from the books of Shubunkin Ltd. at December 31st 19.., after the Profit and Loss Account had been prepared.

	£	£
Authorized and Issued Share Capital 80 000 shares of £1 each		80 000
Share Premium		10 000
6 per cent Debentures		20 000
Freehold Property (at cost)	70 000	
Furniture and Fittings (at cost)	4 000	
Stock-in-Trade at end of year	28 950	
Wages and Salaries Due		350
Provision for Bad Debts, January 1st 19..		400
Provision for Depreciation of Furniture and Fittings		1 200
Trade Debtors	15 000	
Trade Creditors		9 280
Balance at Bank	27 200	
Debenture Interest Due		600
Rates in Advance	50	
Profit and Loss Account Balance, January 1st 19..		3 300
Net Profit for Year		20 070
	£145 200	£145 200

You are given the following information:
(a) The directors propose to transfer £12 000 to general reserve.
(b) They propose a dividend of 10 per cent on the issued capital.
You are required to prepare an Appropriation Account for the year 19.. and a Balance Sheet as at December 31st 19..

Ignore taxation.   (RSA 1 adapted)

2. The following Trial Balance was extracted from the books of Rostrevor Ltd., as on December 31st 19..

Trial Balance

	£	£
Share Capital (authorized and issued)		
80 000 Ordinary Shares of £1 fully paid		80 000
20 000 7 per cent Preference Shares of £1 fully paid		20 000
Motor Vans at cost	14 460	
Freehold Property at cost	95 200	
General Reserve		10 000
Premium on Preference-Shares A/c		2 000
Provision for Depreciation of Motor Vans		10 142
Stock-in-Trade at December 31st 19..	17 754	
Provision for Bad Debts at December 31st 19..		400
Profit and Loss Account Balance at January 1st 19..		10 680
Balance at Bank	14 170	
Trade Debtors and Creditors	28 325	24 150
Rates and Insurance in advance	272	
Wages Due		944
Net Profit for Year		11 865
	£170 181	£170 181

You are told that the directors propose
(a) To place a further £5 000 to General-Reserve A/c.
(b) To pay 7 per cent preference dividend.
(c) To pay a 10 per cent dividend on the ordinary shares.

Draw up an Appropriation Account, and a Balance Sheet as at December 31st 19...   (RSA II adapted)

3. The following Trial Balance was extracted from the books of **Andrew** Ltd. on December 31st 19..

Trial Balance

	£	£
Share Capital, authorized and issued:		
200 000 Ordinary Shares of £1 each		200 000
6 per cent Debentures		40 000
Freehold Properties at cost	265 000	
Furniture and Fittings at cost	12 000	
Trade Debtors	18 950	
Trade Creditors		12 930
Preliminary Expenses	2 000	
Stock-in-Trade, January 1st 19..	18 930	
Provision for Bad Debts, January 1st 19..		300
Debenture Interest to June 30th 19..	1 200	
Provision for Depreciation of Furniture and Fittings		6 000
Bank Overdraft		490
Wages and Salaries	23 360	
Rent and Rates	1 650	
General Expenses	5 120	
Bad Debts	1 510	
Profit and Loss Account: Balance on January 1st 19..		14 740
Purchases	164 740	
Sales		240 000
	£514 460	£514 460

You are given the following information:
(a) Stock-in-Trade at December 31st 19.. amounted to £20 470.
(b) The provision for bad debts is to be increased to £350.
(c) Depreciation at 5 per cent *per annum* on cost is to be charged on furniture and fittings.
(d) Rates paid in advance at December 31st 19.. were £75.
(e) Wages outstanding on December 31st 19.. amounted to £240.
(f) One-fifth of the balance on preliminary expenses account is to be written off.
(g) The outstanding debenture interest is to be paid (to December 31st).
(h) The directors have decided to recommend a dividend of 12 per cent on the share capital.

You are required to prepare a Trading and Profit and Loss Account for the year 19.. and a Balance Sheet as at December 31st 19..

Ignore taxation. (RSA II)

4. The following balances remained on the books of Toleymore Ltd. after the Profit and Loss Account had been prepared for the year to February 28th 19. .

Share Capital £120 000; premium on shares £20 000; 6 per cent debentures £40 000; freehold buildings at cost £75 000; plant and machinery at cost £82 620; provision for depreciation on plant and machinery £41 380; furniture and equipment at cost £25 840; provision for depreciation on furniture and equipment £13 270; stock-in-trade £42 140; Profit and Loss Account (undistributed profit) £21 146; general reserve £35 000; provision for dividend payable £12 000; creditors for goods supplied £21 794; debtors £45 341; balance at bank £23 649; investments £30 000.

The authorized share capital is 120 000 shares of £1 each, all of which are issued and fully paid. The debentures are redeemable in 1986. The investments are entered in the books at cost and consist of government securities. The holding is temporary in character. Their market value at February 28th 19. . is £30 080.

You are required:

(a) to list the above balances in the form of a Trial Balance, and

(b) to prepare the Balance Sheet of Toleymore Ltd. at February 28th 19. . .

5. The following Trial Balance was extracted from the books of Box Ltd. at December 31st 19. .

Trial Balance

	£	£
Share Capital—Authorized and Issued 40000 shares of £1 each		40 000
Stock-in-Trade January 1st 19. .	13 428	
8 per cent Debentures		20 000
Share Premium		10 000
Freehold Property (at cost)	50 000	
Furniture and Fittings (at cost)	3 000	
Bad Debts	601	
Wages and Salaries	9 820	
Purchases	90 620	
Sales		121 498
Provision for Bad Debts, January 1st 19. .		250
Provision for Depreciation of Furniture and Fittings January 19. .		750
Insurance	693	
Office Expenses	1 142	
Balance at Bank	14 294	
Debenture Interest paid to July 1st 19. .	800	
Rates	210	
Profit and Loss Account balance at January 1st 19. .		2 900
Trade Debtors	16 923	
Trade Creditors		12 989
Rent Received		390
Directors' Salaries	6 000	
General Expenses	1 246	
	£208 777	£208 777

You are given the following information:
(a) Stock-in-Trade December 31st 19. . £16 426.
(b) The provision for bad debts is to be increased to £300.
(c) £796 has been included in the wages and salaries account which represents the wages cost of extending the company's freehold property.
(d) Rent receivable due at December 31st 19. . £130.
(e) Insurance paid in advance at December 31st 19. . amounted to £86.
(f) Depreciation of furniture and fittings is to be provided for at the rate of 5 per cent *per annum* on cost.

(g) The outstanding debenture interest is to be paid.

(h) £7 000 is to be transferred to general reserve and provision is to be made for a dividend of 10 per cent on the issued capital.

You are required to prepare a Trading and Profit and Loss Account for the year 19.. and a Balance Sheet in vertical style as at December 31st 19.. Ignore taxation.   (RSA 11)

6. Green and Brown Limited has an authorized share capital of £200 000, divided into shares of £1 each and of which 100 000 shares have been issued.

   After the preparation of the Profit and Loss Account for the year ending March 31st 19.. the following balances remained on the books:

   Share Capital Account £100 000; freehold land and buildings at cost £40 000; Share Premium Account £10 000; machinery at cost £60 000; stock as valued £37 040; sundry creditors £19 743; sundry debtors £43 221; provision for bad debts £524; balance at bank £22 028; General-Reserve Account £25 000; investments at cost £25 000; loan secured on land and buildings £20 000; dividend payable £10 000; provision for depreciation of machinery £32 000; fixtures and fittings at cost £22 506; provision for depreciation of fixtures and fittings £10 006; and Profit and Loss Account, undistributed profit £22 522.

   (a) List the above balances in the form of a Trial Balance.

   (b) Prepare the Balance Sheet of the company. (Investments have a market value of £28 050.)   (RSA 11 adapted)

7. The balances appearing below were those remaining on the books of Ham Ltd. after the profit and loss account for the year ended December 31st 19.. had been prepared:

	£
Share Capital, Authorized, 50 000 shares of £1 each; issued, 40 000 shares of £1 each	40 000
6 per cent Debentures	9 000
Premises at Cost	22 000
Machinery at Cost, *less* Depreciation to date of £5 000	24 000
Creditors	7 430
Debtors	16 150
Stock-in-Trade	12 920
Share Premium Account	4 000
Profit and Loss Account balance at January 1st 19..	3 420
General Reserve	8 000
Fixtures at Cost *less* Depreciation to date of £1 000	1 200
Provision for Bad Debts	250
Balance at Bank	15 030
Profit for year to December 31st 19..	19 200

It was resolved that:

(a) the General Reserve be increased by £10 000;

(b) a Dividend of 10 per cent on the Issued Capital be declared.

Prepare a Trial Balance, the company's Appropriation Account for the year ended December 31st 19.. and the Balance Sheet at that date. Ignore taxation. (RSA II)

8. Excel Traders Ltd. has an authorized capital of £100 000 divided into 100 000 ordinary shares of £1 each.

The following balances were extracted from the books at December 31st 19..

	£
Issued Capital (fully paid)	60 000
General Reserve (January 1st 19..)	10 000
Profit and Loss Appropriation Account (credit balance January 1st 19..)	1 460
Profit for Year to December 31st 19..	14 670
Fixtures and Fittings at cost	4 800
Machinery at Cost	37 000
Provisions for Depreciation:	
Fixtures and Fittings	1 600
Machinery	14 500
Freehold Premises at cost	48 000
Stock	8 850
Sundry Debtors	9 250
Provision for Bad Debts	370
Sundry Creditors	3 440
Bank Overdraft	1 860

The directors decided to transfer £3 000 to reserve and to recommend a dividend of 15 per cent on the issued ordinary shares.

Prepare the Appropriation Account of the company for the year ended December 19.. and a Balance Sheet as at that date.

Notes: The assets and liabilities are to be grouped under appropriate headings. Omission of appropriate sub-headings and inclusion of items under a wrong heading will be penalized.

(University of London O level)

9. Solarheaters Ltd. has an authorized capital of £80 000 divided into 160 000 ordinary shares of £0·50 each.

The following balances were extracted from the books at December 31st 19..

	£
Issued Capital (fully paid)	50 000
General Reserve (January 1st 19..)	20 000
Profit and Loss Account (credit balance January 1st 19..)	1 260
Profit for year to December 31st 19..	15 270
Fixtures and Fittings at cost	6 000
Machinery at cost	35 800
Provisions for Depreciation:	
Fixtures and Fittings	1 200
Machinery	4 900
Freehold Premises at cost	38 400
Stock	9 900
Sundry Debtors	8 200
Provision for Bad Debts	550
Sundry Creditors	3 260
Bank Overdraft	1 860

The directors decided to transfer £6 000 to reserve and to recommend a dividend of 10 per cent on the issued ordinary shares.

Prepare the Appropriation Account of the company for the year ended December 31st 19.. and a Balance Sheet as at that date.

Notes: The assets and liabilities are to be grouped under appropriate headings. Omission of appropriate sub-headings and inclusion of items under a wrong heading will be penalized.

(University of London O level adapted)

10. The following Trial Balance was extracted from the books of Turnip Tops Ltd. as at December 31st 19.. whose authorized capital is £80 000.

Trial Balance

	£	£
Share capital 80 000 ordinary shares of £1 each		80 000
6 per cent Debentures (issued January 1st 19..)		10 000
Share Premium		25 000
Freehold Buildings at cost	70 000	
Plant at cost	40 000	
Motor Vehicles at cost	4 000	
Provision for Depreciation on Plant as at January 1st 19..		18 000
Provision for Depreciation on Motor Vehicles as at January 1st 19..		1 500
Sales		134 720
Purchases	97 468	
Returns In	621	
Returns Out		417
Debtors	13 099	
Creditors		8 698
Bad Debts	427	
Provision for Doubtful Debts January 1st 19..		621
Motor Expenses	1 127	
Rent and Rates	1 850	
Insurances	160	
Salaries	11 206	
General administration expenses	10 426	
Stock-in-Trade January 1st 19..	23 846	
Bank Balance	10 641	
Directors' Fees	5 000	
Profit and Loss Account as at January 1st 19..		11 469
Discount Received		907
Discount Allowed	1 461	
	£291 332	£291 332

You are given the following additional information:

(a) Stock-in-Trade at December 31st 19.. £32 779.

(b) Rent owing at December 31st 19.. £550.

(c) Insurance in advance at December 31st 19.. £40.

(d) Provision for doubtful debts is to be increased to £685.

(e) Debenture interest is payable annually on January 1st and the amount due is to be provided for.

(f) Depreciation on plant is to be provided for at 10 per cent of cost and on motor vehicles at 25 per cent of cost.

(g) £5 000 is to be transferred to general reserve.

(h) A dividend at the rate of 10 per cent on the ordinary share capital is to be provided for.

You are asked to prepare a Trading and Profit and Loss Account for 19.. and a Balance Sheet as at December 31st 19.. Ignore taxation.

(RSA 11)

11. The following Trial Balance was extracted from the book of Dark Shadows Ltd. as at December 31st 19..

Trial Balance

	£	£
Share capital, Authorised and Issued		
40 000 shares of £1 each		40 000
Share Premium		10 000
6 per cent Debentures		20 000
Sales		142 620
Purchases	116 940	
Returns In	227	
Returns Out		359
Bad Debts	348	
Provision for Doubtful Debts		260
Rent and Rates	1 050	
Lighting and Heating	420	
Salaries	12 240	
General Expenses	2 661	
Debtors and Creditors	16 260	9 180
Freehold Buildings at cost	40 000	
Furniture and Equipment at cost	20 000	
Provision for Depreciation of Furniture as at January 1st 19..		7 400
Stock-in-Trade, January 1st 19..	18 260	
Balance at Bank	2 955	
Debenture Interest	600	
Profit and Loss Account as at January 1st 19..		2 142
	£231 961	£231 961

You are given the following additional information:

(a) Debenture interest is paid on January 1st and July 1st each year.

(b) Provision for doubtful debts is to be reduced by £20.

(c) Rates paid in advance at December 31st 19.. amount to £50.

(d) Lighting and heating due at December 31st 19.. amounts to £71.

(e) Depreciation is to be charged on furniture and equipment at the rate of 10 per cent *per annum* on cost.

(f) Stock-in-Trade at December 31st 19.. was valued at £19 621.

(g) A dividend of £4 000 is proposed for 19..

You are asked to prepare a Trading and Profit and Loss Account for the year 19.. and a Balance Sheet in vertical style at December 31st 19.. Ignore taxation.

12. The Trial Balance of Green Swan Ltd. at December 31st 19.. is as follows:

Trial Balance

	£	£
Share Capital, Authorized and Issued		
(80 000 shares of £1 each fully paid)		80 000
5 per cent Debentures		20 000
Freehold Buildings at cost	50 000	
Plant at cost	35 600	
Motor Vans at cost	8 500	
Provision for Depreciation:		
Plant		9 750
Vans		3 980
Purchases	88 792	
Sales		134 689
Rent and Rates	3 000	
Salaries	12 294	
General Expenses	9 946	
Bad Debts	349	
Provision for Doubtful Debts at January 1st 19..		428
General Reserve		10 000
Profit and Loss Account at January 1st 19..		3 296
Debenture Interest to June 30th 19..	500	
Interim Dividend paid July 31st 19..	4 000	
Debtors	13 294	
Creditors		8 491
Stock-in-Trade January 1st 19..	24 269	
Balance at Bank	20 090	
	£270 634	£270 634

You are given the following additional information:

(a) Stock-in-Trade December 31st 19.. is £26 922.

(b) Rates paid in advance at December 31st 19.. £400.

(c) Salaries unpaid at December 31st 19.. £121.

(d) Bank charges for 19.. amounting to £24 have been made by the company's bankers but have not been recorded in the books.

(e) A total dividend for the year of 15 per cent on the issued share capital is proposed.

(f) Debenture interest is payable half-yearly on January 1st and July 1st.

(g) Depreciation is to be charged on plant at the rate of 10 per cent on cost and on motor vans at 20 per cent on cost. No expenditure on these assets was incurred during 19..

(h) The provision for doubtful debts is to be increased to £462.

You are asked to prepare the Trading and Profit and Loss Account of Green Swan Ltd. for 19.. and its Balance Sheet in vertical style as at December 31st 19.. (RSA II)

(See Note on Answers to Questions, page 456.)

Unit Thirty-Two

Interpreting Final Accounts: The Control of a Business

32.1 How To Control a Business

When a business has been running for some time, it becomes possible to compare the current trading period with earlier periods. Such comparisons are almost always interesting, especially if attention is paid to *relative changes* and not *absolute changes*. For example, a manager who tells his employer that sales have increased by £100 per week is telling him the actual figures—the absolute change that has taken place. It sounds very impressive, but before giving him a bonus, the employer should inquire what relative change the increase represents, i.e. what percentage change. If sales have been running at £10 000 per week anyway it is only a one per cent increase and no one would think it miraculous. The success, of an advertising campaign for example, is always best judged in percentage terms.

Even if the business has only been running for a short time it is possible to compare it with similar businesses, if statistics are available from trade associations and similar bodies which analyse the activities of enterprises in their particular field. It is also possible, if a certain amount of planning is undertaken, to draw up in advance estimates of future performance in selling, expenditure, cash turnover, etc. These budgets may then be compared with actual performance as the weeks go by. This is the system known as *budgetary control*.

For the purpose of this Unit it is proposed to consider the most useful control figures which can be derived from the Final Accounts. These are:

(*a*) From the Trading Account,
    (i) the 'gross-profit percentage'
    (ii) the 'rate of stock turnover'
(*b*) From the Profit and Loss Account
    (i) the 'net-profit percentage'
    (ii) the 'expense ratios'
(*c*) From the Balance Sheet
    (i) 'working-capital ratio' or 'current ratio'
    (ii) the 'acid-test ratio'
    (iii) the 'return on capital invested' ratio.

Incidentally, while dealing with these matters, we shall learn many useful pieces of accounting vocabulary, such as the terms *fixed capital*, *floating capital*, *overtrading*, *insolvency* and *capital employed*.

Before preparing any such figures it is essential to have a set of Final

Accounts in good style, prepared in the way suggested throughout this book. When attempting to analyse the affairs of a business whose accounts have been prepared poorly the first step is to rearrange them in good style. Most of the control figures may then be prepared immediately.

32.2 Controlling Trading—A Trading Account for Analysis

Consider the following Trading Account (see Fig. 32.1).

Sunshine Boutique (E. Rawlinson)
Trading Account
(for year ending December 31st 19..)

19..		£	19..		£
Dec. 31	Opening Stock	2 564	Dec. 31	Sales	42 240
	Purchases 29 725			*Less* Returns	240
	Add Carriage In 135			Net Turnover	42 000
	────				
	29 860				
	Less Returns 424				
	────	29 436			
	Total Stock Available	32 000			
	Less Closing Stock	6 500			
	Cost of Stock Sold	25 500			
	Wages	5 500			
	Cost of Sales	31 000			
	Gross Profit	11 000			
		£42 000			£42 000

Fig. 32.1 A Trading Account to be appraised

Last year the gross profit was £9 500 on sales of £32 000, so that both turnover and profit have increased.

The points to consider in analysing the results shown by a Trading Account are

(a) the gross-profit percentage
(b) the rate of stock turnover.

32.3 The Gross-Profit Percentage on Turnover

The Gross-profit percentage on turnover is found by the formula

$$\frac{Gross\ profit}{Turnover} \times 100$$

Turnover is the net sales of the business, i.e. the sales, less returns inwards. In this case the percentage is

$$\frac{£11\ 000}{£42\ 000} \times 100$$

$$= \frac{550}{21}$$

$$= 26\cdot2\ \%$$

One of the interesting things about the gross-profit percentage is that if business trends are steady, the *gross-profit percentage will be constant*, i.e. the same from year to year. For example, supposing business were to double in the coming year? Sales would be twice as great, purchases would be twice as great, we should probably need to take on more workers so that wages would rise, and profits ought to double as well. When we come to work out the gross-profit percentage it would be

$$\frac{Gross\ profit}{Turnover} \times 100 = \frac{£22\ 000}{£84\ 000} \times 100$$

$$= 26\cdot2\%$$

The gross-profit percentage remains the same even if everything has doubled. It shows the relative profitability of the business, this year compared with the previous year. This is the usefulness of the gross-profit percentage. If business conditions are steady, the gross-profit percentage will be steady too.

Returning to Fig. 32.1 it is possible to compare this figure of 26·2 per cent with last year's gross-profit percentage. Last year the figures were £9 500 gross profit and £32 000 sales.

$$Gross\text{-}profit\ percentage = \frac{£9\ 500}{£32\ 000} \times 100$$

$$= 29\cdot7\%$$

Clearly the gross-profit percentage has fallen off from 29·7 per cent to 26·2 per cent. This is a significant fall in gross-profit percentage. It may have occurred for perfectly good reasons, but it certainly detracts to some extent from the performance of the business. Let us examine the possible causes of a decline in gross-profit percentage.

(1) Causes of a Decline in Gross-Profit Percentage

(*a*) **Cash losses.** If the manager takes money out of the till before cashing up the daily takings, the sales figure will be reduced and hence the gross profit, and the gross-profit percentage. It is unwise to accuse a manager of this type of theft, but if his way of life seems excessive for a person earning his salary, it may be necessary to take some corrective action. If the manager is not at fault it may be that someone else is the culprit. Where there are several cash registers it is possible for staff to steal money by incorrect ringing up of receipts. If a till has been deliberately placed so that the customer cannot see the amount being rung up an owner should be suspicious. Modern tills do much to overcome this type of theft by preventing any money being rung up unless the drawer is shut. Every amount rung up is totalled into daily totals which cannot be reset without an automatic record being made. If customers are always given till receipts this also reduces the chances of sharp practice. Staff training to emphasize the ease with which theft of takings can be detected is helpful in reducing cash losses.

(b) **Stock losses.** If the takings are being properly recorded, it may be that the fall in gross-profit percentage is caused by the theft of stock. Regular theft of small quantities of stock by staff will reduce the stock in hand at the end of the trading period. This will increase the 'cost of stock sold' and reduce the gross profit and hence the gross-profit percentage.

Passing out, the deliberate handing over of stock without payment to friends or accomplices, is a common form of theft. *Shoplifting* is a common practice, believed to cost at least £10 million each year to shops in the United Kingdom. The provision of store detectives, two-way mirrors and other devices helps reduce this activity. Where the trader takes home goods for his own use the effect will be similar (see pages 280–1).

Other forms of stock losses include *breakages* in departments where fragile goods are sold. Some assistants are naturally fumble-fisted and should be transferred from departments where this is a disadvantage. Skylarking and tomfoolery should be discouraged and action taken against offenders. Stock losses due to *the spoiling of perishable commodities* indicates bad buying. Too many tomatoes, fresh fruit, etc. may result in stocks going bad, while bad storage may lead to stock losses due to evaporation, blowing away of powdery stocks like meal and flour, and the contamination of foods by other substances or by insects.

(c) **Mark-downs.** Sometimes stock has to be disposed of at reduced prices because it is shop-soiled, or slow-moving. This indicates bad buying. Some buyers may be out of touch with what is fashionable and readily saleable. Products, which for some reason do not achieve anticipated sales figures, may have to be marked down, thus reducing the gross profit and the gross-profit percentage. An appraisal of such 'clearance items' may reveal that a particular buyer is responsible for a high proportion of them. Clearly some action may be needed to end this situation.

(d) **Increased purchase prices.** Sometimes world prices of raw materials change, and result in higher purchase prices for goods. This increased price should be passed on to the consumer as increased selling prices. Sometimes this is not possible because of competition, and the result is falling profit margins and a lower gross-profit percentage. At least a businessman who is aware of these falling profit margins can be ready, when circumstances are less competitive, to recoup past losses. He may also vary his mixture of goods to include more items where competition is less fierce, reducing those where his rivals are particularly efficient and are able to undercut him.

(e) **Expenses.** Even in the Trading Account there are certain expense items. An increase in these may explain a falling gross-profit percentage. This type of change is discussed more fully below under *expense ratios* (see Section 32·7).

(*f*) **Incorrect stock valuation.** One further explanation of a change in gross-profit percentage is that the change may be the result of incorrect stock valuation. An over-valued stock overstates the profit and gives an artificially high percentage of gross profit. As this stock then becomes the 'opening stock' of the next period, it will artificially inflate the 'cost of stock sold' and lower the percentage of gross profit in the following year. This will give a difference between the two successive years which is not the fault of the manager. It is simply caused by the bad stock-taking.

(2) Causes of a Rise in Gross-Profit Percentage

The items listed above explain a fall in gross-profit percentage, indicating dishonesty or incompetence somewhere in the business. Where a *rise* in gross profit percentage occurs it is almost certainly due to increased efficiency in the conduct of the business. More careful supervision, more systematic working or some other improvement has produced the beneficial change. The manager who is more honest, or more efficient should be rewarded with a bonus for his good work.

(3) Gross-Profit Percentage on Cost

Sometimes it is helpful to work out a different gross-profit percentage based on cost price, rather than selling price (turnover). This is not used as frequently as the gross-profit percentage on turnover, but it may be found by the formula

$$\textit{Gross-profit percentage on cost} = \frac{\textit{Gross profit}}{\textit{Cost price of goods sold}} \times 100$$

In the Trading Account shown in Fig. 32.1 it will be

$$\frac{\pounds 11\ 000}{\pounds 25\ 500} \times 100$$
$$= 43\%$$

Note: The gross-profit percentage on cost will always be greater than the gross-profit percentage on turnover because it is a percentage figure and all percentages depend upon the figures that you start with in your calculations. Since cost prices are always less than selling prices (except in a business making trading losses) it follows that the *same* profit will be a higher percentage on cost than it is on sales. It is an old joke in the retail trade for the shopkeeper to tell customers the profit margin on sales, rather than costs. For example

Cost price of a packet of envelopes, 4p
Selling price 6p
Profit 2p

$$\text{Gross-profit percentage on selling price} = \frac{2}{6} \times 100 = 33\tfrac{1}{3}\%$$

$$\text{Gross-profit percentage on cost price} \quad = \frac{2}{4} \times 100 = 50\%$$

The shopkeeper may tell the housewife 'You are buying this for 6p, of which I get one-third, a 33⅓ per cent profit.'

Actually he is getting a 2p profit on an original outlay of 4p which is a 50 per cent profit.

You should now try the simple calculations given below to practise dealing with gross-profit percentages.

32.4   Exercises Set 45: Gross-Profit Percentage

1. Mr A. had the following results in successive years:

	Year 1	Year 2
Sales	£27 000	£35 000
Gross profit	£5 000	£6 000

Compare the two years by finding, and commenting upon, the gross-profit percentage.

2. R. Dawson makes two products, a Junior model and a Senior model of an electrical appliance. His records show the following results at the end of the year.

	Junior	Senior
Sales	£5 800	£25 600
Sales Returns	£1 800	£1 600
Cost of Sales	£3 800	£16 500

He has no room to expand, and at present allocates half his available space to each model. Calculate the gross profit on each model, the gross-profit percentage on each model, and offer Dawson some advice. You may assume that an unlimited market exists for each product.

3. R. Marshall, a retailer, finds that his gross-profit percentage has fallen from 38 per cent last year to 23 per cent this year. Is he justified in considering the following as perhaps responsible for the fall in gross-profit percentage?

(a) The takings have been deliberately reduced by embezzlement.

(b) One of the assistants has been conspiring with friends to charge less than the full price for goods each time they come in to purchase supplies.

(c) The accountant has had a large increase in salary.

(d) A supermarket four doors away has caused him to offer cut prices on many articles.

(e) Marshall's wife has not been well and he has taken home regularly goods for domestic use which have not been recorded in any way.

(f) An assistant buyer has placed several large orders with suppliers for goods which proved to be unpopular and were sold off in an end-of-year sale.

4. (a) What is the meaning of 'gross profit'? (b) What is the meaning of 'gross-profit percentage'? (c) Using the figures given below, prepare the Trading Account of Keith Newing, to find the gross profit and the gross-profit percentage earned during the year.

	£
Stock, January 1st 19..	4 500
Cash Purchases	1 000
Credit Purchases	12 500
Carriage Inwards	500
Returns Outwards (Purchases Returns)	1 000
Cash Sales	23 000
Credit Sales	8 000
Returns Inwards (Sales Returns)	1 000
Stock, December 31st 19..	5 500

5. (a) At December 31st 19.. the Trial Balance of E. Randall contained the following items:

	£
Stock (January 1st 19..)	2 785
Purchases	6 908
Sales	7 642
Returns Outward	195
Returns Inward	262
Wages (Trading Account)	700
Wages owing	20
Import Charges	126

Randall's Stock at December 31st 19.. was valued at £4 440. Prepare the Trading Account for the year ending December 31st 19...

(b) What was Randall's percentage profit or loss on his turnover?

32.5 The Rate of Stockturn

The rate of stockturn, or rate of stock turnover, is a figure which can be calculated to show how many times the stock turns over in a year. Rate of stock turnover is important because every time the stock turns over it yields a profit, so that a rapid turnover will increase the total profit earned in the year. Turnover must be rapid with some merchandise, perishable foods or daily papers, for example, must turn over every day if possible. At least one chain of supermarkets throws away all cut-meat products unsold at the end of the day. Overstocking in such circumstances can be very expensive.

The formula for finding this control figure is:

$$\text{Rate of stock turnover} = \frac{\text{Cost of stock sold}}{\text{Average stock at cost price}}$$

The average stock can be found by one of the following methods:

$$\frac{Opening\ stock\ +\ closing\ stock}{2}$$

or

$$\frac{Sum\ of\ the\ four\ quarterly\ stock\ figures}{4}$$

or

$$\frac{Sum\ of\ the\ twelve\ monthly\ stock\ figures}{12}$$

It depends upon the frequency with which stock is taken as to which method is used.

In the case of the Trading Account in Fig. 32.1,

$$\begin{aligned}
The\ rate\ of\ stock\ turnover &= \frac{25\ 500}{(2\ 564 + 6\ 500) \div 2} \\
&= \frac{25\ 500}{4\ 532} \\
&= 5 \cdot 6\ times
\end{aligned}$$

Is this a satisfactory rate of turnover? The answer is that we must know what the product is before we can say. It would be satisfactory for grand pianos but quite inadequate for groceries. It would perhaps do well enough for antiques, but not well enough for sweets or tobacco.

How long is the average item in stock? The rate of stockturn tells us how many times the stock turns over in a year. If we divide the 52 weeks of the year by the rate of stock turn we find how long the average item is in stock. In this case it is clearly $52 \div 5 \cdot 6 = 9 \cdot 3$ weeks.

32.6 Exercises Set 46: The Rate of Stock Turnover

1. L. Perry carries an average stock (at cost price) of £5 250. Her annual sales are £78 750 (selling price) of which 20 per cent is profit. What is the rate of stockturn in her business?

2. A. Reddington sells cars valued at £159 375 (selling price, of which 20 per cent is profit). His average stock (at cost price) is £8 500. What is his rate of stock turnover?

3. Using the figures available in the Trading Account overleaf, find:
   (a) The average stock held.
   (b) The rate of stock turnover for the year.
   (c) The average length of time an article of stock was in the possession of A. Trader.

Trading A/c of A. Trader
(for year ended December 31st 19. .)

	£	£		£
Opening Stock		2 100	Sales	7 500
Purchases	5 040		Less Returns	20
Less Returns	90		Net Turnover	7 480
	——	4 950		
		7 050		
Less Closing Stock		1 560		
Cost of Stock Sold		5 490		
Gross Profit		1 990		
		£7 480		£7 480

(East Anglian Examination Board)

4. Using the figures available in the Trading Account of M. Lewis, find:
   (a) The average stock held.
   (b) The rate of stock turnover for the year.
   (c) The average length of time an article of stock was in the possession of M. Lewis to the nearest day.

Trading A/c of M. Lewis
(for the year ended December 31st 19. .)

Opening Stock		2 400	Sales	69 540
Purchases	51 550		Less Returns	420
Less Returns	190		Net Turnover	69 120
	——	51 360		
		53 760		
Less Closing Stock		1 920		
Cost of Stock Sold		51 840		
Gross Profit		17 280		
		£69 120		£69 120

5. Using the figures available in the Trading Account of D. Hancock, find:
   (a) The average stock held.
   (b) The rate of stock turnover for the year.
   (c) The average length of time an article of stock was in the possession of D. Hancock (to the nearest day).

Trading A/c of D. Hancock
(for year ended December 31st 19..)

	£		£
Opening Stock	2 500	Sales	24 400
Purchases	20 700	Less Returns	112
Less Returns	400	Net turnover	24 288
	20 300		
	22 800		
Less Closing Stock	2 560		
Cost of Stock Sold	20 240		
Gross Profit	4 048		
	£24 288		£24 288

6. The proprietor of Downtown Do-It-Yourself Stores prepares his Final Accounts annually and the following figures relate to the year ended September 30th 19..

	£
Purchases	12 909
Sales	16 065
Stock at Start	2 134
Stock at Close	2 086
Returns Inwards	873
Returns Outwards	297

You are required to:

(a) Prepare a Trading Account for the year ended September 30th 19..

(b) State the cost of the goods sold during the year.

(c) Calculate the Gross Profit/Sales percentage.

(d) Calculate, in months, the average time for which goods were held in stock.

7. J. F. Roe manufactures bicycles. He holds an average stock of 70 bicycles. The manufacturing cost of each bicycle is £18 and the selling price £25. During 19.. he sold 910 bicycles.

(a) Calculate:

(i) Roe's rate of turnover of stock for the year 19..

(ii) Roe's gross profit for the year 19..

(b) For the next year Roe reduced the selling price by 10 per cent and holding the same average stock, his rate of turnover of stock was 15. His gross profit was £6 825. Calculate:

(i) the value of Roe's turnover for the year;

(ii) the cost of manufacture of each bicycle in this second year.

(University of London O level)

8. M. Regent manufactures vacuum cleaners. He holds an average stock of 80 cleaners. The manufacturing cost of each cleaner is £20 and the selling price £35. During 19.. he sold 1 200 cleaners.

(a) Calculate:

(i) Regent's rate of turnover of stock for the year 19..

(ii) Regent's gross profit for the year 19..

(b) For the next year Regent reduced the selling price by 10 per cent and holding the same average stock, his rate of turnover of stock was 20. His gross profit was £19 200. Calculate:

(i) the value of Regent's turnover for the year;

(ii) the cost of manufacture of each bicycle.

32.7   Controlling Expenses—The Profit and Loss Account

The gross profit is carried forward to the Profit and Loss Account where other profits are added to it and losses are deducted. The resulting net profit can be used as the basis for a *net-profit percentage*, which is found by the formula

$$\text{Net-profit percentage} = \frac{\text{Net profit}}{\text{Turnover}} \times 100$$

Once again this should be constant from year to year, and if it is not the causes of the change should be discovered.

In the case of the Trading Account shown in Fig. 32.1 the gross profit to be carried forward was £11 000.

The Profit and Loss Account may be imagined to be as follows:

Sunshine Boutique (E. Rawlinson)
Profit and Loss A/c
(for year ending December 31st 19..)

19..		£	19..		£
Dec. 31	Salaries	1 500	Dec. 31	Gross Profit	11 000
	Administration Expenses	420		Discount Received	750
	Light and Heat	680		Commissions Earned	1 550
	Rent and Rates	1 650			
	Insurance	450			13 300
	Advertising	1 240			
	Carriage Out	100			
		6 040			
	Net Profit	7 260			
		£13 300			£13 300

Fig. 32.2 A Profit and Loss Account to be appraised

Calculating the net-profit percentage we have

$$Net\text{-}profit\ percentage = \frac{Net\ profit}{Turnover} \times 100$$

$$= \frac{7\ 260}{42\ 000} \times 100$$

$$= 17 \cdot 3\%$$

(1) Analysing the Net-Profit Percentage

The figure of net-profit percentage achieved here seems a fairly adequate percentage. Most firms would be very satisfied to achieve this net-profit margin, and in many of the more competitive industries smaller profit margins than this are commonplace. The chief advantage of the net-profit percentage is that it enables us to compare one year with another, or one trading period with the previous trading period if we take out Final Accounts more frequently. Let us imagine that last year the net profit percentage was 20 per cent. This means that in the last year there has been a fall of 2·7 per cent on the net-profit percentage. What can have been the cause of this decline? Let us imagine that the gross-profit percentage has remained constant, so that clearly there is nothing wrong with the trading activities of the firm.

There can only be two explanations:

(a) The expenses may have increased for some reason.

(b) The 'other profits' may have declined for some reason.

A useful thing here is to prepare *expense ratios*. Expense ratios enable the accountant to compare every expense with the same expense the previous year. He can then see whether they have risen abnormally. The formula is

$$Expense\ ratio = \frac{Expense\ item}{Turnover} \times 100$$

In the case of salaries, for example, the ratio in this particular example is

$$Salaries\ ratio\ to\ turnover = \frac{1\ 500}{42\ 000} \times 100$$

$$= 3 \cdot 57\%$$

Suppose that last year the salaries were £1 000 and turnover £32 000.

$$Salaries\ ratio\ (previous\ year) = \frac{1\ 000}{32\ 000} \times 100$$

$$= 3 \cdot 13\%$$

There has been quite a large increase in the salaries figure relative to the volume of trade done, and this seems to indicate some inefficiency somewhere. Some managers build 'empires' of staff under their control, and this appears to have happened here to some extent.

(2) Falling 'Other Receipts'

If the decline in net-profit percentage does not seem to have been caused by an increase in expenses, it may have been caused by a decrease in 'other receipts', such as commission received, or rent received. If such items have yielded less profit than in previous years, some attempt to discover the reasons should be made. It may be that a sub-tenant has been given notice to quit because his share of the building was required for expansion. In such a case there is nothing we can do about the lost rent. In other cases we might discover that commission previously earned has not been forthcoming for some reason. Extra attention to this matter might ensure that this type of earnings will be pursued more vigorously in the following year.

Regular comparison of the gross-profit percentage and net-profit percentage in successive trading periods is extremely useful, and reveals changes of a favourable or unfavourable nature that are taking place in the business.

Many firms prepare *interim Final Accounts* at three-monthly or even monthly, intervals, so that they can check the profitability of their enterprises.

32.8   Exercises Set 47: Net-Profit Percentage

1. F. Azouqua has the following results for two successive years. Present these two sets of figures in such a way as to make a comparison between them, and state any conclusions you are able to draw.

	Year 1	Year 2
Turnover	£72 000	£80 000
Gross Profit	£14 400	£16 200
Net Profit	£8 000	£9 000

2. K. Penn takes out Final Accounts at six-monthly intervals. He finds the following results. Compare these two sets of figures and comment upon them.

	January–June	July–December
Gross Profit	£18 400	£22 400
Net Profit	£5 520	£7 520
Turnover	£46 000	£80 000

3. How would the following transactions affect (*a*) the gross profit and (*b*) the net profit of R. Spurling's manufacturing business?
   (i) Sold goods on credit (cost price £100) for £120.
   (ii) Paid commission to salesmen £650.
   (iii) Paid bonus to works manager £250.
   (iv) Paid office wages £210.
   (v) Purchased new machinery on credit £2 000.
   (vi) Paid customs duty on raw material £60.
   (vii) Depreciated machinery by £300.
   Your answers are to be given under the two headings:

   Effect on gross profit   *Effect on net profit*

You are required to show, under the appropriate heading, the amount of increase or decrease. Indicate an increase by the sign + (plus) and the amount and a decrease by the sign − (minus) and the amount. If there is no effect write the words 'no effect'.   (University of London O-level)

4. (a) What is meant by the term *expense ratio*? (b) Calculate the expense ratios for the expenses of R. James's business listed below. His turnover is £30 000.

Expense Item	Amount
Discount Allowed	£750
Office Light and Heat	£1 200
Office Salaries	£3 200

5. At January 1st 19.. M. Truman valued his stock in trade at £16 700. For the ensuing year he made the following estimates: sales £60 000; returns inwards £1 500; carriage inwards £1 100; manufacturing wages £9 800; purchases £22 000. The ratio of gross profit on sales was 17½ per cent.

You are required to prepare:

(a) Truman's Estimated-Trading Account showing the estimated value of his Stock-in-Trade at December 31st 19.. and

(b) his Profit and Loss Account, assuming a net profit percentage of 10 per cent.

All Truman's expenses are assembled in a single General-Expenses Account.

6. (a) The following balances were extracted from the accounts of F. Fraser at December 31st 19...

Prepare Fraser's Trading and Profit and Loss Accounts for the year ended December 31st 19...

	Dr.	Cr.
	£	£
Purchases	16 720	
Sales		21 885
Sales Returns	135	
Stock (at cost) January 1st 19..	2 880	
Delivery of Goods Sold	242	
Rent and Rates	1 425	
Bad Debts	103	
Light and Heat	142	
Insurance	45	
Discount Received		204
Discount Allowed	296	
Wages of Shop Assistant	728	
Bank Charges and Interest	41	

The following matters are to be brought into account:

 (i) On December 31st 19.. stock was valued at cost, £2 740.

 (ii) Rates £230 for the half-year to March 31st next were paid and are included in the balance of Rent and Rates Account.

 (iii) Fraser's annual rent was £960. Rent for December 19.. had not been paid.

 (iv) A provision for bad debts of £40 is to be created.

(b) (i) What is the amount of Fraser's turnover for the year 19..?

 (ii) Calculate his rate of turnover of stock for the year.

 (iii) During the year Fraser had purchased a delivery van for £960. To what extent (if any) do you think this would affect Fraser's profit for the year?

 (iv) Calculate Fraser's net-profit percentage.

(University of London O level adapted)

7. From the following information from M. Tyler's accounts ascertain:

(a) Turnover for the month.

(b) Cost price of goods sold during the trading period.

(c) Percentage of gross profit to turnover.

(d) Percentage of net profit to turnover.

(e) The general-expenses ratio to turnover.

	£
Capital	8 000
Stock, December 1st	6 000
General Expenses	180
Purchases	3 080
Stock, December 31st	5 080
Returns Inwards	600
Returns Outwards	80
Sales	5 500

8. (a) During the year 19.. J. R. Tee held an average stock at cost price of £5 640. He marked up his purchases by 25 per cent to obtain his selling prices. His turnover for the year was £84 600.

His selling and administrative expenses were 11 per cent of turnover. Calculate:

 (i) His gross profit for the year.

 (ii) His rate of turnover of stock for the year.

 (iii) His net profit for the year.

(b) For the following year Tee plans to reduce his mark up on cost price to 20 per cent and to spend £1 000 on advertising. What must be his minimum rate of turnover of stock if he is to earn, at least, a net profit of £7 600?

Assume that the average stock remains the same in amount and cost as in 19.. and that selling and administrative expenses, other than the additional advertising, are estimated at £9 448.

(University of London O level)

9. (*a*) During the year 19. . T. Lumley held an average stock at cost price of £8 000. He marked up his purchases by 25 per cent to obtain his selling prices. His turnover for the year was £100 000.

His selling and administrative expenses were 12 per cent of turnover. Calculate:

    (i) His gross profit for the year.

    (ii) His rate of turnover of stock for the year.

    (iii) His net profit for the year.

(*b*) For the following year, Lumley plans to reduce his mark up on cost price to 20 per cent and to spend £2 000 on advertising. What must be his minimum rate of turnover of stock if he is to earn, at least, a net profit of £12 000?

Assume that the average stock remains the same in amount and cost as in 19. . and that selling and administrative expenses, other than the additional advertising, are estimated at £10 000.

(University of London O level adapted)

32.9 The Condition of a Business—a Balance Sheet for Interpretation

By now you are very familiar with the Balance Sheet of a business. You will remember that it is a 'snapshot' of the affairs of a business at a moment of time. Here is the Balance Sheet of Sunshine Boutique, as a basis for discussion.

Sunshine Boutique (E. Rawlinson)
Balance Sheet
(as at December 31st 19. .)

Fixed Assets	£	£	£	*Capital*	£	£
Goodwill			14 000	At Start		58 080
Land and Buildings			28 000	*Add* Net Profit	7 260	
Fixtures and Fittings			3 600	*Less* Drawings	3 600	
Motor Vehicles			1 000			3 660
			46 600			61 740
Current Assets						
Stock		32 540		*Long-Term Liability*		
Debtors	2 560			Mortgage		15 000
Less Provision	320			*Current Liability*		
		2 240		Creditors	12 350	
Cash at Bank		7 800		Wages due	150	
Cash in Hand		60				12 500
			42 640			
			£89 240			£89 240

Fig. 32.3 A Balance Sheet to be appraised

The Vocabulary of Balance-Sheet Appraisal

You have long been familiar with a stylish presentation of the Balance-Sheet figures, sub-divided into fixed and current assets, and into capital, long-term liabilities and current liabilities. You must now learn a further range of terminology, much of which simply amounts to alternative phrases for those you already know. The others extend your knowledge and increase your ability to appraise a Balance Sheet. In appraising a Balance Sheet a most useful idea is to know the total value of the business, and who 'owns' it. The simple answer would be that it all belongs to the proprietor(s), i.e. the sole trader, or the partners, or the shareholders. This would be too simple a view, as we shall see. The new control figures, and ratios, connected with the Balance Sheet are listed and explained as follows:

(a) **The 'capital employed'.** This figure is one which gives some difficulty to trainee accountants. It is defined differently by different people. You will have to make up your mind which version is required according to the circumstances in which you meet the term. To give a complete picture here three possible definitions have been included.

Definition No. 1.

In the Balance Sheet of Sunshine Boutique, the owner's capital at start is given as £58 080, yet the business is worth £89 240, as the total of the Balance Sheet shows. It follows that the capital employed in this business is greater than £58 080, and must have been provided in some other way than by the original contribution of the proprietor, E. Rawlinson. It is easy to see where these extra funds came from. A mortgage provided £15 000, creditors supplied goods without payment £12 350, employees are waiting for their wages and to this small extent are providing funds for the business, while £3 660 was ploughed back out of profits over the year. The capital employed in this business has therefore been provided in five different ways.

One subtle point here however is this: if the creditors are allowing Rawlinson to use their funds in his business, it must equally be true that Rawlinson has allowed the debtors to use *his* funds in *their* businesses, and consequently the figure of £2 240 is being employed not in Sunshine Boutique but elsewhere. We must deduct this from the 'capital employed', so that our formula for discovering the capital employed by this definition is:

$$Capital\ employed = total\ value\ of\ the\ business - debtors$$
$$= £89\ 240 - £2\ 240$$
$$= £87\ 000$$

Definition No. 2.

By this definition, which is usually used in connexion with the accounts of limited companies, accountants refer to the funds invested by the shareholders or ploughed in out of profits during the course of the years since it was founded.

The formula here is:

$$Capital\ employed = Capital\ at\ start + Reserves\ at\ the\ start\ of\ the\ year$$

Definition No. 3.

The third definition, which is not at all satisfactory to the theoretician, is also used by some accountants with reference to limited companies. In this definition the funds contributed by debenture holders are also included as 'capital' employed. This is not really correct, since debentures are loans to companies, not the capital of companies. Debenture holders are creditors, not shareholders. However, the idea does have some validity, in the following way. If you are trying to assess the quality of management of a firm, and its ability to earn profits, you get a clearer picture of their efforts if you measure the profits against *all* the funds at the management's disposal, and this includes the loans from debenture holders.

(*b*) **What is the capital employed in doing?**—'fixed capital' and 'circulating' or 'floating capital'. The 'capital employed' above is being used to provide two classes of assets, fixed assets and current assets. The capital used in this way is called *fixed capital* and *circulating capital*. The latter is sometimes also called *floating capital*. Defining these terms we may say:

Fixed capital is capital tied up in fixed assets, which are in permanent use in the business forming the framework for running its affairs.

Circulating capital or *floating capital* is capital tied up in current assets, which are in the process of turning over, or circulating, in the way shown on page 66, i.e. stock, sold to debtors, which becomes cash again, used to buy stock etc.

For Sunshine Boutique, the figures are:

Fixed capital = total of fixed assets = £46 600
Circulating capital (*floating capital*) = total of current assets = £42 640

It is usual to include the debtors in this figure although, strictly speaking, they are using the capital in *their* business.

(*c*) **Liquid capital.** A third term in common use is the term 'liquid capital'. Liquid capital is capital tied up in liquid assets, which may be defined as cash and 'near cash' items. Liquid assets are cash in hand, cash at the bank, debtors (who have a legal obligation to pay) and any other near liquid assets such as investments which are readily marketable. The best way to define liquid capital is:

Liquid capital = *current assets* − *stock*

In the case of Sunshine Boutique the figure for liquid capital is:

Liquid capital = £42 640 − £32 540
= £10 100

(*d*) **Working capital.** The most important guiding figure when appraising a balance sheet is the *working capital*. This is that portion of the capital employed which is not tied up in fixed assets (fixed capital) but is available to 'work' the business, in other words *meet its revenue expenditure*. The figure is found by the formula

Working capital = *current assets* − *current liabilities*

In the case of Sunshine Boutique it is:

Working capital = £42 640 − £12 500
= £30 140

(e) **'Working-capital ratio' (current ratio) and 'liquid-capital ratio'** (acid-test ratio). These two important figures can be shown as numbers, or ratios.

$$Working\text{-}capital\ ratio = current\ assets : current\ liabilities$$
$$Liquid\text{-}capital\ ratio\ \ = liquid\ assets : current\ liabilities$$

The first tells us *the ratio between the circulating part of a firm's assets and its current liabilities.*

In the case of Sunshine Boutique the ratio is:

$$Working\text{-}capital\ ratio = £42\ 640 : £12\ 500$$
$$= 3\cdot 4 : 1$$

It is generally recognized that 2:1 is a satisfactory working capital ratio, so that this appears to be quite satisfactory. However a more crucial test is the liquid-capital ratio. The liquid-capital ratio tells us *the ratio between a firm's readily available cash or near-cash assets and its current liabilities (due for payment in one month).*

In the case of Sunshine Boutique the ratio is:

$$Liquid\text{-}capital\ ratio = (current\ assets - stock) : current\ liabilities$$
$$= (42\ 640 - £32\ 540) : £12\ 500$$
$$= £10\ 100 : £12\ 500$$
$$= 0\cdot 808 : 1$$

It is clear that this firm is a little short of liquid capital: it could not meet its short-term liabilities easily, and would need to borrow to pay them. Liquid-capital ratio should never be less than 1:1, except where the management has anticipated it as a temporary situation for which they have provided by arranging an overdraft etc. To the investor, considering whether he should invest in a firm or not, the liquid-capital ratio is a particularly valuable guide to the financial position of the firm and it is therefore often called the *acid-test ratio*.

(f) **Capital owned, capital invested and return on capital invested.** You have already been introduced, in Unit 30, to the idea of 'net worth'. The net worth of any business, as explained on page 329, is the difference between the total value of the business and the *external liabilities,* both current and long term. An alternative name for net worth is capital owned, and the formula for discovering it is as follows:

Capital owned (net worth total) = value of the business − external liabilities

Thus, with the balance sheet of Sunshine Boutique, we have

$$Capital\ owned = £89\ 240 - £27\ 500$$
$$= £61\ 740$$

This amounts, of course, to the *capital invested* at the start of the year plus the profits ploughed back during the year. If in any year the losses exceeded the amount of the capital, the resulting debit balance on Capital Account would be called *a deficiency of capital.*

The last of the important figures used in the appraisal of a balance sheet is the *return on capital invested.*

The formula for this figure is as follows:

$$Return\ on\ capital\ invested = \frac{net\ profit}{capital\ invested\ at\ start} \times 100$$

With Sunshine Boutique it is

$$\frac{7\ 260}{58\ 080} \times 100$$

$$= \frac{72\ 600}{5\ 808} = 12\tfrac{1}{2}\%$$

The figures discussed in the last few pages will now be used to appraise the affairs of Sunshine Boutique.

32.10 A Balance Sheet Appraised

In considering the Balance Sheet of any business, we are anxious to decide whether the enterprise appears to be soundly based. In order to be regarded as 'sound' we should expect to find the following:

(a) The *fixed assets* should be appropriate for the type of business concerned, and offer prospects of future profitability when they are used to conduct the enterprise. Too many fixed assets is called *over-capitalization*.

(b) The working capital should be adequate, that is to say the current assets should be great enough to pay the current liabilities, preferably twice over, i.e. a 2:1 ratio. If not, the firm is *overtrading*, that is to say it is buying too much and selling too little, piling up debts which will mean trouble.

The term *insolvency* is used when, after a period of overtrading, a firm is forced to recognize that it cannot pay its debts and continue operations. It must realize its fixed assets, i.e. sell them for what they will fetch, and use the funds so obtained to pay its creditors. Insolvency is not the same as bankruptcy, since many traders who have reached an *insolvent position* will raise enough cash from the sale of fixed assets to pay all the creditors.

(c) The liquid capital should be adequate, that is, sufficient to pay the current liabilities of the firm. This is the *acid test* of a sound firm.

Finally the *return on capital invested* should be adequate, representing a reasonable reward to the proprietor for the effort he has put in.

Appraising the figures for Sunshine Boutique, we find the following:

(a) *Fixed Assets*. These are valued at £46 600. They are, however, a fairly unsatisfactory mixture. £14 000 of the total is made up of a goodwill figure. This is an *intangible asset*: it exists only in the minds of customers, and is a very high proportion of the total fixed assets. The actual part of the fixed assets that are used in the business, £3 600 of fittings and £1 000 of motor vehicles seem rather small for the enterprise. We should need to inspect them to know whether they were adequate.

On the whole we cannot feel very satisfied, at least *prime facie*, with the fixed assets of Sunshine Boutique.

(b) The *working capital ratio* is 3·4:1. This appears to be sound enough, but it is rather illiquid, as is shown by (c) below.

(c) The *liquid capital ratio* is 0·808:1; in other words it is inadequate since it should be at least 1:1. We may therefore advise the proprietor to improve his position by reducing purchases of stock until his present stocks are cleared, and to do everything possible to improve liquidity by selling off his slow-moving items, preferably for cash.

(d) The *return on capital invested* seems adequate. If invested in other ways, for example in a building society, the gross return would probably be about 8 per cent, so that a 12½ per cent return seems reasonable. On the other hand, if Rawlinson, and perhaps his wife, are fully employed in the business, so that some of the net profit of £7 260 may truly be regarded as wages, the return might not be sufficient for the effort involved and the capital required.

'Flow of Funds' Statements

It sometimes happens that businessmen who are not too knowledgeable about book-keeping and accounting complain to their accountants that they cannot understand why they are so short of cash when the business has made excellent profits. To the untrained person it seems that a business which is making good profits must have plenty of funds available. This is not necessarily so. If the businessman watches his expenses carefully, keeping the working expenses as low as possible, and if he keeps capital expenditure down to safe levels, he will usually have cash available to meet his needs. If he does not do these things he will soon find himself in financial difficulties.

A further example which illustrates the same result is the position of a businessman who sells on credit to unreliable customers. Suppose goods costing £1 000 are sold for £2 000 to A. Slowpayer. The profit is £1 000, but when Mr Slowpayer fails to pay at the end of the month the cash position of the business will be adversely affected. The businessman must honour his own obligations to his suppliers, paying £1 000 for the goods now in Slowpayer's possession; but the £2 000 which was to yield such a handsome profit is unpaid. Despite excellent profits on paper the businessman may need an overdraft from his bank. In order to demonstrate the source and applications of funds it is usual to draw up a 'flow of funds' statement. The example given below will illustrate this.

Example

R. Smith, a businessman, points out to you that in the past year he has made excellent profits, yet his bank overdraft has increased. His drawings have been very moderate for such a prosperous business. Where has all the profit gone? Here are his Balance Sheets which record the situation:

Balance Sheets (R. Smith)
(as at December 31st each year)

	Previous Year		Current Year			Previous Year		Current Year
	£	£	£			£	£	£
Fixed Assets					Capital		5 000	8 900
Land and Buildings	7 000		11 500		Net Profit	4 600	5 700	
Fixtures		400	650		*Less*			
Motor Vehicles		260	1 200		Drawings	700	900	
		7 660	13 350				3 900	4 800
							8 900	13 700
Current Assets					*Current Liabilities*			
Stock	4 000		4 500		Creditors	4 800	4 200	
Debtors	2 200		2 500		Bank			
Cash	40		50		Overdraft	200	2 500	
		6 240	7 050				5 000	6 700
		£13 900	£20 400				£13 900	£20 400

'Flow of Funds' Statement

Sources of Funds in the Current Year	£
Net Profit	5 700
Increase in Bank Overdraft	2 300
	£8 000

Application of these Funds	£
Purchase of extra Land and Buildings	4 500
Purchase of extra Fixtures	250
Purchase of extra Motor Vehicles	940
Purchase of extra Stock	500
Extension of credit to extra Debtors	300
Extra Cash in Hand	10
Prompter settlement of Creditors	600
Drawings	900
	£8 000

An alternative way of displaying the same facts to bring out the need for the increased overdraft would be as follows:

Flow of Funds Statement

Activities carried out in current year which required funds: £

Purchase of extra Land and Buildings	4 500
Purchase of extra Fixtures	250
Purchase of extra Motor Vehicles	940
Purchase of extra Stock	500
Extension of credit to extra Debtors	300
Extra Cash in Hand	10
Prompter settlement of Creditors	600
Drawings	900
	8 000
Financed by Net Profit	5 700
Financed by increased Overdraft	£2 300

You should now attempt some of the exercises on the interpretation of Balance Sheets given below.

32.11   Exercises Set 48: The Appraisal of Balance Sheets

1. State from the following Balance Sheet of A. Brewis, showing calculations if necessary.

   (*a*) The capital owned by the proprietor on December 31st 19. .

   (*b*) The capital employed in the business.

   (*c*) The fixed capital of the business.

   (*d*) The working capital of the business.

Balance Sheet
(as at December 31st 19. .)

	£	£		£	£	£
Fixed Assets			Capital			
Land and Buildings	3 000		At Start		5 000	
Furniture and Fittings	1 500		*Add* Profit	2 550		
Motor Vehicles	1 000		*Less*			
		5 500	Drawings	1 000		
Current Assets					1 550	
Stock	2 250					6 550
Debtors	3 000		Long-Term Liabilities			
Balance at Bank	1 050		Mortgage			3 000
Cash in Hand	450		Current Liabilities			
		6 750	Creditors		2 580	
			Wages Due		120	
						2 700
		£12 250				£12 250

2. From the following Balance Sheet of R. Hemingway state, showing calculations if necessary.

    (a) The capital owned by the proprietor on December 31st 19. .

    (b) The capital employed in the business.

    (c) The fixed capital of the business.

    (d) The working capital of the business.

Balance Sheet
(as at December 31st 19. .)

	£	£		£	£	£
Fixed Assets			Capital			
Land and Buildings	33 000		At Start		75 000	
Furniture and Fittings	4 500		*Add* Profit	12 550		
Motor Vehicles	8 000		*Less* Drawings	4 000		
	—	45 500			— 8 550	
Current Assets						— 83 550
Stock	44 300		Long-Term Liabilities			
Debtors	4 800		Mortgage		15 000	
Balance at Bank	9 500		Current Liabilities			
Cash in Hand	150		Creditors	5 580		
	—	58 750	Rates Due	120		
					—	5 700
		£104 250				£104 250

3. The following is the Balance Sheet of Fides Ltd., a manufacturing company:

Balance Sheet
(as at December 31st 19. .)

	£		£
Freehold Buildings	15 000	Share Capital	24 000
Plant and Machinery	10 500	Net Profit	7 000
Stock	8 500	7% Debentures	10 000
Debtors	9 000	Creditors	8 000
Bank Balance	6 000		
	£49 000		£49 000

You are required to calculate:

(a) Capital employed.

(b) Current assets.

(c) Current liabilities.

(d) Working capital.   (RSA II)

4. The following balances remain on the books of Coolbawn Ltd. on March 31st 19. . after the Profit and Loss Account to that date has been prepared:

	£
Share Capital	100 000
Profit and Loss Account	18 922
6% Debentures	30 000
Premium on Shares	25 000
Freehold at Cost	85 000
Plant at Cost	70 600
Provision for Depreciation on Plant	25 400
Stock-in-Trade	32 147
Debtors	21 096
Bank Balance in Hand	15 260
Current Liabilities	24 781

You are asked (a) to prepare the Balance Sheet of Coolbawn Ltd. at March 31st 19.. and (b) to indicate from the figures in that balance sheet the amount of (i) the capital employed and (ii) the working capital as at March 31st 19..

Note: The 'capital employed' referred to in this question is really the sum of the ordinary shareholders' interest and the debentures (see Section 32.9).

5. The following balances remain on the books of Holder Ltd. on March 31st 19.. after the Profit and Loss to that date has been prepared:

	£
Share Capital	180 000
Profit and Loss Account	28 500
7% Debentures	20 000
Premium on Shares	26 000
Freehold at Cost	95 000
Plant at Cost	90 000
Provision for Depreciation on Plant	20 700
Stock-in-Trade	44 155
Debtors	26 250
Bank Balance in Hand	30 500
Current Liabilities	10 705

You are asked (a) to prepare the Balance Sheet of Holder Ltd. at March 31st 19.. and (b) to indicate from the figures in that Balance Sheet the amount of (i) the capital employed and (ii) the working capital as at March 31st 19...

6. A. Trader considers he could earn at least 5 per cent interest on his capital invested in his business without working for it. Assuming he had £5 000 capital in his business on January 1st 19.. and invested a further £400 on July 1st what interest could he rightly claim out of profits at the end of the trading year December 31st 19..?

7. (*a*) On 31st December 19.. the following balances appeared in R. T.'s ledger after preparation of the Trading and Profit and Loss Accounts.

	Dr. £	Cr. £
Capital (January 1st 19..)		40 000
Profit and Loss Account		8 800
Drawings	3 500	
Trade Debtors	4 200	
Trade Creditors		2 400
Expenses Outstanding		100
Freehold Premises	20 000	
Fixtures and Fittings	6 500	
Motor Vans	2 800	
Stock-in-Trade	6 200	
Cash in Hand and Balance at Bank	8 100	
	£51 300	£51 300

Prepare R.T.'s Balance Sheet in such a way as to show *within the Balance Sheet*:
    (i) The total of fixed assets.
    (ii) The total of current assets.
    (iii) The total of current liabilities.
    (iv) The working capital.
    (v) The net book value of the assets.

8. (*a*) On December 31st 19.. the following balances appeared in J. Kay's ledger after preparation of the Trading and Profit and Loss Accounts.

	Dr. £	Cr. £
Capital (January 1st 19..)		26 280
Profit and Loss Account		5 705
Drawings	4 000	
Trade Debtors	3 668	
Trade Creditors		1 946
Expenses Outstanding		72
Freehold Premises	15 000	
Fixtures and Fittings	1 150	
Motor Vans	2 340	
Stock-in-Trade	5 610	
Cash in Hand and Balance at Bank	2 235	
	£34 003	£34 003

Prepare Kay's Balance Sheet in such a way as to show within the Balance Sheet:

- (i) The total of fixed assets.
- (ii) The total of current assets.
- (iii) The total of current liabilities.
- (iv) The working capital.
- (v) The net book value of the assets.

(b) How would the following transactions affect the amount of Kay's capital and the amount of his working capital?

- (i) New fittings were purchased on credit for £120.
- (ii) £342 was paid to trade creditors.
- (iii) Stock valued at £130 on December 31st 19. . was sold on credit for £170.
- (iv) Trade debtors £76 were written off as bad debts.
- (v) Kay withdrew £300 from the bank for private purposes.
- (vi) Motor vans were depreciated by £470.

You are to present your answer in the following form:

Item	Effect on capital	Effect on working capital
(i)		
(ii)		
(iii)		

and so on.

Indicate an increase by the sign + and the amount and a decrease by the sign − and the amount. If there is no effect write the words 'no effect'.

(University of London O Level)

9. Malcolm Peters is puzzled because his business appears to be making good profits yet he is always short of cash to meet end-of-month requirements. With the help of the Balance Sheets presented below you are asked (*a*) to prepare for him a cash flow statement which explains his present position, and (*b*) to suggest to him how he can overcome the situation in the months ahead.

Balance Sheet
(as at December 31st each year)

	Previous Year £	Current Year £		Previous Year £	Current Year £
Fixed Assets			*Capital at Start*	5 000	7 500
Land and Buildings	5 000	8 000	Add Net		
Fittings	600	1 000	Profit 3 800		3 900
Motor Vans	650	1 550	Less		
	6 250	10 550	Drawings 1 300	1 800	
				2 500	2 100
				7 500	9 600
Current Assets			*Current Liabilities*		
Stock	250 1 250		Creditors 550	850	
Debtors	550 850		Overdraft —	2 250	
Bank	850 —			550	3 100
Cash	150 50				
	1 800	2 150			
	£8 050	£12 700		£8 050	£12 700

10. John Wooding is puzzled because his business appears to be making good profits yet he is always short of cash to meet end-of-month requirements. The balance sheets presented below explain his situation. You are asked (a) to prepare for him a cash flow statement which explains the shortage of cash, and (b) to suggest to him how he can overcome the situation in the months ahead.

Balance Sheet
(as at December 31st each year)

	Previous Year £	Current Year £		Previous Year £	Current Year £
Fixed Assets			Capital at Start	18 000	19 200
Land and			*Add* Net		
Buildings	17 000	25 000	Profit 4 000		6 500
Fittings	1 500	2 500	*Less*		
Motor Vans	1 000	3 800	Drawings 2 800		5 500
	———	———		1200	1 000
	19 500	31 300		19 200	20 200
Current Assets			*Long-Term Liability*		
Stock	1 000	950	Mortgage	—	8 000
Debtors	1 500	4 800	*Current Liabilities*		
Cash	150	250	Creditors	2 500	3 300
	———	———	Overdraft	450	5 800
	2 650	6 000		2 950	9 100
	———	———		———	———
	£22 150	£37 300		£22 150	£37 300

Unit Thirty-Three

Departmental Accounts

33.1 Controlling a Business with Several Departments

There has been a tendency in recent years for businesses to grow in size, as there are many advantages of large-scale enterprises. This usually results in a departmental organization of some sort, and in many businesses, particularly wholesale and retail trade, different qualities and experience are required for each department. Thus a buyer of carpets will have very different experience from a buyer of groceries. It follows that the respective chief buyers will regard their own special fields as of paramount importance, and will have to be controlled if they exceed their authorities and destroy the 'balance' of the business.

In order to control departments, a number of systems are available, coming under the general heading of *budgetary control*. This system anticipates the expenditure, growth, etc., of each department and prepares a budget of future performance which can be compared with actual performance to show whether the department concerned is reaching, exceeding or failing to achieve expectations. Budgetary control is one of the more advanced accounting techniques.

Departmental accounts are more routine—they endeavour to show what the performance of each department was like compared with other departments, in such matters as the gross-profit percentage achieved, the net-profit percentage achieved, and the expense ratios to turnover. It might, for example, be found that while the groceries department made a steady profit the fruit and vegetable department frequently resulted in a loss. This would indicate either that this department should be closed down, or that a drastic revision of its activities should be undertaken.

33.2 Figures for Departmental Accounts

If departmental Trading Accounts and Profit and Loss Accounts are to be prepared, the basic figures required must be obtained by a rearrangement of procedures. For example analytical Day Books, and cash books will be needed so that extra columns are available to collect figures for each department. With mechanized accounting a coding system will enable the accountant to tell the expenditure of one department from another. You can see this procedure for yourself the next time you visit a supermarket. Against every item you will find a code number telling the management whether the item is groceries, meat, fruit and vegetables or toiletries.

Analysis of these items will reveal the total sales for each department,

Departmental Trading and Profit and Loss Account
(for year ending December 31st 19..)

Trading Account — Debit

19.. Dec. 31st	Dept. A		Dept. B		Total
Opening Stock		8 400		2 300	10 700
Purchases	28 462		40 246		
Less Returns	462		2 246		
		28 000		38 000	
Total Stock Available		36 400		12 300	48 700
Less Closing Stock		5 840		1 150	6 990
Cost of Stock Sold		30 560		11 150	41 710
Wages		4 440		1 850	6 290
Cost of Sales		35 000		13 000	48 000
Gross Profit		11 000		15 000	26 000
		£46 000		£28 000	£74 000

Trading Account — Credit

19.. Dec. 31st	Dept. A	Dept. B	Total
Sales	47 250	28 360	75 610
Less Returns In	1 250	360	1 610
	46 000	28 000	74 000
	£46 000	£28 000	£74 000

Profit and Loss Account — Debit

19.. Dec. 31st	Dept. A	Dept. B	Total
Salaries	3 184	4 750	7 934
Light and Heat	240	160	400
General Expenses	2 026	3 190	5 216
Advertising	300	200	500
Total	5 750	8 300	14 050
Net Profit	5 750	7 000	12 750
	£11 500	£15 300	£26 800

Profit and Loss Account — Credit

19.. Dec. 31st	Dept. A	Dept. B	Total
Gross Profit	11 000	15 000	26 000
Rent received	500	300	800
	11 500	15 300	26 800
	£11 500	£15 300	£26 800

Fig. 33.1 A departmental Trading and Profit and Loss Account

analysis of the invoices from suppliers will reveal the departmental purchases, while expenses will be similarly allocated to the department responsible. Some expenses are not *direct*, but indirect expenses or overhead expenses. These will be allocated on some logical basis. For example lighting expenses might be allocated on the basis of counter space occupied by the department, and general advertising expenses on the basis of departmental sales.

These rearrangements will make available the figures necessary for the preparation of departmental accounts of the type shown in Fig. 33.1. The layout with which you are already familiar is simply continued into the analysis columns, the cross-totting of which produces figures for the whole business.

33.3   A Comparison of Departments

From Fig. 33.1 it is possible to compare the departments, and the following statistics may be derived.

	Gross-Profit %	Net-Profit %
Dept. A	23·9	12·5
Dept. B	53·6	25·0
Whole firm	35·1	17·2

It is difficult to draw any real conclusions from these figures without actually knowing the business concerned. For example it is clear that Department B is very much more profitable than Department A, and one might feel tempted to suggest that Department B should be expanded and Department A contracted. In real life this might be quite impossible. For example Department A might be selling groceries, and be quite indispensable to the people in the locality, while Department B, selling furniture and furnishings, might be saturating the demand of the neighbourhood and incapable of expansion.

Other figures seem to need investigation, for example Department B, with only about half the turnover, has very high 'general expenses'. It would be interesting to discover why, by analysing these expenditures.

You should now attempt one or two of these simple 'departmental' exercises.

33.4   Exercises Set 49: Departmental Accounts

1. Prepare a departmental Trading Account from the following accounts in R. Rogers' books for the year ending December 31st 19.. Calculate the gross profit on each department and on the business as a whole:

	Dept. A	Dept. B
Opening Stocks	2 800	3 860
Purchases	15 290	27 420
Sales	30 234	41 040

	Dept. A	Dept. B
Carriage In	144	142
Returns In	300	400
Returns Out	460	280
Closing Stock	1 840	1 540
Wages	2 000	3 040

2. Prepare a departmental Trading and Profit and Loss Account from the following information from the books of V. Bartlett at December 31st 19..

	Dept. A	Dept. B
Opening Stocks	3 800	3 210
Purchases	27 000	15 000
Sales	55 000	27 000
Returns Out	450	230
Returns In	950	260
Closing Stocks	2 500	2 650
Salaries	3 500	2 200
Warehouse Wages	4 850	2 700
Rent and Rates	320	180
Sundry Expenses	730	530

Calculate the gross profit and net-profit percentages for each department, and for the business as a whole (correct to one decimal place).

3. Carlingford Ltd. is a large departmental store and the following figures appear in their books for the year ended December 31st 19...

Sales:	£
Dept. A	21 400
Dept. B	33 600
Dept. C	24 800
Dept. D	18 600
Purchases:	
Dept. A	16 900
Dept. B	24 700
Dept. C	22 100
Dept. D	14 900
Stock, January 1st:	
Dept. A	2 940
Dept. B	3 760
Dept. C	4 100
Dept. D	1 670
Stock, December 31st	
Dept. A	3 490
Dept. B	1 900
Dept. C	2 880
Dept. D	1 760

You find that purchases for Dept. D costing £1 000 have been debited against Dept. C and that Sales for £400 for Dept. A have been credited to Dept. B.

You are asked to prepare a departmental trading account in columnar form after making the adjustments for the wrongly analysed items. You should calculate the gross profit percentage for each department. (RSA II)

4. Slumbersweet Ltd. is a large departmental store and the following figures appear in their books for the year ended December 31st 19...

	£
Sales:	
Dept. A	78 000
Dept. B	66 000
Dept. C	58 000
Dept. D	12 000
Purchases:	
Dept. A	42 000
Dept. B	31 000
Dept. C	27 000
Dept. D	11 000
Stock, January 1st:	
Dept. A	5 950
Dept. B	7 280
Dept. C	8 640
Dept. D	2 150
Stock, December 31st:	
Dept. A	7 120
Dept. B	3 380
Dept. C	7 250
Dept. D	6 540

You find that purchases for Dept. C costing £850 have been debited against Dept. A and that Sales for £800 for Dept. D have been credited to Dept. B.

You are asked to prepare a departmental Trading Account in columnar form after making the adjustments for the wrongly analysed items. You should calculate the gross-profit percentage for each department correct to one decimal place. (RSA II adapted)

5. R. Winter, a sole trader runs a business with two departments, A and B. He prepares a departmental Trading Account at the end of his financial year, but then prepares a general Profit and Loss Account, and a Balance Sheet. Draw up the Final Accounts from the figures given below.

Trial Balance
(as at December 31st 19..)

			£	£	£
Capital					22 438
Furniture and Equipment (cost £4 200)				3 240	
Motor Vans (cost £3 400)				2 260	
Purchases	Dept. A	30 200			
	Dept. B	42 382			
			72 582		
Sales	Dept. A	42 620			
	Dept. B	48 624			
					91 244
Provision for doubtful debts as at January 1					538
Stock in trade as at January 1	Dept. A	7 900			
	Dept. B	9 560			
			17 460		
Debtors				8 570	
Creditors					6 328
Drawings				3 400	
Rent and Rates				1 776	
Salaries				7 940	
Bad Debts				560	
General Expenses				2 140	
Bank Balance				620	
				£120 548	£120 548

Stock in trade at the close was

	Dept. A	8 200
	Dept. B	10 656
		£18 856

Unit Thirty-Four

Control Accounts

34.1 The Need for Control Accounts

There are many types of Control Accounts, which as their name implies seek to give management control over some aspect of a business. The work of devising adequate controls over accounting procedures is necessarily fairly advanced. In a book on the principles of accounting it is only possible to illustrate the simplest types of control accounts. Usually the examination syllabuses at this level require an understanding of Sales-Ledger Control Accounts and Purchases-Ledger Control Accounts. In order to understand these the reader must first understand why they are necessary. The reason is that the sub-division of the ledger, as business has grown more complex, has enabled management to delegate the posting of ledgers to less experienced employees. Control Accounts are designed to check on the work of these employees and ensure that errors are discovered.

34.2 The Sub-division of the Ledger

When the work of keeping the ledger became too great for a single counting-house clerk, the ledger had to be sub-divided into sections each of which would provide employment for an individual clerk. First the *cash book* was introduced, with the cashier in charge of it. For security reasons the private accounts were removed into a *Private Ledger*, kept by the proprietor himself, or the accountant. The very numerous debtors' accounts were removed into separate *Debtors' Ledgers*. Later these were mechanized into a card system operated by junior typists. The less numerous creditors' accounts were then removed into loose-leaf *Creditors' Ledger* systems which again were kept by junior staff. This left the *General Ledger*, containing the nominal accounts (losses and profits of the business) and the real accounts (assets of the business). This ledger was usually kept by a chief accounts clerk, whose responsibility included the preparation of the Trial Balance. (See Fig. 34.1.)

34.3 Getting the Trial Balance to Agree

Consider the diagram in Fig. 34.1. It shows the sub-division of the ledger, and the staff in charge of each section. Listing the names, and the number of accounts kept, it is easy to see where the mistakes are likely to occur.

Staff	*Duties*	*Number of Accounts*
Cashier	Three-column cash book	2 (Cash A/c and Bank A/c)
Accountant	Private Ledger	6 or 9

Staff	Duties	Number of Accounts
Chief clerk	General Ledger	200
Junior clerks	Creditors' Ledger	600–1 000
Junior typists	Debtors' Ledger	Up to 100 000 accounts

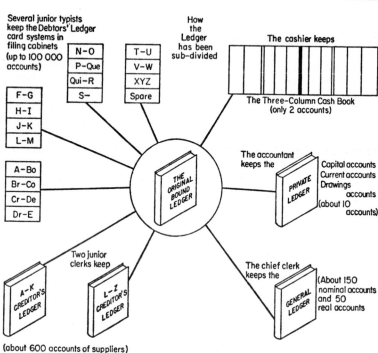

Fig. 34.1 The sub-division of the ledger

Clearly, if the Trial Balance fails to agree it is more likely that the junior staff have made the mistakes, especially as they have so many accounts to keep. For this reason the accountant devises control accounts on the Debtors' Ledgers and Creditors' Ledgers; one for each sub-division if there are several. Thus an A–E Debtors' Ledger would be controlled by an A–E Debtors' Control Account. Sometimes these are called *Total Accounts*.

Each control account will represent exactly the complete ledger section kept by a junior employee, whose work will thus be proved to be right before it is included in the Trial Balance. The accountant, or the chief clerk, will prepare the control accounts from figures obtained from the subsidiary books, and without direct reference to the sources used by the office junior. For example the A–E Debtors' Ledger is prepared from 'posting media', i.e. sales invoices, credit notes, statements, etc. The A–E Debtors' Control Account is prepared from *total figures* obtained from the subsidiary books, without reference to the posting media. Once the total of the book has been found to agree with the Control Account its figures can be included in the Trial Balance. The junior in charge of the book is praised for a creditable performance, and the chief clerk turns to help whichever juniors are in difficulties because their books do not agree with the Control Accounts. This method is often called *Sectional balancing*.

34.4 Preparing a Control Account

When drawing up a Control Account the clerk has to prepare, on a single page, an exact replica of the entire section of the ledger being kept by each junior accounts clerk or accounting machine operator. Naturally the preparation of Control Accounts in mechanized or computerized accounting is very sophisticated, but it follows the basic principles outlined below. In order to follow the procedure it is necessary to consider the types of entry made by— for example—the junior keeping the F–K Debtors' Ledger. The first account in the ledger-card system is A. Farr's Account. In Fig. 34.2 this account is shown with the F–K Control Account immediately below it. You should compare the two, with the help of the notes provided.

			A. Farr A/c				DL 171
19..			£	19..			£
July	1st Balance	B/d	127·50	July	3rd Bank	CB 17	121·12
	9th Sales	SDB 5	68·60		3rd Discount		
	14th Sales	SDB 6	174·75		Allowed	CB 17	4·13
	27th Sales	SDB 9	38·50		14th Contra	J 21	2·25
					17th Returns	SRB 3	15·00
					31st Balance	c/d	266·85
			£409·35				£409·35
Aug.	1st Balance	B/d	266·85				

			F–K Debtors' Ledger Control Account				CL 29
19..			£	19..			£
July	1st Balances	B/d	17 254·50	July	1st Balances B/d		84·50
	31st Sales	SDB 11	8 572·65		31st Bank	CB 29	15 175·65
	31st Carriage	J 9	708·00		31st Contras	J 11	422·50
	31st Dishonoured				31st Returns	SRB 7	202·80
	cheques	J 12	76·30		31st Bad		
	31st Balances	c/d	28·50		Debts	J 13	127·65
					31st Motor		
					Vehicles	J 15	540·00
					31st Balances c/d		10 086·85
			£26 639·95				£26 639·95
19..			£	19..			£
Aug.	1st Balances	B/d	10 086·85	Aug.	1st Balances	B/d	28·50

Fig. 34.2 A debtors' control account compared with an individual debtor's account

Notes:

(*a*) In the Debtors' Ledger we expect to have a large number of debit balances. In this example the total debit balances on the F–K section on July 1st were £17 254·50.

(*b*) We also find on Control Accounts that there is often a credit balance too. This means that somewhere in the ledger there is one account, or perhaps more, bearing a credit balance for some reason. This may be because the debtor, having paid for goods, then finds there is some reason for returning them. He becomes temporarily a creditor instead of a debtor. The existence of this credit balance is recognized on the Control Account.

(*c*) On the debit side of the Control Account appear those items—in total—which appear as individual postings on the debit side of the customers' accounts. These figures will have been obtained from analysis columns in the books referred to in the folio column. For example the Sales figure will have come from the F–K analysis column of the Sales Day Book. An analytical Day Book of this sort is shown in Fig. 23.2. The 'carriage' and 'dishonoured-cheques' figures will have come from the Journal Proper. Since there are very few such items it is usual to analyse them off by turning over the few pages of the Journal for the month, making a note of any items affecting the F–K ledger. The entry 'contras' is explained in Section 34.5.

(*d*) On the credit side of the Control Account appear those items which normally appear on the credit side of the customer's account. These figures will have been obtained from analysis columns in the cash book (see Fig. 23.3) and Sales-Returns Book, or from direct analysis of the Journal, while in firms using mechanized or computerized accounting the figures will be collected in registers or data storage devices.

(*e*) The final balances represent the total F–K debtors' balances. The junior accounts clerk or typist keeping this part of the ledger should find, when she totals her ledger cards, that they agree with the Control Account. If they do, the total debtors' figure is put into the Trial Balance.

(*f*) The comparison of these two accounts thus shows that the Control Account imitates the ordinary Ledger Account of any debtor, but has entries in it to cover every possible type of entry made in the previous month, since these are sure to have occurred on at least one account in the ledger.

Examination work on Control Accounts

Because the preparation of Control Accounts is an excellent test of the ability of students, they are popular questions with examiners. The student is given information referring to either a Debtors' Ledger or a Creditors' Ledger, and is asked to draw up the Control Account. This information will have been derived from the appropriate records in analytical Sales Day Books, Purchases Day Books, Cash Books, etc. An example of this type of exercise is given below.

Example

Tom Jones keeps his Creditors' Ledger controlled by drawing up monthly a Creditors' Ledger Control Account in two parts A–K and L–Z. The following figures are available at January 31st, 19.. when there is a difference on the Trial Balance of £1 000.

		A–K	L–Z
Jan. 1	Balances on Creditors' Ledger (credit side)	4 200	1 800
1	Balances on Creditors' Ledger (debit side)	25	42
Jan. 1–31	Purchases	7 256	3 686
1–31	Returns	500	326
1–31	Sundry charges by suppliers	100	22
1–31	Cheques paid to suppliers	3 990	1 710
1–31	Discount received from suppliers	210	90
31	Balances carried down to debit side	25	16

The book-keeper in charge of the A–K ledger makes his accounts total £7 856 while the clerk in charge of the L–Z ledger makes his ledger balances total £3 356. Draw up the two Control Accounts and draw any conclusion you can from them.

Preparing the two accounts we find the following situation:

Creditors' Ledger Control Account A–K

19..		£	19..		£
Jan. 1	Balances B/d	25	Jan. 1	Balances B/d	4 200
1–31	Returns	500	1–31	Purchases	7 256
1–31	Bank	3 990	1–31	Sundry charges	100
1–31	Discount received	210	31	Balances c/d	25
31	Balance c/d	6 856			
		£11 581			£11 581
19..		£	19..		£
Feb. 1	Balance B/d	25	Feb. 1	Balance B/d	6 856

Creditors' Ledger Control Account L–Z

19..		£	19..		£
Jan. 1	Balances B/d	42	Jan. 1	Balances B/d	1 800
1–31	Returns	326	1–31	Purchases	3 686
1–31	Bank	1 710	1–31	Sundry charges	22
1–31	Discount received	90	31	Balances c/d	16
31	Balances c/d	3 356			
		£5 524			£5 524
19..		£	19..		£
Feb. 1	Balances B/d	16	Feb. 1	Balances B/d	3 356

The Control Accounts reveal that there is a difference of £1 000 between the Control Account for the A–K ledger and the totals discovered by the book-keeper in charge of that ledger. The L–Z ledger seems to be correct. The obvious solution is to check the ledger entries in the A–K ledger very carefully. Almost certainly it is an adding-up mistake—it nearly always is when there is an error of £1, or £10, or £100, or £1 000, etc.

34.5　Contra Accounts in the Ledger

When the ledger is sub-divided it often happens that a firm will appear in two sections of the ledger, as a debtor in the Debtors' Ledger and as a Creditor in the Creditors' Ledger. It means that we have dealings with this firm in both capacities; selling to it and buying from it. Keeping two accounts in this way is the most convenient method, since the two sets of ledgers may be in quite different parts of the building. At the end of the month the smaller account will be set off against the larger account, and the words 'per contra' or 'contra' written to explain that an 'opposite' account is being cancelled out by this entry. This is a rather different kind of 'contra entry' from the type you are familiar with in the three-column cash book (see Section 14.2).

34.6　Other Names for the Control Account

Control Accounts are often called by other names. Sometimes they are called Total Accounts, or Adjustment Accounts, and sometimes the system is called the 'self-balancing ledger system'. Each of these names is simply a variation on Control Accounts, and you should treat any exercise referring to them as being identical with the control-account system described in this section.

34.7　The Control Account which is Wrong

The purpose of the Control Account is to discover mistakes in the work of junior members of staff. It is therefore very regrettable if the Control Account is incorrectly prepared, since it may mean that staff are kept behind because their ledgers do not balance when in fact the accountant is at fault. To save loss of face, the young accountant should be particularly careful in the preparation of the Control Accounts, and should approach the discovery of errors in a set of ledgers in a friendly and conciliatory way. Until the books agree it is never absolutely safe to say where the error lies.

34.8　Exercises Set 50: Control Accounts

1. R. Martin maintains a system of self-checking ledgers. You are asked to prepare the Sales-Ledger Control Account from the following figures:

	£
Debit balances January 1st 19..	35 850
Credit balance January 1st 19..	127
Sales	38 560
Cash received from customers	29 726
Discount allowed	743
Returns and allowances	1 026
Bad Debts	154
Credit balance January 31st 19..	36

2. Sheering Ltd. maintain a system of self-checking ledgers. You are asked to prepare the Sales-Ledger Control Account from the following figures:

	£
Debit balances January 1st 19..	34 296
Credit balance January 1st 19..	26
Sales	51 264
Cash received from customers	28 629
Discount allowed	824
Returns and allowances	968
Bad Debts	426
Credit balance January 31st 19..	32

(RSA II)

3. L. Renton keeps several Sales Ledgers and a Purchases Ledger. From the following details relating to his No. 1 Debtors and his Creditors, write up Renton's Sales-Ledger No. 1 Control Account and the Purchases-Ledger Control Account for the month of November 19..

19..			£
November	1st	Balance of Sales Ledger No. 1 Control Account	2 670
		Balance of Purchases Ledger Control Account	4 140
	30th	Sales for month (No. 1 A/c)	2 890
		Purchases for month	3 960
		Receipts from debtors (No. 1 A/c)	2 405
		Payments to creditors	3 920
		Discounts allowed (No. 1 A/c)	125
		Discounts received	95
		Sales returns (No. 1 A/c)	65
		Purchases returns	145
		Transfer of a debit balance from the Purchases Ledger to Sales Ledger No. 1	120

(University of London O level)

4. M. Lucas keeps several Sales Ledgers and a Purchases Ledger. From the following details relating to his No. 1 Debtors and his Creditors write up

Lucas's Sales-Ledger No. 1 Control Account and the Purchases-Ledger Control Account for the month of November 19..

19..			£
November	1st	Balance of Sales Ledger Account No. 1	3 875
		Balance of Purchases Ledger Control Account	4 182
	30th	Sales for month (No. 1 A/c)	3 525
		Purchases for month	4 395
		Receipts from debtors (No. 1 A/c)	3 650
		Payments to creditors	3 973
		Discounts allowed (No. 1 A/c)	91
		Discounts received	209
		Sales returns (No. 1 A/c)	127
		Purchases returns	382
		Transfer of a credit balance from the Purchases Ledger to Sales Ledger No. 1	36

(University of London O level)

5.   (a) S. Hardy keeps a Sales Ledger, a Purchases Ledger and a General Ledger. What kind of accounts would you expect to find in each of these ledgers?

(b) In which ledger would the following accounts appear?

F. J. Doe—a supplier of Hardy's stock-in-trade.

R. T. Ray—a customer.

Sales Account.

Stock Account.

(c) On May 1st 19.. Ray's Account had a debit balance of £329. On May 10th Hardy received payment of this amount by cheque and sold goods on credit to Ray £189. On May 20th Ray was allowed £17 on the goods sold to him on May 10th.

Prepare Ray's Account as it would appear on May 31st 19.. and balance it as at that date.

(d) Hardy keeps a Sales-Ledger Control Account and a Purchases Ledger Control Account. From the following details relating to the month of May 19.. draw up these accounts as they would appear on May 31st 19.. and balance them as at that date.

	£
Balances at May 1st 19..	
Sales-Ledger Control Account	3 107
Purchases Ledger Control Account	4 201
Sales on credit	3 406
Receipts from trade debtors	2 905
Sales returns and allowances	146

	£
Purchases on credit	2 803
Payments to trade creditors	3 800
Discounts allowed	75
Discounts received	210
Bad debts	36

6. L. Martin keeps a Sales-Ledger Control Account and a Purchases-Ledger Control Account. From the following details relating to the month of May 19.. draw up these accounts as they would appear on May 31st 19.. and balance them as at that date.

	£
Balances at May 1st, 19..	
Sales-Ledger Control Account	4 206
Purchases-Ledger Control Account	5 107
Sales on credit	3 815
Receipts from trade debtors	4 101
Sales returns and allowances	386
Purchases on credit	6 258
Payments to trade creditors	4 680
Discounts allowed	105
Discounts received	120
Bad debts	136

7. The following figures are taken from the books of Bartlow for 19...

	£
Sales-ledger balances (Dr.) January 1st 19..	7 249
Sales-ledger balances (Cr.) January 1st, 19..	62
Sales	81 296
Amounts received from customers and lodged at the company's bank (including the relodging of a cheque for £39 which had been returned by the bank)	76 424
Returns and allowances	1 291
Discount allowed	3 468
Bad debts written off	421
Sales ledger balances (Cr.) January 31st, 19..	149

You are asked to prepare a Sales-Ledger Control Account for the month.

(RSA II)

8. There is a difference in the balances on the books of Clover Ltd. In an attempt to locate the difference, total accounts for the Purchases and Sales Ledgers are prepared from the following figures:

19..		£
January 1st	Balances on Purchases Ledger	40 921
1st	Balances on Sales Ledger	50 420
31st	Purchases during month	498 216
31st	Sales during month	628 421
31st	Discounts received	8 289
31st	Discounts allowed	10 498
31st	Purchases returns during month	825
31st	Sales returns during month	1 422
31st	Bad debts written off	623
31st	Cash paid to suppliers	456 227
31st	Cash received from customers	582 989

Prepare the total accounts. You are now told that the Purchases-Ledger balances total £73 976 and the Sales-Ledger balances total £83 309. What conclusions do you draw?

9. From the following particulars prepare (a) the Bought-Ledger Control Account, and (b) the Sales-Ledger Control Account for January, for Colvin and Hodge.

	£
Purchases	19 000
Sales	40 000
Total Creditors balance on January 1st	7 000
Total Debtors balance on January 1st	6 000
Discounts received	210
Discounts allowed	400
Returns outwards	20
Returns inwards	300
Cash paid	16 000
Cash received	35 000
Bad debts written off	500

You are now told the following facts:
(a) The Trial Balance for Colvin and Hodge fails to agree by £820·50.
(b) The typist keeping the Sales Ledger on a card index system makes her debtors' account balances total £9 800.
(c) The book-keeper who keeps the creditor's ledger makes his creditors' ledger come to £9 770.
What conclusion do you draw about the error on the Trial Balance?

Unit Thirty-Five

Amalgamations

35.1 Definition of Amalgamation

An amalgamation is a joining together of two businesses. It usually results in more efficient operations, because the economies of large scale can be achieved. There are many economies of large scale, administrative economies, financial economies, marketing economies, etc. For example a sole trader who wishes to take a short holiday may have to employ a qualified manager to take his place. A reliable man may demand a sizeable salary for such a short assignment. If the sole trader amalgamates with another sole trader one will be able to take care of the joint enterprise while the other is away, in return for similar services later when he needs a vacation. Advertising may be beneficial to both parties, and hence more economical, while the joint properties may provide better security for bank loans or overdrafts, making them easier to obtain. What are the accounting problems of amalgamation?

35.2 Arrangements Between the Parties

Clearly both parties in a proposed amalgamation will have some existing assets and liabilities which could be set out in a balance sheet or statement of affairs at the date of amalgamation. This existing condition may, or may not, be acceptable to the proposed partner. Usually some adjustments will be made to one, or both, of the balance sheets to take account of objections raised by the other party. One may feel that the other's motor vehicles are overvalued. The other may feel that the debtors' figure shown by the first is excessive, and includes a number of debts that should be regarded as bad. Such objections will result in the adjustment of their respective balance sheets.

Another point that may be raised is the question of goodwill. This would particularly arise where the new business was to make use of the business premises of one partner only, the other's premises being sold. The partner whose premises are to form the base of the new joint enterprise may insist upon some payment for goodwill, or its recognition as part of the asset values to be taken over.

35.3 An Example of Amalgamation

The following example will illustrate the procedures necessary when an amalgamation of businesses is arranged.

A. Brown and B. Green have businesses in the same district, with assets and liabilities as shown below.

A. Brown
Balance Sheet
(as at December 31st 19. .)

	£	£		£
Fixed Assets			*Capital*	8 520
Premises		6 000	*Long-Term Liabilities*	
Furniture and Equipment		2 000	Mortgage	5 000
Motor Vehicles		350	*Current Liabilities*	
		———	Creditors	1 850
		8 350		
Current Assets				
Stock	4 750			
Debtors	1 250			
Cash at Bank	880			
Cash in Hand	140			
	———	7 020		
		£15 370		£15 370

B. Green
Balance Sheet
(as at December 31st 19. .)

	£	£		£
Fixed Assets			*Capital*	8 839
Premises		3 000	*Current Liabilities*	
Furniture and Fittings		1 850	Creditors	2 081
Motor Vehicles		2 500		
		———		
		7 350		
Current Assets				
Stock	2 920			
Debtors	650			
	———	3 570		
		£10 920		£10 920

They agree to amalgamate, using the premises and furniture of Brown, and the motor vehicles of Green. Brown will sell off his motor vehicles privately, Green will sell his premises and all the fixtures and fittings except weighing machines valued at £100. In place of these assets he will bring in £3 000 cash as extra working capital. Brown will open up a provision for bad debts of £200 and Green will do the same for £100.

Brown will create a Goodwill Account of £2 000 and Green will create one of £500.

Modify the Balance Sheets to take account of these arrangements, and then amalgamate them to show the Balance Sheet of the new business as at January 1st 19. .

The solution then proceeds as follows. The modified Balance Sheets are given below. In each case they must be adjusted to include only the assets actually brought into the new business—the capitals of each partner being altered to take account of the changes in the net worth he is contributing.

A. Brown
Adjusted Balance Sheet
(as at December 31st 19..)

	£	£	£		£
Fixed Assets				*Capital*	9 970
Goodwill			2 000	*Long-Term Liabilities*	
Premises			6 000	Mortgage	5 000
Furniture, etc.			2 000	*Current Liabilities*	
			———	Creditors	1 850
			10 000		
Current Assets					
Stock		4 750			
Debtors	1 250				
Less Provision	200				
		—— 1 050			
Cash at Bank		880			
Cash in Hand		140			
		——	6 820		
			£16 820		£16 820

B. Green
Adjusted Balance Sheet
(as at December 31st 19..)

	£	£	£		£
Fixed Assets				*Capital*	7 489
Goodwill			500	*Current Liabilities*	
Furniture and Fittings			100	Creditors	2 081
Motor Vehicles			2 500		
			———		
			3 100		
Current Assets					
Stock		2 920			
Debtors	650				
Less Provision	100				
		—— 550			
Cash at Bank		3 000			
		——	6 470		
			£9 570		£9 570

Upon amalgamation all that is now required is to merge these two adjusted Balance Sheets into an amalgamated Balance Sheet as shown below.

A. Brown and B. Green
Balance Sheet
(as at January 1st 19..)

	£	£	£			£
Fixed Assets				*Capital*		
Goodwill			2 500	A. Brown		9 970
Premises			6 000	B. Green		7 489
Furniture, etc.			2 100			17 459
Motor Vehicles			2 500			
			13 100	*Long-Term Liabilities*		
				Mortgage		5 000
Current Assets				*Current Liabilities*		
Stock		7 670		Creditors		3 931
Debtors	1 900					
Less Provision	300					
		1 600				
Cash at Bank		3 880				
Cash in Hand		140				
			13 290			
			£26 390			£26 390

35.4 Exercises Set 51: Amalgamations

1. A. Young and B. Old are to amalgamate their businesses. Young will contribute a motor vehicle valued at £500 and capital in cash of the same amount £500. Old will bring in his premises £5 000; his fixtures and fittings £800; his stock £2 500 and debtors of £1 000. He has creditors to be paid of £2 200. Draw up the opening Balance Sheet, on January 1st 19...

2. Maker and Seller are to amalgamate their businesses, whose assets and liabilities are given below.

	Maker	Seller
	£	£
Premises	2 500	7 500
Furniture and Fittings	1 000	1 800
Motor Vehicles	2 000	1 800
Stock	450	5 250
Debtors	—	1 850
Creditors	650	1 650
Bank Balance	2 850	800 (overdraft)
Cash in Hand	130	50

All assets and liabilities will be brought into the new business except the following.

(*a*) Seller will dispose of his vehicles privately and use the funds made available to pay up his overdraft. He will also bring in a bank balance of £500

(*b*) Seller's Stock will be valued by the new business at £5 000, and Maker's at £350.

(*c*) Seller will create a provision for bad debts of £250.

Draw up the Balance Sheet of the new business when it commences operations on January 1st 19. .

3. W. Sandon and M. Sandon agree to amalgamate as from January 1st 19. . On that day their records show the following situation.

	W. Sandon £	M. Sandon £
Land and Buildings	6 000	4 000
Machinery	2 500	1 500
Furniture and Fittings	1 800	1 500
Stocks:		
Raw material	800	600
Work in progress	230	450
Finished goods	1 720	850
Cash	25	85
Bank	1 520	450
Creditors	850	1 450
Rents due	50	—
Debtors	650	850

W. Sandon will open a provision for bad debts for £150. M. Sandon will sell her land and buildings and furniture and fittings. She will then pay off all her creditors and bring in £1 000 extra in the Bank Account. W. Sandon will be allowed to open a Goodwill Account for £2 000. Draw up the amalgamated Balance Sheet. (*Note*: The rents due are owing on a lock-up garage W. Sandon has rented to store materials prior to manufacturing.

4. A and B have businesses in adjoining premises. They agree to combine and trade as partners from January 1st 19..

On that date they agreed the value of assets and liabilities of each business as follows:

	A £	B £
Freehold Premises	10 000	8 000
Furniture and Fittings	650	440
Motor Vans	1 170	1 840
Stocks	3 250	2 170
Trade Debtors	1 890	1 640
Provision for Bad Debts	160	140
Trade Creditors	2 980	1 965
Rates Outstanding	170	—
Insurances Prepaid	20	15
Bank Overdraft	—	320
Cash at Bank	840	—

(i) Before combining the businesses A paid off his outstanding rates from his business bank account and B paid off his bank overdraft from his private bank account.

(ii) The goodwill of A's business was agreed at £3 490 and of B's business at £2 000.

(iii) On amalgamation A made a loan of £1 000 at 7 per cent *per annum* to the partnership as additional working capital.

(iv) It was agreed that current accounts should be kept and that profits and losses should be shared equally.

(a) Draft the opening Balance Sheet of the partnership at January 1st 19..

(b) At the end of 19.. the partnership had made a net trading profit of £6 770 before allowing for interest on A's loan. It was agreed that £500 should be written off goodwill.

During the year each partner had withdrawn £3 000.

Prepare (i) the Appropriation Account of the partnership for the year ended December 31st 19.. and (ii) the Current Accounts of the partners balanced as at December 19..

(University of London O level)

5. X and Y have businesses in adjoining premises. They agree to combine and trade as partners from January 1st 19..

On that date they agreed the value of assets and liabilities of each business as follows:

	X £	Y £
Freehold Premises	12 000	10 000
Furniture and Fittings	1 000	800
Motor Vans	2 500	2 000
Stocks	4 750	2 600
Trade Debtors	1 500	1 450
Provision for Bad Debts	250	200
Trade Creditors	2 000	1 670
Light and Heat outstanding	180	—
Insurances Prepaid	30	20
Bank Overdraft	—	450
Cash at Bank	1 650	—

(i) Before combining the business X paid off his outstanding light and heat bill from his business bank account and Y paid off his bank overdraft from his private bank account.

(ii) The goodwill of X's business was agreed at £4 000 and of Ys business at £2 000.

(iii) On amalgamation X made a loan of £2 000 at 7 per cent *per annum* from his private funds as additional working capital.

(iv) It was agreed that current accounts should be kept and that profits and losses should be shared 3:2.

(a) Draft the opening Balance Sheet of the partnership at January 1st 19...

(b) At the end of 19.. the partnership had made a net trading profit of £6 320 before allowing for interest on X's loan. It was agreed that £1 000 should be written off goodwill.

During the year Drawings were X £2 500, Y £1 500.

Prepare (i) the appropriation account of the partnership for the year ended December 31st 19.. and (ii) The current accounts of the partners balanced as at December 31st 19..

(University of London O level adapted)

Unit Thirty-Six

Purchase of a Business

36.1 Introduction

The purchase of businesses is an everyday affair. Some sensational take-overs capture the national headlines for days on end. There is little difference as far as accounting records are concerned between the purchase by one small trader of another's business, and the purchase of one huge public company by another. The basic elements in any purchase of a business may be listed as follows:

(*a*) The purchase price has to be agreed, between the *vendor* and the purchaser.

(*b*) The effective date of the transfer of ownership has to be decided upon and the necessary conveyances arranged if land and buildings are to change hands.

(*c*) The purchaser will review the assets being taken over to decide whether they are correctly valued. He will bring the new assets on to his books at the valuation he places on them, irrespective of what the vendor considered them to have been worth.

(*d*) He may also be taking over certain liabilities of the old business. Usually he cannot vary these from the vendor's figures, and they will have to be honoured in full, except that a settlement discount of some sort may be earned.

(*e*) The difference between the asset values and the liabilities taken over will be the net value of the business to the new owner. Yet nearly always it will be found that he is paying a price in excess of this net value. The difference between what the assets are worth and what he is paying for them must be the goodwill figure, i.e. the amount he considers it is worth paying the previous owner for the hard work he has done in years gone by.

The recording of these matters in the books of the new business is best considered by taking an example and following the procedures we have discussed.

36.2 The Purchase of a Business—An Example

Consider the following set of circumstances.

J. Brown agrees to sell his business to M. Regan as from July 1st 19.., at a price of £20 000. The assets and liabilities on June 30th were as shown in J. Brown's Balance Sheet below. Regan will not take-over the cash at bank or the cash in hand.

J. Brown
Balance Sheet
(as at June 30th 19..)

	£	£		£
Fixed Assets			*Capital*	15 000
Premises		6 000	*Current Liabilities*	
Fixtures and Fittings		2 500	Sundry Creditors	1 530
Motor Vehicles		800		
		9 300		
Current Assets				
Stock	4 250			
Debtors	2 650			
Cash at Bank	300			
Cash in Hand	30			
		7 230		
		£16 530		£16 530

Regan decides on the following changes in value:

(*a*) Premises will be revalued to £8 500.

(*b*) Fixtures and fittings will be valued at £2 000, and motor vehicles at £500.

(*c*) Stock will be valued at £3 500 and a provision for bad debts of 10 per cent will be created.

Regan brings in capital of £15 000, arranges a mortgage of £8 000 on the premises, and pays Brown on July 1st in full by cheque.

(1) Calculation of the 'Goodwill' Figure

The goodwill is calculated as follows:

		£
Value of assets taken over: Premises		8 500
Fixtures		2 000
Motor Vehicles		500
Stock		3 500
Debtors	2 650	
Less Provn.	265	
		2 385
		16 885
Less Current Liabilities		1 530
Net value of assets		£15 355

Purchase price	=	£20 000
Less net value of assets	=	£15 355
Goodwill	=	£4 645

Since Regan is prepared to pay £20 000 for assets valued at a net figure of £15 355, he must be prepared to consider the goodwill as worth £4 645.

(2) The Opening of the Books of the New Business
This requires a series of simple Journal entries. The following stages are required to complete the opening entries.

(a) **Take on the Vendor as a creditor, and debit a Purchase of Business Account.** This is simply a convenience account, opened for a few minutes while the double-entry is carried out.

19.. July	1	Purchase of Business A/c Dr. J. Brown A/c Being agreed purchase price at this date	L 1 L 2	£ 20 000	£ J 1 20 000

Purchase of Business A/c			L 1
19.. July 1st J. Brown J 1	£ 20 000		

	J. Brown A/c		L 2
	19.. July 1st Purchase of Business		£ J1 20 000

Fig. 36.1 The vendor becomes a creditor

(b) **Take in the assets, including goodwill, and credit the Purchase of Business Account.** Of course each asset account will be debited.

19..
July
	1	Goodwill A/c Dr.
		Premises A/c Dr.
		Fixtures and Fittings A/c Dr.
		Motor-Vehicles A/c Dr.
		Stock Dr.
		Debtors A/c Dr.
		   Purchase of Business A/c
		Being assets taken over at
		   agreed valuations
			L 3
			L 4
			L 5
			L 6
			L 7
			L 8
			L 1
				£
				4 645
				8 500
				2 000
				500
				3 500
				2 650
					£ J 1
					
					21 795

Goodwill A/c			L 3
19.. July 1st Purchase of Business J 1	£ 4 645		

(contd. on page 423)

Premises A/c   L 4

19..		£	
July 1st Purchase of Business J 1	8 500		

Fixtures and Fittings A/c   L 5

19..		£	
July 1st Purchase of Business J 1	2 000		

Motor-Vehicles A/c   L 6

19..		£	
July 1st Purchase of Business J 1	500		

Stock A/c   L 7

19..		£	
July 1st Purchase of Business·J 1	3 500		

Sundry-Debtors A/c (Really there would be many)   L 8

19..		£	
July 1st Purchase of Business J 1	2 650		

Purchase of Business A/c   L 1

19..		£	19..		£
July 1st J. Brown	J 1 20 000		July 1st Sundry Assets J 1	21 795	

Fig. 36.2 Taking over the assets purchased

(c) **The liabilities must now be taken on, including the provision for bad debts.**

19..					£	£ J 1
July	1	Purchase of Business A/c Dr.	L 1	1 795		
		Creditors	L 9			1 530
		Provision for bad debts	L 10			265
		Being liabilities taken over at this date				

Purchase of Business A/c   L 1

19..			£	19..			£
July 1st J. Brown	J 1	20 000		July 1st Sundry assets	J 1	21 795	
1st Sundry liabilities	J 1	1 795					
		£21 795				£21 795	

(contd. on page 424)

Sundry-Creditors A/c (Really there would be many)　　　L 9

	19..	£
	July 1st Purchase of Business	
	J 1	1 530

Provision for Bad Debts A/c　　　L 10

	19..	£
	July 1st Purchase of Business	
	J 1	265

Fig. 36.3 Recording the liabilities undertaken on purchase

(d) The capital is brought in, the mortgage arranged and the vendor is paid.

19..						£	£
July	1	Bank A/c	Dr.	CB 1	15 000	
		Capital A/c		L 11			15 000
		Being capital brought in at this date					
July	1	Bank A/c	Dr.	CB 1	8 000	
		Mortgage on Premises A/c		L 12			8 000
		Being mortgage arranged at this date					
July	1	J. Brown A/c	Dr.	L 2	20 000	
		Bank A/c		CB 1			20 000
		Being payment of vendor as agreed					

Bank A/c　　　CB 1

19..		£	19..		£
July 1st Capital	J 1	15 000	July 1st J. Brown	J 1	20 000
1st Mortgage	J 1	8 000	1st Balance	c/d	3 000
		£23 000			£23 000
July 2nd Balance	B/d	3 000			

Capital A/c　　　L 11

	19..	£
	July 1st Bank	J 1	15 000

Mortgage A/c　　　L 12

	19..	£
	July 1st Bank	J 1	8 000

(contd. on page 425)

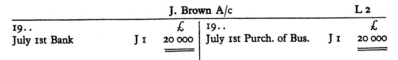

	J. Brown A/c			L 2
19..		£	19..	£
July 1st Bank	J 1	20 000	July 1st Purch. of Bus. J 1	20 000

Fig. 36.4 Paying the vendor his purchase price

(e) Finally, a balance sheet of the new business is drawn up

M. Regan
Balance Sheet
(as at July 1st 19..)

Fixed Assets	£	£	£	*Capital*	£
Goodwill			4 645	At start	15 000
Premises			8 500	*Long-Term Liabilities*	
Furniture and Fittings			2 000	Mortgage	8 000
Motor Vehicles			500	*Current Liabilities*	
			———	Creditors	1 530
			15 645		
Current Assets					
Stock		3 500			
Debtors	2 650				
Less Provision.	265				
	———	2 385			
Bank Balance		3 000			
		———	8 885		
			£24 530		£24 530

Fig. 36.5 The balance sheet of the new business

36.3   Exercises Set 52: Purchase of a Business

1. On December 31st 19.., A. Robertson purchased the business of R. Long. The assets were as follows:

	£
Freehold property	5 000
Furniture and fittings	2 200
Stock-in-Trade	1 800
Debtors	550

The purchase consideration was £12 000, to be paid by cheque on January 1st. Robertson decided to revalue the premises at £6 000, and the Stock at £1 500. He brings in cash at the bank, £15 000 and pays Robertson as arranged.

Show the Journal entries opening the books of Robertson's new business and the Balance Sheet on January 1st 19..

2. The Balance Sheet of P. Fitzpatrick at December 31st 19.. was as follows:

Balance Sheet
(as at December 31st 19..)

	£		£
Freehold property	12 000	Capital	22 500
Plant	8 500	Creditors	4 400
Motor Vehicles	4 100	Bank overdraft	950
Stock-in-Trade	3 250		
	£27 850		£27 850

He sold the assets only to R. Killinchy on January 1st 19.. for the agreed price of £33 350.

Killinchy valued the freehold at £16 000, plant at £8 800, motors at £3 600 and stock at £2 950.

You are asked to give the Journal entries necessary to record these matters in the books of R. Killinchy, who brings in capital of £35 000, cash at Bank and pays Fitzpatrick by cheque on January 1st 19.. Then draw up the opening Balance Sheet of the business.

3. The Balance Sheet of R. Morgan at December 31st 19.. was as follows:

Balance Sheet
(as at December 31st 19..)

	£		£
Freehold property	15 000	Capital	26 300
Plant	8 000	Creditors	1 500
Motor Vehicles	4 000	Bank overdraft	1 200
Stock-in-Trade	2 000		
	£29 000		£29 000

He sold all the assets to M. Phillips on January 1st 19.. for the agreed price of £36 000; Phillips also agreeing to pay up the creditors.

M. Phillips valued the freehold at £20 000, plant at £7 500, motors at £3 000 and stock at £1 800.

You are asked to give the Journal entries necessary to record these matters in the books of M. Phillips, who brought in cash at bank of £25 000, and arranged a mortgage of £12 000 to provide further cash. The vendor was paid on January 2nd. Then draw up an opening Balance Sheet.

4. On September 30th, 19.. R. Lyons arranged to take over the business carried on by J. Kelleher. The assets were taken over at the following valuations: fixtures and fittings £1 850; stock £6 250; motor vehicles £850. Trade creditors amounted to £785 and it was also found that

(*a*) Telephone charges accrued on the date of transfer were £9·55.

(*b*) Electricity due amounted to £37·45 against which could be set a deposit for the original connection of £25, which would be effectively transferred to the new owner.

(*c*) Rent had been paid in advance of £50 for the month of October.

(*d*) Rates £30 had been paid in advance for the quarter to December 31st.

The purchase price was agreed at £10 000, which Lyons paid on October 1st from funds he contributed on that date. These consisted of £11 900 in the bank account and £100 in cash.

Open the affairs of R. Lyons business with appropriate Journal entries, and show the opening Balance Sheet. There is no need to post the Journal entries to the ledger accounts.

5. The Balance Sheet of White, Rock and Sandy on December 31st 19. . was as follows:

Balance Sheet
(as at December 31st 19. .)

	£	£		£	£
Fixed assets			Capitals		
Freeholds		58 000	White		50 000
Plant		37 400	Rock		40 000
Transport		10 500	Sandy		30 000
		105 900			120 000
Current assets			Current Accounts		
Stock	15 426		White	1 722	
Debtors	11 319		Rock	—	
Bank	3 869		Sandy	—	
		30 614			1 722
			Current Liabilities		
			Creditors		14 792
		£136 514			£136 514

On January 1st 19. . the partners bought the net assets of R. Ardmillan for £50 000. The purchase consideration was satisfied in cash, which was contributed by White £30 000 and Sandy £20 000.

The Balance Sheet of Ardmillan on January 1st 19. . immediately prior to the sale of its net assets was:

£　　　Balance Sheet　　　£

(as at January 1st 19..)

		£			£
Fixed assets			Capital		44 600
Plant		29 600			
Transport		9 600			
Current assets		39 200	Current liabilities		
Stock	8 430		Creditors	7 980	
Debtors	5 110		Bank overdraft	160	
	——	13 540		——	8 140
		£52 740			£52 740

You are asked to prepare the balance sheet of the partnership immediately after all these transactions have been completed. The assets and
liabilities of Ardmillan Ltd. which appear in its Balance Sheet at January
1st 19.. are taken over at their book value.

Value Added Tax Accounting

37.1 What is a Value Added Tax?

A value added tax is a tax imposed on consumers when they purchase goods, but collected at several points along the chain of production, distribution and trade, wherever value is added.

Suppose a farmer plants flax, and in due course harvests the crop and sells it to a merchant. At that point of sale the farmer makes his profit on the farming activity, and we say value has been added—the original seed the farmer saved to plant has grown and is now worth more. The merchant transports the flax to a factory and sells it to the factory owner at a profit. More value has been added, for the flax is worth more now that it has been shifted away from the lonely farmland into the city where the works is situated. The linen master separates the fibres and makes the linen into linen goods. He sells them to a retailer. More value has been added for the flax is now turned into a convenient article, ready to be used. The retailer sells the linen goods to the housewives who visit his shop, charging them a profit margin to pay for the services he provides. More value has been added, in that the housewife is able to buy conveniently small quantities to suit her needs and her family budget. At this point the Value Added Tax is paid by the housewife, and for convenience we will say that the rate of tax is 15 per cent as it is at the moment in the United Kingdom. If we imagine that the price of each item is £5, the tax of 15 per cent will add 75 pence to the price to be paid by the housewife, who will therefore pay £5·75.

It might appear to be sensible that the retailer should now pay over the tax collected to the revenue authorities, and that would be the end of the matter, but this is not how VAT is collected. VAT is collected at every point along the chain from production to consumption where value has been added. This can best be followed if we take the actual example given above, but instead of one item we will think of about fifty items. On these the total value will be £250 + £37·50 tax, so that the final price will be £287·50 to the housewives concerned. Note that in VAT anything purchased for use in a business is called an 'input', and the tax on it is called *input tax*. Anything supplied by a business, such as a good sold to a customer or a service performed for a customer is called an 'output'. The tax charged on the output is called *output tax*. Table 37.1 and the note below it explain exactly what happens.

Note: This Unit is written as if there were only one rate of VAT, a standard rate of 15 per cent.

Table 37.1 Value Added Tax calculations

Nature of Activity	Summary of Transaction Excluding VAT		VAT Movements	£	Payable to HM Customs and Excise £
Farmer — Uses seed saved to grow flax. Sells flax to merchant. Value of sale is £100 plus VAT at 15%	Value of inputs Value of outputs Value added	Nil 100 100	Collected from merchant £100 × 15% =	 15·00	15·00
Merchant — Buys flax from farmer, £100 plus 15% VAT. Sells flax to factory, £120 plus 15% VAT	Value of inputs Value of outputs Value added	100 120 20	Paid to farmer Collected from factory £20 × 15% =	15·00 18·00 3·00	3·00
Factory Owner — Buys flax from merchant, £120 plus 15%. Sells household linen to retailer, £200 plus 15% VAT	Value of inputs Value of outputs Value added	120 200 80	Paid to merchant Collected from retailer £80 × 15% =	18·00 30·00 12·00	12·00
Retailer — Buys linen goods from factory, £200 plus 15% VAT. Sells linen goods to housewives, £250 plus 15% VAT	Value of inputs Value of outputs Value added	200 250 50	Paid to factory owner Collected from housewives £50 × 15% =	30·00 37·50 7·50	7·50
Housewives — Buy linen goods, £250 plus 15% VAT	Value of goods purchased	£250	Tax paid to retailer £37·50 Total tax paid to HM Customs and Excise in four separate payments as shown		Nil —— 37·50

Note: The housewives are the only persons who have really paid tax on the goods purchased. The total of £37·50 paid was collected at each point where value was added.

VAT can be fixed at any rate, and originally was intended to be a very widespread tax at a low rate—say about 3 per cent. For political reasons it was decided not to impose the tax on foodstuffs. At once this meant that the tax spread was much reduced, so that a 3 per cent level would not raise the money required, and when a number of other controversial items, such as children's clothes, were also zero-rated the rate for other goods had to be increased. At the time of writing this Unit, a single unified rate of 15 per cent (apart from the zero rate) is in use, and this will serve to illustrate the principle of VAT. At times this rate may vary, or a multi-rate system may be introduced. Very small businesses (with turnover less than an agreed figure—at present £18 000 per annum) need not register for VAT, but cannot claim back VAT on inputs. If they feel aggrieved about this, they may register voluntarily. The current rates for VAT and details about the VAT system, registration, returns, etc., are obtainable in the United Kingdom from local VAT officers (see HM Customs in your local telephone directory).

37.2 Criticisms of VAT

Opponents of the VAT system claim with some justification that it is a cumbersome way to collect tax. When we think that every single firm has to keep VAT records to play their part in the collection system, and is required to issue tax invoices on every good or service it supplies, we can see how cumbersome it is. It is quite impossible for some firms to issue tax invoices when they supply goods—for example a confectioner cannot issue a tax invoice each time he sells a bar of chocolate. So HM Customs have had to invent a wide variety of ways of collecting this tax. There are nine schemes for retailers, explained in a special booklet issued by the government through local VAT offices. This is Notice No. 727, and has nine sub-booklets to explain the different schemes.

This book is not the place for a full discussion of VAT; it is dealt with more fully elsewhere in specialist publications. What we must look at here is the VAT Account, and its position in the double entry system.

37.3 Double Entry and the VAT Account

What the VAT system has done to the books of most businesses—apart from creating a tremendous amount of extra work in keeping records—is to add one new account, the VAT Account. This is the account of the firm with HM Customs and Excise Department, and since the Department will usually be a creditor it might reasonably be placed in the Creditors' Ledger. Most firms add value to the goods they buy, and they sell them at a profit as finished (or more highly processed) goods, so it stands to reason that the VAT they charge their customers (output tax) will be higher than the VAT they pay to their suppliers when buying the goods or raw materials (input tax). This can be seen from Table 37.1. They will therefore finish up with extra money, which is the tax they have collected, and must pay it to HM

Customs. A typical VAT Account would therefore look like Fig. 37.1. Note that the 'output tax' on sales is a credit item at the end of each month, coming from a special column in the Sales Day Book where the VAT on sales can be accumulated as the month goes by. The 'input tax' on purchases comes similarly from a special column in the Purchases Day Book. Where VAT is paid on capital items like furniture it may be reclaimed. As a result the debit side of the account includes VAT on capital items. The difference between the two sides is the amount payable to HM Customs and Excise Department at the end of the VAT quarter. This sum has to be settled before the last day of the following month, and in Fig. 37.1 it was settled on April 8th, by cheque.

HM Customs and Excise Department VAT Account							CL 27
19..			£	19..			£
Jan. 31	VAT on purchases	PDB3	328·27	Jan. 31	VAT on sales	SDB 5	712·48
Feb. 17	Capital item	J7	42·50	Feb. 28	VAT on sales	SDB 8	498·25
Feb. 28	VAT on purchases	PDB4	436·25	Mar. 31	VAT on sales	SDB12	1 385·66
Mar. 11	Capital item	J14	27·40				
Mar. 31	VAT on purchases	PDB9	492·60				
Mar. 31	Balance	c/d	1 269·37				
			£2 596·39				£2 596·39
Apr. 8	Bank	CB5	1 269·37	Apr. 1	Balance	B/d	1 269·37

Fig. 37.1 A typical VAT Account

Some traders sell goods which are zero rated, such as foods, books, newspapers and children's clothing. In these circumstances they may find that the debit side is greater than the credit side, for they are not charging VAT to their customers. In this case HM Customs and Excise Department are not creditors but debtors. The Department owes the retailer money. Since it might cause hardship to retailers paying VAT if they had to wait for these refunds for three months, it is possible for them to receive the refunds on a monthly basis. The VAT Account would therefore be in the Debtor's Ledger and might appear as shown in Fig. 37.2. Note that as the Customs and Excise Department are debtors they settle up each month, not quarterly. Note that the firm concerned does have some input tax to pay on capital items, services and also on expense items such as stationery, telephone, etc., which are labelled Nominal Ledger items in the account. The firm does not appear to deal in any standard rated items as neither purchases nor sales appear on the account.

19..			£	19..			£
Apr. 1	Balance	B/d	147·52	Apr. 12	Refund from	CB8	
8	Capital	J5			HM		
	item		23·62		Customs		147·52
9	Capital	J6		30	Balance	c/d	135·83
	item		17·25				
30	Services	J12	56·40				
30	Nominal	N63					
	Ledger		38·56				
			£283·35				£283·35
May 1	Balance	B/d	135·83				

Fig. 37.2 A VAT Account in a zero-rated trade

Some types of business deal in both zero-rated and standard-rated items, in which case HM Customs may sometimes be a debtor and sometimes a creditor. The trader must decide whether to ask for his account to be settled monthly or quarterly. The latter may be preferable if HM Customs are only occasionally the debtor—since the VAT payable by the trader can be in a deposit account for three months earning the trader interest. A trader who exports goods (exports are exempt from VAT) may also find HM Customs is a debtor, and may therefore prefer a prompt (monthly) settlement.

37.4 VAT Figures for the Accounting Entries

The figures required for the preparation of the VAT Account are obtained from the original documents, the invoices and credit notes dispatched or received. These original documents are of course entered in day books, as illustrated in Units 9, 10, 11 and 12. A number of important points arise as a result of the need to keep VAT records. These are:

(a) The figures for VAT must be distinguished from the purchase price of the goods bought, and the selling price of the goods sold. The figures taken to Purchases Account and Sales Account must be the 'net of VAT' figures.

(b) The customer must be debited with the full sale price, including VAT, and the supplier must be credited with the full purchase price, including VAT.

In order to obtain these figures the four day books have been modified with a VAT column as shown in Figs. 37.3–37.6. For capital items recorded in the Journal Proper the journal entry will be as shown in Fig. 37.7.

Date	Details	F	Value excluding VAT	VAT	Total Purchases
					See Note (a)
			See Note (b)	See Note (c)	

Fig. 37.3 The modified Purchases Day Book

Notes:
(a) Credit each supplier's account with the total value of the purchase (including VAT).
(b) Debit the Purchases Account with the 'net-of-tax' price charged by the supplier.
(c) Debit the VAT Account with the VAT charged by the supplier (input tax).

Date	Details	F	Value excluding VAT	VAT	Total Sales
					See Note (a)
			See Note (b)	See Note (c)	

Fig. 37.4 The modified Sales Day Book

Notes:
(a) Debit each customer's account with the total value of the goods or services supplied (including VAT).
(b) Credit the Sales Account with the 'net of tax' charge to the customer.
(c) Credit the VAT Account with the VAT charged to the customer (output tax).

Date	Details	F	Value excluding VAT	VAT	Total Purchases Returns
					See Note (a)
			See Note (b)	See Note (c)	

Fig. 37.5 The modified Purchases Returns Book

Notes:
(a) Debit each supplier's account with the total value of the returns (including VAT).
(b) Credit the Purchases Returns Account with the 'net-of-tax' value of the returned goods.
(c) Credit the VAT Account with the VAT no longer being charged by the supplier (input tax cancelled).

Date	Details	F	Value excluding VAT	VAT	Total Sales Returns
					See Note (a)
			See Note (b)	See Note (c)	

Fig. 37.6 The modified Sales Returns Book

Notes:
(a) Credit each customer with the total value of the goods returned (including VAT).
(b) Debit Sales Returns Account with the 'net-of-tax' value of the returned goods.
(c) Debit VAT Account with the VAT no longer being charged to the customer (output tax cancelled).

19.. July	14	Plant and Machinery Dr. VAT Account Dr. XYZ Machine Co. Ltd. Being purchase of shaping machine ML 127356 at this date	L 76 L 125 L 63	£ 1 500·00 225·00	£ 1 725·00

Fig. 37.7 A Journal entry showing VAT on a capital item

37.5   The VAT Account and the Balance Sheet

The final point to note is that the VAT Account will always be either a creditor account (the businessman owes money to HM Customs and Excise Department) or a debtor account (HM Customs and Excise Department owe money to the trader in zero-rated goods). The VAT Account will therefore be included in one of these two figures when the Balance Sheet is prepared. For most traders the sum due to HM Customs will be part of the item 'Creditors'. It need not be separately disclosed. For zero-rated traders the sum receivable will be part of the item 'Debtors' on the Balance Sheet.

37.6   Exercises Set 53: Value Added Tax

1. What is VAT? Explain the terms 'zero rate', 'standard rate' and 'higher rate'.
2. Draw up an imaginary VAT Account for a trader who sells goods only at the standard rate. Insert three monthly sets of figures, also some capital items. Balance off the account at the end of the three months and bring down the balance. Then show the payment due to Customs and Excise Department during the following month.
3. R. Jones is a wholesale ironmonger. His VAT figures reveal the following for his tax quarter which begins on February 1st 19.. and ends on April 30th.

> *Input tax on invoices from suppliers of goods*
> February   £4 274·94
> March   £3 887·67
> April   £2 995·55
>
> *Input tax on other items (consumables, etc.)*
> February   £371·50
> March   £298·65
> April   £725·35
>
> *Output tax charged to customers*
> February   £17 284·24
> March   £19 327·62
> April   £14 326·56

Draw up the VAT account for the three-month period and balance it off on April 30th. This balance is paid to Customs and Excise Department on May 25th, by cheque.

4. N. Bennett is a retail grocer selling zero-rated items under one of the special retailers' schemes. According to this scheme he sold £8 726·54 of goods during January, all of it zero rated. At the same time he paid VAT on goods for use in his business, £181·75 input tax. He also paid tax on services £86·24. You are asked to draw up his VAT Account for the month of January. Besides the facts given above you are told:

(a) The VAT Account had a debit balance of £131·75 on January 1st.

(b) Customs and Excise refunded this balance on January 16th.

(*See Note on Answers to Questions, page 456.*)

The Basic Concepts of Accounting

38.1 The Place of Accounting in the Economy

Now that we know a good deal about elementary accounting we are ready to stand back and take a look at the place of accounting in the modern economy, and the general concepts of accounting which have developed in recent years. In earlier times, when production was largely domestic in nature, there was little need to lay down principles of accounting to be adhered to by everybody. Today, wealth is created in a complex way, by people in vast organizations, and it can be moved quickly from place to place by means of sophisticated electronic systems. Governments want their share of the nation's wealth and have large Inland Revenue departments to collect it. Consequently we have to have systems of accountancy that everyone understands, and rules that all must keep. In this way, it is arranged that we pay our fair share of taxes, account to shareholders, creditors and employees for the wealth our company has created, and discover fraud, embezzlement and theft as soon as they occur—we hope.

The following basic principles are known as the *concepts* of accounting:

(*a*) the concept of business entity;
(*b*) the prudence concept;
(*c*) the going-concern concept;
(*d*) the accruals concept;
(*e*) the substance and materiality concepts;
(*f*) the consistency concept;
(*g*) the objectivity concept;
(*h*) the stable-money concept.

Having studied this book, you will already be familiar with many of the ideas involved in these concepts.

38.2 The Concept of Business Entity

A business entity is a separate business unit, distinct from all other business units. A sole trader business is separate from all other sole traders, partnerships, limited companies, friendly societies or co-operative societies, etc. It is even distinct from the owner of the business, who may sometimes act for the business (e.g. when he is buying goods for re-sale) and at other times act as an individual (e.g. when he buys food to take his family for a picnic).

The concept of business entity is recognized by law, and in some cases the business is given a special legal status—an incorporation. Thus a limited liability company is an incorporation—a body set up by process of law. This process is called the *registration* of the company. Some companies are set up by special Act of Parliament (a statutory company) and some are set up by royal decree (a chartered company).

Partnerships, sole traders and clubs are not incorporations and do not have separate legal status from the partners, proprietors or members of the club. However, the accountant still separates them off from one another; the business has its own accounts, and these are quite distinct from the partners' accounts, the sole trader's personal records, etc.

A development from the concept of business entity is the *concept of stewardship*. Those who run a business must account to the owners of the business for all its financial affairs. A sole trader, of course, only has to account to himself (and to the Inland Revenue for the tax due). Partners must account to one another. The treasurer of a club must account to the members, and the directors of a company must account to the share-holders. It is necessary to keep honest books of account, produce receipts (or paid cheques) for all money spent, balance our books every month in a Trial Balance, and every year produce a set of Final Accounts in a Balance Sheet showing the affairs of the business at the end of the last day in the financial year. You have already learned how to do all these things.

38.3   The Prudence Concept

The prudence concept holds that a person in business is most likely to be successful if he is prudent (cautious) in everything he does, i.e. he tries to avoid such things as overspending, and overtrading (see page 387), etc. You are already familiar with most of the basic ideas associated with the prudence concept. You have learned the rule 'Stock is valued at cost or net realizable value whichever is lower' (Section 25.1). If stock has risen in value and we value it at this increased price, we are taking the profit on it before we have sold it. This is imprudent because we may never sell it and so may never actually achieve the profit. Similarly, if stock has fallen in value, it is prudent to take the loss into account at once and not leave it to be suffered at a later date. A prudent businessman never takes a profit until he has actually made it, and always accepts a loss at once even if there is a chance he may recover it later. If we hear that a debtor is in financial difficulties and a receiver has been appointed to deal with a debtor's affairs, the prudent businessman treats the debt as bad at once, while doing what is possible to claim in the bankruptcy. Similarly, as we know from learning about provisions for bad debts (Section 26.8) and provisions for discounts (Section 26.9), the prudent businessman anticipates some bad debts, even when he does not know which debtor is likely to go bankrupt. By deducting some-thing from our profits to provide for bad debts, we put away the profits for a future emergency.

There is, however, another side to this prudent behaviour. If we reduce our profits more than is reasonable we shall also pay less taxes, for, as we know, the Government's revenues partly come from a share of business profits. Many legal cases result from disputes between the Inland Revenue and businessmen about the amount of profit they are retaining for future hard times. We are allowed to be prudent—but not to defraud the revenue authorities.

38.4 The Going-Concern Concept

This concept holds that an accountant is entitled to work out the Final Accounts of a business, and draw up a Balance Sheet, on the basis that the business will continue for the conceivable future—in other words it is a 'going concern'. If he has some reason to believe that it does not intend to continue, it is, of course, fraudulent to prepare the accounts as if it were.

The reason for the going-concern concept is that the value of things can change to a considerable extent according to their usefulness to the business as a going concern. If you visit a large engineering works or factory you will see expensive machinery producing the goods the company sells. As a going concern the machinery is valuable. If you visit the same factory six months after it has shut down, much of the machinery may only be worth what it would fetch as scrap metal. Therefore, if there is some prospect that the business, or some major part of it, may shut down or cease to operate, the accountant must reflect this in the accounts he prepares, and in particular in the Balance Sheet of the business.

The assumption is, in all businesses, that the accounts have been prepared for a business that is a going concern, and that no intention or necessity to reduce activity or sell off parts of the business is envisaged.

38.5 The Accruals Concept

The accruals concept is the basis of preparing Final Accounts. It holds that the profits we earn and the costs we bear are recognized at the time they take place, and not at the time they are actually paid for (which may be several months later). For example, if we sell goods in January and they are paid for by our debtors in March, there is no problem of accrual for a business which keeps its accounts on a calendar year basis, for both the sale and the payment are made in the same year. By contrast, if we sell goods in November and they are paid for in February, there is a problem of accrual. When did the profit on these goods accrue—when we sold them or when we actually recovered the payment? The answer, according to the accruals concept, is that the profit was earned when we sold the goods, and it must be counted as a profit for the year, when we do the Final Accounts in December of that year. Similarly with expenses—an expense incurred in November counts as an expense of that financial year even though we don't actually pay the account until February of the following year. These are examples of 'adjustments' (see Unit 26).

There is one exception to this rule: the prudence concept (see Section 38.3) can override the accruals concept in so far as is reasonable. We can carry forward a provision for bad debts, if there is some prospect that some of the sales we are making in November may not actually be paid for when payment time comes round.

This exception apart, the basic idea of the accruals concept is a concept of 'matching' profits with the expenses of earning these profits. The basic rule which the Inland Revenue Department follows when deciding whether our accounts are satisfactory is as follows:

(a) on the credit side of the Trading and Profit and Loss Accounts appear *all the profits we have earned this year, whether they have actually been received or not*; and

(b) on the debit side of the accounts appear *all the expenses incurred in earning these profits, whether they have actually been paid or not.*

You have already met all these ideas when learning how to prepare the Final Accounts of all types of organizations.

38.6   The Substance and Materiality Concepts

These concepts deal with the problem of excessive detail in the accounts. The Final Accounts of a firm might be very complicated and take pages and pages of typescript to reproduce. We have to be allowed to group some things together to reduce the amount of detail. Thus flour, eggs, etc. can be put together as stock. Should lorries and private cars be lumped together as 'motor vehicles'? The answer is provided by these two concepts.

First, the accounts must show the true *substance* of the firm's financial position. Suppose we have loaned one of the directors £100 000 to buy a house. He is in debt to the company for this amount. If we hide this debt from the shareholders by including it in the 'debtors', we shall not be revealing the true substance of the matter. Similarly, if we are a company engaged in road haulage, and all our lorries are old, but all the cars we have purchased for the use of the directors are new, it would not reveal the true state of affairs if we put them together as 'motor vehicles'. Compare the following Balance Sheet entries:

Balance Sheet
(as at December 31st 19..)

Fixed Assets	At Cost	Less Depreciation	Current Value
Motor Vehicles	£100 000	£50 000	£50 000

Balance Sheet
(as at December 31st 19..)

Fixed Assets	At Cost	Less Depreciation	Current Value
	£	£	£
Heavy Lorries	60 000	45 000	15 000
Motor Cars	40 000	5 000	35 000
	£100 000	£50 000	£50 000

Clearly, the first entry hides the true state of affairs, for it appears that all vehicles still have half of their useful life ahead of them. The second entry reveals the true substance of the firm's situation. Its heavy goods vehicles are almost at the end of their useful life and before long we can expect very heavy costs to replace them.

So the substance concept requires the accounts to be prepared in such a way that they bring out the true state of affairs. The materiality concept is very similar. If an item is 'material', i.e. sufficiently important to affect our judgment of the true position of the firm, it must appear as a separate item. If it does not affect our judgment, it can be merged with other items. Thus the item 'Petty cash' does not appear on a Balance Sheet—it is merged with 'Cash in hand', even though most of the cash is in the cashier's cash box and the petty cash is in the petty cashier's till.

38.7   The Consistency Concept

When we prepare the accounts of any organization we expect management to compare this year's records with the records of earlier years. For this reason we must be consistent from one year to the next. If we show the Balance Sheet headings in a different way from the headings used the year before, management will be confused and unable to detect 'trends', such as:

(a) Are sales increasing or decreasing?
(b) Are stocks building up or declining?
(c) Are wages costs rising or falling?
(d) Are profit margins increasing or decreasing?

We have studied all this in Unit 32, Interpreting Final Accounts.

If, for any reason, it is impossible to follow the same pattern as in previous years, we must give a full explanation in the form of a *Note to the Accounts*. This explains why this year's accounts cannot be compared strictly with last year's accounts. If, for example, the basis of valuing stock has changed from FIFO to LIFO we must explain why we have changed, and the effect it has had on the profits. Similarly, if a revolution has affected our trading activities in an overseas country, we should explain the situation and give a brief assessment of its likely effect on the firm.

38.8   The Objectivity Concept

The objectivity concept holds that the accounts should be prepared objectively, not subjectively. This means that they must be viewed not from the viewpoint of someone inside the firm, but from the point of view of an outside observer, looking at the firm and all other firms with the same attitude. If this doesn't happen, we may get into serious trouble. Many 'takeover bids' succeed because of such mistakes. Suppose I purchased a piece of property in the City of London twenty years ago for £10 000. It is still valued on my books at cost price. An outside observer may know that this property is now worth £1 million. If he takes over my business he can sell this asset for its full value, and I shall not realize the profit, but he will. Had I valued my assets objectively I would have raised that value on my books in line with its change in value over the years, and when he tried to take over my business he would have had to pay the full value. Of course, he wouldn't have tried to take it over—and I should still be in business.

38.9   The Stable-Money Concept

At one time money was stable in value. From 1745 to 1939 the British Government always borrowed money at $2\frac{1}{2}$ per cent interest, and could always get as much as it wanted without any difficulty. Today money suffers from a disease called 'inflation'. With this disease prices of goods and services rise, so that the value of money falls, and rates of interest are variable and often very high. The basic idea in accounting is that money is stable in value; if I borrow £500, I expect to repay £500 in the future. Although this is how the records in our ledgers look, in real life I don't repay £500, I repay £500 in *depreciated* currency. The notes I pay are worth much less than those I borrowed. That is why interest rates are so high. The interest payable makes the true value of what I repay about 'right' in an inflationary period.

In 1980 rules were laid down requiring large firms to take inflation into account by making adjustments to the value of assets, stock, etc. This is fully explained in *Success in Accounting and Costing*.

The best way to illustrate the effects of inflation is to consider the FIFO/LIFO/AVCO problem, referred to earlier (see Section 25.3).

FIFO, LIFO and AVCO

Where stock consists of a collection of items purchased in inflationary times at a variety of prices it can be allocated for use in jobs or contracts in several different ways. Let us imagine motor vehicle tyres, all of the same type and quality purchased at £18, £20 and £24. The stock card might look like this:

Tyres Type 2D radials	£
16 – cost £18 each – value	288
12 – cost £20 each – value	240
20 – cost £24 each – value	480
	£1 008

A customer now buys 4 tyres at £36 each (current cost £24 + 50 per cent mark-up).

The three most common methods of accounting for this transaction are as follows:

(a) FIFO—first in, first out. The first tyres cost £18 each. The stock would decrease by 4 × £18 = £72.

(b) LIFO—last in, first out. The last set of tyres to be delivered cost £24 each. This time the stock would decrease by 4 × £24 = £96.

(c) AVCO—This stands for 'average cost' and the tyres would be regarded as having all cost the same average price, i.e. £1 008 ÷ 48 = £21. The value of the stock would decline by 4 × £21 = £84.

Whichever method of valuation we adopt, it does involve keeping careful stock records. In the case of AVCO we have to recalculate the average price each time we take delivery of a new batch of stock.

Now consider the effect of these different valuation policies on the profits of a business. We will do a comparative Trading Account to see what the situation is, assuming that 30 tyres have been sold.

The sales value would be 30 × £36 = £1 080.

The tyres would be used as follows:

FIFO	(16 × £18) + (12 × £20) + (2 × £24)	= £576
LIFO	(20 × £24) + (10 × £20)	= £680
AVCO	(30 × £21)	= £630

The stock left would be as follows:

FIFO	(18 × £24)	= £432
LIFO	(16 × £18) + (2 × £20)	= £328
AVCO	(18 × £21)	= £378

The profit may be calculated as follows:

	FIFO	LIFO	AVCO
	£	£	£
Sales	1 080	1 080	1 080
Cost of sales	576	680	630
Profit	£ 504	£ 400	£ 450

We get the most profit with FIFO and the least profit with LIFO, while with AVCO we fall between these two extremes. Note that in this example the customer has been charged the same price, £36, in each case. Had we wished to do so, we could have maintained a more competitive stance in the market place by continuing to sell at old prices so long as we had 'old' items in stock. This would not have affected our stock valuation policy, but it would have altered our profits for the year, because the 'sales' figure would have been reduced.

The stock values at the end of the year are in the same order. Under FIFO we have the dearest stock left, valued at £432, whereas under LIFO it is valued at £328 and under AVCO at £378. The alert student will notice that it is not easy to comply with the rule about showing the value of stock at cost or net realizable value, when using AVCO. We have the stock valued at an average price and do not really know what the true original cost of any particular unit was.

Note also that the order in which we value stock is an accounting problem and not necessarily connected with the order in which we use the stock. Just because we supply a customer at the latest price (+ profit margin) does not mean we actually give him the latest item to come into stock. It is usual to use stock in the order in which it came into stock—oldest items first—irrespective of our accounting policy for valuation of stock.

38.10   The Law and Accounting Concepts

For centuries, governments made no attempt to legislate on accountancy matters. It was an age of 'laisser faire', a French phrase meaning 'to let people work things out for themselves'. It was thought that when a businessman succeeded in making himself rich, he was bound to make the whole nation richer to some extent. The accounting concepts grew up as a body of rules which right-minded businessmen and their accountants were glad to follow.

More recently there has been some attempt to regulate accounting practices. It began with the Companies Act 1948, when for the first time it was set down that accounts must give a 'true and fair view' of the affairs of a company. It was still left to the accountants to decide what was 'true', and what was 'fair'. For about twenty-five years accountants seemed to arrive at fairly satisfactory results, and complied with the spirit of the law—not just the letter of the law. Then some accountants became less scrupulous about abiding by the statutory requirements.

One result of this was that a body was set up—the Accounting Standards Steering Committee—which looked at all the difficult areas in accounting practice and began to publish SSAPs—*Statements of Standard Accounting Practice*. These are sets of rules which act as guidelines in accountancy, and have undoubtedly helped a good deal to ensure that all accountants work in the same way. These are fully discussed in other books in this series: *Success in Financial Accounting* and *Success in Accounting and Costing*.

Another result was that some of the concepts of accounting were laid down as statutory duties in the Companies Act of 1981. The going-concern concept, the accruals concept, the consistency concept, the prudence concept and the substance and materiality concepts are now effectively embodied in the Act, and have become a legal requirement of the accounts of companies. This means that accounts prepared without due regard to these basic principles could be the subject of criminal charges if the company gets into financial difficulties. This explains why these concepts are now of greater importance to accountants than previously.

38.11   Exercises Set 54: The Concepts of Accounting

1. What is meant by an accounting concept? List the concepts with which you are familiar and explain any *one* of them in detail.

2. (*a*) What is meant by 'prudence' in accounting? (*b*) Peter Jones has just completed a contract for Bigboy Ltd. for the erection of plant at a

factory. The profit amounts to £334 000, but £134 000 has to be kept in a special provision account in case the plant fails to work satisfactorily in the first six months. Peter Jones is a prudent accountant. How much should he declare as profit for the present financial year, which ends on Friday of this week?

3. (a) What is meant by the going-concern concept? (b) AB Ltd. have decided to cease trading on the last day of the present financial year. What difference will this make to the accountant's thinking as he considers the preparation of the Final Accounts for the year?

4. Would you include the following items in your Final Accounts under a separate heading as being important items affecting the substance of your Final Accounts, or merge them with other items as being immaterial?

(a) £350 000 paid to a firm of experts who extinguished a fire at No. 3 well which had caused a £15 million loss to the company;

(b) £30 paid to a member of staff who worked overtime to cure a plumbing leak;

(c) Timber worth £750 was used to rebuild a store damaged by vandals. Our annual turnover of timber is £3·5 million, and we frequently lose stock as valuable as this by theft, or fire, or road accident.

(d) The purchase of property valued at £85 000. Our total property is valued at £650 000.

Give your answer in the form of a list (a) to (d) with the words 'separate item' or 'immaterial item' written alongside. You do not need to give a written explanation.

5. (a) What is meant by the consistency concept? (b) Up to now your firm has always valued stock on a FIFO basis, but you are in favour of adopting the LIFO system. Explain what this means in terms of the profit situation. How would you draw your shareholders' attention to this change of policy?

6. On January 1st 19.. a trader has the following items in stock. They are identical but were purchased at different times as prices rose during the previous year:

    5 which cost £10 each;
    8 which cost £14 each;
    7 which cost £17 each;
    10 which cost £20 each.

He always sells at a mark-up of 50 per cent on current cost price. What will be his profit, and what will be the value of closing stock on January 31st 19.., if he sells 18 items in the month and accounts for them on a FIFO basis?

7. Using the same figures as in question 6, what will be the profit and what will be the value of the closing stock if he accounts for the 18 items on a LIFO basis instead?

8. On January 1st 19.. a trader has the following items in stock. They are identical but were purchased at different times as prices rose during the previous year:

        3 which cost £50 each;
        8 which cost £55 each;
        4 which cost £60 each;
        5 which cost £65 each.

He always sells at a mark-up of 60 per cent on current cost price. What will be his profit, and what will be the value of closing stock on January 31st 19.., if he sells 15 items in the month and accounts for them on a FIFO basis?

9. Using the same figures as in question 8 above, what will be the profit and the value of the closing stock on January 31st 19.. if he accounts for the 15 items on a LIFO basis?

(See Note on Answers to Questions, page 456.)

Unit Thirty-Nine

The Computerization of Elementary Accounting

39.1 What is a Computer?

A computer is an electronic device which can perform very simple functions (like addition and subtraction) so rapidly that it can outpace any human calculator. The associated storage devices such as magnetic tapes and discs can retain vast amounts of information. Not only do computers vary considerably, but the rate of development in the computer field is such that current machines require updating or even replacing every few years. However, the basic concepts of computer applications remain the same even if the methods or machines change. They have important applications in many fields, particularly in scientific projects where calculations would otherwise be very laborious, and in technology where they can sample products and institute control procedures in such activities as oil refining and control of water pollution. This is called *Control Engineering*.

39.2 The Computerization of Accounting

Computers are as useful to commerce as they are to science and technological projects. There is a vast range of computers available to commercial businesses from small mini-computers to large configurations with enormous capacity and processing power. More and more businesses now use computers in their day-to-day running, including their accounting procedures.

It is unlikely that anyone working in accounting will not, at some time, find himself in a computerized accounting environment. The purpose of this section is to give some idea of computerized accounting procedures and how they modify the tasks and procedures of manual accounting.

There are three basic activities in the computerization of accounting. They are:

(*a*) the input of information (data);
(*b*) the manipulation and organization of data (data processing);
(*c*) the output of information.

The Input of Information (Data). The computer has to be given basic information. Just like an invoice typist the computer requires the details of a customer's order if a sales invoice is to be prepared which in turn can be posted to the customer's account in the sales ledger. Similarly, the details of a supplier's invoice are required if it is to be posted to the Purchases Ledger. Such facts together with details of the relevant names and addresses have to be put into the computer system. The information is usually abbreviated as much as possible by the use of codes such as supplier codes, customer codes, account codes, etc. Static information (information which changes rarely) such as suppliers' names and addresses can be 'input' once only and held by the computer on a file. The dynamic information (information which changes from order to order) is input quoting codes which the computer can cross-reference to connect the current order with the relevant names and addresses.

The Manipulation and Organization of Information. This is achieved in the computer by means of programs and storage devices such as magnetic tapes and magnetic discs. Programs are written by computer programmers and are coded instructions which are performed in the computer. Programs act like clerks and typists—they can perform the tasks on the basic input data creating files of information, collating suppliers' invoices for each supplier, calculating discounts, preparing invoices from customer orders, etc. and producing printed reports or reports to be displayed on the screen of a *Visual Display Unit (VDU)*. Organized information, such as a set of information relating to suppliers (for example, names, addresses, payment dates, unpaid invoices), is collated by the program and stored on a magnetic tape or disc as a file. This file and many others can be accessed time and time again by the program to add further information, delete obsolete information and to prepare such things as reports and sales details.

The Output of Information. Vast amounts of information relating to sales accounting, purchases accounting, etc. can be held as files in the computer, accumulating as further daily or weekly information is added. All this information is useless unless we can have access to that information in an understandable form rather than as magnetized particles on a magnetic tape. Programs are therefore written which give access to the information we require, sort it into the order we need and *output* the information in a readable form. This can be a printed report, a visual display on a VDU or a microfilm which can be read in a special viewer.

39.3 An Example of Computerization

Fig. 39.1 (pp. 450–51) shows in diagrammatic form how one of the basic accounting systems (the Purchases Day Book and Creditors' Ledger) would be computerized. Methods and applications may vary depending upon the computer and particular requirements of the business concerned but the basic concepts will remain the same.

The reader is advised to follow the diagram through stage by stage, in conjunction with the notes in this section.

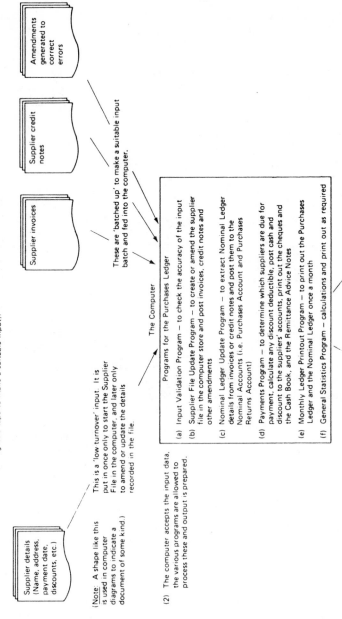

(1) The original documents and other information have to be fed into the computer (this is done by punching the information onto punch cards, or encoding it onto magnetic tape to make a suitable input).

Supplier details
(Name, address,
payment date,
discounts, etc.)

Note: A shape like this
is used in computer
diagrams to indicate a
document of some kind.

This is a 'low turnover' input. It is
put in once only to start the Supplier
File in the computer, and later only
to amend or update the details
recorded in the file.

Supplier invoices

Supplier credit
notes

Amendments
generated to
correct
errors

These are 'batched up' to make a suitable input
batch and fed into the computer.

The Computer

Programs for the Purchases Ledger

(a) Input Validation Program — to check the accuracy of the input

(b) Supplier File Update Program — to create or amend the supplier
    file in the computer store and post invoices, credit notes and
    other amendments

(c) Nominal Ledger Update Program — to extract Nominal Ledger
    details from invoices or credit notes and post them to the
    Nominal Accounts (i.e. Purchases Account and Purchases
    Returns Account)

(d) Payments Program — to determine which suppliers are due for
    payment, calculate any discount deductible, post cash and
    discount to the suppliers' accounts, print out the cheques and
    the Cash Book, and the Remittance Advice Notes

(e) Monthly Ledger Printout Program — to print out the Purchases
    Ledger and the Nominal Ledger once a month

(f) General Statistics Program — calculations and print out as required

(2) The computer accepts the input data,
the various programs are allowed to
process these and output is prepared.

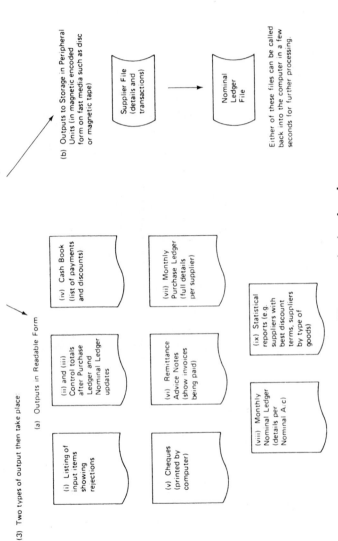

(3) Two types of output then take place

(a) Outputs in Readable Form

(i) Listing of input items showing rejections

(ii) and (iii) Control totals after Purchase Ledger and Nominal Ledger updates

(iv) Cash Book (list of payments and discounts)

(v) Cheques (printed by computer)

(vi) Remittance Advice Notes (show invoices being paid)

(vii) Monthly Purchase Ledger (full details per supplier)

(viii) Monthly Nominal Ledger (details per Nominal A/c)

(ix) Statistical reports (e.g. suppliers with best discount terms, suppliers by type of goods)

(b) Outputs to Storage in Peripheral Units (in magnetic encoded form on fast media such as disc or magnetic tape)

Supplier File (details and transactions)

Nominal Ledger File

Either of these files can be called back into the computer in a few seconds for further processing.

Fig 39.1 The computerization of purchases

Notes on Fig. 39.1

(*a*) *The basic input data.* Some parts of the input data are *static data*, or *low-turnover input.* For example, the names, addresses, and other details about suppliers will not vary greatly, and once the whole collection has been fed into the computer and recorded *on file* in the computer a very small *updating input* each month will keep this information up to date by including new suppliers, taking note of changes of address, etc.

Other information will be *dynamic* (for example, invoices received from a supplier for goods supplied, credit notes and documents or correspondence to correct errors) and will need to be coded and fed into the computer.

(*b*) *The programs.* Once the data are input the computer can call upon the various programs it has stored away in its data banks. They will be loaded into the core—the chief working area—and will process the data according to the program. To prevent errors, the input material is checked, and any items which appear inaccurate are output as *rejections.* This program is called the *Input Validation Program.* Other programs will post the invoices, credit notes, etc. to the suppliers' accounts, post the Purchases Account and Purchases Returns Account, print out cheques when accounts are due for payment and work out any statistical details.

(*c*) *Maintaining the files.* All these new data lead to changes in the computer's records which are called *files.* These are stored in *fast media* magnetic tapes and discs, which can be accessed by the machine when required to find an account and other relevant details. In this case a Supplier File and a Nominal Ledger file will be affected by the various entries and will be changed before being put back into store.

(*d*) *Output of readable material.* The situation of any account in the supplier file, the statistical results of any calculations made and many other details must be made available in readable form for those who need them. The output may be a document of some kind (such as a cheque, remittance advice note or report), a visual display in a cathode ray tube or a microfilm which can be read in a microfilm-reader.

39.4   Other Systems

Where other areas are computerized, such as Sales Accounting and Payroll, other programs can be written to collate the information from each system even to the extent of producing *final accounts* if required. How sophisticated a computerized system becomes is a management decision. For some firms the routine work of the various day books and ledgers is computerized and the final accounts are prepared manually. Other firms may feel that the writing of Final Accounts programs is a worth-while exercise, and the whole system will be computerized.

Micro-computers. In recent years there have been significant advances in micro-computer systems. These small computers make use of the latest developments in silicon chip technology and are sufficiently powerful to perform many of the functions described above. Micro-computers are often called home computers since they are portable and can be plugged into a normal electric socket. They can also be connected to a floppy disc input device or to a cassette tape recorder, and with these attachments can be used to store data and computer programs. The data are displayed on a visual display unit like a television set and a printer can also be connected if a printout is required. Safety devices can be built into the system whenever a vital entry is being made. For example, the visual display unit shows messages such as 'You are asking me to post this to Bank Account. Is this OK?' If the operator presses the 'Yes' key the posting will be made in a fraction of a second. A complete audit trial can be printed out on request, showing a full record of the accounts. With the present low cost of micro-computers it is quite feasible for even the smallest businesses to use a home computer to perform management and accounting functions. For example, the very simple system described in Section 19.3—the Simplex System—is now available as Micro-Simplex. The entire system, that is,

  (a) a micro-computer,
  (b) a disc-drive unit,
  (c) a printer,
  (d) a visual display unit, and
  (e) the software (programs),

can be purchased for about £1 000. When a document arrives it is entered using an appropriate program, and all the necessary postings are done instantaneously. Weekly and monthly printouts give a complete audit trial and at the end of the financial year the figures for the Trading, Profit and Loss Account and Balance Sheet will be provided (although Balance Sheets are not usually drawn up by computer).

Unit Forty
Covering the Syllabus

40.1 Introduction

You have now been through all the Units of this book and if you have worked a reasonable selection of the exercises, you will know enough accounts to run a small business, and would certainly be ready to take any type of routine accounts post. You would similarly be well prepared to take most preliminary examinations of the examining boards in professional and commercial examinations. Listed below is a check list of the items covered in this book. You should consider each item and ensure that you have become knowledgeable about each point. The list looks imposing, but in fact it is only what a good junior accountant would be familiar with. By checking off the items as you consider them, and referring to the index to find appropriate pages where you are hazy or unsure, you will soon see that, in fact, you are very knowledgeable after your course of study.

40.2 A Check List of Points on the Syllabuses of Examination Boards

You should check that you are familiar with the following:

(a) *Documents*

(i) Invoices
(ii) Credit notes
(iii) Statements
(iv) Receipts
(v) Cheques
(vi) Debit notes
(vii) Remittance advice notes
(viii) Wages slips
(ix) Petty cash vouchers
(x) Bank reconciliation statements

(b) *Books of original entry*

(i) The Journal Proper
(ii) The Purchases Day Book
(iii) The Purchases-Returns Book
(iv) The Sales Day Book
(v) The Sales-Returns Book
(vi) The Three-column Cash Book
(vii) The Petty Cash Book

(c) *The Journal Proper* (details)

(i) Opening entries
(ii) Closing entries
(iii) Purchase of assets
(iv) Sale of worn-out assets
(v) Depreciation
   (a) Straight-line method
   (b) Diminishing-balance method
   (c) Revaluation method
   (d) Amortization of leases
(vi) Correction of errors
(vii) Dishonoured cheques

(viii) Bad debts
    (a) Wholly bad
    (b) Partially bad
    (c) Bad debts recovered

(ix) Goodwill
(x) Loans
(xi) Bank interest and charges

(d) *The Ledger*

(i) Personal Accounts
(ii) Nominal Accounts
(iii) Real Accounts
(iv) Continuous-balance Accounts
(v) Extracting a Trial Balance
(vi) What to do if a Trial Balance fails to agree

(vii) Errors of omission
(viii) Errors of commission
(ix) Errors of principle
(x) Compensating errors
(xi) Original errors
(xii) Suspense Accounts
(xiii) Control Accounts

(e) *Final Accounts*

(i) Sole trader Final Accounts
(ii) Partnership Final Accounts
(iii) Club Accounts

(iv) Limited Company Final Accounts
(v) The increased net-worth method of finding profits

(f) *Interpretation of Final Accounts*

(i) Current assets
(ii) Fixed assets
(iii) Intangible assets
(iv) Fictitious assets
(v) Current liabilities
(vi) Long-term liabilities
(vii) Capital owned
(viii) Capital employed
(ix) Net worth
(x) Fixed capital
(xi) Floating capital
(xii) Working capital
(xiii) Gross-profit percentage
(xiv) Net-profit percentage

(xv) Rate of stock turn
(xvi) Average time in stock
(xvii) Return on capital invested
(xviii) Working capital ratio (current) ratio
(xix) Liquid-capital (acid-test) ratio
(xx) Turnover
(xxi) Cost of stock sold
(xxii) Cost of sales
(xxiii) Expense ratios
(xxiv) Accumulated Fund of a club
(xxv) Ordinary-shareholders' interest

(g) *Abbreviations*

(i) Dr.
(ii) Cr.
(iii) E and OE
(iv) C

(v) COD
(vi) FIFO, LIFO and AVCO
(vii) VDU

(h) *Further matters*

(i) Stock valuation	(b) The prudence concept
(ii) Capital and revenue expenditure	(c) The going-concern concept
	(d) The accruals concept
(iii) Amalgamations	(e) The substance concept
(iv) Purchase of a business	(f) The materiality concept
(v) The basic concepts of accounting	(g) The consistency concept
	(h) The objectivity concept
(a) The business-entity concept	(i) The stable-money concept

Note on Answers to Questions

The answers to all questions in this reprint are given in the 1984 version of the companion volume, *Success in Principles of Accounting: Answer Book*. The answers are fully worked out so that you can see exactly how they should be displayed.

Students using earlier versions of the *Answer Book* should note the following:

Unit 31—Exercises Set 44: Company Final Accounts (*pages 356–67*)
Printings of the *Answer Book* before 1982 do not display the answers to the questions in this exercise in the format now required by the Companies Act 1981 and described on pages 350–5 of this book. A careful study of the text will reveal the differences caused by the 1981 Act.

Unit 37—Exercises Set 53: Value Added Tax (*pages 436–7*)
In earlier reprints of the book this Unit appeared as an Appendix, Unit 38. Printings of the *Answer Book* before 1984 have the answers to the questions in this exercise listed under Unit 38, not Unit 37.

Unit 38—Exercises Set 54: The Concepts of Accounting (*pages 445–7*)
This is a new Unit in the 1984 reprint of this book. The answers to the questions in this exercise are given below:

(**1**) Check your answer with the text.
(**2**) (a) Check your answer with the text.
    (b) He should declare £200 000 as profit.
(**3**) (a) and (b) Check your answers with the text.
(**4**) (a) Separate item; (b) immaterial; (c) immaterial; (d) separate item.
(**5**) (a) and (b) Check your answers with the text.
(**6**) Profit £293; value of closing stock £234.
(**7**) Profit £207; value of closing stock £148.
(**8**) Profit £730; value of closing stock £325.
(**9**) Profit £665; value of closing stock £260.

Index